1 MONTH OF
FREE
READING

at
www.ForgottenBooks.com

By purchasing this book you are eligible for one month membership to ForgottenBooks.com, giving you unlimited access to our entire collection of over 1,000,000 titles via our web site and mobile apps.

To claim your free month visit:
www.forgottenbooks.com/free57311

ISBN 978-0-483-31107-7
PIBN 10057311

PROCEEDINGS

OF

THE THIRD AMERICAN PEACE CONGRESS

HELD IN

BALTIMORE, MARYLAND
MAY 3 to 6, 1911

EDITED BY
EUGENE A. NOBLE
CHAIRMAN OF PUBLICATIONS COMMITTEE

PRICE, 75 CENTS

COMPOSED AND PRINTED AT THE
WAVERLY PRESS
By the Williams & Wilkins Company
Baltimore, U. S. A.

OFFICERS

iii

258062

COMMITTEES

Executive Committee

THEODORE MARBURG, Chairman.

TUNSTALL SMITH,   SAMUEL T. DUTTON,
EDWARD C. WILSON,   BENJAMIN F. TRUEBLOOD.
EUGENE A. NOBLE,

Executive Secretary

TUNSTALL SMITH, "The Preston," Baltimore, Md.

Publications Committee

EUGENE A. NOBLE, Chairman.
JAMES L. TRYON.

Resolutions Committee

THEODORE MARBURG, Chairman.

E. H. GRIFFIN,   W. I. HULL,
HAMILTON HOLT,   JAMES BROWN SCOTT,
W. W. WILLOUGHBY,   LYMAN ABBOTT,
TUNSTALL SMITH,   S. C. MITCHELL.
THEODORE E. BURTON,

Banquet Committee

FRANK N. HOEN, Chairman.

WM. A. BOYKIN,   E. K. PATTISON,
W. W. CATOR,   P. BYRD THOMPSON,
W. D. GILL,   W. W. SYMINGTON,
KEY COMPTON,   CARTER G. OSBORNE,
DANIEL C. AMMIDON,   O. B. BIDWELL.

School Committee

JAMES H. VAN SICKLE, Chairman.

A. A. J. MILLER,   MISS MARY E. HOLMES,
DAVID WEGLEIN,   EDWARD C. WILSON.

Finance Committee

RICHARD J. WHITE, Chairman.

J. HENRY BAKER,   FRANCIS M. JENCKS,
THOMAS H. BOWLES,   EUGENE LEVERING,
FRANK H. HOEN,   EUGENE A. NOBLE,
FRANCIS T. HOMER,   ALBERT C. RITCHIE.
DOUGLAS M. WYLIE,

Entertainment Committee

DOUGLAS M. WYLIE, Chairman.

WILLIAM F. LUCAS, JR.,   MRS. WILLIAM M. ELLICOTT.

iv

DELEGATES AND ORGANIZATIONS

The following States were represented by Delegates appointed by their respective Governors:

Colorado, 8 delegates, appointed by His Excellency, JOHN F. SHAFROTH
Connecticut, 7 delegates, appointed by His Excellency, SIMEON E. BALDWIN
Florida, 10 delegates, appointed by His Excellency, ALLEN W. GILCHRIST
Georgia, 6 delegates, appointed by His Excellency, JOSEPH M. BROWN
Hawaii, 2 delegates, appointed by His Excellency, W. F. FREAR
Idaho, 3 delegates, appointed by His Excellency, JAMES H. HAWLEY
Kansas, 1 delegate, appointed by His Excellency, WALTER R. STUBBS
Kentucky, 6 delegates, appointed by His Excellency, AUGUSTUS E. WILSON
Mississippi, 20 delegates,appointed by His Excellency, E. F. Noel
Missouri, 23 delegates, appointed by His Excellency, HERBERT S. HADLEY
Minnesota, 7 delegates, appointed by His Excellency, A. O. EBERHART
Massachusetts, 2 delegates, appointed by His Excellency, EUGENE N. FOSS
Michigan, 6 delegates, appointed by His Excellency, CHASE S. OSBORN
New Mexico, 6 delegates, appointed by His Excellency, WILLIAM J. MILLS
New York, 10 delegates, appointed by His Excellency, JOHN A. DIX
New Hampshire, 5 delegates, appointed by His Excellency, ROBERT P. BASS
North Carolina, 15 delegates, appointed by His Excellency, W. W. KITCHIN
Oregon, 8 delegates, appointed by His Excellency, OSWALD WEST
Oklahoma, 7 delegates, appointed by His Excellency, LEE CRUCE
Pennsylvania, 9 delegates, appointed by His Excellency, JOHN K. TENER
South Dakota, 6 delegates, appointed by His Excellency, ROBERT S. VESSEY
South Carolina, 6 delegates, appointed by His Excellency, Cole L. BLEASE
Texas, 9 delegates, appointed by His Excellency, O. B. COLQUITT
Vermont, 5 delegates, appointed by His Bxcellency, JOHN A. MEAD
Virginia, 5 delegates, appointed by His Excellency, WILLIAM HODGES MANN
Wisconsin, 6 delegates, appointed by His Excellency, F. C. McGOVERN
West Virginia, 6 delegates, appointed by His Excellency, WILLIAM E. GLASSCOCK
Wyoming, 3 delegates, appointed by His Excellency, JOSEPH M. CAREY
Washington, 5 delegates, appointed by His Excellency, M. E. Hay

The following organizations were represented. The corporate name and name and address of the Secretary are as follows:

American Peace Society, DR. BENJAMIN F. TRUEBLOOD, Secretary, 313-14 Colorado Bldg., Washington, D. C.
New York Peace Society, Prof. WM. H. SHORT, Executive Secretary, 507 Fifth Avenue, New York, N. Y.
Pennsylvania Arbitration and Peace Society, Dr. WM. I. HULL, Secretary, Swarthmore, Pa.
American Society for Judicial Settlement of International Disputes, THEODORE MARBURG, Secretary, 14 Mt. Vernon Place, W., Baltimore, Md.

Maryland Peace Society, EDWARD C. WILSON, Secretary, 1925 Park Avenue, Baltimore, Md.

American Peace and Arbitration League, ANDREW B. HUMPHREY, Secretary, 31 Nassau Street, New York, N. Y.

Chicago Peace Society, Rev. CHAS. E. BEALS, Secretary, 30 N. La Salle Street, Chicago, Ill.

Connecticut Peace Society, Rev. RODNEY W. ROUNDY, Secretary, Hartford, Conn.

Pennsylvania Peace Society, MISS ARABELLA CARTER, Secretary, 1305 Arch St., Philadelphia, Pa.

Buffalo Peace Society, FRANK F. WILLIAMS, Secretary, Buffalo, N. Y.

Peace Society of Southern California, ROBERT C. ROOT, Secretary, 619 O. T. Johnson Building, Los Angeles, Cal.

American Academy of Political and Social Science, Dr. CARL KELSEY, Secretary, University of Pennsylvania, Philadelphia, Pa.

American School Peace League, MRS. FANNIE FERN ANDREWS, Secretary, 405 Marlboro, Boston, Mass.

New York Italian Peace Society, GIOVANNI DANIELE, Secretary, 2039 First Avenue, New York, N. Y.

Universal Peace Union, AMOS R. ELLIS, Secretary, 1305 Arch Street, Philadelphia, Pa.

Peace Association of Friends in America, MISS H. LAVINIA BAILEY, Secretary, Richmond, Ind.

National Assn. for Arbitration, MRS. BELVA A. LOCKWOOD, 619 F Street N. W., Washington, D. C.

Washington Peace Society, F. L. SIDDONS, Secretary, Bond Building, Washington, D. C.

Great Lakes International Arbitration Society, RUBY M. ZAHN, Secretary, Detroit, Mich.

The League of Peace, SAML. BELL THOMAS, International Secretary, 203 Broadway, New York, N. Y.

Bahai Assembly, CHAS. MASON REMEY, Chairman, 1517 H Street, N. W., Washington, D. C.

American Group of the Interparliamentary Union, St. Louis, Mo., ROBERT F. BROUSSARD, Secretary, New Iberia, La., and House of Representatives, Washington, D. C.

American Association of International Conciliation, Dr. FREDK. P. Keppel, Secretary, 501 W. 116th St., New York, N. Y.

World Peace Foundation, EDWIN D. MEAD, Secretary, 29 A. Beacon Street, Boston, Mass.

Lake Mohonk Conference on International Arbitration, H. C. PHILLIPS, Secretary, Lake Mohonk, Ulster County, N. Y.

Japan Society of New York, EUGENE WORDEN, Secretary, 165 Broadway, New York, N. Y.

National Committee for the Celebration of the 100th Anniversary of Peace Among the English Speaking People, JOHN A. STEWART, Chairman Executive Committee, WM. H. SHORT, Secretary, 50 Church Street, New York, N. Y.

The Peacemakers of Washington, C. M. SCARFF, Secretary, Seattle, Wash.

Kansas State Peace Society, ORMAN EMERY, Secretary, Wichita, Kans.

Delaware Peace Society, CHARLES S. PHILIPS, Secretary, 1805 Monroe Street, Wilmington, Del.

Friends Peace Association of Philadelphia, WALTER HAVILAND, 20 S. 12th St., Philadelphia, Pa.

Virginia Peace League, MRS. R. A. RICKS, Secretary, 113 N. 3d Street, Richmond, Va.

Rhode Island Peace Society, WM. B. WHITE, Secretary, Providence, R. I.

Peace Department of Women's and National Women's Christian Temperance Union, Mrs. H. J. BAILY, President, Winthrop Centre, Me.

Women's International Peace League of America, Mrs. MARY F. EVANS, President, Care of B. E. EVANS, Port Collins, Colo.

Committee of Peace and Arbitration of the National Women Suffrage Association, Mrs. LUCIA AMES MEAD, 39 Newbury Street, Boston, Mass.

Young People's International Federation, Miss MARY J. PIERSON, 318 E. 15th St., New York, N. Y.

The American Scandinavian Society, CARL LORENTZEN, Secretary, 507 Fifth Avenue, New York, N. Y.

Ministerial Peace Association, Rev. J. B. REMENSNYDER, 900 Madison Avenue, New York, N. Y.

The following abstract from the official program is presented:

On Thursday all delegates and out-of-town visitors are invited to be the guests of the Congress at lunch at McCoy Hall, Johns Hopkins University, at one o'clock. Delegates should register and procure badges, on arrival, at the Headquarters of the Congress, McCoy Hall; and visitors may procure tickets to the luncheon by registering and giving their home address. Delegates may also procure badges at the Lyric on Wednesday, May 3, until 2 P.M.

The Arundel Club, Charles and Eager Streets, has generously extended the privileges of the Club to women visitors and delegates. The University Club, Charles and Madison Streets, and the Johns Hopkins Club, Monument and Howard Streets, extend a like privilege to men visitors and delegates.

Orders for the printed proceedings of the Congress (price, 75 cts.) may be left at the Headquarters of the Congress; or sent to the Waverly Press, 2427 York Road, Baltimore.

Subscriptions to the Banquet (Five Dollars) are limited to 350, and will be received by Richard J. White, Treasurer, 10 South Street, before the opening session of the Congress, and thereafter at McCoy Hall, Johns Hopkins University.

PROGRAM

PROGRAM

THIRD SESSION

Thursday, May Fourth

McCoy Hall, Ten o'clock A.M.

Hon. Huntington Wilson, Assistant Secretary of State, *Presiding Officer*
Address by the Presiding Officer
James S. Speyer, New York,
Embargo on War Loans
Prof. John H. Latané, Washington and Lee University,
The Panama Canal in Relation to the Peace Movement.
(Not present in person but address to be printed in proceedings.)
Hon. Richard Bartholdt, Member of Congress, Missouri,
Universal Arbitration
Prof. E. H. Griffin, Dean Johns Hopkins University,
An Argument from Hobbes "Leviathan."
Hon. James L. Slayden, Member of Congress, Texas,
Relation of the United States to other American Governments, as They Are and as They
Should Be.
F. W. Boatwright, President Richmond College,
The College and Arbitration.

FOURTH SESSION

Thursday, May Fourth

McCoy Hall, Two o'clock P.M.

Topic: The Aims and Activities of some of the Societies participating
in the Congress—Addresses limited to ten minutes each.
Hon. Theodore E. Burton, Senator from Ohio, *Presiding Officer*
Address by the Presiding Officer
Hon. John Barrett, Pan-American Union.
A. D. Call, Connecticut Peace Society.
Mrs. Belva A. Lockwood, National Association for Arbitration.
Alfred H. Love, Universal Peace Union, Philadelphia.
Robert Stein, Washington Peace Society.
James Brown Scott, American Society of International Law, The Carnegie Endowment
for International Peace.
John A. Stewart, New York.
National Committee for the Celebration of the 100th Anniversary of Peace Among
English Speaking People.
W. H. Short, New York Peace Society.
Rev. Gilbert Reid, International Institute of China.
Mrs. Elmer E. Black, Henry Clews, American Peace and Arbitration League, New
York.
Daniel Smiley, Lake Mohonk Conference on International Arbitration.
Rev. Charles E. Beals, Chicago Peace Society.

The annual meeting of the American Peace Society will be held at the close of this
session.

FIFTH SESSION

Thursday, May Fourth

McCoy Hall, Eight o'clock P.M.

Rev. Lyman Abbott. *Presiding Officer*
Address by the Presiding Officer
Dr. E. D. Warfield, President Lafayette College, Easton, Pa.,
The Why, When and How of Disarmament.
Price Collier,
What are We Doing for Peace in the Far East?
Mrs. Fannie Fern Andrews, Boston, Mass.,
Education and International Peace.
Prof. William I. Hull, Swarthmore College,
The Abolition of Trial by Battle.
Rev. Milton Fairchild,
Law and Order and International Peace.

SIXTH SESSION

Friday, May Fifth

McCoy Hall, Ten o'clock A.M.

Eugene A. Noble, President Goucher College, *Presiding Officer.*
Address by the Presiding Officer
James Brown Scott, Washington, D. C.,
The Carnegie Endowment for International Peace.
Dr. T. Iyenaga, Japan,
Peace in Asia.
Allen S. Will, Baltimore, Md.,
Popular Intelligence One of the Best Preventives of War.
Edwin Ginn, Boston, Massachusetts,
Education for Peace.
Samuel P. Brooks, Pres. Baylor University, Waco, Texas,
The Schoolroom in the Peace Propaganda.
Prof. Philander P. Claxton, University of Tennessee,
Universal Education as a Factor in International Peace.

SEVENTH SESSION

Friday, May Fifth

McCoy Hall, Two-thirty o'clock P.M.

Hon. John W. Foster, Former Secretary of State, *Presiding Officer*
Address by the Presiding Officer
Prof. Samuel T. Dutton, Columbia University,
New Propaganda for Peace.
Isaac Sharpless, Pres. Haverford College,
The Education of Peace Men.

S. C. MITCHELL, President University of South Carolina,
America as Peacemaker.
PROF. HENRY WADE ROGERS, Dean Yale University Law School,
The United States in the Peace Movement.
RT. REV. JOHN G. MURRAY, Bishop of Maryland.
World-Peace, Proper, Practical and Profitable.

BANQUET

Friday, May Fifth

BELVEDERE HOTEL, SEVEN O'CLOCK P.M.

HON. CHAMP CLARK, Speaker of the House of Representatives, *Toastmaster.*
THE MAYOR OF BALTIMORE.
Welcome to Baltimore.
SENATOR BARON D'ESTOURNELLES DE CONSTANT, Member of The Hague Court,
Co-operation of the Nations.
REV. FREDERICK LYNCH, New York City,
Some Untabulated Signs of World Unity.
MRS. MAY WRIGHT SEWALL, Boston, Mass.,
Woman's Part in the Promotion of Internationalism.
SENATOR HENRI LA FONTAINE, President of Permanent International Peace Bureau of
Berne, Switzerland,
Internationalism as a Science.
SPECIAL RESOLUTIONS.

EIGHTH SESSION

Saturday, May Sixth,

McCOY HALL, TEN O'CLOCK A. M.

JOHN HAYS HAMMOND, *Presiding Officer*
Topic: The Interest which Business Men have in the Peace Movement.
Address by the Presiding Officer
JOHN BALL OSBORNE, Chief of Bureau, Trade Relations, Department of State,
How Commerce Promotes Peace.
CHARLES YATES, U. S. Coast and Geodetic Survey
The importance of the Geographic Delimitation of Boundaries.
U. J. LEDOUX, Canada,
The Business Man in World Politics.
CHARLES MASON REMEY, Washington, D. C
The Bahai Movement and The Occident-Orient Unity.
REV. CHARLES E. BEALS, Chicago, Ill.
The Patriotism Required by an International World.
DR. J. W. MAGRUDER, General Secretary Federated Charities, Baltimore, Md.,
Peace as a Prevention of Poverty.

PROGRAM FOR SCHOOLS

MARYLAND TEACHERS' MEETING

Tuesday, May Second

ASSEMBLY ROOM, WESTERN HIGH SCHOOL, 3 o'clock P.M.

HONORABLE M. BATES STEPHENS, State Superintendent of Public Instruction, *Presiding Officer*

MRS. LUCIA AMES MEAD

YOUNG PEOPLE'S MEETING

Thursday, May Fourth

ASSEMBLY ROOM, WESTERN HIGH SCHOOL, 3 o'clock P.M.

MR. JAMES H. VAN SICKLE, City Superintendent of Schools, Baltimore, President of the American School Peace League, *Presiding Officer*

MRS. LUCIA AMES MEAD

(Music by public school choruses)

PHILOSOPHY OF THE THIRD AMERICAN PEACE CONGRESS

[Introductory]

THEODORE MARBURG

The aim of the peace movement is not a subject of controversy. Where difference of opinion enters is as to method: whether armaments or courts are the best instruments for preserving peace. And here the militarists have been put on the defensive; *i.e.*, armaments, as well as war, are universally recognized as an evil to be dispensed with just as soon as a practical plan for their suppression presents itself.

War involves biological and moral loss as well as economic loss. The reign of law between nations would promote the cause of justice by extending its sway, by increasing men's respect for, and love of, justice, and by strengthening the habit of doing justice. The new system is already partly inaugurated and must prevail; but armaments will be maintained while it is being put to the test.[1]

The period of time this process will occupy will depend on the extent to which men direct their energies toward it and especially on the measure of attention they succeed in getting their statesmen to give to it. When conditions are ripe the act of a single man charged with power may advance a cause a full generation. If, on the other hand, the opportune moment is allowed to pass, a series of untoward events may distract and discourage its advocates and divert the popular interest.

The most pressing peace measure before the country today is the proposed all-inclusive treaty of arbitration with Great Britain.[2] A common language, literature, and kinship of institutions and law, all offer reasons why this treaty should be consummated.

[1] Richard Bartholdt.
[2] Theodore E. Burton.

These two countries have been more happy than others "in reconciling and adjusting legitimate authority with personal liberty."[3] Such a treaty will not only insure peace between the two contracting nations, but by offering an example which other nations are bound to follow "will prepare the way for enduring peace throughout the world."[4] It may therefore prove to be an epoch-making event.

"The only way for a man to rise above the presidency of the United States is to ascend into the international realm."[5] This President Taft has done by the utterance of which the pending treaty with Great Britain is the outcome: namely, his declaration in favor of a treaty with some power by which all questions not resolvable by diplomacy shall be referred to an arbitral court. President Taft has laid the axe "to the root of international war."[6] But such a treaty must not be regarded as bringing an end to war at once.[7] It is only a step toward the goal "to be followed by other steps as rapidly as possible." Now that mediation is recognized as a friendly act and a duty, the various chancelleries of the world are themselves agencies for the promotion of peace. Having become a powerful nation the United States has duties to discharge to weaker nations and a responsibility for the peace of the world in its neighbourhood. With the aid of certain South American countries it has during the present administration succeeded in averting wars in four separate instances.[8,9]

A great source of war today is found in the governments which "do not exercise complete control over their people." It is the duty of the United States and of the other great republics in the two Americas to exercise their "kindly and peaceful influence to prevent such outbreaks." Unfortunately suspicion is cast on the motive of the United States in tendering its good offices, a suspicion which is baseless because we have ample territory in which

[3] James Cardinal Gibbons.
[4] James Cardinal Gibbons.
[5] Hamilton Holt.
[6] Andrew Carnegie.
[7] President Taft.
[8] President Taft.
[9] Huntington Wilson.

to work out the experiment of popular government and there is therefore among us an entire absence of any desire for aggrandisement of territory.[10] While interference in the internal affairs of a state has been a prolific source of oppression and of war in the past, it is equally true that a broad rule of non-interference is unworkable.[11] Misgovernment is bound to lead to foreign complications. It was the injustice and oppression practiced by the Turkish state which drew down upon Turkey the vengeance of other powers. If just government had obtained in Cuba the island would still belong to Spain; and unless the Johannesberger had been oppressively taxed there would have been no South African war. Why is it that there is danger of interference by the United States in the internal affairs of Mexico and no such danger with respect to Canada where there is an ever-growing number of Americans?

Is it not simply because of the difference with which justice is meted out by the law and the courts in the two countries? The modern world insists upon a standard of government as well as upon a standard of living. "Peace rests on justice" and not on the "international figment that the internal affairs of a nation are of no consequence to another."[12] It cannot be secured by machinery which leaves "unavenged and unredressed the misery of millions and the worst of all human wrongs, injustice at the fount of justice, spoliation under the guise of taxation" and the denial of rights to men. This principle is definitely set up in the Platt Amendment by which the United States requires of Cuba the stamping out of pestilence, the maintenance of order and the enforcement of contracts. It would be well to extend the principle by organizing under an international commission all countries whose protracted internal disorder makes of them danger-points.[13] Such a commission would make more secure the independence of such countries by taking away the excuse for interference on the part of a single power whose act may result in permanent occupation with or without previous intent.

[10] President Taft.
[11] Talcott Williams.
[12] Talcott Williams.
[13] Talcott Williams.

War is a plentiful source of injustice and suffering, but it is not the only source.[14] There may be a steady denial of justice which results in profound human misery. In time of peace there may be actual loss of life—as in the massacres in Turkey—greater than that which results from war. War is to be condemned especially because it is such a source of injustice; but "what we are seeking is first justice and next peace."[15] Disarmament must therefore follow the establishment of justice, not precede it. Men laid aside their rapiers when they found they were safe without them. Just so armaments will drop away of their own accord when they are no longer needed.[16] We all desire to see the rule of reason supplant the rule of force, but suppose there is no reason? "You cannot appeal to reason when facing a pack of wolves." Within the leading nations, as a rule, there is internal order, a love of justice and respect for law. Between certain of them the rule of reason has likewise long prevailed in external relations, and as to such states it is quite safe to set up treaties which provide for the peaceful settlements of all disputes between them.[17]

Ignorance of each other is a source of distrust. Mixture of upright intentions and downright ignorance produces folly. We can do much for peace by simply knowing each other better.[18] As great as will be the uses of the Panama Canal as a commercial artery, they will be outweighed by its usefulness in bringing the nations closer together.[19]

The Pan-American Union, devoted to the development of commerce among the twenty-one nations of the western hemisphere acts upon this principle. The seven million people who compose Latin America are looking to the United States for leadership and sympathy and help, and the Union aims to be the channel through which it may all flow.[20]

The frequent internal disturbances in South American coun-

---

[14] Lyman Abbott.
[15] Lyman Abbott.
[16] Price Collier.
[17] Lyman Abbott.
[18] Price Collier.
[19] Champ Clark.
[20] John Barrett.

tries must not blind us to the fact that in international relations they have displayed forbearance and a sense of justice of a high order.[21] In the past three generations the map of South America has not changed nearly so much as the map of Europe. If the methods which were applied to Poland had obtained at the end of the war between Argentina, Brazil and Uruguay on the one hand, and Paraguay on the other, the latter country would have been effaced from the map of South America. Despite the fact that Paraguay was the aggressor, no territory was taken from it. Its victors magnanimously recognized the fact that the conflict was due to the acts of a dictator and they refused to penalize a people simply because they were in a backward stage of political development.[22]

In South America it is not so much the conscious desire to appropriate another state's territory as the uncertainty as to where the boundary line runs that leads to difficulty. The dense tropical jungles of the interior are only now being explored and shadowy territorial claims are found to conflict. What is needed is a geographical delimitation of boundaries[23] to be followed by an agreement that hereafter in the two Americas "no territory shall be transferred as a consequence of war."[24]

Like geographical delimitation of boundaries is needed in Africa and Asia. For example, in the case of the Chinese Empire, her "practically unmarked and geographically undefined boundaries" extend more than eight thousand miles, abutting the possessions of the British, French, Germans, Portuguese, Russians and Japanese.[25]

The Monroe Doctrine should not be used as an excuse for undue interference in the affairs of Latin America nor for imposing on it our own views of government.[26] To the extent to which it retards European immigration into that region, the doc-

[21] Leo. S. Rowe.
[22] Leo. S. Rowe.
[23] Charles C. Yates.
[24] James L. Slayden.
[25] Charles C. Yates.
[26] James L. Slayden.

trine is injuring it. The foreigner, including the citizen of the United States, who locates in a Latin American country, has no right to claim security of person or property superior to that which the citizen of that country enjoys. He can demand only the equal protection of the laws. This applies equally to times of political upheaval and to times of peace. "If the forms of law be more rigorous than are known at home, if their manner of execution be more severe, if the government be less able than his own to insure him the blessings of liberty," be it remembered that in the eye of international law he consents to this order of things when he enters the land.[27] Spanish American countries suspect us of desiring to control their foreign relations and to regulate their internal affairs. "They have a right to demand that we shall treat them as we would have them treat us if they were strong and we were weak."[28]

The behavior of the private citizen abroad is a considerable factor in giving direction to international relations. As governmental action is influenced powerfully by popular opinion, the impression conveyed in foreign lands by honest dealing and considerate conduct on the part of the stranger, as well as the color given by newspapers to events in foreign lands, are of much importance.[29]

The good relations of the world are markedly promoted by candid and well-meaning diplomacy, by acts which in private life would be regarded as gentlemanly and which advance international morality; acts such as England's cession of the Ionian Islands to Greece, the withdrawal of the United States from Cuba after the latter had been aided in the difficult task of establishing an independent government, and the repayment by the United States to China of the Boxer indemnity.[30, 31]

If international institutions eventually furnish as satisfactory a method of settling disputes between nations as municipal institutions now offer for the adjustment of differences between

[27] James L. Slayden.
[28] James L. Slayden.
[29] Huntington Wilson.
[30] Robert Stein.
[31] Huntington Wilson.

private individuals, it is reasonable to assume that public war will disappear just as the rule of private war has disappeared.[32]   The perfection of such institutions is therefore the duty of the hour. It is the practical means of attacking the problems of war and of armaments.   The defect which has characterized arbitrations— namely the tendency to compromise in lieu of declaring exact justice—has been less marked since the establishment of The Hague Court which seems to feel its responsibility to act more as a court and less as an agent merely to compose differences.   An analysis of nine decisions by the court leads to the conclusion that only one, the Casablanca decision, is a manifest compromise, that two others are affected with the spirit of compromise, and that the remaining six are free of this suspicion.[33]   The question is raised whether compromise should not be left to the field of negotiation and whe- ther a court should not be held strictly to the law and the facts. The establishment of a true international court of justice might, in course of time, bring this about through the gradual neglect of the Permanent Court of Arbitration.   The worst form of com- promise is that which colors the very reasoning of the court, there- by affecting the development of international law.   This tendency is encouraged by permitting the president of the court and one other official to sign the award—as under the present Hague con- vention—in lieu of requiring each judge to signify separately his approval not only of the award but of the reasoning of the court.

The element of compromise in arbitration may be reduced by letting the arbitrators understand that unless the terms of the submission are respected, the decision may be set aside by a higher tribunal clothed with authority to entertain an appeal; by the adoption of a code of procedure; by the exclusion of nationals from the tribunal; and by establishing either the right of challenge in the selection of judges, or, better still, the practice of selecting judges by direct agreement as provided in article 46 of The Hague convention of 1907.[34]

[32] William C. Dennis.
[33] William C. Dennis.
[34] William C. Dennis.

The peace movement is an endeavor to substitute law for force in the relations of nations, to do between the nations what has already been done within the nations.[35] To what extent actual federation of the nations is required to bring this about is at present not clear. The mind, starting with the analogy of a federal state, soon enters this domain of speculation. It finds a measure of coöperation already existing among the nations. It finds in embryo certain institutions which might readily be developed into federal institutions. Such is The Hague Peace Conference, (which will probably meet hereafter at fixed intervals,) a quasi-legislative body whose members are appointed by the executive branches of the various governments and whose conclusions have great weight with the home governments. Such again is the Inter-parliamentary Union, an annual unofficial gathering whose position it is proposed to strengthen by having its members selected by the various home legislatures. These two bodies, if joined together, would thus be constituted on the principle of an upper and lower house.

Still another essential of a federated world state is found in embryo in The Hague Court which is certain of rapid growth. The least developed of the three great branches of a world state is the executive; though its beginnings are found in the international bureaus which we owe so largely to conscious effort on the part of one man, Henri La Fontaine. The policing of Morocco, the North Sea, and the Behring Sea, likewise come under this head.

Whether we shall proceed to actual world federation is not a problem for present day politics. The formation of the American Union out of a people speaking a common language and inheriting common institutions was a simple matter when compared with the problem of uniting nations which have common interests, it is true, but which are controlled by widely differing motives and ideals. The impelling motive for the union of the American colonies was defense against an outside aggressor rather than the desire to avoid armed conflict among themselves. This motive

[35] Hamilton Holt.

cannot exist for the great powers, including Japan and presently China, because no formidable outside enemies would remain. Moreover, is actual federation necessary to the world's peace? If the attitude of the United States toward European aggrandisement in the western hemisphere has substantially prevented European countries from waging war here, why cannot the united will of the great powers prevent it over the world generally?[36]

The creation of a deliberative assembly which shall meet periodically to help regulate international relations,[37] the firm establishment of a high court or courts to compose differences and to interpret the regulations declared by the deliberative assembly, together with an international police to operate in backward countries—a body which shall be purely a police and not a military force—is perhaps all that is needed and all that we may safely project for the present. Force will not be needed to induce the more progressive nations to respect the award of an international tribunal. Furthermore the attempt to use it against any of the leading powers would be disastrous. The principle of the international court, once introduced, must win by sheer weight of its reasonableness. No nation which has justice for its guiding star need ever fear the award of such a tribunal. If that which a nation has done or is planning to do is just, certainly it should not hesitate to enter it. Under such a régime some of us may be restrained from doing again what we have done in the past; others of us may be allowed the fulfilment of just ambitions which powerful rivals have previously forbidden to us.

The world is changing its mind about the difficulty of submitting purely political questions to international tribunals. The two Hague Conferences not only created new machinery for dealing with international disputes, but, by that fact as well as directly, greatly enlarged the scope of arbitration by increasing the kind of questions which may be dealt with by arbitration. Questions supposedly involving national honour actually have been solved by these new institutions at The Hague, namely the Commission of

[36] W. O. Hart.
[37] Hamilton Holt.

Inquiry and the Permanent Court of Arbitration; and questions of national policy so often turn upon questions of fairness and justice that nations may soon learn to submit these as well.   Whereas in the past peace has been preserved over wide areas by empire, *i.e.*, by force, the tendency now is to preserve the peace by leaning on the power of the intellect, *i.e.* upon reason as defined by some authorized agency.[38]   It is significant that we are beginning to think in terms of arbitration and the peaceful settlement of disputes rather than in terms of war.   As international institutions for the settlement of disputes grow, the minds of men will turn naturally to them when difficulties arise and the possibility of war growing out of such disputes will not be the first thing on men's lips.[39], [40]

Since the Second Hague Conference the United States has been more active than any other government in promoting the establishment of institutions and practices calculated to make war difficult.[41]   Secretary Root negotiated many treaties looking to the reference of future disputes to arbitration.   Secretary Knox has taken the lead in endeavoring to bring into being the court of arbitral justice.   The Congress, by joint resolution, invited the President of the United States to appoint a commission to consider the question of armaments and the question of coöperation by the powers to make the peace of the world more secure; and President Taft is favoring and actually negotiating an all-inclusive treaty of arbitration.

In respect of the nature and enforcement of her neutrality laws, however, the United States has not only not kept the position in advance of the world which it once enjoyed, but has fallen markedly behind the best practice.[42], [43]   The wholesale participation of citizens of the United States in the revolution in a neighboring state with which we were at peace is a matter of common knowledge.   They crossed and recrossed the frontier with arms, seek-

[38] Edwin M. Borchard.
[39] Frederick Lynch.
[40] Madelaine Black.
[41] Benjamin F. Trueblood.
[42] John W. Foster.
[43] Leo. S. Rowe.

ing temporary refuge on American soil when worsted. The President should have power to control the intercourse with other countries so as to avoid having American soil made the base of operations against such countries whether in time of insurrection or in time of war.[44] Our neutrality laws were put in their present shape in 1818. President van Buren (1833) and President Arthur (1884) both urged upon Congress a revision of them. Great Britain visits with fine and imprisonment the enlistment of its citizens in the forces of a country engaged in war against another power with which it (Great Britain) is at peace; and the larger countries of Latin America have followed its lead. During the recent disorders in Uruguay its neighbor Argentina assumed an admirable attitude in this respect.[45]

As against the adoption of strict neutrality laws we are sometimes reminded that the American Colonies would not have achieved their independence except for the aid of the French. But the important assistance which France gave to us, it must be remembered, was an open and public act, amounting to an alliance against England. Lafayette's greatest service to us was in securing that alliance rather than in any personal service, however chivalrous, in the field. The government can never prevent its citizens from aiding a foreign cause which appeals to their sympathy. But backward neutrality laws and lax enforcement of existing laws certainly engender a feeling of resentment on the part of foreign governments which are made to suffer by reason of them.

America, holding aloft ideals of liberty at home, should be foremost in a liberal foreign policy.[46] Its wealth, geographical position and the fact that England, formerly its opponent, is now its best friend, gives it less excuse for failure to live up to the highest ideals in all its international relations.[47] Its actions should fit its creed. "I believe it weakens a man, a society or a nation to have purposes that find no plans."[48]

[44] John W. Foster.
[45] Leo S. Rowe.
[46] Price Collier.
[47] S. C. Mitchell.
[48] Price Collier.

America's people are the children of so many lands that so far as blood is concerned the greater part of Europe is their mother country. That fact should excite America's interest in the welfare of Europe.[49] Moreover it is not afflicted with an excess of population for which an outlet may be required. "It is in the power of America to insure the peace of the world." This is the biggest task of the twentieth century and "if America, richly endowed with energy of will springing out of popular sympathy with progressive causes and exhaustless material resources, once gets a vision of the active part it can play in bringing the blessings of peace to the world" it will prove resistless.[50] To arouse the people so that they will take up this question in earnest is a long and difficult task.[51] "You can hardly expect people who do not exert themselves on the side of honest and fair dealing in local and state affairs to be alert or enthusiastic respecting those problems which call for an intelligence or a patriotism transcending the bounds of state or nation. They need to be impressed with the moral grandeur of a world united in seeking the good of mankind, and of governments honestly, sincerely, devoutly striving to establish justice."[52] It is the duty of America to reconcile outside its borders the peoples it has reconciled within its borders.[53]

There is a close analogy between the growth of law between the nations and within the nations.[54] Wrong to the individual was formerly redressed by him without let or hindrance from the state. Next, the wrongful act of the individual involved a collective responsibility on the part of all related to him by blood, just as today still the acts of malevolent or stupid rulers bring out people from peaceful pursuits to be killed on the battlefield. When tribal responsibility succeeded to family responsibility an elaborate system of money compensations took the place of private or family retaliation; and gradually as society became better

[49] S. C. Mitchell.
[50] S. C. Mitchell.
[51] Samuel T. Dutton.
[52] Samuel T. Dutton.
[53] Henri La Fontaine.
[54] W. I. Hull.

organized, crime and misdemeanor came to be recognized as a
wrong against the body politic, something which it was the business of the latter to punish.   The struggle of society to regulate
private war was long and arduous.   The trial by ordeal of fire
and water allowed to ecclesiastical courts, and the trial by battle,
both practised for such a long period of time as supposed methods
of inviting divine intervention in favor of the right, are looked
upon now as the crude inventions of a stupid age.   But are we
not equally stupid today when we resort to war between nations
as a means of determining the right or wrong in an international
dispute?   The work of evolving between the nations a system
of justice such as obtains within the nations is still before us.   We
have still to lay down the principle that a wrong by one state
against another is a matter with which the society of nations must
concern itself; that the International Commission of Inquiry, like
the grand jury in English municipal law, must not stop with the
inquiry but must evolve eventually a body which shall exist for
the purpose of passing upon international wrong-doing, and must
present the culprit for trial by a permanently constituted tribunal;
that, in other words, the society of nations and not the individual
nation will set right an international wrong.[55]   Under such a
system occasional miscarriage of justice may be expected exactly
as in municipal law; but how insignificant will this be when compared with the wholesale injustice, private and public, which
flows from war.   So, too, must we expect an occasional war on a
mighty scale when numbers of states shall be divided on a question, just as we have civil war today within the state; but such
catastrophes should be increasingly rare.

A modern development which is most promising for the eventu-
al peace of the world is the growing extent to which political
power is passing from a ruling class into the hands of the people,
from those who stand to gain by war to those who forever stand
to lose by it.[56]

Immanuel Kant remarked long ago that wars would not cease

[55] W. I. Hull.
[56] Allen S. Will.

till autocratic government ceased.   The problem now is to get
the people to think on their political affairs and not follow their
leaders blindly.   It is the informed will of the people and not the
emotional will of the people that must lead to higher things in
the people are still the last body to trust when the war spirit is
government.   Even today in the very best governed countries
abroad.   The most conservative body in a democracy is the
elective cabinet.   Its chief and its members know that no matter
what the popular passion or the passing vagaries of the legislature, it is they, the cabinet, who will be pilloried before history
and held responsible for an unjust or disastrous war.

This state of things may be changed.   The dangerous flaming
up of popular passion into an appetite for war is possible only
because the masses do not measure the consequences either of
war or peace.   They are too quick to rush to war, and, if reverses
come, are too quick to tire of it.   There is still unreasoning assent
to the leadership of demagogues.   The average man "has the
impression that he is not in a position to know the facts and that,
if he did know them, he would not be qualified to reach a proper
conclusion" about war and peace.   When war is threatening the
people should be made to realize how absurd it is to take "one
hundred thousand lives to settle a question which can be better
adjusted without the loss of any."[57]

In private affairs the settlement of disputes by reference to an
impartial tribunal has for centuries been an accepted principle:
"the strongest minds in the world have long given their best
thought to its application."[58]   The invention of man which supplied the tribunal for individuals must in time prove adequate to
the task of creating a similar tribunal for the nations.

The present suspicions and hostile attitude of states is portrayed in the vast war preparations and in actual conflicts.   The
recent decade, 1895–1905, has been the most warlike since Waterloo.   "In fact the most disquieting and discouraging feature
of the moral and political life of our time is the profound dis-

[57] Allen S Will

trust with which the leading nations of the world regard one another."[59]

Europe has for many centuries been a greater offender in respect of war than Asia.[60] In Europe military power has long been an essential to national greatness. Japan's rapid development in the arts of peace brought to her no such recognition among the powers as did the conduct of two successful wars. A coalition of European powers seemed bent on the partition of China. Territory was seized, railway and mining concessions demanded, and the Chinese Empire actually mapped out into spheres of influence. It was only by waging war against the principal aggressor that Japan succeeded in stopping the movement.[61]

The state of war conceived by Hobbes in the *Leviathan* as the condition of man previous to the social compact is found in international relations in the twentieth century.[62] It was by surrendering certain liberties that primitive society rose out of the condition of private war, the institution of the state presupposing a tacit compact under which men mutually agree to abstain from certain acts for the sake of the general good. It was the need of defense against a common enemy more than the love of justice or desire for peace and order within the group which gave rise to primitive organization and eventually to the state. Group struggle, which arose early in the history of animal life, called for coöperation which could only arise with the development of altruistic qualities and obedience to a common superior. The interdependence of nations has not yet reached a point where one state may not dispense with the coöperation of others. This fact helps to explain the continuance of a state of war among nations long after private war has ceased. In order to rise out of the intolerable condition of war in which the nations as such still labor, there must be a general surrender of certain privileges at present still regarded as essential elements of sovereignty. Whether it will be a group movement undertaken to protect the interests of the more liberal-minded against the stubbornness of cer-

[59] E. H. Griffin.
[60] F. Iyenaga.
[61] F. Iyenaga.
[62] E. H. Griffin.

tain powerful entities which insist on continuing in the old condition of armed peace, or whether it will develop through general coöperation of all the leading powers, depends on the men who are guiding the destinies of the several states as well as on the general public sentiment which a statesman in the end is compelled to obey. "It is through some wisely conceived application of this idea"—the idea of the surrender of certain rights by tacit or express compact such as took place when the American Union, the Swiss Confederation and the German Empire were formed—"that the peace of nations is to be safeguarded.[63] An indispensable feature of such a régime, whether it be secured by all-inclusive treaties of arbitration or by a governing council, is an international supreme court, because, subsequent to public justice is the tribunal which is to decide among the complex and varying acts of men what is just and what unjust, as well as an agreement on the standards by which the acts shall be adjudged.[64] States could safely agree to submit to such a tribunal all questions except independence. "It would certainly seem reasonable to say that, as a man may not contract himself into slavery, so a nation may not submit to any tribunal the question of its own existence."[65]

The bearing of war on eugenics is disclosed by the most casual examination of history. The losses in war, both in Greece and in the Roman state, are principally responsible for the decline of Greece and Rome.[66] Mommsen estimates that three hundred thousand Italians, chiefly Romans of the best stock, perished in the Punic wars. Added to the loss in war was of course the judicial murder of the most talented and most enterprising in Greece, due to the jealousy of princes, and the wholesale proscriptions in Rome, where, on one occasion, ninety senators and twenty-six hundred knights, and on another, one hundred senators and two thousand knights were the victims. The decline of the Roman Empire was physical rather than moral; it perished be-

[63] E. H. Griffin.
[64] E. H. Griffin.
[65] E. H. Griffin.
[66] Eleanor L. Lord.

cause the Roman stock was killed off. This reversed selection, as David Starr Jordan has termed it, has gone on throughout European history.[67]

Internationalism was born of intercourse. It practically did not exist in the days when travel and communication were difficult and costly. Improvement of transportation, leading to the enormous steady flow of persons, commodities and ideas from nation to nation, is the force which is making for better relations between the peoples of the earth.[68] Nationality is no longer as preponderant a bond of union among men as formerly. Strata of interests, extending beyond the boundaries of the nation, constitute a warp and woof which are slowly weaving mankind into a united whole. Out of the practical need of removing hindrances to communication and of protecting property and rights beyond the borders of one's own country have grown the numerous international bureaus. Supplementing these are the societies designed to promote the interests of a particular science, art or industry. There exist today over three hundred international institutions, and every meeting or congress of an international character is making for peace.[69] The Central Office of International Associations at Brussels convoked in 1910 the first congress of such associations; one hundred and thirty-six separate organizations were represented. Conscious effort, supplementing the natural process, can promote and quicken the growth of international bureaus and associations.

The annual value of international commerce today is thirteen thousand five hundred million dollars, to which must be added the international transactions involved in navigation, railway traffic, telegraph, financial investments abroad, remittances on account of them, remittances by emigrants and the money expended in travel abroad.[70]

The thorough commercial organization effected by business men indicates what could be accomplished by the great world of busi-

[67] Eleanor L. Lord.
[68] Henri La Fontaine.
[69] Henri La Fontaine.
[70] John Ball Osborne.

ness for peace provided it gave serious attention to the problem. In many European countries associations of business men, besides furthering local interests, are consulted through their federated organizations by the commerical and industrial departments of the government. "In Austria the Chambers are entitled to four seats in Parliament."[71] In other places they supervise "the industrial, commercial and vocational schools" and public docks. Through the International Chamber of Commerce, which is composed of the various national chambers, business men have been instrumental in having their governments call three international conferences relating to trade matters.[72]

The business man, having as his constant aim elimination of waste, sees most clearly the waste involved in war and in the preparations for war, preparations which leave the nations in the same relative position at the end of each succeeding year.[73] They see the inconsistency of preserving the natural resources of the country and piling up a legacy of debt by militarism. They recognize the interdependence of nations, the prosperity of one being reflected in the prosperity of others. They realize what ameliorations—industrial, philanthropic, and public,—would be made possible by diverting to such uses the treasure now expended on armaments. Therefore, when any practical measure is proposed, such as President Taft's all-inclusive treaty of arbitration with Great Britain, they are found zealously coöperating.[74]

The real struggle before the world is the commercial struggle. Europe is handicapped in this by the mistakes of the past. If America follows in her footsteps it will be deliberately throwing away a great advantage which it is still possible for it to enjoy.[75]

China might be saved from a similar burden by neutralization. If the great powers jointly entered into such an agreement with it, China could feel confident that the agreement would be faith-

[71] U. J. Ledoux.
[72] U. J. Ledoux.
[73] John Hays Hammond.
[74] John Hays Hammond.
[75] d'Estournelles de Constant.

fully kept, and could then bend all its energies to the development of its neglected natural resources.[76]

Heavy foreign investments make a people cautious about going to war with a country in which they have such investments.[77] The Russian loans held in France constitute a guarantee of peace equal to the "entente cordiale." In the light of this fact the present practice of discriminating against foreign securities by an extra tax and by forbidding trust estates and savings banks to hold them is impolitic.

Few nations have within themselves the resources for a protracted war. Japan would hardly have undertaken the struggle with Russia unless assured of foreign financial support. Certainly she could not have continued it for many weeks unless that support had been forthcoming. Therefore an agreement among the leading powers to discourage the placing of foreign war loans in the home market until the intending belligerents had exhausted peaceful methods would act as a deterrent of war.[78]

In this connection it is significant that attempts are seldom made to place government loans abroad without first securing the open approval of the chancellery of the country from which the loan is expected.

ARMAMENTS

The expenditures of the United States government on the army and navy and on pensions, the legacy of past wars, amounts to twenty-five dollars a year for every family of five persons. Inasmuch as the incidence of taxation causes this burden to fall ultimately in large part on the wage earner and so many wage earners even in our best-conditioned cities are on the border line of poverty, the tax for armaments means to them the difference between a promising and a hopeless struggle against poverty.[79]

In many cases the initial cost of a United States battleship is greater than the value of the grounds and buildings and produc-

[76] John Hays Hammond.
[77] James Speyer.
[78] James Speyer.
[79] J. W. Magruder.

tive funds of all the colleges and universities in the state whose
name the battleship bears.[80]   This is true of Oregon, New Hampshire, Alabama, Louisiana, Georgia, Nebraska, Delaware, Vermont, Rhode Island, Idaho, Mississippi, North Dakota, South
Carolina, West Virginia and Montana.   The annual cost of maintaining the largest ships is over three-quarters of a million dollars
apiece.   There are but few universities whose annual budget
exceeds that sum.   The total cost of maintaining the battleships
of the United States during 1910 was a little over twenty-four
and one-half million dollars.   The total revenues of all the colleges
and universities in the United States for 1909, from tuition fees
and productive funds, was about twenty-five million dollars.
Taking into account depreciation, the cost of the "thirty-eight
battleships for a single year is greater than the administration of
the entire American system of higher education."[81]

We may proceed on the assumption that the world already
realizes the waste of armaments as well as the horrors and injustice
of war and seeks only a means of escape from them.[72]   Institutions which offer a substitute for war may be set up by a few
nations and used by few or many.   Progress has therefore been
made along this line.   The difficulty with the question of armaments is that only by joint agreement of all the great powers can
their growth be arrested.

Russia issued the call for the First Hague Conference for the
avowed purpose of stopping the growth of armaments.   England, France, Japan and the United States would unquestionably
favor concerted action directed to that end.   Austria and Italy
would follow the lead of their ally, Germany; and as this exhausts
the list of great powers it is therefore on Germany that the world
waits.

So long as Germany declines to discuss the matter of an agreement to regulate the growth of armaments the question is not a
question of practical politics.   If the time be ripe—as many
believe it is—for such a step, it needs only some great German with

[80] Charles F. Thwing.
[81] Charles F. Thwing.
[82] Daniel Smiley.

a mind and heart equal to the task to lift this burden from his own country and from the world. When we remember how Germany has been trampled upon in past centuries for lack of military organization we cannot blame it for wanting a strong army and navy. But a frank discussion of plans with the nations might disclose the fact that Germany's relative strength as against probable foes is likely to remain the same after years of steady increase in military budgets and that an agreement to limit expenditures, to say the present budgets even, will leave Germany relatively just as strong and save millions to all of us.

EDUCATIONAL

The educational side of the peace movement has practical value because it must depend ultimately upon the attitude of the people whether the peace institutions which the world is endeavoring to set up will be respected and used, or whether, in moments of popular excitement, they will all be brushed roughly aside and the nations rush to war despite of them.

This education cannot begin too early in life. "As the boy stores up impressions, prejudices, sympathies, so the man legislates and the nation makes friends or foes."[83]

Of course, it is the beauty of the world and not its gloom which is to be pointed out to little children; but the peace question may be dealt with from that side. Inspiring in the child a friendly attitude toward the world, prompting it to be fair by acquiring the habit of putting itself in "the other fellow's place," showing it how much each nation owes to other nations, these are the ideas which make possible an intense patriotism without chauvinism.

While of course preserving a study of war on account of the important part it has played "in both social and national evolution" it is highly desirable to avoid the waste at present resulting from a study of the details of campaigns.[84]

Help children to realize that the lessening of suffering and saving of life are the heroic things. Cause them to feel profoundly

[83] Lucia Ames Mead.
[84] Fannie Fern Andrews

the overwhelming importance of justice in human affairs and how little the ends of justice are served by war. "Prosperity depends on peace, and peace depends on justice, and justice depends on far-sighted organization."[85]

Is the teaching of history at all adequate unless young people are informed of the leading facts about the Hague Conventions, what they have accomplished and what their promise? Let them know how much their own country has done for peace and the things still to be striven for.[86] Young people must come to feel that only the right is in the long run the expedient; in other words, be given a moral basis which alone will enable them in times of excitement to withstand popular clamor for war.[87] There should be conveyed to them the philosophy of law and justice, its meaning in the life of every boy and girl, beginning with the laws of the schoolroom, the town and the state, and proceeding thence to the international field where the operation of justice is interrupted by war.[88] The teaching of international arbitration, humanity and brotherhood is already prescribed as part of the curriculum in the primary, secondary and normal schools of France.[89]

But it is during the college period principally that character and purpose take shape. The college and university represent homes widely scattered. They are gardens by the sea whence wind and tide carry "seeds to fructify distant lands."[90] War is emotional and thoughtless. To cultivate in men the habit of thought is to undermine the institution of war. The college preeminently stands for thought.[91] The mind of the under-graduate is in a receptive mood, ready for ideals, ready for noble causes, weighing motive and the appeals of life. "It is the dream time and yet the time when impulses harden into life purposes."[92] Great public causes which are not controversial and not ephem-

---

[85] Lucia Ames Mead.
[86] Lucia Ames Mead.
[87] Isaac Sharpless.
[88] Milton Fairchild.
[89] Fannie Fern Andrews.
[90] F. W. Boatwright.
[91] Charles F. Thwing.
[92] F. W. Boatwright.

eral should therefore be espoused where youth congregate, since nowhere may they be so effectively advanced.

The young are naturally combative; the doctrine of non-resistance is not apt to appeal to them.[93] But show them that here is a great cause with its roots deep down in the past, that Christianity, which moved slowly toward the abolition of the slave, is moving likewise toward the abolition of war; that causes which were formerly fought over are now settled by arbitration and inquiry; that certain definite institutions which are calculated to make war less common have actually come into being and are in operation; and let them feel that in the light of the recent past the cause does call for struggle still—long and gigantic struggle—and they will become interested.[94] Show them that today still "Nations as soon as they become self-conscious are associations of people for the purpose of taking other people's land"[95] and that it is a far cry from this to a family of nations "united in international bonds which shall make it at once the duty and the interest of each nation to seek and maintain the integrity and freedom of every other."[96] The peace movement in point of practical achievements has only just begun. Its tasks are all before it. No headway whatever has been made against armaments. To the establishment of a court of law for the nations we may look forward with confidence; but such a court cannot function wholly satisfactorily until the nations reach an agreement on the subject of the law which the court is to administer.[97] Jurists in their private capacity, though preferably in coöperation, may do much toward formulating such a law, its formal acceptance by the nations coming in good time. The firm establishment of the international court and the formulation of international practice into accepted and definitive law are two most urgent needs to which the coming generation must bend its energies, for "peace between nations is as impossible in the absence of law and justice,

[93] Thos. S. Baker.
[94] Thos. S. Baker.
[95] Poesche and Goepp, quoted by Thos. S. Baker.
[96] Ethelbert D. Warfield.
[97] James Brown Scott.

as peace is impossible among men in the absence of law and orderly administration."

Procedure, the peaceful means by which rights are preserved and wrongs redressed, must be extended into the international field.

We need furthermore a scientific study of the causes of the disease of which war is a symptom and an examination of the social cost of war in all its aspects[98]—biological, ethical and economical.

[98] James Brown Scott.

PROCEEDINGS

OF

The Third American Peace Congress

At the First Session of the Third American Peace Congress held in the Lyric Theatre, the Presiding Officer, Mr. Hamilton Holt, of New York City, introduced as the first speaker, His Eminence, James, Cardinal Gibbons, as follows:

"On Easter Sunday, 1896, Cardinal Vaughan of England, Cardinal Logue of Ireland, and Cardinal Gibbons of the United States, issued an appeal to the English speaking nations of the world for a permanent tribunal of arbitration 'as a rational substitute among the English speaking races for a resort to the bloody arbitrament of war.' This appeal has always been regarded as one of the many great forces which brought about the First Hague Conference, that Magna Charta of International Law. Throughout his long and distinguished career, Cardinal Gibbons has lost no opportunity to make his great influence felt for peace and justice. He is a true, constant and consistent follower of the Prince of Peace. I now have the great honor to introduce to you His Eminence, James, Cardinal Gibbons."

ADDRESS OF HIS EMINENCE, JAMES, CARDINAL GIBBONS

Mr. Chairman: I shall make my remarks, Ladies and Gentlemen, as brief as possible, as I do not wish to detain the honored President of the United States, who is soon going to address you. I was requested to offer a prayer at the opening of this great convention of peace, but I regard a specific invocation quite unnecessary on this occasion, inasmuch as I am satisfied that all the addresses that shall be made from this place today will be prayers for peace.

I assume that the purpose of this great and distinguished gathering is to create, to promote closer and more friendly relations between the United States and Great Britain, and I am firmly persuaded that a treaty of arbitration between England and the United States would be not only a source of infinite blessing to both of the nations concerned, but also will prepare the way for enduring peace throughout the whole world. There are many reasons why there should be a closer alliance between England and the United States. We speak the same noble English language, a language by the way which today is more generally employed than any tongue in the civilized world. Not only do we speak the same tongue, but we also enjoy the same literature; the classic literature of England is ours, from Chaucer down to Newman, and the classic literature of the United States is claimed also by England. The literature of both countries is a common heritage to both.

And again, we are living practically under the same form of government. The head of our nation is the honored President before us. The head of England is the King. We are ruled by a constitutional republic; England is ruled by a constitutional monarchy, and I venture to say, without any disparagement whatever of other nations, that England and the United States have been more happy in reconciling and in adjusting legitimate authority with personal individual liberty than any other nations on the face of the earth.

We all know the vast dominions of the British Empire. England's empire embraces about ten million square miles or about one-fifth of the surface of the globe. Great was the extent of the Roman Empire in the days of the imperial Cæsars. The Empire of Rome extended into Europe as far as the River Danube; it extended into Asia as far as the Tigris and the Euphrates and into Africa as far as Mauretania. And yet the extent of the Roman Empire was scarcely one-sixth of the British Empire of today.

Daniel Webster, the great statesman, about sixty years ago made a speech in the United States Senate in which he thus described the vast extent of the British Empire: "She has dotted the whole surface of the earth with her possessions and military forces, whose morning drumbeat, following the sun and keeping company with the hours, encircles the whole earth with one unbroken strain of the martial airs of England."

The United States today houses one hundred millions of happy and contented people, and our nation, our government, exercises a certain dominant but still more a very salutary influence on the many republics of America that are south of us. We all know that its influence is not to destroy but to save. This influence is not to dismember, but the aid of our President is always with the cause of peace and righteous economy. Oh, my friends, how happy will the day be when those two great nations unite together in the cause of permanent friendship.

We are told in Holy Scripture, that when the waters receded from the earth in the time of Noah, Almighty God made a solemn covenant with the patriarch and his posterity that from that time forth never again would this earth of ours be deluged by water, and as a sign, as a symbol, as an evidence of this covenant which He made, He caused an arch to appear in the Heavens, a rainbow to appear in the Heavens. Let Britannia and Columbia join hands across the Atlantic, and their outstretched arms will form a sacred arc, a sacred rainbow, a sacred arch of peace, that will cause and excite the admiration of the world and will proclaim to mankind that with God's help never more again shall this earth of ours be deluged with bloodshed, fraticide or war. I am sure that the time is most auspicious for the consummation of this great event, this great alliance. It sees us start with the help of one whom we all honor, the President of the United States, who brings his own strong personality and also the influence of his official position. I trust also that it will meet with the endorsement of our Congress, and we all know that it receives the encouragement of Sir Edward Grey, the Minister of Foreign Affairs of England. Looking around me here, I see that we have many distinguished men sent upon the same glorious mission. They come to uphold the hands of the President in this mission just as the people of Israel upheld the arms of Moses when he addressed them.

I pray that all you gentlemen who are participating in this glorious work will deserve to receive that title bestowed upon the friends of peace by the Prince of Peace, "Blessed are the peacemakers, for they shall be called the children of God."

PRESIDENT HOLT: I am asked by the Committee on Resolutions to state that all resolutions must be presented in writing and given without debate to the Committee on Resolutions, which will report at the end of the meeting on Friday afternoon.

It is now my painful duty to introduce to you the next speaker. Though his name appears on the official program as the President of the Congress, I feel bound.to state that he is mostly a figurehead. All the credit of making this Peace Congress the great success it is, belongs to Mr. Theodore Marburg of Baltimore, and his most efficient hardworking and public-spirited fellow citizens. You will now have the doubtful pleasure of listening to Mr. Hamilton Holt of New York, who will read a paper entitled:

A LEAGUE OF PEACE

The first National Peace Congress of the United States was held in New York City from the 14th to the 17th of April, 1907— just two months before the convening of the Second Hague Conference. In the personnel of its officers, speakers and delegates, it was the most distinguished unofficial gathering ever held in the United States.

As was to be expected, the main attention of the Congress was focused on the coming Hague Conference. Nearly all the speakers discussed it, and the two most important resolutions passed were those favoring the negotiation of a general treaty of arbitration and the turning of The Hague Conference into a permanent international body.

The Hague Conference, thanks in large measure to the leadership of the United States delegation, took a long step towards making these two propositions realities. The principle of obligatory arbitration was unanimously adopted by all the nations, and had not Germany and Austria and a few of the smaller European states objected so bitterly, a general treaty in accordance with that principle would have been drafted and approved.

The nations also took the first steps towards turning The Hague Conferences into an automatic and periodic World Congress, by taking the Third Conference out of the hands of Russia and putting it in charge of an international preliminary committee which was to meet about 1913 and determine its method of organization and progress.

When the Second National Peace Congress of the United States was convened in Chicago exactly two years ago this very day and hour, the Second Hague Conference had already passed into history and the world was just beginning to realize what a great work it had accomplished for international justice and peace. As Elihu Root has so truly said, that Conference "presents the greatest advance ever made at a single time towards the reasonable and peaceful regulation of international conduct, unless it be the advance made at The Hague Conference of 1899."

The Chicago Congress was not content, however, with passing congratulatory resolutions on things already accomplished. Like the New York Congress it set its face towards the future and spoke out brave and strong. Not only did it declare that war was "out of date" in this age of Hague Conferences courts and arbitration treaties, but it demanded as the most pressing "next steps" in the peace movement the creation of a peace commission by our government to study the whole peace question, a general treaty of obligatory arbitration, and the establishment of a League of Peace, to make the recurrence of war impossible. Two years have now elapsed since these three recommendations were uttered. Has any progress been made towards their realization?

Last June the Congress of the United States passed unanimously the following resolution:

"RESOLVED, etc., 'That a commission of five members be appointed by the President of the United States to consider the expediency of utilizing existing international agencies for the purpose of limiting the armaments of the nations of the world by international agreement and of constituting the combined navies of the world an international force for the preservation of universal peace, and to consider and report upon any other means to diminish the expenditures of government for military purposes and to lessen the probabilities of war.' "

In his annual message to Congress, dated December 16, 1910, President Taft stated:

"I have not as yet made appointments to the commission because I have invited and am awaiting the expressions of foreign governments as to their willingness to co-operate with us in the appointment of similar commissions or representatives who would meet with our commissions and by joint action seek to make their work effective."

It is impossible to overestimate this epoch-making document and the action of the President upon it. When the President appoints the members of the Commission for the first time in the annals of history a great nation in time of peace will prepare for peace.

It is in the realm of arbitration, however, that the greatest cause for rejoicing exists. The world, to be sure, has not yet obtained the desired general treaty of obligatory arbitration. It has got, however, what is of vastly more importance. President Taft's statement that he is willing to settle all disputes, even those involving national honor, by arbitration, is the most momentous declaration ever made by a man in his position in favor of peace. The proposed arbitration treaty of unlimited scope with Great Britain is the practical application of this declaration. Already it has transfigured the whole peace movement and has rendered the code of war obnoxious if not obsolete. And this is the situation that confronts the world as we assemble here today at the opening of the Third National Peace Congress of the United States. It is our duty to look ahead through the vista opened up by President Taft's high statesmanship and to take as resolute and progressive a stand here as the New York and the Chicago Congresses did four and two years ago.

There are many pressing problems before us waiting to be

solved. The judicial arbitration court created by the Second Hague Conference, all but the detail of the method of the selection of the judges, is yet to be constituted. No attention has yet been paid to the requests of both the First and the Second Hague Conferences that the governments give themselves over to the serious study of the limitation of armaments. It is not yet provided that the future Hague Conferences become automatic, periodic and self-governing bodies, as our delegation suggested at the Conference of 1907. The Peace Commission is not yet appointed. We should consider all these and many other questions where our voice may be of help to governments, and peace societies both here and abroad. But the one all-important issue before us is the pending arbitration treaty with Great Britain; for this treaty is destined to make war hereafter impossible between the English speaking people of the earth.

The peace movement, we have now come to realize, is nothing but the process of substituting law for war. The world has already learned to substitute law for war in hamlets, towns, cities, states and even within the forty-six sovereign civilized nations. But in that international realm over and above each nation in which each nation is equally sovereign, the only way at the present moment for a nation to secure its rights is by the use of force. Force, therefore, or war as it is called when exerted by a nation against another nation—is at present the only legal and final method of settling international differences. The world is now using a Christian code of ethics for individuals, and a pagan code for nations, though there is no double standard of ethics in the moral world. In other words, the nations are in that state of civilization where without a qualm they claim the right to settle their disputes in a manner which they would actually put their own subjects to death for imitating. Thus the peace problem is nothing but the ways and means of doing *between* the nations what has already been done *within* the nations. International law follows private law. The "United Nations" follow the United States.

At present international law has reached the same state of development that private or municipal law had attained in the

tenth century. Furthermore a careful study of the formation
of the thirteen American Colonies from separate states into our
present compact union discloses the fact that the nations today
are in the same stage of development that the American Colonies
were at about the time of their first confederation. As the
United States came into existence by the establishment of the
Articles of Confederation and the Continental Congress, so the
"United Nations" at this very moment exist by the fact of The
Hague Court and the recurring Hague Conferences, The Hague
Court being the promise of the Supreme Court of the World and
The Hague Conferences being the prophecy of the Parliament
of Man. We may look with confidence therefore to a future in
which the world will have an established court with jurisdiction
over all questions, self-governing conferences with power to legislate on all affairs of common concern, and an executive power of
some form to carry out the decrees of both. To deny this is to
ignore all the analogies of private law and the whole trend of the
world's political history since the Declaration of Independence.
As Secretary Knox has said in his great address delivered last
June at the commencement of the University of Pennsylvania:

"We have reached a point when it is evident that the future
holds in store a time when war shall cease; when the nations of
the world shall realize a federation as real and vital as that now
subsisting between the component parts of a single State."

I recall no more far-visioned statement than this ever emanat-
ing from the chancellery of a great State. It means nothing less
than that the age-long dreams of the poets, the prophets and the
philosophers have at last entered the realms of practical statesmanship, and the world is on the threshold of the dawn of universal peace.

The political organization of the world, therefore, is the task
of the twentieth century. But the formation of a world government must be a very slow process. Such a federal government
when complete would be as the historian Freeman has said, "The
most finished and the most artificial production of political
ingenuity." To accomplish it is surely not the work of a day
or a year.

How then can this movement be hastened? There are only two ways. First by the education of the public opinion of the world so as to compel the governments to move at successive Hague Conferences or at special international conferences, and, second, by a few of the more enlightened nations organizing themselves together for peace in advance of the others. This latter method is already being adopted extensively. The Judicial Arbitration Court will be constituted by only a few of the nations at first. England and the United States will not wait for a general treaty of obligatory arbitration before establishing a model one between themselves. Chile and Argentina did not delay for concurrent action on the part of the whole world before they commenced to disarm, as the statue of the Christ on the summit of the Andes so eloquently attests. Why, then, should not a few nations here and now form among themselves a League of Peace to hasten the ultimate world federation?

The idea of a League of Peace is not novel. All federal governments and confederations of governments, both ancient and modern, are essentially Leagues of Peace, even though they may have functions to perform which often lead directly to war.

The ancient Achaian League of Greece, the Confederation of Swiss Cantons, the United Provinces of the Netherlands and the United States of America are the most perfect systems of federated governments known to history. Less perfect, but none the less interesting to students of government, are the Latium League of thirty cities, the Hanseatic League, and in modern times the German Confederation. Even the Dual and Triple Alliances and the Concert of Europe might be called more or less inchoate Leagues of Peace.

Any League of Peace, however, likely to be established in the immediate future and designed to be of real and lasting benefit to humanity must differ from all previous and present leagues, alliances and confederations in total abstinence from the use of force. The ancient leagues as well as the modern confederations have generally been unions of offense and defense. They stood ready, if they did not actually propose, to use their common forces to compel outside states to obey their will. Thus they were as frequently Leagues of Oppression as Leagues of Peace.

The problem of the League of Peace is therefore the problem of the use of force. Shall the members of the League "not only keep the peace themselves but prevent by force, if necessary, its being broken by others," outside of the League, as ex-President Roosevelt has suggested? Or shall it exercise its force only within its membership and so be on the side of law and order and never on the side of arbitrary will or tyranny? Or rather shall it never use force at all? Whichever of these three possibilities is ultimately adopted, I think that at first it would be unwise for a League of Peace to attempt to use force for any purpose whatsoever. Besides, the use of force will probably be found unnecessary. When nations arrive at that state of civilization where they are ready to settle their differences by arbitration rather than by war, they are ready peaceably to abide by the decision of arbitral tribunals. The history of arbitration clearly demonstrates this. With but one or two insignificant exceptions, the nations have lived up to all arbitral awards, both in the letter and the spirit of the judgment and there have been hundreds of such awards. We need a policeman to use force on criminals. But happily there is no such thing nowadays as a criminal nation.

Moreover to project a League of Peace at the present moment with a specially constituted international force at its disposal would instantly beget suspicion, if not alarm, on the part of all nations not invited to join. They would consider it an alliance against themselves and would very likely proceed forthwith to start a counter alliance to preserve the balance of power.

With the idea in view then, that the League of Peace shall not have any specially constituted common army and navy at its disposal, I offer herewith, for whatever it may be worth, the following constitution for a proposed League of Peace in the hope that it may possibly serve as a basis for further study.

1. The nations in the League shall refer all disputes of whatsoever a nature to arbitration.

2. The Hague Court or other duly constituted courts shall decide all disputes that cannot be settled by diplomacy.

3. The League shall provide a periodical convention or assembly to make all rules for the League, such rules to become law unless vetoed by a nation within a stated period.

4. Each member of the League shall have the right to arm itself according to its own judgment.

5. Any member of the League shall have the right to withdraw on due notice.

The advantages that a nation would gain in becoming a member of such a League are manifest. The risk of war would be eliminated between the members of the League, and a method would be devised whereby they could develop their common intercourse and interests as far or as fast as they could unanimously agree on ways and means. It is conceivable that such a league might in time reduce tariffs and postal rates and in a thousand other ways promote commerce and comity among its members. Indeed the possibilities of such a League are almost infinite, even though it attempts to employ no force at all to compel obedience to its will.

Assuming, then, the desirability of such a League of Peace, how is it to be brought about?

Surely the first step is to conclude the arbitration treaty now being negotiated with Great Britain. Once this treaty is upon the international statute books, and as surely as daylight follows dawn, it will be followed by similar treaties with other nations. Japan and France are said to be ready—even anxious—to negotiate similar treaties with us. Indeed it is by no means impossible that there will be a race between England and Japan on the one hand and France and the United States on the other to see which can conclude the second model arbitration treaty of the world.

Thus the time is likely soon to come when several of the nations having bound themselves each to each by eternal chains of peace will be ready to take the next logical step and negotiate a general treaty of arbitration among themselves. This, to all intents and purposes, would constitute a League of Peace. And it would inevitably grow in power and prestige until all the nations of the world entered its concordant and prosperous circle.

Indeed it might be a stroke of statesmanship if an article were added to the proposed arbitration treaty between Great Britain and the United States, inviting other nations to adhere to it. This would save much time and effort, and obviate the necessity for each of the forty-six nations to negotiate a special treaty with every other.   Thus only one treaty would have to be negotiated instead of 1034.   But whether Great Britain and the United States ask other nations to adhere to their model treaty or not, the principle of unlimited arbitration will grow—first by a few nations adopting it, then by more, until finally the whole world will agree to enthrone reason rather than might as the great arbiter of their destinies, and war shall reign no more.   First, an unlimited arbitration treaty between Great Britain and the United States.   Second, a League of Peace.   Third, the Federation of the World.

Is all this a dream?   I have already quoted the weighty words of Secretary Knox prophesying the coming of a world federation. Let me close with the equally prophetic utterance of an equally responsible and distinguished statesman.   On the 17th of March, at the dinner of the International Arbitration League, the Right Honorable Sir Edward Grey, the British Secretary of State for Foreign Affairs said:

"If an arbitration treaty is made between the two great countries on the lines sketched out by the President of the United ·States. . . . don't let them set narrow bounds to their hopes of the beneficent results which may develop from it in the course of time—results which I think must extend far beyond the two countries originally concerned.   The effect on the world at large of the example would be bound to have beneficent consequences.   To set a good example is to hope that others of the great powers will follow it, and if they did follow there would eventually be something like a League of Peace."

The President of the United States was introduced by the presiding officer, Mr. Holt, as follows:

The President of the United States occupies the greatest national office in the world.

Not only does he preside over a confederation of forty-six sovereign States—the greatest peace society known to history, and a living example to the forty-six civilized nations of the world of the way to obtain peace through political organization—but he holds his exalted office by the deliberate choice and sanction of ninety million free and enlightened people.

The only way for a man to rise above the level of the presidency of the United States is to ascend into the international realm.

By far the greatest and noblest thing to be done in the international realm is to organize the world for peace. Peace is the outcome of justice, justice of law, law of political organization. Emanuel Kant, one of the greatest intellects the world has ever produced, proclaimed this as the true philosophy of peace, when in 1795, he said, "We never can have universal peace until the World is politically organized," and it will never be possible to organize the world politically until all the nations have a representative form of government.

This afternoon we have with us not only the man who is President of the United States, but also the man who has taken the highest stand ever taken by the head of a great nation in favor of law instead of war as a method of settling international differences. If peace hath her victories no less renowned than war, its greatest victory during the present century if not during the entire human era is the declaration of President Taft that he is willing to refer *all* questions, even those involving national honor, to arbitration.

This declaration exalted him at once and forever to the position of leader in the peace movement of the world, and offers to the nations a guiding principle that they will support with ever-increasing favor and fervor until it is made a universal law.

And so when this unlimited arbitration treaty now being negotiated between Great Britain and the United States is ratified by the Senate—it is already ratified by the people of England and America—and is followed by similar treaties with all the remaining nations, great and small, President Taft will have done more than any man in all history to hasten that day sure to come, when as Victor Hugo prophesied in 1849, "the only battlefield will be the market opening to commerce, and the mind to new ideas."

The Third American Peace Congress of the United States will now have the unprecedented honor of being opened and addressed by the President of the United States.

ADDRESS BY THE PRESIDENT OF THE UNITED STATES

It expresses my feelings when I say that I am frightened by the introduction of the Chairman. I have been told before that I exercise in the presidential office greater power than any man on earth. I have been able to take that idea in, and I know how much of it is real fact and how much of it is eloquence turning a good period.

It is possible that the President does exercise greater power than that of any other ruler in the world, but I am able to give you a little information from the standpoint of one with some opportunity to observe, and I am bound to say that the burden and responsibility of the position are brought home to him much more clearly than the power.

Your Chairman has been good enough to refer to something that I had said with reference to a hope for general arbitration, and the expression of opinion that an arbitration treaty of the widest scope between two great nations, would be a very important step in securing the peace of the world. I do not claim any patent on that statement, and I have no doubt that it is shared by all who understand the situation at all. I have no doubt that an important step—if such an arbitration treaty can be concluded —will have been taken, but it will not bring an end of war at once. It is a step, and we must not defeat our purposes by enlarging the expectation of the people of the world as to what is to happen and then disappointing them. In other words, we must look forward with reasonable judgment, and look to such an arbitration treaty as one step to be followed by other steps as rapidly as possible; but we must realize that we are dealing with a world that is fallible and full of weakness—with some wickedness in it—and that reforms that are worth having are brought about little by little and not by one blow. I do not mean to say by this that I am not greatly interested in bringing about the arbitration treaty or treaties that are mentioned, but I do think that we are likely to make more progress if we look forward with reasonable foresight and realize the difficulties that are to be overcome, than if we think we have opened the gate to eternal peace with one key and within one year.

I am not going to dwell upon the question of the arbitration treaty which is in the process of negotiation. The truth is I would much rather stand upon the platform and refer to such a step as taken, to such a treaty as made and acquiesced in, than to discuss it during its negotiation when I am part or one of the negotiators. Therefore, I would wish to make the few remarks which I will address to you this afternoon upon one or two other subjects than that of the general arbitration treaty.

Since the matter of the arbitration treaty has been suggested, I have received a great many invitations from various associations whose titles indicated that their purpose was the promotion of peace, and it seemed to me that in the number of those associations and in their lack of coöperation we might find some opportunity for an improvement in the movement and for giving greater force to organized expression for peace. You have a Congress here, and in this Congress I assume that a good many associations take part. Have you any basis of organization and union which unites your efforts in anything but this Congress? Don't you think you had better unite your peace associations and make your efforts united toward the one object you have in view? Aren't you likely to squander a little of your force if you maintain isolated associations and do not come together for the purpose we all have in view?

The second thought that I would like to bring to you is that one of the evidences of an improvement in the world for peace is the fact that all the state departments, all chancellories of foreign affairs are themselves now organized into agencies for the promotion of peace by negotiation. The State Department at Washington has no more important or absorbing duty than to lend its good offices to the republics—the twenty republics of this hemisphere—to prevent their various differences from leading into war. And, not to go back of this administration, there have been four instances in which the action of the State Department, taken in connection with some of the influential countries of South America, has absolutely prevented wars which twenty or thirty years ago would certainly have ensued. The difficulties with respect to war are not now so large, although, of course, the danger from them is not absent—but not now so large with stable and powerful governments, maintaining law and order with something like perfection, but it is in those governments which do not exercise complete control over their people and in which revolutions and insurrections break out, not only to the injury and danger of the people and their property as well as of the government itself, but to the disturbance of all the world in their neighborhood. It is with reference to disturbances of this kind that the United States and the other great republics of this hemisphere must exercise their kindly and peaceful influence as much as possible. One of the difficulties that the United States finds is the natural suspicion that the countries engaged have of the motive which the United States has in tendering its good offices. Now, asseveration, I presume, helps but little where the suspicion is real, and yet I like to avail myself of an opportunity in such a presence as this to assert that there is not, in the whole length and breadth of the United States, among its peoples, any desire. for territorial aggrandizement, and that its people as a whole will not permit this government, if it would, to take any steps in respect to foreign governments except those which will aid those foreign governments and those foreign people in maintaining their own government and in maintaining peace within their borders. We have had wars, and we know what they are. We know the responsibilities they entail, the burdens and losses and horrors— and we would have none of them. We have a magnificent domain of our own in which we are attempting to work out and show to the world success in popular government, and we need no more territory in which to show that.

p. 16, line 21, read asseveration *in place of* asservation

But we have attained great prosperity and great power. We have become a powerful member of the community of nations in which we live, and there is, therefore, thrown upon us necessarily a care and responsibility for the peace of the world in our neighborhood, and a burden of helping those nations that cannot help themselves, if we may do that peacefully and effectively.

Now, we have undertaken such a duty in respect to Santo Domingo. She was torn with contending factions. Foreign nations held her bonds and desired to collect what was due. We entered into an arrangement by which we put in our revenue officers to collect the revenue. We took charge of the custom houses, and that agency gave us an instrumentality by which we have enabled that nation to go on, until she is rapidly paying off her debts, and while we have been there has had no factions or revolutions.

I may add that our position with respect to Santo Domingo enabled us to intervene when she and Haiti thought it was necessary to fight about something, and to persuade those two nations to submit their difference to The Hague.

I do not think we can avoid the discharge of a duty like that. It helps the world, it helps the country which we help, and it helps ourselves by showing that a nation ought to have a conscience and ought to have a neighborly feeling as well as an individual one.

Now, my friends, I am not going on with these desultory remarks. I am glad that I could come here to this Congress of Peace, and any personality that I may have of a representative character I wish to lend to your Congress, and lend to it the support of the United States.

In introducing Mr. Andrew Carnegie as the next speaker Mr. Holt said:

This Congress has the great honor of having on its platform this afternoon Mr. Andrew Carnegie, President of the First National Peace Congress of the United States and Honorable J. M. Dickinson, Secretary of War, President of the Second National Peace Congress of the United States.

As to Mr. Carnegie, I think it is fair to say that no man in the whole world during the past generation has stood more conspicuously and worked more zealously, constantly, and untiringly for international peace than he.

You have all heard of the sinews of war. When we think of him we cannot help thinking of the sinews of Peace.

The year 1910 will forever be memorable in the annals of the American Peace movement. In that year President Taft made his epochal declaration in favor of unlimited arbitration, Congress created the United States Peace Commission, Mr. Edwin Ginn was the first citizen of the world to give $100,000 to Peace, and then Mr. Andrew Carnegie electrified all Christendom with his princely $10,000,000 endowment, for a peace foundation.

Mr. Carnegie's gift is the noblest and crowning benefaction of his life. As long as capital draws interest, this endowment will yield its half million a year, and when wars cease as they inevitably will, when nations learn the better way, it will be used to abolish the next greatest scourge of mankind.

Let us congratulate ourselves that this great gift has been given by an American to Americans for the world.

I now have the honor of introducing to you the donor of the first Dreadnought in the Navy of Peace—Mr. Andrew Carnegie.

THE PEOPLE WHO LIVED IN DARKNESS HAVE SEEN A GREAT LIGHT

ANDREW CARNEGIE

Gentlemen: I rise with diffidence to address the members of our various peace societies here assembled in the presence of the great peace-compelling ruler—the bearer of the message from on high, who, through his trumpet with one blast, has blown down the stronghold of international war, which lay in the fallacy that nations could not submit to arbitration questions affecting their honor or vital interests without losing their sovereignty, which only meant, however, their fancied dignity, the truth being that the nation which could not submit any and every question was already bereft of sovereignty, which means power to do what it pleases. When a nation agrees to settle all disputes, she possesses her sovereignty.

There had been slight glimpses of a coming dawn for some years. A few small stars twinkled at intervals in the sky for a moment and all again was darkness, denser than before. No steady flame was visible until the brilliant sun burst forth proclaiming its sovereignty over all things, and revealing to our leader the true path. Then, but not till then, the people that had walked in darkness saw a great light.

To President Taft's appeal to the world, in which both his heart and head went forth for one great nation to join his country in proving their sovereignty by agreeing to submit all disputes to peaceful settlement, behold there came such responce across the sea from the other branch of our English-speaking race, as had never been made to any appeal before. The leaders of parties in Britain sunk the partizan in the patriot, touched by the President's appeal. The nation was unanimous; all parties fused into one. Today the representatives of the two lands are formulating the treaty, and here Britain knows nothing of party, for all parties coöperate, a sublime spectacle, proving that party issues fade in the presence of the high moral issue which leads nations to peace. What of our own statesmen, leaders of party? Are they to emulate their compeers of Britain? My prediction is that they will, and that our republic will prove to the world that politics with us are only skin deep, and that our statesmen rise above party when a great moral world-wide victory is within our grasp. I am not without some basis for the faith that is in me.

Mr. Chairman, upon the subject which demands attention today in our mission as peace advocates, I am somewhat disposed to exclaim: "Farewell the plumed steed, the ear-piercing fife, the spirit stirring drum, the royal banner, and all pomp and circumstance of glorious war."

"Othello's occupation gone," what use to preach to the converted, and where is the peace orator to find the unconverted today in our land? Whither has the mailed champion fled who insisted that war was the mother of valor and heroism, ever warning us that "When roll of drum and battle's roar shall cease upon the earth, O! then, no more the deed, the race of heroes in the land!"

The heroes who stand on land and shoot at each other scarcely discernible, miles distant, or in ships at sea firing through space seven miles away, for such has modern war become—the courage required for this does not strike one as obviously very heroic. The truth is that the ranks of industrialism are revealing daily in many lands true heroes who excel those of the war-worn past as much as civilization excels barbarism, for they risk their own lives to save those of their fellowmen. Thus peaceful civilization is at last producing a race of genuine heroes, not such as kill, but such as save their fellowmen at the risk of their own lives. Such the true, the only heroes of our age. Brute courage man shares with the brute. The moral courage of today's true heroes is alone divine.

In 1759 there flashed upon the mind of Franklin the idea of the federation of the States. This was to be under the monarchy. Although this had the almost unanimous concurrence of the conference, the measure was almost unanimously rejected by the provincial legislatures of the States. In this measure of Franklin's we have the germ which blossomed into the unrivaled American Constitution, which Gladstone pronounced the most wonderful work ever produced at one time by the brain and purpose of man.

Franklin guarded and developed this germ until it blossomed, and now it astonishes the world, keeping forty-seven states, comprising the wealthiest nation the world has ever seen, in peaceful, harmonious relations ever growing closer, in a territory as large as Europe, all citizens under the reign of law; no citizen permitted to redress his real or fancied wrongs, but all compelled to plead before a court of justice. Franklin is one of the immortals. Matthew Arnold has pronounced his the weightiest voice that ever sounded across the Atlantic, and the people of our republic through him had seen a great light. We now rest upon peaceful federation; but what Franklin did for his country, the President standing here in the flesh before us has done what promises to be for all countries. He has laid the axe to the root of international

war and it will soon be banished from the face of the earth, and
as long as history endures and records of great events are kept,
so long must one name shine with glorious luster. Gentlemen,
in an inspired moment our leader saw the great light. How,
when, where, we know not. Probably the message came to him
in a flash and he was guided he knew not how, but surely the
Angel of the Lord appeared and entrusted to him the divine mission.

I was beholding the greatest natural wonder in the world, the
Grand Canyon, last spring, when the New York papers arrived
and I read the President's divine message, and was exalted. I
could not refrain from writing him a letter which perhaps surprised
him, but gentlemen, I have seen the great light. I occupy a
strange position; Britain is my Motherland, the Republic my
Wifeland. I love them both, as Mother and as Wife, and to see
my native and adopted lands hand in hand leading the world
to peace would add a new charm to my life. I cannot imagine
to what extremes I might go, even to murmuring "Now let thy
servant depart in peace, for he has seen the Glory of the Lord!"

In introducing the next speaker, the Presiding Officer referred
to the Reciprocity Treaty that had been presented to the Congress
of the United States and said, "No man in Canada has exerted
a greater influence in favor of this Reciprocity Measure than the
speaker whom I now have the honor to introduce, Dr. James A.
MacDonald, Editor of the *Toronto Globe*."

Dr. MacDonald then delivered the following address:

Three things only would I say and say them in six minutes.

First, speaking for Canada—half the continent—if the proposal for unlimited arbitration between the empire to which I
belong and the republic to which you belong is ratified into a
treaty, the name of William Howard Taft will be mentioned in
the world's future history, and so long as men love peace, and
when the day comes that nations shall not lift up swords against
nations, that name in the long line of American presidents will
be mentioned with honor.

My second word is this: Above all other parts of the world, the Dominion of Canada has the greatest stake in that proposal. Canada has most to gain through peace; most to lose through war. The sovereignty of Britain and the sovereignty of the United States meet at the Canadian boundary line and meet nowhere else. There would be the storm center, the battle ground and the loss. An Anglo-American treaty of arbitration would determine forever that the boundary between these two English speaking nations on this continent shall be, not a danger point, but along its three thousand seven hundred miles, and for all time to come a bond of union, a tryst of friendship, a pledge of peace.

Canada stands on the northern hand of this American continent, a free nation in the British Empire, the nearest neighbor and next of kin to the United States, embodying in herself the perfect understanding and mutual confidence by which for a hundred years the international boundary has been without a fort or battleship, the wonder of the nations and the hope of the world.

Canada is now at the parting of the ways: Not in politics or in national relationship; there our heart is fixed. The deepest resolve of the Canadians is to stand, as for half a century they have stood, loyal Britons, free Canadians, surrendering not one atom of the rights of self-government, attracted neither by the jingo imperialism on one side, nor by the dreams of continentalism on the other. I know, sir, there is no precedent for such a national ideal, but let us have a chance, and by the blessings of the God of Nations, we will make a precedent for nations that follow after.

And that is not all. Canada has a problem of her own, the great problem of Canadian democracy to work out. It is our ambition, sir, so to develop the life and resources of our country that in our nation democracy may have a new birth of freedom, and "government of the people, by the people and for the people," a new chance to secure for all citizens not only "life, liberty and the pursuit of happiness," but a full measure of justice as well.

But, sir, to do that we must have peace. We cannot afford the waste and loss of war. The taxes of our people will all be needed for the development of our resources and for making Canada the

home, not for eight millions, as she has now, but for eighty millions of contented and prosperous people before the century shall
close. Before we are forced into war, to military burdens for
battleships and armaments, we pause and make our appeal to
the mother country beyond the sea and to the sister republic at
our side—we make this appeal for you to join hands and lift this
barbaric obligation out of our way. In God's name why should
that young nation be tricked out in the false and faded glory
of the war régime, or cursed with the discredited inheritance of
an outgrown and repudiated past? The waste of money Canada might survive, but not the waste of men. In the quiet of
our northern homes we have been reading history, and not in
vain. We have seen Great Britain robbed of the best of her
breed, paying the awful price of degeneracy for the mastership
of the sea. We have seen every province of it, every shire of it,
every glen of it, every moor of it, robbed of its best. Kipling
told us the ghastly truth:

>We have strawed our best to the wood's unrest
> To the shark and the sheering gull;
>If blood be the price of admiralty,
> Lord God, we've paid in full.

Blood was the price, the best blood of England, the best of
Scotland, of Ireland and of Wales. And that waste of the best
has meant the later breeding from the worst. The sad story of
decay in every shire, on every moor, and in every glen, is the result, relentless and inevitable, of the wanton waste of the fittest,
in camp and on the field of war.

The short history of your own republic—and we have had it
open to us, and opened so that we have seen it—is charged with
the same stern warning. What means all this confusion and
crime in politics and business and in the Halls of Justice? Who
bred these enemies of your nation? Not your best, your million
men and boys who fell in your Civil War. Had they been spared,
the problem of American sovereignty would have been solved
today.

And, sir, Canada cannot afford to take the risk or to pay the price. Not from weakness, not from cowardice, not from fear—not that—the best blood of the best races is red and hot in our veins. But, sir, the thing would be the maddest folly, an unimaginable crime against humanity. Before it need be done we ask that the necessity for it be swept away. And Canada desires this pact of peace not for her own sake alone but for the world's. We want no alliance for offense or for aggression. We covet the territory of no kingdom or ruler anywhere. We covet not their wealth. The flag of Canada could wave, fold in fold with the flag of your republic on the Atlantic and on the Pacific, not to threaten, not to inspire fear, but to guard all the commerce of the world that sails the seas and to keep the peace for all the people that line the shores.

My last word is this: The time to do it is at hand. The hour has begun to strike. The tide is swelling to the flood, and if ever at any time, or anywhere, I have the right to speak for the country where I was born, where my father was born before me, my father's father before him, and where his father, and his father before him lived and died—if ever I had the right to speak for my country, or for the empire to which I belong, it is here and now, and to ask that the Parliament of Great Britain and the Congress of the United States, the King and the President joining hands, shall do this thing, and do it for good and do it forever.

President Holt introduced the next speaker as follows:

The international interests of the United States up to the present time have usually followed the longitudes rather than the latitudes. Happily we have at last begun to realize that Canada to the north and Latin America to the south offer as profitable fields for travel, commerce and friendship as Europe and Asia. If it is true that Europe is the land of yesterday and North America the land of today, it is equally certain that South America is the land of tomorrow. No man in the United States has realized the duty of cultivating friendship with Latin America more than the next speaker. Whether as a delegate to the Pan-American Conference at Rio de Janeiro in 1906, as president of the American delegation to the First Pan-American Scientific Congress at Santiago, Chile, as adviser to the Mexican government last September when the great University of Mexico was being established, or here at home as economist, editor, educator and statesman, he has ever been foremost in promoting amity and commerce among the nations of the New World. I now have the pleasure of introducing to you Professor Leo F. Rowe of the University of Pennsylvania, the subject of whose address is "The Contribution of Latin America to the Cause of International Peace."

THE CONTRIBUTIONS OF LATIN AMERICA TO THE CAUSE OF INTERNATIONAL PEACE

DR. LEO. S. ROWE

If the topic which I have selected required any special justification, the inquiries which I have received during the last two weeks would amply furnish it. From many different quarters the question has been put to me "Is it possible to speak of the contributions of Latin America to the Cause of International Peace?" "Would it not be more accurate to refer to these countries as disturbing factors in the present international situation?" This fundamentally erroneous view of the part played by the countries of Latin America in the development of the principle of international arbitration is due in large part to the fact that we have failed to interpret the development of Latin American affairs in the same broad, philosophic spirit that has been applied to the study of international relations on the continent of Europe. In fact, throughout the United States, there is a marked tendency to interpret Latin American international relations as if they were determined by the personal feeling of a few self-constituted leaders rather than by the same fundamental economic and social forces that have shaped European relations.

When the present international situation on the American continent is studied in a truly scientific spirit, we are surprised to find how many have been the contributions of the countries of Latin

America to the principle of international arbitration. No other section of the world has shown a more remarkable degree of self-control in the adjustment of international affairs. The merit of this achievement is all the greater because of the exceptionally difficult and delicate international problems involved.

The countries of Latin America emerged into independence with most of their frontiers either entirely unsettled or in an extremely unsatisfactory condition. Many of these disputes have presented questions which are usually regarded as so vital as hardly to permit of settlement by arbitration. Nevertheless, the countries of South America have given to the world some of the most striking instances of a pacific settlement of such controversies. Time and again they have been brought to the verge of war because of a seeming impossibility to reach a solution by any other means, but in almost every case the governments have found that the principle of arbitration is in no sense antagonistic to any of the vital interests involved.

It is well for us to bear in mind that the early history of the United States was characterized by an uncompromising attitude toward all questions involving national boundaries. The fixed and determined purpose to secure control of the mouth of the Mississippi, the aggressive position assumed in the settlement of the northwest boundary, our attitude toward the annexation of Texas and the control of California, stand in marked contrast with the position of the Latin American countries on questions quite as vital to their welfare. It is no exaggeration to say that had the countries of Latin America taken the same position with reference to their boundary disputes as that assumed by the United States during the first half of the century of our national existence, the history of the last one hundred years would be a record of continuous and bloody struggles.

The international questions confronting the countries of Latin America during the latter half of the nineteenth century and the beginning of the twentieth have been far more difficult and delicate than those confronting the countries of Europe, and yet, with two exceptions they have all been adjusted either through direct diplomatic negotiation or by means of arbitration.

The spectacle presented to the world at the close of the Paraguayan War when that country lay crushed and bleeding at the feet of Argentina, Brazil and Uruguay, may well serve as an example to all the nations of western civilization. For a time it looked as if Paraguay would be made the Poland of South America. If the usual European standards as to rights acquired by conquest had been applied, Paraguay would today no longer exist on the map as an independent country. At the suggestion of the Argentine Republic, it was agreed by the conquering triple alliance that victory does not carry with it the right to dismemberment and although Paraguay had been the aggressor in the struggle, the people of the country were not made to suffer because of the ambitions of a political dictator. The territorial integrity of the country was respected and whatever sacrifice this may have involved to the countries which had achieved so signal a victory their forbearance and self-control saved South America from a series of subsequent conflicts which the partition of Paraguay would undoubtedly have involved.

The Argentine Republic and Uruguay are today confronted by an international question so difficult and delicate that it can only be compared with our own policy with reference to the mouth of the Mississippi. Neither the government nor the people of the United States would for a moment entertain any compromise with reference to our complete and absolute control of the Mississippi River. Difficult and dangerous as is the question of the control of the River Plate, both the governments and people of Argentina and Uruguay are conscientiously endeavoring to find a satisfactory solution.

If time permitted, instances of this conciliatory spirit might be indefinitely multiplied. My main purpose is to show that in the settlement of the many difficult international questions confronting the countries of Latin America, they have shown a degree of forbearance and self-control which deserved far greater recognition, and which may well serve as an inspiration to all those who are interested in the maintenance of international peace. Public opinion in the United States has been misled by reason of the fact that the few instances in which arbitral awards have been rejected have been given such prominence as to create the impression that the countries of Latin America are unmindful of the obligations of an arbitral award.

The fact that the history of the countries of Latin America has been marked by many internal disturbances has obscured the fact that in their international relations they have been shown quite a different spirit. As time goes on we will recognize more and more fully the debt which the world owes to the forbearance and self-control which have made the history of international relations in South America a record of consistent attempts to preserve international peace in the face of great difficulties and, at times, great provocation.

The services of the countries of Latin America to the cause of international peace have not been confined to the advance of the principle of arbitration. They have made positive contributions to other branches of international law which may serve as an example even to the United States.

At the opening of the nineteenth century the United States took the lead in the development of the law of neutrality. Important as were our contributions at that time to this branch of the subject, we have not maintained our position of leadership. One of the fruitful sources of international irritation is the participation of the citizens of one country in the domestic disturbances of another. Our present law of neutrality is inadequate to prevent the international complications which arise from this cause.

Great Britain took up the great work of developing the law of neutrality at the point at which it was abandoned by the United States. By declaring it an offense for any of her subjects to accept, or agree to accept without the permission of the British government, any commission or engagement in the military or naval service of any foreign state at war with a state, with which Great Britain is at peace, an important step was taken in the development of neutral obligations. The position of leadership assumed by Great Britain in this respect has been followed by some of the larger Latin American countries and the world is now waiting to see the United States uphold its reputation as the historic defender of neutral rights and obligations by enlarging the scope of neutral obligations of our citizens and giving to the executive ample power to enforce such obligations.

The opportunity is now offered to the United States to take a step in advance of that taken by Great Britain by making it an offense for our citizens to participate in the internal disturbances of another country. Some way must be found to overcome any constitutional difficulty which may arise respecting the possibility of punishing a citizen for an offense committed in foreign territory. It is also high time that our federal legislation strengthen the arm of the executive in dealing with the forwarding of arms, munition and supplies to insurrectionary movements. The advanced position taken by the Argentine Republic during the recent uprising in Uruguay affords an excellent instance of the possibility of a broader interpretation of neutral obligations.

At the present moment on our Mexican border the executive is powerless to prevent such shipments because we still hold to the theory that such shipments are made in the ordinary course of trade and commerce, and cannot, therefore, be interfered with by our government. Here again the United States is given the opportunity to broaden the interpretation of neutral obligations, and in so doing we will be rendering the same service to international peace as the Argentine rendered by the advanced position which she took during the Uruguayan disturbances above referred to.

With a century's record of achievement of which they may well be proud, the countries of Latin America enter into the present world situation as important factors in sustaining and developing the principle of arbitration. When the final balance sheet of America's contribution to civilization is made up, a leading position must be given to the important part which the new world has played in promoting the cause of international peace. In this final estimate the far-reaching importance of Latin-America's contribution will not be overlooked.

President Holt introduced the next speaker as follows:

The next gentleman on the program has rendered great and enduring service to his country and to the cause of peace as an officer in the State Department. He particularly deserves the gratitude of all good men for the invaluable services he rendered the cause of international justice when he was agent for the Department of State in 1909–1910, at the trial of the Oronoco case between the United States and Venezuela before The Hague Tribunal.

We shall now have the great profit and pleasure of hearing from William C. Dennis, Esq., of Washington, D. C., whose subject is Compromise—the Great Defect of Arbitration.

COMPROMISE—THE GREAT DEFECT OF ARBITRATION

WILLIAM C. DENNIS

"Respect for the rights of others is peace" was a famous saying of a great Mexican patriot, lawyer and statesman, whose whole life was consecrated to the endeavor to establish the reign of law but whose entire career by the bitter irony of fate was spent in the midst of warfare. For Juarez found, as many great and good men have found before and since, that the world is full of those who are not yet willing to respect the rights of others, and as he was unable, owing to adverse circumstances, to secure justice for his countrymen through law they took up arms to obtain justice through force.

Force and law have long been competitors and rivals in the history of the individual. For hundreds of years trial by combat and trial by jury were competing remedies in England and only by slow, painful degrees did trial by jury prove its fitness to survive because it was a cheaper, surer, better way of obtaining justice.

In the same way arbitration and war are now competing remedies. War is "the state in which a nation prosecutes its right by force,"—arbitration is, or ought to be, an appeal to reason to do justice according to law. History seems to show that rightly or wrongly nations like men will continue to appeal to force to secure what they deem to be their just right until they become convinced that there is some surer and better way of obtaining justice, and arbitration can only hope to replace war as it demonstrates its superiority in actual practice. *Prima facie* this would not seem to be a very severe requirement for it would appear that anyone who looks at the matter philosophically must admit that the worst arbitral sentence which has ever been rendered is infinitely more to be desired than any war, but unfortunately most men are not philosophers and they cannot be expected in weighing the relative advantages of arbitration and war to consider ultimate results. If the municipal courts only replaced private warfare among individuals after the courts had been brought to a relatively high state of perfection through long experience, it can hardly be expected that nations will be more reasonable than men or that they will discard their swords for ploughshares in order to submit their difficulties to tribunals less efficient than those which have been found necessary for the settlement of disputes among men. In other words, it is reasonable to suppose that before international arbitration can banish warfare it must afford at least as satisfactory a method of obtaining justice between nations as our municipal tribunals now afford between individuals.

It therefore becomes the most pressing duty of the hour for all those interested in the abolition of war to study the present system of international arbitration with a view to so eliminating its defects that it may speedily emerge victorious in the struggle for the survival of the fittest which is now going on between arbitration and war.

The most striking characteristic of arbitration as it exists today between individuals, as a supplement to the regular courts, a characteristic which is peculiarly apparent when arbitration is applied to matters of general public interest, such as labor disputes, is the irresistible tendency shown by arbitrators to compromise and split-the-difference instead of doing justice though the heavens fall.

Almost every American who has represented the United States

before an international tribunal has made a record of his conclusion that international arbitration shows the same tendency. Gallatin, who represented the United States in the Northeastern Boundary arbitration with Great Britain correctly foresaw the results of that and many other arbitrations when he said:

"An arbitrator, whether he be king or farmer, rarely decides on strict principle of law; he has always a bias to try if possible to split the difference."

And General Harrison, counsel for Venezuela in the British Guiana boundary arbitration, General Foster, Agent of the United States in the Behring Sea and Alaska boundary arbitrations, Mr. Carter, counsel in the Behring Sea arbitration, and Mr. Root, counsel for the United States in the recent North Atlantic Fisheries arbitration, all have told the same story.

Passing from the argument from analogy and the argument from authority to the argument from history, a necessarily brief review of the actual results in certain typical and important arbitrations fully sustains the conclusions reached by the American lawyers and statesmen who have had the best opportunity to judge arbitration at first hand.   Take, for instance, what may perhaps be fairly regarded as five typical and leading arbitrations in which the United States and Great Britain were concerned prior to the inauguration of The Hague Tribunal: The arbitration between the United States and England over the Northeastern Boundary, before the King of the Netherlands, under the treaty of September 29, 1827; the Alabama arbitration with Great Britain under the treaty of Washington; the arbitration between the United States and Great Britain regarding the northwestern or San Juan boundary before the Emperor of Germany under other articles of the same treaty; the Behring Sea arbitration with Great Britain, and finally, the arbitration between Great Britain and Venezuela over the British Guiana boundary which, in view of the circumstances may well be classed with the other Anglo-American arbitrations.

In the first of these cases, the Northeastern Boundary arbitration, the royal arbitrator frankly admitted his inability to render a judicial decision and recommended a compromise, a course which amounted to such a clear departure from the terms of the submission that the United States refused to abide by the award and Great Britain acquiesced in this decision. And it is generally admitted that the Behring Sea award and the British Guiana award, however useful they may have been in disposing of very troublesome difficulties which might have led to war, cannot be deemed to rank as judicial decisions. This leaves only the San Juan and Alabama arbitration awards which can fairly claim to stand as decisions which, whether right or wrong in their results, were judicial decisions upon the law and the facts as understood by the arbitrators—a ratio of three compromises out of five arbitrations.

Turning to the arbitral decisions of The Hague Tribunal, now nine in number, the result, as was to be expected, is more encouraging. In the first decision of The Hague Court, in the Pious Fund case, the Tribunal found in favor of the United States on every point except one, and that one point was of such difficulty that it is believed without unjust suspicion that the decision was the result of a compromise based on the fact that it was re-solved in favor of the defeated litigant. In the next two cases, the Venezuela Preferential case and the Japanese House Tax case, the decisions were all one way and consequently the idea of compromise, at least as to the result, is precluded, and the same may be said of the recent Savaker extradition case between Great Britain and France. In the fourth and seventh cases before The Hague Tribunal, the case of the Muscat Dhows and the Norway-Sweden Boundary arbitration, the decisions, while not absolutely in favor of either party appear to an outsider at least to be so reasonably founded on the law and the facts as to be fairly exempt from the charge of being matters of compromise. Indeed, it is submitted that the Norway-Sweden decision is upon the whole, from a technical point of view, one of the most creditable achievements of The Hague Tribunal. This leaves for discussion the Casablanca arbitration between France and Germany, the North Atlantic Coast Fisheries case between the United States and Great Britain, and the Orinoco Steamship Company case between the United States and Venezuela.

In the Casablanca case The Hague Court probably rendered its greatest contribution, so far, to the peace of the world. That case of all those decided by the Tribunal was sent to the court under the imminent threat of war, and although its decision depended upon matters of law and fact, it also, under the circumstances of the case, was thought to involve what are commonly called questions of national honor. It is an ungracious task to criticize a decision which was accepted as satisfactory by the people of both countries litigant, and which has been of such practical benefit to the world as has this decision, but of course this case cannot pretend, either in the result reached or the opinion rendered, to rank as a judicial decision. Dr. Lammasch, four times a member and three times a president of tribunals sitting under The Hague Conventions, has expressed the well-nigh universal opinion when he refers to this case in a recent magazine article as having a "preponderatingly diplomatic character."

As regards the remaining two decisions of The Hague Tribunal, the North Atlantic Coast Fisheries arbitration and the Orinoco Steamship case, the situation is more complex. The general result in the Fisheries case was a decision in favor of the United States, although some of the American contentions were not sustained, and it would require an intimate acquaintance with and an elaborate discussion of the decision to reach any conclusion as to just how far certain findings of the court were affected by the spirit of compromise. It is significant, however, that Dr. Lammasch, the president of the Tribunal, has himself said, in the article already referred to, that the judgment in the North Atlantic Coast Fisheries case "contained elements of a compromise."

Dr. Lammasch defends this course on the ground that "the court had received special and extraordinary full powers for this purpose." It is submitted with all deference however, that the very specific and detailed terms of submission under which the court was sitting will be searched in vain when justly construed for any authority to compromise.

The situation in the Orinoco Steamship case in which Dr. Lammasch also presided is much the same. The decision upon the great question of principle involved, the right judicially to revise an international award, and in all its larger aspects, is in favor of the United States, although the holding of the tribunal on one point resulted in the failure to allow the principal item of damage claimed by this Government. The decision has, however, been very sharply criticized in Venezuela in articles which bear every earmark of having emanated from someone connected with the Venezuelan Agency at The Hague, chiefly on the ground that it was a compromise. In view of Dr. Lammasch's admission with regard to the North Atlantic Coast Fisheries case, and in the light of the terms of submission and the contentions of the parties in case, counter-case and argument, it seems reasonable to infer that certain portions of this opinion, which was likewise written by him, also contain elements of compromise.

Summing up the results of this necessarily brief examination of the decisions of The Hague Court, so far rendered, it would seem that there are six decisions which at least, on the face of the record are not open to the criticism that they are based on compromise so far at least as the actual decisions are concerned; one decision, the Casablanca award, which is unquestionably a compromise, and two decisions which are fairly subject to the suggestion that they are, as to some points at least, affected by the spirit of compromise.

Stating this result as strongly as possible against the court, it would give six judicial decisions to three decisions in whole or in part affected by the spirit of compromise, a marked improvement over previous conditions and a very short ground for encouragement; but it remains true, that arbitration even at The Hague Tribunal still frequently results in compromise.

It is, however, a fair question whether or not, after all, this can properly be said to be a defect in arbitration, and it has been and is argued by those whose opinions are entitled to the greatest respect, that the tendency of arbitrators to compromise, so far from being a defect is in fact an advantage, or at most, under present conditions, a necessary condition to peaceful settlement. Bourgeois, at the Second Hague Conference, in discussing the establishment of the proposed permanent court of arbitral justice, maintained that even if the new judicial tribunal were established, the present so-called Hague Tribunal should be continued for the disposition of matters which the nations were not yet ready to submit to a judicial tribunal, and it has been suggested quite recently that if the proposed judicial tribunal were established, that tribunal and the present Hague Court would "probably operate side by side for several decades before the more perfect one finally supplants the other."   It may well be doubted, however, whether there is any real field for admitted compromise outside the domain of diplomacy and mediation. As President Harrison said, when vainly appealing to the Umpire of the British-Guiana Boundary Commission for a judicial decision,

"If conventions, if accommodations, and if the rule of give and take are to be used, then let the diplomatists settle the question.   But when these have failed in their work, and the question between two great nations is submitted for judgment, it seems to me necessarily to imply the introduction of a judicial element into the tribunal."

If once a judicial tribunal were really established it is believed that there would be little recourse to arbitration before the present tribunal, which would in that event be discredited as an open effort to secure a compromise and would lose its present facility for affording a compromise under the guise of a judicial decision. It is not intended to suggest that a compromise is not frequently, even generally more to be desired than an international law suit, but it is suggested, that when a compromise is desired, diplomacy, mediation, and a reference to an amiable *compositeur* afford ample and open means for reaching this result.   Compromise reached through negotiation, diplomacy, mediation, is in the interests of peace and good neighborship; compromise reached by a tribunal, such as The Hague Tribunal which is under an obligation to judge according to the law and the facts, and which may know little or nothing of the consideration of sentiment and expediency, which are properly considered in reaching a compromise, is, it is submitted, in the long run, a stumbling-block in the pathway to peace through justice.

Having reached the conclusion that arbitration has in the past frequently resulted in compromise rather than in justice according to the law, and that this is still the case although in a less degree and that this condition of affairs although natural is most regrettable, it remains to consider briefly the causes of this situation and to suggest some possible remedies. Doubtless it is true that the fundamental cause lies in the nature of arbitration itself, for as Gallatin says "an arbiter, whether he be king or farmer . . . . is always biased to try if possible to split the difference." Doubtless it is also true that the fundamental and ultimate remedy, therefore, for compromise and arbitration is to substitute for arbitration a permanent judicial tribunal to do justice between nations, but the difficulties in the way of the establishment and successful operation of such a tribunal are still serious. These difficulties will doubtless all yield in time to intelligent and broadminded diplomacy, but whether the time required be short as we all hope, or considerable as some of us fear, it is believed that there are certain suggestions which can be immediately put into operation and which will make for the elimination of compromise in arbitration. These suggestions have reference first to the framing of the terms of submission, second to the selection of the judges, and third to the procedure before international tribunals, and finally to the importance of maintaining and perfecting the right to revise and set aside arbitral awards and the establishment of a regular system of appeal in certain cases.

Perhaps no better illustration of the difference between terms of submission framed with a view to a compromise and terms of submission framed with a view to securing a judicial decision, can be found, than by a comparison of the compromise between German and France providing for the submission of the Casablanca incident to The Hague Court and the provisions of the Treaty of Washington submitting the San Juan Boundary dispute between the United States and Great Britain to the arbitrament of the Emperor of Germany.

The Casablanca compromise after reciting that the two governments had agreed "to submit to arbitration all the questions raised by the events which happened at Casablanca on the 25th of last September," provided in articles 1 and 9 as follows:

"ARTICLE I.   An arbitral tribunal constituted as· here stated is empowered to decide the questions of fact and law raised by the events which happened at Casablanca on the 25th of last September between the officials of the two governments."

ARTICLE IX.   After the tribunal shall have decided the questions of fact and law which are submitted to it, it shall determine in accordance therewith the situation of the individuals arrested on the 25th of last September in regard to which there is a dispute."

It may be well that the negotiators who framed the compromise in the general terms were really seeking a compromise and not a judicial decision, and this suggestion becomes the more plausible when it is remembered that it is the general understanding that Messrs. Renault and Kriege, respectively the advisers of the foreign offices of France and Germany, framed the terms of the compromise and that these same eminent juris-consults were the national members of The Hague Tribunal which rendered the Casablanca award.   If there is reason to expect that a case will be compromised instead of decided, it would seem most desirable that nationals who understand the questions of policy involved should be members of the tribunal.   Under these circumstances it is perhaps not quite fair to score up the Casablanca compromise against international arbitration in general.   Contrast with the compromise in this case articles 34–40 of the Treaty of Washington which provided for the submission of the San Juan Boundary dispute to the Emperor of Germany.

It will be remembered that this dispute grew out of the terms of the Treaty of 1846 between the United States and Great Britain, governing the boundary between the United States and Canada west of the Rocky Mountains, which provided for the continuation of the boundary line along the "49th parallel of North latitude to the middle of the channel which separates the continent from Vancouver's Island; and thence southerly through the middle of said channel and of Fuca's Straits to the Pacific Ocean: Provided, however, that the navigation of the whole of the said channel and straits, south of the 49th parallel of North latitude, remain free and open to both parties."

The Treaty of 1846 was negotiated under the threat of the war cry of "Fifty-four forty or fight," as a last effort to prevent war between the two contracting parties. It was a case where it was deemed more important to reach some agreement than to reach a precise and definite agreement, and accordingly the treaty was negotiated, signed and ratified although both parties were aware that the channel between Vancouver's Island and the mainland was filled by an archipelago of islands, through which there were at least two distinct channels, the Canal de Haro and the channel subsequently known as Rosario Straits, one on the British and one on the American side shown by the maps used by the negotiators and yet the negotiators contented themselves by referring to the "middle of the channel" without specifying any particular channel.

Under these circumstances it was not remarkable that a dispute almost immediately arose as to whether the boundary line should be drawn through the Canal de Haro or the Rosario Straits; in 1869 a convention was negotiated by Reverdy Johnson and Lord Clarendon providing for the submission of the San Juan Boundary dispute to the President of the Swiss Federation. The terms of this convention authorized the referee in case he "should be unable to ascertain and determine the precise line intended by the words of the treaty. . . . to determine upon some line which in his opinion will furnish an equitable solution of the difficulty and will be the nearest approximation that can be made to an accurate construction of the words of the treaty."

The Johnson-Clarendon Convention was not approved by the Senate, and the matter came up for adjustment in the negotiation leading up to the Treaty of Washington. During these negotiations the British commissioners proposed compromise on a middle channel "generally known as the Douglas Channel." This proposal was declined and it was decided to submit the matter to arbitration. Thereupon "the British commissioners proposed that the arbitrator should have the right to draw the boundary through an intermediate channel. The American commissioners declined this proposal, stating that they desired a decision not a compromise."

In accordance with the desire of the American commissioners for a judicial decision the question was submitted in perfectly clear-cut form. The American claim of the Canal de Haro and the British claim of Rosario Straits were stated and the umpire was asked to decide "which of those claims is most in accordance with the true interpretation of the treaty of June 15, 1846.

The award of the Emperor of Germany was precisely responsive to the question submitted. The Emperor's decision reads as follows:

"Most in accordance with the true interpretations of the treaty concluded on the 15th of June, 1846, between the governments of Her Britannic Majesty and of the United States of America, is the claim of the government of the United States that the boundary-line between the territories of Her Britannic Majesty and the United States should be drawn through the Haro Channel."

The San Juan Boundary arbitration is an instance of an arbitration relating to that class of questions which of all others is most prone to breed compromise, namely, boundary disputes, submitted to a foreign sovereign (and the head of a state is perhaps of all arbitrators most under the temptation to compromise) and yet a clear-cut judicial decision was obtained because the American negotiators who framed the terms of submission "desired a decision not a compromise," and said so in the treaty.

Even with all possible care in making definite the terms of submission and with the utmost good faith on the part of the arbitrator, compromise will doubtless occasionally result. Such for instance was the case in the Northeastern Boundary arbitration between the United States and Great Britain where sufficiently definite questions appear to have been submitted to the royal arbitrator, and yet, nevertheless, the King of the Netherlands, acting upon the advice of commissioners, to whom the case had been referred, practically confessed inability to answer the questions of construction submitted upon the evidence before him and recommended a compromise line. In this case, however, the perfect good faith of the arbitrator in stating the method by which his award had been reached enabled the United States, with the acquiescence of Great Britain, to decline to accept the award on the ground that it amounted to a departure from the terms of submission. Against possible bad faith or stupidity on the part of an arbitrator no care in framing the terms of submission can wholly provide, but the recent decision of The Hague Court in the Orinoco Steamship case setting aside the award of the umpire of the United States and Venezuela Mixed Commission of 1903 in that case, on the ground that he had exceeded the terms of submission, suggests that arbitrators in the future who expect their decisions to stand, must at least make a reasonable showing of abiding by the terms of the submission from which alone they draw their authority.

With respect to the selection of judges so much has been said that little can be added to any purpose. It has repeatedly been pointed out that nationals should be excluded from arbitral tribunals if compromise is to be avoided. It has furthermore been pointed out that every effort should be made to exclude partisans from the tribunal, and under partisans, of course, should be excluded those judges who are prejudiced for or against either of the parties litigant or who have irrevocably made up their minds in advance upon any of the questions submitted. It has been suggested that partisanship upon the bench might be eliminated by permitting the right of challenge in the selection of judges under The Hague Convention, as in the case of the selection of jurymen in our municipal courts.

It is submitted, however, that such an arrangement might easily operate as a similar right of challenge did operate in the English House of Commons in making up committees to judge contested election cases, where the process of challenging was familiarly referred to as "knocking the brains out of the committee." And, moreover, such a process might easily tend to create international misunderstanding and friction which it is the very purpose of arbitration to avoid. It is suggested that the benefits to be secured by the right of challenge could be largely obtained without these disadvantages if in every instance the parties litigant made an earnest effort to designate all the judges by "direct agreement" as suggested in article 46 of The Hague Convention of 1907, rather than by the more elaborate formula provided in the same article.

It is believed that if both parties litigant are really desirous of a capable and impartial tribunal, selection by direct agreement would be the best of all methods available so long as resort is to be had to the present Hague Tribunal.

With respect to procedure, it is perhaps sufficient to point out that the provisions of the present Hague Conventions still leave much to the imagination of the tribunal and agents of the two litigating governments. There is no generally accepted system of pleading in international arbitrations. There seems to be no agreement upon what the case and counter-case ought to contain. Under the present system, as it works out in practice, argument is mixed with the statement of the case and new evidence is introduced in the midst of oral argument, all with apparent impunity. There is no general understanding as regards such matters as discovery, interlocutory motions or order of argument.

And finally, the question of language remains one of the most serious practical questions connected with international arbitration. It is submitted that irrespective of what may be thought as to the advisability of the codification of substantive international law, the framing of at least a simple code of arbitral procedure is one of the present needs of international arbitration and one of the most effective steps which can be taken to eliminate compromise.

One further matter of procedure, directly affecting the tribunal seems to be worthy of more attention than it has received. Arbitral tribunals generally, and the various tribunals sitting under The Hague Conventions in particular, have striven valiantly for unanimity. The president of the British Guiana Boundary tribunal, one of the worst offenders in the matter of compromise, in his closing remarks laid special stress upon the unanimity of the decision in that case which he contrasted favorably to the decision in the courts which decided the Alabama and Behring

Sea arbitrations. And Sir Richard Webster, counsel for Great Britain, followed the president in a similar strain.

In his remarks at the close of the Pious Fund arbitration the president of that tribunal also expressed the opinion that the unanimity with which the tribunal had arrived at its decision was a guarantee of the correctness of its conclusions. Professor Matzen, however, was able to say in that case that "each judge for himself and all together" had arrived "at the same conclusion." When this truly can be said, unanimity is indeed persuasive of the correctness of the decision reached and of the arguments upon which it is founded.

But it is believed that too often in the history of arbitration unanimity has been purchased at the price of mutual concession— of compromise—and of the subtlest and in some respects the most injurious of all forms of compromise, namely, compromise as to the reasons given for the decision, reasons which may affect not only the particular arbitration in question but the development of international law. Unanimity purchased by the emasculation and befogging of the opinion of the court comes at too high a price.

Dr. Drago's clear-cut dissenting opinion on question 5 of the North Atlantic Coast Fisheries case, irrespective of the merits of the conclusion which he reaches, is, it is believed, one of the most hopeful incidents in the recent history of arbitration.

Article 52 of The Hague Convention of 1899 required the award to be "drawn up in writing and signed by each member of the Tribunal," whereas, according to the present Hague Convention, it is merely required that the word award be "signed by the president and registrar, or by the secretary acting as registrar."

It is submitted that this change is unfortunate. It is much easier for a judge to silently acquiesce in a compromise opinion which is entirely satisfactory neither to him nor to anyone else, than it is to sign his name to such an opinion. It is suggested that future agreements for arbitration should require, as did the special agreement in the North Atlantic Coast Fisheries arbitration that the opinion and award be signed by every arbitrator assenting thereto. And it is suggested that it might even be well to go farther and require a specific statement in the opinion that not only the result but the reasoning in the opinion is concurred in by all who sign.

Finally, it is suggested that in addition to the limited right to revision secured by the present Hague Convention and in addition to the right to disregard and have judicially annulled a judgment which has disregarded the terms of the submission (a right which has just been vindicated by The Hague Tribunal) it is worthy of serious consideration whether or not the next Hague Conference should not make some provision for appeal in certain cases for the correction of error similar to that which has been found necessary in municipal law. A precedent for such provision indeed can be found in the unratified Olney-Pauncefote Treaty of 1897.

It is submitted that with care in the framing of the terms of submission, direct argument as to the selection of the judges, a simple, clear code of arbitral procedure and maintenance and amplification of the right of revision, and the right to set aside an award which disregards the terms of submission, together with provision for appeal in proper cases for the correction of error, compromise may be largely banished from international arbitration, even before the establishment of a permanent court of arbitral justice.

In introducing the last speaker at the First Session of the Congress, President Holt remarked that no man in the United States had a more intimate and detailed knowledge of the Peace Movement than Dr. Benjamin F. Trueblood, formerly of Boston, and now of Washington. "As secretary of the oldest and best known Peace Society in this country, he has rendered invaluable service to this great cause. He saw the vision of the world's peace long ago and consecrated his life to make the vision actual. When he began his work, agitation in behalf of peace seemed like the pious dream of sentimentalists, and the movement was often regarded as a little cult nursed by cranks. The world is now coming to see the light which Dr. Trueblood perceived in its first glimmerings. He will tell us of 'Events in Connection with the Peace Movement Since the Previous Congress.'"

Dr. Trueblood delivered the following address:

EVENTS IN CONNECTION WITH THE PEACE MOVE-
MENT SINCE THE PREVIOUS CONGRESS

BENJAMIN F. TRUEBLOOD

It is always peculiarly difficult to speak at the end of a long program. It is particularly difficult when all that you intended to say has been said, and a good deal of it said two or three times, and when most of the people whom you would like to reach have gone out of the house. I hope, then, I have your very sincere and profound sympathy. I suppose that you would all like to compromise with me and have me sit down. You will find in my paper at least one merit, possibly the only one, and that is the merit of brevity. A good many of our later day peace-makers are apt to forget that the peace movement has a history and is not a thing of today. While these distinguished speakers from the government, and from our institutions of learning, and from our great journals, and Mr. Carnegie, were speaking this afternoon, I was on the platform here on which they were stand-ing, borne up by the shoulders of the great pacifists of nearly a century ago, I mean Noah Worcester, Dr. Channing, William Ladd, William Lloyd Garrison, Charles Sumner, and Judge Jay, and—on the other side of the water,—William Allen, Joseph Sturge, John Bright, Richard Cobden, Henry Richard and still later men like Frederick Passy of France. I saw these men who worked for the cause of peace when it was not fashionable to go to gatherings addressed by the President of the United States or the president of anything else, who worked under the disadvantage of having no constituency, and I thought how much more difficult the task of these men was than the task of us mod-ern men, who are building on the past and at present under most encouraging conditions.

This Third American Peace Conference with an opening audience, such as I have almost never looked on before at a peace gathering, is only the top branch, or one of the top branches of a great tree whose roots go down deep into the past century and whose top will reach into the skies. We are not to forget this if we wish to appreciate the point we have reached.

One of the most encouraging things about the peace movement at the present time is the fact that it has grown too big to be summarized in a brief address.

I am very much afraid, therefore, that what I shall present will resemble very closely the action of the Greek pedant who carried about with him a brick to show what sort of a house he lived in.

At the Second National Peace Congress at Chicago two years ago, we were rejoicing over the work of the Second Hague Conference, trying to interpret to ourselves the full significance of that great world gathering, the meaning of what it did and the still greater meaning of what it just failed to do. We were also trying to find out what were the next tasks to which we should devote ourselves.

Since that time, the efforts of the friends of peace have been turned very largely toward securing the completion of what The Hague Conferences left well advanced but not actually accomplished. What did The Hague Conferences do? What have the pacifists done within the past two years toward further advance? The answer to these two questions will show us the point which our movement has reached.

The results of The Hague Conferences, in briefest outline, are as follows:

1.   The establishment of an International Court of Arbitration for the voluntary use of the nations, to which all the governments of the world are parties.

2.   The prohibition of the bombardment from the sea of unfortified coast cities, towns and ports.

3.   The extension and strengthening of the rights of neutrals as against the rights of belligerents.

4.   The prohibition of the attempt to collect contractual debts from debtor nations by force until arbitration has first been tried or refused, thus extending the principle of obligatory arbitration to all that numerous class of controversies between nations involving money claims.

5.   The prohibition of the dropping of projectiles and explosives from balloons, thus practically neutralizing the air.

6. The prohibition of the laying of submarine mines so as seriously to endanger neutral commerce.

7. The most important actual accomplishment of the Second Hague Conference was the adoption of the principle of periodic conferences and the fixing of the date of the Third Hague meeting, thus actually laying the foundations of a World Congress or Parliament. Though much yet remains to be done, in substance the thing is done and the world will never go back upon this momentous step forward.

What The Hague Conference of 1907 came near doing but just failed to do, was the most significant part of its accomplishments.

1. It voted, about six to one of the delegations, in favor of a general treaty of obligatory arbitration to be signed by all the nations in common, thus recording the judgment of more than five-sixths of the people of the world in favor of the substitutes of reason and law for war in the settlement of controversies between nations.

2. The Conference came near putting all unoffending private property at sea in wartime beyond the reach of the ravages of violence and failed in this through the opposition of only two or three of the great powers who, in spite of the progress of our time, still persist in reserving to themselves the savage's right of making war on private property in order to accomplish their designs against a public enemy.

3. It declared itself without a dissenting delegate, in favor of the creation of a regular International Court of Justice, with judges always in service and holding the regular sessions of the tribunal; and it failed to bring such a Court into existence only because of its inability to agree upon a method of selecting the judges satisfactory to the small and the great powers alike.

4. The Conference pronounced its solemn judgment, as the Conference of 1899 had done, against the present colossal armaments and urged upon the governments the duty of making a serious study of the problem of getting rid of the exhausting burdens laid by these immense armaments upon the economic welfare and progress of the world.

The Conference did a number of other important things, but those cited are the leading and most constructive ones.

Since 1907, the friends of peace have thus had their program of practical work laid out for them by this first great representative gathering of substantially all the nations of the world. For the most part they have worked steadily and energetically for the accomplishment of these central objects. On the side of the governments, one regrets to have to say that action has been confined, for the most part, to our own government. We are all very glad, of course, that our national authorities at Washington have taken the splendid lead which they have taken. But not very much can be finally accomplished until a number of other important powers move in the same direction, as they are certain to do, sooner or later, under the stimulus of the example of the United States.

Three momentous steps have been taken at Washington since the last Conference at The Hague which have greatly impressed the world and led to the most sanguine hopes ever yet entertained of the early establishment of such a system of pacific adjustment of international disputes and of world organization as will result in the early realization of the dream of the disappearance of war and the establishment of universal and permanent peace. These proposals have recently been so much before the public and have been so widely and thoroughly discussed that they only need mentioning: They are:

1. The proposition of Secretary Knox that the establishment of a permanent International Court of Justice need not wait until the Third Hague Conference, but may be brought about by the investment of the Prize Court, agreed upon at The Hague in 1907, with the functions of a regular Court of Arbitral Justice.

2. The action of Congress last year in authorizing the President to appoint a Commission to study the problem of limitation of armaments and other allied subjects.

3. The memorable action of President Taft in declaring himself in favor of the arbitration of all international disputes without reservation of even questions of vital interest and of national honor, and his more recent effort to put this idea into practice by

securing a treaty of unlimited arbitration with Great Britain. This latter action of President Taft and the splendid, enthusiastic response made by the British government and people through Sir Edward Grey is far and away the most striking and hope-inspiring event in the recent annals of the international peace movement. All thoughtful and progressive men, not only in the United States and Great Britain, but in all other countries also, have become impressed with the feeling that the moment is one of great solemnity and that extraordinary developments in the direction of peace are soon to take place.

It is the point herein to call attention once more to the fact that within the past two years the two great gifts of Edwin Ginn and Andrew Carnegie for the promotion of the peace cause have been made. These munificent foundations have given assurance that at last the peace movement, which has so far made its way almost without resources, is at last to be adequately financed.

On the popular side of the peace propaganda, the efforts of the pacifists have been directed with unwonted energy, faith and hopefulness toward the bringing about of the very end which the government of our country has so prominently brought to the attention of the world. In this direction there has been a sudden and enormous development of public opinion among all classes of society somewhat resembling the great physical upheavals of geological history. The peace societies of the world, now six hundred in number, the international and the national peace congresses, the Interparliamentary Union, special organizations like Mohonk, the International Conciliation Association, the Society for the Judicial Settlement of International Disputes, and other like bodies have steadily thrown the weight of their influence, some emphasizing one phase and some another, toward the stronger and deeper development of international goodwill and trust, toward the pacific, judicial settlement of all international controversies and toward the earliest possible limitation and reduction of the great military and naval establishments of our time. This wide-spread and increasingly powerful movement of public opinion upon these strategic points in the conflict with the savage and irrational system of war which remains, in Mr.

Carnegie's vigorous phraseology "the foulest blot upon our civilization" is, after all is said and done, the chief pillar on which our movement rests, and on the further development and strengthening of which we must build our future hopes of the speedy triumph of the cause in whose interests we have gathered together for this Congress.

Following the address of Dr. Trueblood, President Holt announced that telegrams had been received from various friends of peace in different parts of the world, and that some of those telegrams would be read.

Following the reading of these, the First Session of the Congress adjourned.

SECOND SESSION

At the Second Session of the Third American Peace Congress, held Wednesday evening, May 3, in McCoy Hall, of the Johns Hopkins University, President Ira Remsen, of the Johns Hopkins University, called the meeting to order, and delivered the following address:

Ladies and Gentlemen: It is my pleasant duty to welcome you to the Johns Hopkins University. When we learned last year that this Congress was to meet in Baltimore, we at once offered the use of our halls for the purpose of the meeting, and we were very glad to have that invitation accepted. We should have been glad, indeed, to have all the meetings here, but plainly this hall would not have accommodated the great gathering of this afternoon. From this time forward until the end of the session, unless something unexpected happens, this hall will be the meeting place of the Congress.

I need not tell you that we all feel pleased and gratified to have such a distinguished gathering of delegates meeting in our city. There have been a great many important meetings held at the Johns Hopkins University, and in this particular hall, but I doubt if there has ever been a meeting of the same importance with as far-reaching possibilities as the meeting which is now assembled here or as this Congress which is now meeting in Baltimore. I am very glad to have a modest part in the work of this great gathering.

When the moving spirit of this Congress, Mr. Theodore Marburg, suggested to me that as the meetings were to be in the Johns Hopkins University for the most part, it would be appropriate that I should preside at one of the sessions, I must confess that I hesitated very much, but finally accepted, for we all felt that anything Mr. Marburg asked this week should be granted for the sake of peace.

There is one very good reason why a Peace Congress should meet in the halls of the Johns Hopkins University, or some other university or educational institution, for fundamentally the work which these congresses are doing, which all peace societies are doing, is educational work. Without education in this line nothing can be accomplished. The education of young people is difficult enough, as those who have been engaged in that kind of work know very well. But the education of those who have passed the stage of youth is a good deal more difficult, and the difficulty increases as time passes. These peace congresses have students who have grown up, and whose minds have become somewhat fixed, who have lost that plasticity which is the first condition of success in education. The first and great difficulty is to get the attention of those who are to be educated. No doubt that is the difficulty in all lines of education. It is a good deal easier to get the attention of young people than of those who are not so young. We can easily discuss that problem and show why it is so. But I will not change this meeting into a psychological seminary. Each of us has had some experience in educating ourselves in connection with this particular problem before this Congress.

I confess I had difficulty myself. It so happened that in early life I was brought in close relation with two important wars. The first was the Civil War, which was during the time that I was a boy, and the second, the Franco-Prussian War, when I was living near the borders of Germany and France, and the general impression which I got was that war was a necessity. I recall an incident illustrating the conditions then existing. I was living, after my return from France and Germany, in a very quiet nook in New England. There was there an old clergyman, whose chief claim to distinction was that he was a classmate of David Dudley Field. He often told us that, and frequently amused some of us by his references to that fact. He came into the room one day and said, "I have just had a letter from David Dudley Field, and what do you think, they have abolished war." That was an announcement sufficient to cause one to think. It seemed to me that the problem these good people were undertaking, that of abolishing war, was perfectly hopeless. It was almost silly that they should meet and talk over such a problem as that. All of you who have reached my age have gone through such experiences, and I dare say you have often wondered with me whether it was worth while. It does seem almost impossible that within a period of forty years there should have been a feeling that to advocate peace was a perfectly useless sentiment.

What has happened in the meantime? Look at that great audience this afternoon and hear these great speakers, saying with such confidence what would happen in the future. The contrast between that and forty years ago is as great as can be imagined. The cause has triumphed, and it is extremely gratifying to those who, in the early days, gave only a weak adherence to it and doubted its success. The results are far beyond the greatest expectations of the majority of people, I should say, who lived at the time of which I am speaking. They thought that at some time in the dim future there might be some results, but now we have reached the stage where we think war in the future will be the exception, peace the rule. That is as great a change as the world could possibly experience.

This has all come about through education—no, not wholly, I beg your pardon; there have been other causes. It was not education that caused this wholly, but there were other causes with which peace societies had nothing to do, causes which were far-reaching, but I will not go into those, because there might be some disagreement with my views. I do not believe, though, that the peace societies have accomplished all this. The world generally is moving forward, and there are a number of forces at work which have tended to improve it, forces which are not always of such a high character, but economic reasons, reasons connected with inventions, and other reasons which are not operating in the same direction, but endeavoring and helping to bring about the result which the peace societies are aiding so materially. It has sometimes been said that these reform movements of one kind or another hasten the coming of the inevitable. That sounds a little deep, perhaps, but if you will think it over, it has a meaning. I will leave it with you in that form. This peace is coming, and what these societies do, these movements, these meetings, is to hasten the coming of that which will come sometime whether the societies operate or not; but in all good causes societies play their part, and without them undoubtedly progress would be much slower than it now is or would be without them.

It is not, however, my purpose to address you at any length. I was asked to preside at this meeting and I rested calmly upon the presumption that that was my only function. When I received the program I found there was an address called for, which was entirely undesirable to the presiding officer. My duty is to introduce the speakers. I find there are five present now, and if we keep on we may get more. There are other causes interfering here also, which have an effect upon the prompt attendance of the speakers. But I have nothing to do with that. My duty is to preside, whether there are speakers here or not.

Let me introduce now Dr. Charles F. Thwing, President of the Western Reserve University, who will speak on the subject announced in the program.

THE PEACE MOVEMENT AND THE AMERICAN COLLEGE AND UNIVERSITY

CHARLES F. THWING

Perhaps the greatest service which the American college or university can render to the cause of peace lies in the prosaic process and the triumphant result of making the thinker. For the man who thinks is the man who by nature and instinct is opposed to war. It is as true that the doors of academic halls are closed in times of war, as it is true that the laws are silent among arms. The college man who thinks, sees truth broadly: war interprets life narrowly, at the point of the bayonet. The college man who thinks, sees truth deeply: war makes its primary appeal to the superficial love of glory, of pomp and of circumstance. The college man who thinks, sees truth in its highest skyey relations: war is hell. The college man who thinks sees truth in long ranges and in far off horizons: war is emotional, and the warrior flings the years into the hours. The college man who thinks,

thinks accurately, with logic, with reason: war does not think,—war strikes. Strike, may also say the college man, but hear, he cries, yes, think. If the college can make the student think, it has created the greatest force for making the world and the age, an age and a world of peace. The cause of peace can do much for the college and the university. The triumph of the cause would put gold into the academic chest, and gold is silent symbol of what the college stands for. To build a battleship costs the endowment of a university, and its annual maintenance is larger than a university budget.

The total cost of the battleship *New Hampshire* was more than seven million dollars. The total value of the grounds and buildings of all the colleges in New Hampshire is less than two and a half million dollars, and the total amount of productive funds, three millions. The cost of the battleship *Indiana* was more than five millions. The total value of grounds and buildings of colleges and universities in Indiana is slightly more than seven million dollars, and the productive funds are four millions. The total cost of the battleship *Oregon* was more than six millions. The whole value of grounds and buildings of the universities and colleges of Oregon is less than two million, and the productive fund amounts to less than one million. The cost of the battleship *Iowa* was more than five million dollars, and the productive funds of all its colleges and universities is also five millions. The battleship *Kentucky* cost more than four millions. In the colleges of that State the total amount of productive funds is only two millions, and total value of grounds and buildings, three millions. The battleship *Alabama* cost more than four millions, and the entire property, real and personal, of all universities and colleges in that State is less than four millions. The cost of the battleship *Wisconsin* is more than four million dollars. The whole value of all grounds and buildings of its colleges and universities is only slightly more than six millions. The battleship *Maine* cost more than four millions, and the entire value in grounds, buildings, and productive funds of the colleges and universities of that State is little more than five millions. The cost of the battleship *Connecticut* was more than five million dollars. The total value of grounds and buildings is slightly less than that amount. The battleship *Kansas* cost more than seven million dollars. The value of the grounds and buildings of the colleges and universities of Kansas is less than six millions, and the productive funds, little more than a million. The cost of the battleship *Louisiana* was more than seven million dollars. The whole value of the grounds and buildings and the productive funds of that State is little more than six millions. The battleship *Minnesota* cost more than seven millions, and the total value of grounds and buildings of its universities and colleges is only about five millions, and the productive funds little more than two millions. The cost of the battleship *Vermont* was more than seven million dollars, and value of the property of its colleges is scarcely more than two millions, and the productive fund little more than a million. The battleship *Georgia* cost more than six million dollars, and the total amount of property and productive funds of the colleges and universities of the State is less than four millions. The cost of the battleship *Nebraska* was more than six millions, and the entire property, real and personal, of the universities and colleges is less than four millions. The cost of the battleship *New Jersey* was more than six million dollars. The total value of the grounds and buildings of the colleges and universities is but little more than two millions. The cost of the battleship *Rhode Island* was more than six million dollars. The total value of all the property of its universities and colleges is less than six millions. The battleship *Virginia* cost over six millions For education in that State, and the total productive funds are but little more than three millions. The cost of the battleship *Idaho* was more than five million dollars. The total value of the grounds, buildings and productive funds of the colleges and universities of the State is less than one million. The battleship *Mississippi* cost more than seven millions, and the value of all property, real and personal, of its universities is only about three millions. The battleship *Delaware* cost more than seven million dollars, while all the productive funds of the colleges and universities of the State amount to less than one million. The battleship *North Dakota* cost over eight million dollars. The value of the grounds and buildings of the colleges and universities is little more than two millions, and the productive funds about three millions. The cost of the battleship *Michigan* was more than six millions, while the value of the grounds and buildings of its universities and colleges is less than that sum, and the productive funds little more than three millions. The battleship *South Carolina* cost more than six million dollars. The total value of all the property of its colleges and universities is little more than three millions. The cost of the armored cruiser *Colorado* was more than five millions, and the total value of all property available for its colleges and universities is but little over four millions. The cost of the armored cruiser *West Virginia* was more than five million dollars, while the value of all productive funds is less than two millions. The armored cruiser *Tennessee* cost more than six millions. The value of all grounds and buildings is slightly more than three millions. The armored cruiser *Washington* cost more than six millions, while the value of all productive funds of the colleges and universities is but little over three millions. The cost of the armored cruiser *North Carolina* was more than five millions. The total value of all productive funds of its colleges and universities is about five millions. The armored cruiser *South Dakota* cost more than five millions. The total amount of productive funds of the universities and colleges of that State is less than two millions. The cost of the armored cruiser *Montana* was more than five millions. The total value of all property, real and personal, of its colleges and universities is less than two million dollars. The cost of maintaining many of these cruisers, for a year of twelve months, approaches a million dollars. The cost of maintaining the *Colorado* is \$877,919.57; the *Maryland*, \$875,425.31; the *West Virginia*, \$958,997.99; the *Tennessee*, \$961,370.76; the *Washington*, \$892,870.16; the *North Carolina*, \$742,754.50; the *South Dakota*, \$804,866.67; the *Montana*, \$750,333.78. The number of universities in this country whose annual budget exceeds these sums, can be numbered on your fingers. When one takes into view the depreciation which belongs to an armored cruiser or battleship, it is safe to say that it costs more to maintain a battleship for one year than to maintain Yale College for a year, and several times what it costs to maintain a college like Amherst or Williams.

Of the five hundred colleges and universities in this country, the value of the grounds is estimated at $67,000,000, the value of buildings, at $219,000,000, and the productive funds amount to $260,000,000. Leaving out those battleships which are now in course of construction, the *Utah, Florida, Arkansas, Wyoming, New York* and *Texas*, the total cost of the *Indiana, Oregon, Iowa, Kentucky, Alabama, Wisconsin, Illinois, Maine, Missouri, Connecticut, Kansas, Louisiana, Minnesota, Vermont, Georgia, Nebraska, New Jersey, Rhode Island, Virginia, Idaho, Mississippi, New Hampshire, Delaware, North Dakota, South Carolina, Colorado, Maryland, West Virginia, Tennessee, Washington, North Carolina, South Dakota,* and *Montana,* is $236,551,438.57. But, be it also said, that the cost of maintaining these battleships during the fiscal year of 1910, many of which were in commission but a small part of the year, amounted to no less than $24,624,739.55.

The amount which all the colleges and universities in this country received in the year 1909, in tuition fees, was only fourteen million dollars. And the entire income received both from fees and productive funds was only about twenty-five million dollars. In other words, when one takes into view the *depreciation in the battleship or armored cruiser, the entire cost of the thirty-eight battleships for a single year, is greater than the administration of the entire American system of the higher education.*

Is it not very clear that the cause of peace can do much for the college and for the university, and what is infinitely more important, that the cause of peace can do much for humanity? The money which is thus wasted on naval armament and equipment would put the cause of the higher education of America upon a most efficient basis.

CHAIRMAN REMSEN: The next speaker I will call upon is the Dean of Goucher College, Baltimore, Miss Eleanor L. Lord. I take pleasure in presenting Miss Lord, whose subject is

WAR FROM THE STANDPOINT OF EUGENICS

ELEANOR L. LORD, PH.D.

At the outset it may be well to explain that for obvious reasons the present paper is not an attempt to treat exhaustively or technically the physiological aspects of war. In the first place, the limit of time would preclude any comprehensive treatment of the subject; and, in the second place, a student of history who essayed to enter into the details of so highly specialized and, as yet, indeterminate a field as that of heredity in the human species, would be guilty of an unwarrantable incursion into the realm of biological science.

I trust, however, that it may be permitted to a layman, upon whom those who arranged this significant congress have conferred the honor of a place on the program, to emphasize the importance of one aspect of warfare that has received comparatively little attention on the part of writers and speakers on the peace movement.

My attention was first called to the connection between war and eugenics by the address of President David Starr Jordan, last July, at the opening meeting of the National Education Association at Cambridge, Massachusetts, and by his fuller treatment of the same theme in a book entitled, The Human Harvest, to which my attention was subsequently directed.

Briefly stated, President Jordan's thesis, repeated in various forms in his essays on war, is this: With men, as with animals, "like the seed is the harvest." Men have learned through science the art of selective breeding, upon which all progress is conditioned. Permanent advance depends upon advance in the type of parenthood, and decline results solely from breeding from the second-best instead of the best. This is true of races as well as cattle. War tends towards the elimination of the best and therefore towards the decline of the race, since those who are left behind determine the future.

Eugenics, both as a field of biological science, and as a possible instrument of social regeneration, is still in its infancy, but it has taken sufficient hold upon the trained imagination to warrant serious consideration of the question whether we are not approaching some social questions from the wrong end; whether, for example, the advocates of the eradication of the socially unfit by eliminating the conditions of environment which produce poverty, vice and crime are not putting the cart before the horse. Such at least is the view of many biologists who hold that the advocates of *euthenics*, as the theory of reform through environment has come to be called, are seeking what is after all likely to be only a palliative; while the eugenists look to the control of heredity as the ultimate instrument of racial salvation.

It is, of course, an axiom of biology that the survival of the fittest results from a process of selection by which weak or defective individuals give place in the struggle for existence to the stronger and more resistant. Natural selection may be improved upon by artificial selection as in the process of cattle-breeding, or by such experiments as those of Burbank with plants. In any case the evolution of a higher type through selective breeding is essentially a simple process and obviously depends for ultimate success upon the deliberate mating of the fittest with the fittest, and not with the unfittest, rather than upon artificial improvement of the environment. As one writer has put it, no amount of fertilization of the soil, that is, improvement in environment, will produce figs from thistles.

But is not the Darwinian theory of the survival of the fittest in the struggle for existence an excellent argument for the indirect benefits of warfare—a sort of consolation to the sentimentalists who deplore the destruction of human life which war involves— in that the weaker and the unfit succumb to the strength of the victors, who thus prove themselves worthy to replace the degenerate races and so check the decline of civilization corrupted by luxury and vice? It has even been argued that in primitive tribal warfare, the victors married the women of the defeated tribe and so effected a cross-breeding favorable to the race. A moment's reflection will show, I think, that this is by no means a usual occurrence, since, the fiercer the struggle, the more recklessly do the picked warriors rush into the thick of the fray and engage in hand-to-hand encounter with the champions of the enemy. One has only to read the *Iliad* or certain passages of the *Nibelungenlied* to realize that primitive warfare is virtually a species of duelling in which pairs of warriors, more or less equally matched, struggle on till either the accidents of war or some momentary unguardedness lays low not alone the weakling but the glorious hero. In fact it is the weaker and the less heroic who most frequently survive in that type of encounter, since, when the most valiant who led the charge in the vanguard have fallen, the less daring are prone to retreat if opportunity offers. Often nearly as many of the victorious party are killed as of the conquered. History records many victories that proved frightfully expensive when the roll-call of the survivors revealed the true results.

The postulate that warfare results in the survival of the unfittest rests, however, not so much upon the effects of the fighting itself, whether by modern or ancient methods of procedure, but rather upon the operation of the system of recruiting armies, by which the best physical specimens of the nations are carefully selected to be for a very brief hour the nation's pride, the flower of chivalry, and then, too often to become "food for cannon."

With a view to high efficiency in fighting and endurance of the hardships and exposure incident to military campaigns, all governments have pursued the policy of recruiting their armies from the best available material. Young men in the plenitude of their powers have been singled out for long terms of service sometimes from seventeen to fifty years of age, leaving the very immature, the defective and the older men at home to be the propagators of succeeding generations. As early as the regal period the Roman army was classified as Juniors and Seniors, the Juniors, *i.e.*, the fittest, being detailed for the more active service, where the chances of survival were least good. In the earlier wars Rome never allowed the slaves and inferior citizens to serve in the army. The word legion is derived from legere, to *select*. The wars for the possession of Italy and the Punic wars were fought by the pick of the Italian stock; but as the fighting force became depleted by expensive victories the recruits were drawn more and more from the lower classes or, when war became distasteful to he citizens, from alien races. Mommsen estimates that three hundred thousand Italians, chiefly Romans of the best stock, perished in the Punic wars, and at least four hundred townships were destroyed.   It became necessary to fill up a gap of one hundred and seventy-seven in the membership of the Senate.   Professor Seeley, in his study of Roman imperialism, states positively that "whatever the remote and ultimate cause may have been, the immediate cause to which the fall of the empire can be traced is a physical, not a moral, decay.   In valor, discipline and science the Roman armies remained what they always had been; but the problem was how to replenish those armies.   Men were wanting; the empire perished for want of men."

Rome could replenish her armies from the barbarians, but was destined in the end to perish by those same barbarian hordes— an excellent illustration of the law of diminishing returns.

It is not merely in the waste of the choicest specimens of a nation's manhood in aggressive war that the parenthood of the next generation is vitiated, but also in civil wars and revolutions in which unscrupulous usurpers or hostile factions seek to strengthen their own position by the destruction of their able-bodied or able-minded rivals.

Dr. Otto Seeck, in his philosophical history of the downfall of the ancient world, has a most illuminating chapter on *Die Ausrottung der Besten*, The Rooting out of the Best, in which he relates the anecdote of Periander of Corinth who sent to Thrasybulus of Melos and asked his advice as to how to strengthen his power. The latter conducted the messenger to a field and cut off the ears of corn that reached above their fellows and threw them to the ground until the finest ornament of the field was ruined.   Periander understood the parable and had all the leading citizens executed or banished.   Many other Greek tyrants followed this plan of getting rid of the strong, and not merely the fathers but the sons who might wreak vengence upon their father's enemy. This destruction of the *aristoi*, *i.e.*, the best, killed off thousands of the pick of the Greek race who might have become the parents of strong sons.

The same method was pursued by Marius and Sulla and by the Triumvirs of Rome without any thought of what the results might be for the future breed of Romans. No wonder Sulla found the Roman Senate unfit to save the state as he had fondly dreamed. The calibre of the senatorial families had been reduced physically and mentally by the frightful proscription of Marius, which is estimated at ninety senators and two thousand six hundred knights. The second triumvirate, in order to get rid of the few men of energy and capacity still remaining in Italy among their political opponents, says the historian Ferrero, condemned to death and confiscated the property of one hundred senators and two thousand knights. And he adds: "The generation of Octavian was far weaker than the men of Caesar's day in its fear of death and poverty, and it displayed a corresponding timidity and cowardice."

We have no reliable statistics of the mortality due to warfare in the middle ages, but the selective grading of feudal society and the incentives to rivalry in reckless exposure in the hand-to-hand encounters of the age of chivalry suggest that war by no means tended to secure the survival of the fittest elements for parenthood. It is necessarily impossible to distinguish definitely between the physically and the morally fit, since the two classes are not invariably identical; nor is it true that the so-called aristocracies of the nations are always more fit than the middle classes to rear the generations of the future. Yet one cannot avoid the feeling that the loss of so many noble and high minded men and women by the guillotine in the Reign of Terror seriously affected the succeeding generations of Frenchmen.

In Germany during the wars of religion the loss by war is estimated at six million lives, and while historical writers dwell on the fact that, economically speaking, the progress of Germany was crippled for over a century, who shall say that the dynamic power of the Germans, from the physical standpoint, was not similarly paralyzed or atrophied?

Proscription by triumphant usurpers and wholesale massacre of the leading citizens of beleaguered towns which fall into the hands of the enemy have passed out of fashion, most fortunately, but the casualties of regular field engagements are sufficiently appalling to give us pause. It is claimed that three million were killed in the Napoleonic wars—the choicest manhood of France between eighteen and thirty-five years of age. The Grand Army, computed at six hundred and fifty thousand, was probably the largest army ever mustered since the time of Xerxes, but it had already become necessary to fill up the ranks with striplings under age and with older men less capable of endurance. The ghastly Russian campaign devoured one hundred and fifty thousand youths under twenty years of age. Professor Seeck confidently attributes the subsequent decadence of the French physique and the decrease in stature of the modern Frenchmen to this wholesale elimination of the finest physical specimens of the nation.

If any phase of this subject can be regarded as humorous, the spectacle of Frederick William of Prussia proudly drilling his giant grenadiers, his "dear blue children," might at this historical distance provoke a smile; but the new scheme for compulsory service instituted in 1733 was no joke to the subjects of the royal drill master. The nobles resisted the proscription not only because it withdrew serfs from the fields, but because their own sons were gathered into the training school at Berlin. Many parents in their despair tried to prove that they were not noble. Had it not been for the motive which called forth his ingenuity, Frederick William might almost be claimed as one of the early advocates of eugenics, since he seriously undertook to influence the propagation of heroic specimens by forcing marriages between tall men and women who had never seen each other until ordered to the altar.

But what is the use in harking back to the barbaric past or even to the eighteenth century, says the military expert, when the conditions of warfare were fundamentally different from those of the present day? Civilized nations no longer plunge recklessly into wars for the purpose of seizing the lands or movable wealth of their neighbors; nor do they any longer raze flourishing cities to the ground and massacre or enslave the inhabitants. Standing armies are now maintained in order to *prevent* war and its evil consequences.

It is true that there is at present comparatively little inducement for European states to engage in aggressive wars for territorial expansion; that there are no longer vast treasure houses of unutilized capital to tempt the covetous; that the wealth of nations can be made available through trade and peaceable competition; that slavery is no longer regarded as a legitimate or desirable method of increasing the man-power of a country.

It is also true that there has been a marked improvement in the psychological incentives to war. Revenge, greed in its grosser forms, lust for power, religious fanaticism have given place to what one might call low temperature stimuli, and the brutalities of the blood-feud and even the duel of honor have yielded to more rational methods of deciding issues between individuals. But has not this progressive refinement of civilization respecting the provocation of war quite out-distanced the evolution of ways and means of adjudicating the claims of rival nations?

Reduced to its lowest terms, war is collective murder. The purpose of a battle, whether in the open field, in siege operations or upon the sea, is to seize a strategic position by killing off its defenders in sufficient numbers to ensure abandonment of the position. When, after a series of such progressive moves, all the points of defence have been won and the defenders numerically reduced beyond the danger of recovery, the aggressor is enabled to control the situation either by demanding whatever he likes as a price of surrender or by violently seizing all the material resources of the enemy and effecting a complete paralysis of national vitality. From antiquity to modern times, from savagery to civilization, the evolution of warfare has meant the serious business of inventing means to destroy the greatest possible numbers of the enemy in order to bring the remnant to terms. The ethnological museums and the art galleries of the civilized world are full of specimens of life-destroyers ranging from the barbed arrow and the tomahawk, to the lyddite shell.

One would at least be glad to felicitate modern civilization upon the disappearance of much of the ferocity of ancient warfare with the substitution of long-range fighting for the hand-to-hand encounter which brought human beings inflamed with the lust

of conflict face to face in a life and death struggle. The range
of the modern rifle is from two to three miles, and that of a tor-
pedo fifteen to twenty miles. A five-millimetre Mansen rifle,
we are informed, will penetrate five carcasses of horses, used for
experiment, at twenty-seven yards, or one carcass at one thousand,
eight hundred and seventy yards. All this remoteness tends to
a more impersonal attitude towards the business in hand and
makes its deliberation more cold-blooded; but whatever may be
the gain through the restraint of passion in the individual soldier, the nervous tension of modern warfare is immensely
increased and this contributes materially to physical break-down.
Modern shells, filled with strong explosives like melinite and per-
oxylene, tend to explode prematurely and must be handled with
extreme caution. Smokeless powder and the practically noise-
less discharge of the weapon signify that death comes invisibly,
inaudibly, unheralded; so that, along with the improvements in
the efficiency of weapons, there has been an equally deplorable
progress in devices for deceiving the enemy and catching him
unawares—a ghastly contribution to the possibilities of destruction on a gigantic scale. Smokeless powder, mines, long distance
explosives, the high-speed turbine engine, wireless telegraphy,
and aërial navigation furnish ample illustration of the con-
trasts between primitive and up-to-date warfare. Through
improvements in sighting apparatus accuracy of fire has been
greatly increased and the bullet of the modern small calibre
rifle has such a momentum that it will penetrate earthworks $78\frac{1}{2}$
inches thick and pierce through a tree; or it may penetrate even
the third rank of soldiers. The rapidity of revolution and the
deformation of bullets in contact with a hard substance increase
the seriousness and fatality of wounds. Thus the field of death
has become incredibly enlarged. I need not dwell further upon
the sickening details of similar so-called "improvements" in the
projectiles used in the modern battleship and in artillery field
pieces. An estimate made over ten years ago that in a two-
days' battle the armies of the Triple Alliance and the Dual Alliance
could kill forty-one million men with five hundred rounds of
ammunition per gun, *i.e.*, could destroy more armies than could

be put in the field, is to such an extent a *reductio ad absurdum* that the tension of one's horror is almost relieved.

Early in the sixteenth century, the humanist Erasmus wrote to the Abbot of St. Bertin,—"The brute beasts fight with their natural arms, not, like us, with machines upon which we spend an ingenuity worthy of devils." The twentieth century also is confronted with the paradox that more time, money and intelligence have been concentrated upon military apparatus for the destruction or mutilation of human beings than upon appliances for the prolongation or the comfort of existence. As Mr. H. G. Wells has recently pointed out, "the house of today is still almost as ill-ventilated, badly heated, clumsily arranged and furnished as the house of 1858, but the rifle or battleship of fifty years ago was beyond all comparison inferior to those we possess, in power, in speed, in convenience alike. No one has a use now for such superannuated things."

Even the professional soldiers and the war-lords of the present era stand aghast at the possibilities of slaughter, should a serious war break out in Europe. The thought of twelve million men, armed with the most powerful engines of destruction ever devised, hurled at each other in a titanic struggle ought to be sufficient to prevent any government from turning loose the dogs of war save as a last resort. Napoleon himself once declared that war was the trade of barbarians, and Wellington wrote to Lord Shaftsbury: "If you had seen but one day of war, you would pray to God you might not need to see another." General Sherman in a moment of revulsion from the horrors of war exclaimed: "It is only those who never fired a shot nor heard the shrieks of the wounded, who cry aloud for more blood, more vengeance, more desolation! War is Hell!"

The captains of industry and the political economists thoroughly appreciate the disturbances of commerce, finance and other economic conditions involved in the outbreak of a war. Consequently the war situation today presents itself as a supreme effort to maintain an equilibrium; to avoid war by the maintenance of navies and standing armies and, finally, by the balancing of armaments through triple or dual alliances of those powers which are likely to stand together on the issues of war but which are too weak in armies or fleets to engage single-handed against their more formidable neighbors.

The maintenance of these huge armaments at enormous expense implies the deep rooted conviction that war is the inevitable solution of international quarrels. In times of general security when there is no occasion for jingoism or for the appeal to false patriotism by a sensational press, it is comparatively easy to arouse the public to a realization of the horrors and the folly of war; but it is a very different matter to persuade military enthusiasts on the one hand and government officials on the other that the solution of the problem of avoiding war does not lie in the establishment of a large army or navy either by voluntary enlistment or by conscription. At all events, disarmament, partial or complete, appears to them the delusive dream of the idealist who has theories but no appreciation of the practical difficulties involved; the standing army is a deplorable but inevitable necessity.

Hence, in addition to the atrocities of actual warfare, we have a second aspect of militarism to consider: the evils of the maintenance of a standing army during the inactivity of intervals of peace.

The "national army" system presents several features that bear upon the question of race culture. In the first place, there is the recruiting system which withdraws the most perfect specimens of manhood from productive labor and family life to the military service of the state. Vegetius, a Roman military writer of the fifth century, advocated the most careful choice and training of soldiers on the ground that not only upon physical but moral superiority must Rome depend for the restoration of her military power—*Non tam prodest multitudo quam virtus*. Modern nations emphasize physical perfection on the whole more than moral qualities, doubtless on the assumption that the service requires perfect physical machines. In so far as intemperance or criminal propensities impair the fighting power or the morale (which is not synonymous with morality) of the army, inebriates and ex-convicts are rejected.

I have carefully read the circular issued by the United States government relating to the enlistment of men for the navy, which may be taken as typical of the qualifications of most modern nations whether enlistment is voluntary or compulsory.

The age limit is eighteen to thirty-five years, i.e., the period of greatest physical perfection. A carefully graded standard of weight, height and chest measure has been prepared for the guidance of examiners. Physical disqualifications are grouped under three heads: (1) feeble constitution, general poor physique, or impaired health; (2) any disease or deformity that would impair efficiency; (3) any acute disease.

So thorough-going is the examination that among the list of physical disqualifications mentioned above are such defects as color blindness, catarrh, impediment of speech, corns, unsound teeth, twenty sound or properly filled teeth being required. Were the list of forty or more disqualifying diseases or imperfections of more serious character made to apply to the eligibility of candidates for marriage and parenthood instead of to men withdrawn to a greater or less extent from the possibility of marriage at the age of maximum physical perfection, what might not be the effects upon the character of our population, and upon the graver problem of the care and support of the insane, and of the defective and delinquent classes,—at present an enormous burden to the state.

In the corresponding circular for army recruits, number 69, are to be found the following significant paragraphs: "Married men will be enlisted *only upon the approval of a regimental commander, or other proper commanding officer if for other than a regimental organization.*" Again, "A favorable opportunity is afforded for active, intelligent young men of temperate habits, who may enlist as privates and develop the necessary qualifications, to secure promotions to the grade of a non-commissioned officer. *Unmarried soldiers under thirty-five years of age, who are citizens of the United States, who are physically sound, who have served honorably not less than two years in the army, and who have borne a good moral character before and after enlistment, are permitted to compete by examination for promotion to the rank of second lieutenant.*"

Do these regulations suggest selective breeding for the improvement of the population, or what President Jordan has significantly designated as reversed selection pointing to the survival of the unfit?

Another feature of the standing army system is the education of the prospective soldier or marine in training schools. It is on this matter of education that defenders of the military system and compulsory service base their strongest claim for the advantages of military training and the barracks system; and they most reproachfully accuse the advocates of peace of unfairness and ignorance of the actual conditions of military life.

Karl Berthing, in an article written for the *Outlook* a few years ago in defense of Professor Münsterberg's assertion that conscription is not a burden to the German nation, dwells with pride upon the broad educational training afforded by the military school. It is not a mere matter of mechanical drill, it seems, but instruction about the history of Germany, her resources, her colonies, etc., and that actually at the hands of *college bred men!* He also says that the best practical training of individual talent is afforded and that commercial houses are constantly advertising for men who have "served."

Much is made, also, of the superior athletic training. "Military life takes the place of athletics and encourages clean games," it is claimed. So far as my limited observation goes, the games of naval and military academies are encouraged rather for the purpose of offering inducements to enter the schools and of providing the sort of relaxation or sport furnished by rival educational institutions; and as far as the efficacy of the setting-up-drill is concerned, I have seen it performed with equal proficiency and apparent benefit in collegiate and public gymnasiums. It would seem a somewhat unwarrantable expense for a government to maintain elaborate equipment for gymnastics or athletic contests if this phase of the military régime were really worthy of serious consideration. As a matter of fact the practice of athletics and sports appears to be in inverse ratio to militarism. A comparison between England or America, with Russia, Austria and other

European nations among which compulsory military service prevails will throw some light upon that aspect of the case.

If it could be justly claimed, however, that the alleged physical benefits of military education tended to eliminate disease or to raise appreciably the physical standard, there might be some real justification for the military school on the ground of race improvement, so far as those are concerned who return to the life of the civilian after the expiration of their terms of service. James Anson Farrer arguing against the proposed introduction of compulsory service in Great Britain, takes Switzerland as an illustration of the results of military training on the physique. The Swiss conscript begins his military education at ten years of age, and at twenty he reports to the recruiting board for examination: defective men are rejected. After all this systematic training and with the presumption of a good record of heredity, 42 per cent fail to pass muster on account of bad eyesight or disease. The official report of the German war office for 1903 is quoted for the statement that 46 per cent of German recruits are rejected as physically unfit—this after compulsory training for a period of one hundred years. Such testimony, superficial as it undoubtedly is, points quite clearly to the fact that the military régime has not succeeded conspicuously in preventing disease or improving the physique of the recruit.

As to morals, the testimony is contradictory. One French author says that compulsory service far from being a school for morals, as is sometimes asserted, is a school for drunkenness, idleness and debauchery. A French preacher is quoted by Farrer as saying: "The family gives to the army a young man clean in mind and body: the army gives back that same young man steeped to the very lips in debauchery, suffering from disease and degrading vices." A professor at Leland Stanford University, who served about ten months in France, his native country, describes in the *Popular Science Monthly* for April, 1911, his experience at Le Havre, where he, a widow's only son, strictly reared, first came into contact with the gross immorality of a barracks town. The first instructions given out by the officer in charge on the day after his arrival, gave him a shock from which, he says, he was long in recovering.

In the recent Harden libel case in Germany, the leader of the Catholic Centre is reported to have declared in the Reichstag that "the trial had revealed a state of things within and without the barracks that recalled the conditions in the heathen Rome of ancient days."

The illustrated pamphlet entitled, *The Making of a Man-o'-Warsman* issued by the United States Bureau of Navigation with a view to alluring recruits by its graphic portrayal of the fascination of the life of Uncle Sam's sailors, emphatically denies that the prevailing opinion that blue-jackets are of loose moral character has any foundation. Doubtless much of the wholesale denunciation of the military service from the point of view of morality is exaggerated, and yet one must bear in mind that standards vary and that we are confronted today by an aspect of morality that formerly escaped public notice, partly because of a false or at least a mistaken conception of duty, and partly because it was regarded purely as a moral problem.

The recent activities of the medical profession and of other agencies interested in the propagation of the new gospel of sanitary and moral prophylaxis, seem destined to revolutionize previous notions as to the dangers to society, present and future, from the alarming results of the social vices upon the health and productivity as well as upon the morality of the human race. It will not be necessary on this occasion to discuss in detail the bearing of this grave question upon the conditions of barracks life, especially in countries where large numbers of conscripts are segregated in one sense, but in another sense especially exposed to all forms of intemperance.

If we accept Francis Galton's definition of Eugenics as "the science which deals with all the influences that improve the inborn qualities of a race," we may logically include within the scope of its application the effort to reduce the standing army and do away with compulsory military service, thereby limiting disease and mortality among the best specimens of manhood and calling a halt in that process of reversed selection which sets apart the fittest for training in legalized murder or, it may be, for untimely death, while the less fit are excused from the dangers and disadvantages of military service and left to pursue the economically productive callings and to propagate their kind.

But the military enthusiast will object that the career of the soldier is full of compensations and attractions and that the percentage of withdrawals from productive labor is very small and the time of service very limited; while the possibilities of death in actual service are almost negligible in this era of armed peace. It is true that the glamor of the soldier's life is still potent. Gorgeous uniforms, waving plumes, inspiring martial music and the gay nonchalance of Tommy Atkins on parade, stir the blood of young and old of both sexes; nevertheless, in spite of all the inducements offered by governments to secure voluntary enlistment, the profession has undoubtedly become unpopular with the better class of citizens in most civilized countries. Why is it necessary for the United States government to issue such a pamphlet as the one to which I have already referred, with its detailed description and alluring illustrations of the sunny side of life in the navy? Why was it that, when the British war office enlisted men for three year color service believing that a closer acquaintance with the service in peace would render young men eager to extend the term and perhaps choose to devote their lives to a military career, these young soldiers showed a strong disinclination to "extend"— greatly to the amazement of the war office?

Much of the attraction for army life is traceable to admiration for such countries as Germany, where military service is popular and is believed to be the most potent factor in the prosperity and efficiency of the nation. The habit of being educated to attribute national greatness to the "blood and iron" policy of Bismarck's day, naturally creates a strong prejudice in favor of the continuance of the present system; and the more men kept in training, the stronger the inclination to fight when any incident arises that touches the sensitive pride of the military patriot.

An excellent illustration of this inability to commit national causes to any other solution than the arbitrament of war, may be found in this utterance of Colonel Maude of the British army in an article which appeared in the *Contemporary Review* some years ago. After quoting Lord Overstone as ending his remarks about the consequences of a great war, in which England might become involved with the words, "It must never be," Colonel Maude argues in this extraordinary fashion: "Unfortunately it does not lie with us to prevent it. To many of us who have devoted our lives to the general question of such a war, this conclusion seems uncalled for. . . . and since the Almighty allows the ordeal of battle to remain as the only form of national appeal to Him, the problem cannot in itself be insoluble. War is the opportunity given to every nation to regenerate itself." Having stated his belief that when a nation "goes under," investigation invariably shows that the ultimate cause is corruption and the want of honesty between man and man, such as filling cartridges with harmless sawdust, supplying men with rotten provisions, etc., he consoles himself and the British nation with the thought that "at least in these respects the British are not worse than their probable enemies;" and he piously concludes that, if this be so, then "we may await the decision of the Supreme Arbiter without fear of failing, certain that we shall come through our trouble as our fathers before us."

Such gatherings as peace congresses afford a striking refutation of utterances like the above, and yet the hesitation of the intelligent and influential classes of all countries to admit the absurd logic of the present situation is difficult to explain. No one would deny that there is manifested everywhere a growing repugnance for the barbarities and the wastefulness of war; and that all movements for the alleviation of the sufferings incident to battle receive hearty support. As to the economic danger and the percentage of mortality being negligible quantities, the infrequency of war in modern times is, of course, to be taken into account; but there is no less logic in the assumption by the advocates of peace than by the war department that a serious war may break out. The statistics of recent wars show a by no means negligible mortality and, moreover, they reveal the startling fact that the losses from disease far exceed those from wounds. In the Civil War the ratio was one hundred thousand deaths from wounds and four hundred thousand from disease; in the recent Madagascar campaign, the French lost seven thousand from preventable diseases; in the Boer War there were ten times as many deaths from disease as from battle, and in the Spanish War the ratio was fourteen to one.

Modern science has made it possible to reduce very appreciably the death rate in large cities, and the public is much concerned about race suicide. Why, then, since there are, according to a recent estimate, some two hundred thousand commissioned officers and about four million men regularly under arms in Europe alone, and that on a peace footing, should governments fail to take into account even the smallest percentage of mortality among the men who are selected to risk their lives in war and the effects of such sacrifice of the life upon the survival of the fittest in race evolution?

Interest in the conservation of forests, coal mines, oil fields and water-power sites has gained an immense momentum in the past two years, but the proposal to establish a federal department of health in the United States for the conservation of human life has met with open opposition. And yet the absurdity of deliberately encouraging the destruction of the highest physical types of the civilized races of the earth, instead of spending revenue and brain power in exterminating those insidious pests and scourges of humanity that are more deadly than our hypothetical enemies must be patent to every patriotic citizen.

If we admit that the instinct to struggle is inherent in human nature and lies dormant beneath the veneered surface of civilization; if we admit also that this element of pugnacity has tended to prevent stagnation and degeneration of races and that it has developed the heroic virtues of courage, perseverance and self-sacrifice; if, to use the phrase of Professor James, war is "human nature at its highest dynamic" and its abolishment would weaken our fibre and quench our spirit; in other words, if we agree with those who insist that the benefits of war have been worth the price, how are we to extricate ourselves from the horns of this logical dilemma?

I am not so sure that the proposition of Professor James, some-

what quizzically suggested perhaps, does not contain the germ
of a rational solution. His plan is that the youth of the land
be enlisted by conscription in a disciplined, intelligently directed
campaign against the forces of nature in coal mines and swamps,
and in those occupations that develop manliness and hardihood,
"toughness without callousness." Such service might seem
an odd substitute for military campaigning, but the suggestion
that the "moral equivalent of war" is to be found in economic,
political and intellectual struggle is highly valuable and practical. Novicow, in his book on *War and its Alleged Benefits*, puts
the same philosophy of conservation in a somewhat more practical form, when he affirms that "man has many enemies besides
man, when such elements of destruction as droughts, famine,
floods and microbes challenge the intelligence and energy of mankind. Why should we consent to such a prodigious waste of
economic effort in the destruction of our fellow men or in the
attempt to prevent them from destroying us when those other
elements of destruction surround us on every side?"

Men are already coming to realize that the heroic virtues are
not the monopoly of the soldier. An editorial in a recent number
of the *World's Work* drew attention to the results of a voting
competition among the subscribers to one of the Paris journals,
who were asked to name the greatest hero in French history.
The contest resulted in favor not of Napoleon, but of Pasteur.

If history is studied from the psychological view-point, I think
it will be discovered that the instinct to unite, to federate, is as
strong as the instinct to fight: certainly we shall never reach the
culmination of human civilization until man becomes the ally,
not the enemy of man. Many pleas will be heard during this
Congress for the application of judicial procedure to the settlement of international disputes. Personally I am not concerned
for the moment with the practical wisdom of disarmament or
the immediate abolition of war. I am, however, a firm believer
in the maxim that "no evil was ever got rid of by the reiteration
of its inevitability."

If this paper shall have made the smallest contribution to the
movement for discouraging that conception of patriotism that

would dedicate the flower of manhood to the anti-social consequences of war and the standing army; if it has pressed home more convincingly the logical absurdity of spending more national energy upon the means of destruction than upon the agencies of conservation of the human species, it will have served its purpose. Perhaps no more fitting close could be devised than that noble plea of Erasmus for the restoration of man to that dignified supremacy over the brute creation for which he was endowed with the choicest gifts of nature's God:

"What evil spirit," he exclaims, "what pestilence, what mischief, what madness put first in man's mind a thing beyond measure beastly, that this most pleasant and reasonable creature, man, the which nature hath brought forth to peace and benevolence, which one alone she hath brought forth to the help and succor of all other, should with so wild wilfulness, with so mad rages, run headlong one to destroy another."

To ambitious princes he exclaims, "Ye say ye make war for the safeguard of the commonwealth, yea; but noway sooner nor more unthriftily may the commonwealth perish than by war. For before ye enter into the field, ye have already hurt more your country than ye do good getting the victory. Ye waste the citizens' goods, ye fill the houses with lamentation, ye fill all the country with thieves, robbers and ravishers. For these are the relics of war. If ye love your own subjects truly, why revolve you not in mind these words: 'Why shall I put so many, in their lusty flourishing youth, in all mischiefs and perils? Why shall I depart so many honest wives and their husbands, and make so many fatherless children? . . .' If there be any rights that admit of being defended by war they are rights of a grosser kind, which savor of a Christianity already becoming degenerate and burdened with the wealth of this world."

CHAIRMAN REMSEN: The third speaker this evening is Mr. Talcott Williams of the *Philadelphia Press*, and I have the pleasure of introducing Mr. Williams.

INTERNATIONAL RESPONSIBILITY FOR INTERNAL ORDER

BY MR. TALCOTT WILLIAMS

Mr. President, Ladies and Gentlemen: I speak between the upper mill stones of the clock and the lower mill stones of two speakers who are to follow me. I shal¹ therefore abridge the discussion which I propose to present to you. My topic is International Responsibility for Internal Order. We are met here in this Congress not to palliate the evils of war and diminish them by any method whatsoever, but to endeavor to end them.

Peace is the health of nations. War is disease. Peace is normal. War pathological. War never comes without some deranging cause which destroys the natural desire of all civilized men, of all men above the imbruted savage, to live at peace with their neighbors. By nature and her hereditary instincts, man is neither a beast of prey nor descended from a primitive line red with teeth and claw. His animal ancestors were peaceful. Peace for him was earlier than war and shall outlast it, for

> Its foundations builded are
> Below the tides of war.

War will never cease from among men until we know its reasons and remove them. War will end when the causes that make war end. These causes men widely mistake. Desire for conquest, thirst for territory, conflicting ideals of race, polity, religion, struggles over trade and between industrial systems—these have been the great causes of war in the past. When the modern European system emerged from the wreck of feudalism, all wars were of this character. They were wars of personal ambition, as between Francis I of Valois and Charles V of Hapsburg; wars of race and religion, as between Christian and Moslem; wars of religion only, as in the Reformation; wars of freedom and religion, as between the Low Countries and Spain, civil polity playing as large a share as faith; wars of trade, as those over India, and of opposing industrial systems as between our North and South, to be followed, it may be, by some gigantic struggle yet to come between differing ideals on the ownership of property, and the distribution of its usufruct.

These causes still remain and may at any time recur, but they have not been dominant in the wars of the past sixty years. From them only three or four wars in that period have sprung— our Civil War, from opposing industrial systems intertwined with opposing political ideals; the Franco-German War, and the two with Denmark and Austria, sheer struggles as to which nation should be the stronger in the European world. Misgovernment and internal disorder were the immediate and compelling causes of other wars, since the constitutional period in Europe, established some form of self-government as the normal rule to which all civilized lands were tending. Had the small Italian states been as well administered as Belgium, there might have been and probably would have been a federated Italy as there is a federated Germany, but an Italian kingdom would have been long in coming because the one force which moved the lower deeps of Italian revolution and European sympathy was the shameless oppression, disorder and peculation of the petty kingdoms which divided Italy, evils shared in Austrian Lombardy and Venice. Had Turkey been as well governed, one need not say as a European state, but had its administration matched that of a Moslem kingdom such as is ruled over by the Nizam of Naidarabad—who has, let us remember, a population under his rule nearly one-half as large as that of the Sultan of Turkey, four-fifths of it Hindoos, idolatrous in the eyes of every Moslem— neither the Crimean War nor the Turko-Russian War would have ever occurred. A well administered Turkish state, without oppression, preserving religious liberty and dealing fairly by all its motley races, would have never occasioned the successive steps from the destructions of the Turkish fleet in the harbor of Navarine to its second destruction in Sinope, which ended in the interference of England and France with the advance of Russia. This advance would never have been taken up a second time if the Balkan massacres had not moved the Slav world. Had the Turkish constitution of 1876 established the same liberal régime as exists today in Turkey, had it been as now a realm in which

all faiths were able to live at peace and in which the reckless use
of irregular Oriental troops in a peaceful population had not
moved the mingled horror and wrath of Europe, it would have
been impossible for Alexander II in 1817 to cross the Danube.
If today Turkey becomes a fairly governed state and is wise enough
to permit the gradual civilization of Albania, instead of rashly
attempting its subjection, the territory of Turkey will remain
intact. Macedonia has been a danger point, liable at any moment to invite attack, because it was wretchedly governed. . Had
the international police proposed by the Macedonian Convention of 1903 been organized, instead of being frustrated by the
covert determination of the Sublime Porte to have no interference with its oppression and rapine and the open readiness of
Russia and Austria to keep a running sore which weakened the
Turkish Empire, the Balkan peninsula would not be as it is and
promises long to remain, the center of danger to eastern Europe.
It was the misgovernment of Turkey which brought on the Greek
revolution and the Greek War of fourteen years ago. It was
misgovernment in Crete which repeatedly brought the European
Powers close to strife. It was misgovernment in Egypt which
made it the possible causes of European war in 1881. Egypt
would be as safe as Belgium had Egypt been as well governed by
Ismail as Belgium was by Leopold, and the world would have
allowed the former ruler to amass a prodigious private fortune as
readily as it allowed Leopold, had there not been in Egypt that
combination of avarice and oppression, of heavy taxation on industry, and faithless disregard of public obligations which in modern
times creates conditions which breed war. Given a well governed
Korea, and its annexation by Japan would have never taken place.
Given a China equal, one need not assume to military prowess,
but to the maintenance of a fair and reasonable order for foreign
commerce and domestic industry, and the conditions would have
never existed which led step by step to one small war after another,
in time to the collision between Japan and China, the Boxer revolt,
the Russo-Japanese War, and today, the impending disturbance
in Canton which threatens and may prove perilous to the safety
of the Chinese Empire. Had Spain governed Cuba well, one need
not say as England governed Jamaica, but even as well as Holland

governs Java or Japan, Formosa, our war with Spain would never have come. A stable Mexico would never have seen on the Rio Grande the first American army corps mobilised since the Civil War. Had President Diaz to his amazing powers as a despotic ruler added the prescience for the future self-government of Mexico which the United States has shown in the Philippines, there would never have come the explosion which is devastating our sister republic, for there is no way in which men so certainly court an explosion as by sitting on the safety valve of free discussion. With Canada war is impossible, incredible, unbelievable, because Canada and the United States, with all the shortcomings of each —and they are many on both sides of the line—are fairly well governed nations, meeting their obligations, preserving order, and maintaining civilization. Given a Mexico as well governed as Canada, and the Rio Grande, like the St. Lawrence, would be a frontier which one would cross scarcely aware that it had been traversed. What is true of the great wars in the past sixty years is true of the small ones. If Servia and Bulgaria fell out, it was because neither was properly administered. If Chili and Peru flew at each other's throat thirty years ago each of us is well aware it was because the government of each was defective, and the more effective government tore from Bolivia the provinces of Tarapaca and Africa, which both Peru and Chili were proposing to rend from a republic which has not from the time it adopted the name of the liberator had a single year of even respectable administration. One could run through all the acquisition of territory of the past sixty years—the occupation by France of Tonquin, Tunis and Madagascar, the English conquest of the Boer States, and the many English annexations, like those of Burmah, Asam and Beloochistan—and each is due to the fact that within the area annexed the level of administration, the security of life and property, the protection of trade, and the taxation of foreign capital had taken the form of spoliation. Were the five small countries of northern Europe—Sweden, Norway, Denmark, Holland and Belgium—to sink to the same level of misrule as some of the powers which have just been mentioned, to begin the same reckless taxation of foreign ports which cost the Transvaal its independence, to make their territory the source of devastating epidemics as did Spain in Cuba, and to stand the visible example of a country in which oppression was supported by cruelty and every movement toward self-government stifled by armed force, these countries would be absorbed by their neighbors and cease to be, after some war which would set all Europe ablaze.

When the ambassador of the king of Spain, admitted to the House of Commons, under the English Commonwealth, told the body which had just tried a king and beheaded him that his master held to the doctrine that each country had a right to decide what manner of government it desired and none other had a right to interfere with it, he laid down the broad and general doctrine of the mutual independence of all states in internal affairs which Grotius had just developed into recognized international law, accepted as almost fundamental and still asserted as a primary postulate in international relations. The past half century has seen grave modifications worked in this ancient doctrine. It was easy to maintain this doctrine when the alien population of a nation was small, intercommunication difficult, and neither railroad nor steamship brought all lands into constant and close relations. Investments are today universal. Where a century ago nations were by treaty permitting the citizens of each to secure a domicile within their sovereignty, today this right is granted by statute in most civilized states and accepted by all as the natural right of humanity between nations sufficiently similar to create no serious danger from the admixture of differing standards of living, ideals of behavior, or social and moral habits. In the family of civilization there has come to be a standard of living almost as distinct as that which exists in any society with reference to the family. United Europe took Switzerland to task sixty years ago for harboring political refugees. Lord Palmerston a little over a half century ago challenged the administration of Naples on the open ground that its misgovernment was likely to involve Europe in war and could not be accepted without protest. From the Congress of Paris at the close of the Crimean War through a series of nearly a score of gatherings since of the signatory powers, the internal condition of Turkey has been held to be a subject of European concern, and to this have been successively joined the internal conditions of Egypt, Tunis, Morocco, Persia, the waters which surround the Arabian peninsula, and parts of the peninsula itself, because any one may bring war. The internal conditions of Turkey, in spite of the division of the continent, are accepted as a just subject of international discussion and protest for a like reason. Just as there is a certain standard of internal order for a civilized state, so there has grown to be a certain standard in the management of a colony. Belgium and Portugal have both been called to account for departing from it. Holland has been the subject of criticism. It has come to be generally recognized that any power is bound, if it has colonies, to maintain a certain level of administration, to avoid oppressive taxation, and to use a colony, not for the profit of its suzerain, but in order to secure the internal development of the colony itself.

This profound change has taken place in the last half of a century which began with every civilized power, England included, excluding all aliens from its colonica. Spain at the opening of the nineteenth century was treating as pirates luckless American skippers whom profit led into the Spanish main, and its policy which closed not only the territories under its flag but the seas and ocean about them to alien vessels was universal. Instead today all colonies are equally open to all. The management of colonies is a subject of mutual concern, and nothing is more certain than that the persistent and continual failure of Portugal properly to govern its possessions in Africa will be ended by their loss.

If a standard of living is now recognized among civilized nations, it is because its absence is liable to bring collision. If standards of colonial administration are accepted and any departure from them brings the culprit, if not under diplomatic protest, under public discussion, it is because an ill governed colony sooner or later brings collision. Morocco is today liable again to embroil France and Germany because its government is not strong enough to keep order. Were Morocco now as well governed as it was by Mulzi-Hassan, the father of the present Sultan, there would be no French occupation at Casablanca or Oudja and the relations of the Sherifian Empire would be as peaceful as they were from

1873 to 1894, the limits of his reign. It is idle to suppose that either treaties or courts, international arbitration or agreements limiting armaments can ever prevent war when in any one of the units which make up the world of humanity today there is visible disorder. Inevitably where this exists international issues will arise whose final settlement will bring war near and whose ultimate adjustment will probably only be possible with the sword. Peace rests on justice. If a government weak and unable to maintain order, dealing injustice on a colossal scale to helpless human beings instead of justice which governments are organized to administer, if life is unsafe, if property is insecure, if debts cannot be collected, if contracts are unenforced, if courts are venal, if administration is corrupt, if differences of faith are visited with persecution and differences of race with oppression and massacres —by mobs of single victims or many—the moment is sure to come when the cup will fill, and for every drop which has been shed by the innocent and the helpless victims of oppression or prejudice there will fall on some battlefield the plentiful rain of war.

The remedy for all this does not lie in the attempt to maintain the international figment that the internal affairs of each nation are of no consequence to another, because this is not true. Every nation suffers from the disorder of every other nation in a greater or a less degree. Peace cannot be secured by laboriously endeavoring to adjust machinery by which open and definite issues between countries over some trifle of territory, claim or jurisdiction shall be settled when there is left untouched, unavenged and unredressed the misery of millions and the worst of all human wrongs, injustice at the fount of justice, spoliation under the guise of taxation, and the denial of human rights to humanity. The clock of international justice is not always striking twelve, but when it does the high noon of retribution has come and nothing can prevent nations which have permitted these evils long to remain without redressing them by peaceful measures from being led into that costliest of all punishments, wars which might have been prevented if the evils which caused them had been earlier removed.

Instructed by paying this costly penalty, the United States

wrote a new chapter in international responsibility for internal disorder when in what is known as the Platt amendment, it required of Cuba as the price of its independence the maintenance of what I have already termed the standard of living as between civilized nations. As long as Cuba prevents pestilence, maintains order, and enforces contracts, the independence of the island remains as secure as though it were protected by the fleets of the world. When it lapses from this standard, the United States, having learned once for all that such lapses bring their penalty not only for those who suffer the wrong but for those who permit it, discharges the international responsibility for internal order by occupation. The same task has been undertaken in Santa Domingo, whose condition was once likely to lead to hostile action on behalf of bondholders. Steps have been taken towards it in Haiti. A tyrant has been excluded from Venezuela, where his policy narrowly escaped bringing war, as tyranny is always liable to do. A beginning has at least been made to require the observance of a civilized standard of living in Central America. In Mexico it will be seen in the end that nothing is quite so costly as the hallucination that material development can be safely purchased at the expense of human rights and the postponement of self-government. In some way, by some means, through some path, it will be necessary to secure in Mexico that standard of living among nations which preserved peace and which alone can preserve peace.

This great task assumed in whole for Cuba by the United States and in part for other lands, opening a new chapter in international relations under which nations maintain their mutual independence but are required, as members of a common international system, to preserve certain standards, is too near our own experience to enable us to appreciate its momentous importance. Were this same principle in practice applied to the world, were all the various lands which are today points of danger, liable at any moment to become the pivots of international conflict, were Morocco and Persia, for instance, to be taken in hand by an international commission backed by the overwhelming force of the civilized world, given the benefit of a thorough reorganization, and then left independent to work out their own salvation under their own flag, free from any subjection to any power, peace would be rendered more certain and war less liable in the European system.   What is true of these two lands is true in a lesser degree of a great country like China.   Could Korea have had this treatment, Japan would not be ruling an unwilling dependency and the prospect of bitter hate would not cloud all the future of the Korean peninsula.   It is too early in the development of human affairs to expect full appreciation of the large-minded magnanimity of the United States in dealing with the weaker nations south of our borders.   In time, if war is to be prevented, some such plan is necessary.   Mere arbitration over definite issues will never prevent all war if the causes of every war but three or four during the last sixty years are permitted in one land and another to fester until the only apparent remedy for the diseased member seemed to be the surgery of the sword.   The United States has had a comparatively easy duty to discharge in launching this new international practice and openly acknowledging international responsibility for internal order, because its ninety millions constitute an overwhelming majority in numbers, in force, in material wealth, and in all resources of civilization of the Western Hemisphere.   A like task is immeasurably difficult in Europe, because its balance of powers divides and renders impossible the discharge of common duties, so that one war has succeeded another through the last two centuries.   But in the end this new duty will be recognized and is unconsciously now in the attempt to organize an international police for Macedonia and Morocco, in the commissions which managed the debts of Greece and Egypt, and in a sense of Turkey, in the effort to create similar bodies for China, in the consent of European countries that a neutral power like the United States should furnish the commission that is reorganizing both the debt and the finances of Persia, in the similar task which is being discharged in Siam, in our own adjustment of the debts of Santa Domingo, Honduras and Liberia, a course which in due time will be taken for every bankrupt nation in the American system and probably in the old world.   The future will see that it is cheaper, more efficacious, and more just to deal with disorder before it has brought war, even if force is necessary to accomplish this, than to permit neglected disorder to breed a pestilencc of war as neglected sanitation breeds epidemics whose effect can never be limited to the foul place which produced them. Nor can it be forgotten that the international responsibility for internal order is mutual. ˙ If strong nations are responsible for the internal order of the weak, strong nations are responsible also to the world for their own internal order. Whatever of evil any great nation permits within its borders weakens its moral force and position in requiring of lesser lands a due standard of living in their internal administration. If a great nation like our own is careless over the protection of aliens like Chinese and Japanese within its borders, if violent injustice to its own citizens passes without rebuke or protest and is permitted to continue from decade to decade, it ceases to be able in the forum of nations to raise an effective voice for justice, for order, for peace, and for the protection even of its own citizens in other lands. Into that great court of equity, the public opinion of man, a nation must come with clean hands if it is to require of other lands the maintenance of the due standards of civilized society. Every fault we permit in our own land, every weakness or worse, in our own administration, every lack of justice, every prejudice which brings bitter fruit, and every failure to remember the common claims of all humanity to common rights and common justice, weakens before all the world the influence of the great republic in requiring of all lands the discharge of all the duties of a civilized state. The international responsibility for internal order is therefore within as well as without. It is a responsibility as direct and immediate with reference to the internal administration of a country exercising responsibility as in requiring of other lands a due regard for the maintenance of justice, order and self-government. In short, the best guarantee of peace which can exist to day is not only based on universal arbitration and the reduction of armaments, but it rests also on the exercise and discharge of the duty which every nation bears to all the world that its internal order shall be such that is itself a model and gives the ground upon which it has a right to demand that other lands shall give to its citizens, its investments, and its relations with every other country the same just tribunal, the same honest administration, and the same jealous protection of all human rights which it provides.

The great danger of peace today is from the weakness of nations which pass from one failure in administration and justice and order to another, some of them, like Morocco and Persia, national derelicts, some of them like China, great hulks, caught unaware by storm and explosion, and refitting, while all the world doubts if there is still time to prevent the great craft which, not for a thousand, but for three thousand years has braved the battle and the breeze from foundering. The cause of peace needs nothing today more than the clear conscious apprehension of international responsibility for internal order, the unhesitating discharge in the foreign policy of every civilized state of this duty, and the machinery, rapidly developing under one precedent and another, of an orderly procedure by which international direction shall be assumed of these national derelicts which, like vessels flying the signal "not under control," are a peril to all about them in the voyage of nations to the common haven of peace in which all battle flags shall be at last furled.

Dr. Thomas S. Baker, of Port Deposit, Maryland, was unfortunately detained from the Second Session of the Third National Peace Congress, but was thoughtful enough to submit the address which he had prepared on "Education and the Peace Movement," which is printed as part of the Proceedings:

EDUCATION AND THE PEACE MOVEMENT

THOMAS S. BAKER

The idea of universal peace, which has gained greater prominence in recent years than ever before, has had a long period of preparation before it reached its present definite form. The object of this paper is to urge, First: The desirability of showing the historical background in which the present Peace Movement is fixed. Second: The necessity of emphasizing *facts* rather than indefinite aspirations. Both of these topics fall well within the range of educational effort.

There are many advocates of universal peace who believe that the only solution of the question lies in doing way with national distinctions. They are in favor of what they conceive to be a higher form of altruism than is implied in the word patriotism. They advocate what might be called for lack of a better word "cosmopolitanism" rather than nationalism. The good of the whole race is a higher ideal to strive for than the good of any nation. If such a principle can find general acceptance, it will inevitably do away with the necessity of war. Such a conception is, when first considered, somewhat shocking, but although it may seem revolutionary, it was expounded a hundred years ago, and then as now, it was received with some misgivings. It is not proposed to discuss the merits of this idea, but merely to show that the present tendency to universalism or cosmopolitanism has had a long history.

Many of the catch words and phrases which are used at the present time seem to be entirely novel, but as is not infrequently the case, one is surprised to find that they have been used before. The expression, "The Federation of the World," and the idea conveyed by it, would seem to be one of the newest and most original contributions to the whole subject. As a matter of fact, however, it, too, has a previous history. Probably the idea has been carried further by the Germans than by any other nation. Goethe himself has been accused of a lack of patriotism, of being a cosmopolitan, but the charge has been resented by his biographers. However, if the conception, that it is better to strive for the good of the entire race rather than for the good of a particular nation, gains acceptance, it may not always be necessary to apologize for Goethe's so-called lack of patriotism.

The cosmopolitanism of Goethe was, however, carried far beyond his intentions by many Germans of a later generation. This cosmopolitan tendency in German thought reached its height at the time of the Revolution of 1848. Its most bizarre features showed themselves in the writings of the German refugees

who came to the United States after this uprising.   Many of these
men were revolutionists in every sense of the word.   They were
opposed to the constituted government authorities, they were
anti-military men, they objected to the existing social conditions.
They were, however, above all things universalists or cosmopoli-
tans.   Patriotism was frowned upon.   They believed that a
national literature should be discouraged and that a literature
of the world should take its place.

In the discussion of the federation of the world which has been
taking place in recent years, an absurdly grotesque book, the
joint work of two of these German refugees, has been completely
overlooked.   This book has as its plan for the federation of the
world, the expansion of the United States along international
lines.   The book is entitled, *The New Rome, or the United States
of the World*.   It is the joint work of Theodore Poesche and
Charles Goepp.   It was published by G. P. Putnam and Company, New York, 1853.   It is dedicated to Franklin Pierce,
President of the United States, "being a guess at the spirit in
which he was elected."   In spite of its absurdities, many of its
phrases have a strangely modern sound.   The authors say on
page 67, "Wars are the results of mistaken ideas of interest and
pride, possibly only so long as the individual identifies his personal interests, not with those of humanity at large, but with
those of a certain portion of humanity, with whom he speaks the
same language, and whom he terms a nation.   Nationality is the
root of war.   Nations, as soon as they become self-conscious,
are associations of people for the purpose of taking away other
people's land; a nation may be defined to be an organization for
making war on other nations, killing their subjects and pillaging
their property, or of robbing them of their substance by the
peaceful means of commercial and industrial competition.   Wars
require armies; recurring wars, standing armies; and armies,
generals; generalissimos are monarchs; and thus the fictions of
nationality are the causes of all the woes under which Europe
is struggling."

And again on page 119, "The time is past for comparing man to
the vermin on the leaf, of which each species can only infest its

particular plant. History now advances with great strides, to hasten on the day when all the nations of the earth shall be one people, united in a single state. No longer a circumscribed portion of lands, the new 'orbis terrarum' shall encircle the globe; and as ancient Rome assembled all the gods of her empire in a single Pantheon, so shall the ideas of all nations be marshalled into unity. The signs of the times are clear and unmistakable, and 'The New Rome' awakens to her task, and is resolved upon its execution. Let her raise her banner of stars over land and sea, the token of perdition to the despots and redemption to the peoples, who may be convinced: *In hoc signo vincit!*"

Further, on page 8, the authors say, "The following essay is a map of the future of mankind, drawn from surveys of the past and present. It professes to tell neither what might nor what should, but simply what must be." Again on page 9, "Russia . . . . dreams of universal empire; while the American repub-lic, with the motto 'E pluribus Unum,' flaming in her fillet, is developing her resources of mind and body with an external force and an internal freedom, which mark her the germ of a World's Republic.

"This 'New Rome,' the American Union, is a reflection of the old, even in its geographical position. The Roman Empire, embracing the 'orbis terrarum' of the geography of those times, was a political organization of the circle of lands that skirted the Mediterranean Sea, in the midst of which, like a great line-of-battle ship, was moored the Italian peninsula. . . . In the middle of these peninsulas were founded, respectively, the Etru-rian and the British colonies. Each looks to the lands of the East for the sources of its civilization. Each casts its eyes first upon its native peninsula, and strives to reduce it to its undis-puted sway. Thus, the acquisition of all Italy was an important epoch in Roman politics; it supplied the base for further opera-tions. Thus 'The continent is ours,' is becoming more and more distinctly a leading American aspiration."

The history and the plan of the book can be described in a very few words. In the early part of the year 1852, certain Revolu-tionary Societies were founded in the most important cities of the East and also in a few of the western cities.   The headquarters of the new league was at first in Philadelphia, afterwards in Boston.   Its object was to form an universal republic with the United States as the centre.   In other words, to annex all the countries of the world to the United States.   The motto of the United States, *E pluribus Unum*, was taken in the broadest possible sense.   Out of all the political divisions an universal empire would be formed, just as this country was an aggregation of states. The originator of this movement was Carl Goepp, a young German, who had been compelled to leave Europe because of the part which he took in the disturbance of 1848.   The radical doctrines proposed by Goepp were first published in a pamphlet entitled *E pluribus Unum* in 1852.

These peculiar theories found further elaboration in the book already referred to by Theodore Poesche and Charles Goepp. The authors say that the confederation of all the states of North and South America is a question of only a few years.   The time seemed ripe, California and New Mexico had just been annexed and the annexation of Cuba was being discussed.

No pent-up Utica can hold our powers
The whole, the boundless continent is ours,

was a favorite sentiment.   With the whole of the American continent at its back, the United States would be in a position to contest for the possession of some of the English colonies.   In this connection Australia is discussed at considerable length and is easily disposed of.   They say, "With all the continent and Australia in the American scale, the addition of the rest of the world will be a question of time regulated by American convenience."   The infederation of England is treated as a very easy matter.

According to the authors, Russia is the only nation of the earth that will offer any real resistance to the march of the United States.   Russia dreamed also of an universal empire.   When, therefore, the United States and Russia confront each other, "Then will the mastery of Europe be the prize of the death struggle between the Union and the Czar."   "Thus the lines are drawn.

The choirs are marshalled on each wing of the world's stage; Russia leading the one, the United States the other. Yet the world is too small for both, and the contest must end in the downfall of one, the victory of the other." Victory is, of course, prophesied for the Union.

What I have said about *The New Rome* shows its most crass features. There are many passages of very great interest, especially for those who are occupied with this conception of a federation of all nations. In the few moments at my disposal I have been able to select a small number of the most striking paragraphs. *The New Rome* was published by a publisher of good standing, but as far as can be ascertained, it made hardly a ripple on the surface of public opinion. It would hardly deserve being rescued from its obscurity, were it not for the fact that these mad revolutionaries were the mouth-piece of a larger idea which they distorted in their effort to appeal to the vanity of the American nation.

II.

In promoting any great idea, in making propaganda of any sort, it is important that especial attention should be given to young people. This is not a debatable question; its importance is recognized by the various peace associations, and a vast amount of work has already been undertaken with a view to bringing before students in schools and colleges what is being done to promote the cause of universal peace.

The Peace Movement is now beyond the sentimental stage and is concerned rather with ways and means. Many enthusiastic military men acknowledge the desirability of universal peace. They are sceptical merely concerning its realization; they are sceptical concerning human nature. And in their scepticism they have on their side the overwhelming power of tradition. But reformers are the enemies of the past, and no great reform has ever been consummated without breaking with tradition.

The average boy is a very militant figure. Any theory of passive non-resistance makes no appeal to him whatever. It will be recalled that when some of the early Germanic versions

of the Gospels were made by the devout missionaries, it was
found necessary to leave out all reference to humility, to submission, to meekness. Christ was represented as a great Lord
surrounded by twelve heroic figures. Only gradually was it
possible to teach the human race that there were higher triumphs
than military triumphs. In the thousand or more years that
have passed since the childhood of Germanic Christianity this
has been accomplished. But the boy remains a combative,
struggling type. And these characteristics constitute some of
his most important and valuable qualities. It would be unfortunate to have any element introduced into a boy's life that would
lessen his energy, his power of initiative, or his interest in courageous and heroic deeds. I doubt whether the doctrine of peace
merely as a theory makes an appeal even today to the average
boy, but the facts and the possibilities the practical human advantages interest him profoundly and he is eager to learn about
them. We do not realize how little is known even today by our
school boys or even by the man in the street of the great things
that have been accomplished by the workers for peace. In spite
of the fact that boys are worshipers of storm and stress they
are also idealists at heart, and will welcome any positive help
in realizing their ideals. Boys cannot accept abstractions which
are far removed from their experience and their interests, but
they will receive heartily all efforts that are made to show them
the reasonableness of this great historical movement.

Education rests upon the principle that childhood and youth
is the period when information is acquired upon which theories
and principles are later developed. I should then advocate in
all efforts to interest boys in the Peace Movement that attention
be paid first to the practical features and the historical features
of what has been accomplished, and of what is being accomplished. It is not generally realized that our anti-military efforts
are a part of a great humanitarian movement which dates from
the birth of Christ and which has its ramifications in every department of human society. Certainly boys do not realize that the
prevention of a war in which hundreds of thousands of men may
be killed is more logical than the prevention of disease. They
do not realize that the great philanthropist who endows an insti-

tution whose object is the prevention of war is attempting a greater task than the man of wealth who devotes his fortune to the prevention and cure of disease. The prevention of war would seem to be the crowning victory for which humanitarianism has fought during the nineteen hundred years of its history. The relation between the Peace Movement and education is then concerned first with this idea of the historical sequence that is implied in the very existence of this congress.

Furthermore, education in its relation to peace should disseminate a knowledge of what is being done. It need concern itself very little with the arousing of sentiment in favor of peace. This will take care of itself when it is realized that much has already been accomplished, and very definite and very practical plans are being considered at the present time 'to further the aims of such a congress as this. The world of the schools does not yet know the full significance of The Hague Conferences, of such expressions as "Federation of the World," "Courts of Arbitration," "Treaties of Arbitration." It is, however, not sufficient to present what has been accomplished by the movement; the world should be told very fully of what remains to be done and the gigantic difficulties that remain to be overcome. It is a subject that admits of vast flights of eloquence but it is unfair especially to young people to have the presentation one-sided and to gloss over in any way the great struggles that must yet be won. Great ideals are much more effective when they are promoted by practical men, and this fact should never be lost sight of in everything that the cause of education is called upon to do in favor of promoting universal peace. The world must know about the realities and the difficulties which are to be met. With Bismarck dead only thirteen years it is obvious that much hard and detailed work and much serious thought must be devoted to the realization of the ideal.

CHAIRMAN REMSEN: I shall call upon Mr. Edwin M. Borchard, the Law Librarian, in Washington, who was the expert on international law in the North Atlantic Coast Fisheries arbitration, and who will speak on "Peace, its Evolution and Present Status."

PEACE—ITS EVOLUTION AND PRESENT STATUS

EDWIN M. BORCHARD

The progress made in the last twelve years by international law and its corollary, the movement for peace, has been nothing short of remarkable.   And yet, viewed in the light of the history of human institutions, it is a natural concomitant of advancing civilization.   The development of international law and relations toward a condition of relative peace finds close analogy in the development of private law.   Private war and vengeance, which once enjoyed legal sanction, are now considered criminal; it is our desire to bring public war under the same opprobrium. When the thinkers of the present day, who even *now* regard war as unmoral, shall have convinced the large majority of the people of the civilized world that it *is* unmoral, and that the economic and industrial welfare of mankind depends absolutely upon providing international peace with a legal sanction, war will have taken its place among the illegal agencies for settling international differences.

I.

The peace we now enjoy in our private relations is directly attributable to the gradual perfection of our legal institutions. The relative peace under which we live in our international relations has been largely brought about by the development of international law.   The road by which private peace was secured was a long and thorny one; and there are many indications that we still have a long road, precarious and full of pitfalls, to travel before we shall have registered our arrival at the final goal of international peace.

Misunderstanding of the facts as they exist, a misconception of the nature, hereditary instincts and history of the international society whose ills we desire to cure is the greatest danger confronting the Peace Movement.   Henry IV with his Great Design for a European Confederation and James Mill who two centuries ago advocated an international tribunal, with general disarmament as a preliminary, and others after them, made the great mistakes of not taking into account the existing facts, and seeking to regenerate society at one bold stroke. War is too ancient an evil to submit to any single panacea.

At the present time, however, we have reached a point where remedies can be suggested and applied with an assurance of their reasonable consideration by states; and with the growth of an international public opinion in their favor, an assurance of their ultimate acceptance. Various remedies for settling international differences have been suggested; the most effective in practice has been a court of arbitration, or court of justice.

Private individuals did not always display their present willingness to submit their disputes to the arbitrament of courts. The struggle was a long one and fiercely waged, extending from the beginning of history until modern times. But old as are the beginnings of society—tribal relations—international society in such form as we can recognize it did not begin until two or three thousand years later. It is therefore natural that it will take a little longer to arrive at the same stage of social development that our private relations have reached, but the analogies between the two are clearly traceable.

The bond of primitive society was kinship. The first stage in the social relations between the units of that society is marked by universal belligerency, a very natural rule. Disputes were accompanied by a limitless resort to private war and private vengeance. Such action was unrestrained by any humanizing agencies, uncontrolled by any superior, and unlimited in its devastating effects.

In the international society, some analogy to this first stage may be discovered in the utter license and unrestrained cruelty with which the wars of the Reformation were waged—the period when the modern society of states had its origin. This very barbarity had much to do with the writing by Grotius of his epoch-making work, in which the beginnings of a system of international law are presented.

The second stage in private relations discloses a gradual limitation upon the waging of private war, by confining vengeance to certain members of the family or kindred, by restricting it to certain offenses and by inaugurating a system by which pecuniary compensation for minor offenses could be paid.   Sir Henry Maine regards these money fines for private wrongs, such as the Wehrgeld of the Germans and the Eric fine of the ancient Irish, as evidence of a very early conscious effort to prevent war or mitigate it. Pollock and Maitland suggest that the amount of compensation was probably fixed by some form of arbitration.

This second stage in international relations is marked by the introduction of humanizing agencies in war, first through the influence of great writers, principally Grotius and Vattel, then through the influence of progressive civilization and the growing wisdom of states.   Such agencies are exemplified in the codification of the rules of neutrality and the rules of war principally in ameliorating its hardships.   This was largely the work of the Geneva, Brussels, St. Petersburg, and Hague Conferences.

The third stage in private relations is marked by the growth of the kingly power and the gradual waning of the self-helping autonomy of the kindred.   As Maitland remarks "private war is controlled, regulated and put into legal harness."   In this period we find the beginnings of a system by which an issue is submitted to the arbitrament of some impartial agency.   Private vengeance, however, was not abolished, but merely regulated. The king was not yet strong enough to compel his warring subjects to come before the court; but side by side with regulated private war there grew up a system of trial, by battle, by compurgation, and later by jury.   But the institution was weak; there was no jurisdiction save by consent of the parties.   As the king grew stronger, a scale of compensation for injuries, a sort of tariff was decreed.   Compensation had to be accepted, if offered, and private war was lawful only when the adversary obstinately refused to do right. [Heinrich Brunner gives an able presentation of the difficulties in the path of the judicial adjustment of private disputes.]

International relations in this third stage are exemplified by the coördinate existence of a regulated public war and a system of international arbitration, our present condition.

From the conflict between the two agencies in our private

relations, private war and the courts, the judicial method emerged victorious; and the fourth stage finds us practically under the full dominion of a judicial method of adjusting our private disputes. Among the systems of trial, however, trial by jury had to carry on a fierce struggle for supremacy with trial by battle. The prevalence of perjury and other disadvantages influenced a preference for trial by battle, even long after trial by jury had been established. It is a mistake, too, to assume that trial by battle did not satisfy the sense of justice of the litigants. It did. They believed that an impartial spirit was acting as judge, who in letting fall the mantle of victory, indicated the right. But superstition has given way to reason. We now realize that a belligerent method of settling controversies does not do justice; that is why arbitration is replacing war as the only equitable agency for adjusting an international difference.

The analogies we have traced, in particular the evolution from the third into the fourth stage in private law, give us every reason to believe that the conflict between the two agencies on the international side, public war and arbitration, will result in a victory for the judicial system, and that a submission to the arbitrament of judicial agencies will take its place among our permanent social institutions.

II

Peace in the international community is a social need. States were never so willing as now to listen to practical suggestions for its realization. History explains the reason. With the break-up of the Holy Roman Empire and the destruction of the idea of universal sovereignty, of a common superior, spiritual and temporal, a chaos resulted, exemplified in the horrible wars of the Reformation. From that time until the Congress of Vienna in 1815, the states of Europe were engaged in a tremendous struggle of territorial adjustment. The influence of Grotius, which first bore distinct fruit at the Peace of Westphalia, brought certain rules into this process of adjustment, but the ideal of international peace engaged thinkers and not statesmen.

The nineteenth century, however, was marked by a movement

for national unification throughout the world, and while the force of arms played a small part in this nationalization, commerce and industry were the great factors in the process. This century witnessed the most important changes in the legal position of aliens. From his original status as an enemy *eo nomine*, the alien has gradually become practically assimilated to the national in his legal rights. The facilities for immigration and naturalization, and rapid communication, have brought about the democratization of the world, cosmopolitanism. With the growth of social and commercial intercourse among nations, the discoveries of science, and the extreme mobility of capital, nations have come to recognize the unity of their interests. An international consciousness has been awakened. The result has been a growing solidarity of international organization. This present century is to be one of international development or as Prof. Lorimer puts it, "from independence has emerged interdependence." International law has kept pace with the necessities of the new order, as is shown by the great number of international conferences during the last thirty years. The many international unions and agreements on industrial, economic, scientific and legal matters indicate that nations have become convinced of the necessity for coöperation and international arrangements of an administrative nature. In addition almost two hundred international conferences of an unofficial character within the last seventy years, covering almost all fields of human thought and activity, are evidence of the solidarity of world interests.

It is therefore apparent why war is now a greater catastrophe than ever before. While we have been endeavoring to localize war by enlarging the obligations of neutrals—and much still remains to be done along this line—it is nevertheless true that a public war between any of the units of the international community shakes the security of the entire structure and impairs the welfare of all. It is therefore not difficult to realize why all states are now willing to coöperate to prevent an international war and adopt the necessary means to this end.

No society can exist without some rules for the conduct and mutual intercourse of its members. Just as the judicial order of national life springs from, at the same time that it ministers to, its development, so has international arbitration proved itself to be a factor in the development of the society of nations, which has made it possible and of which it is the outcome. Yet up to the present time statesmen and lawyers believe that arbitration has its limitations. As we have said there exists in the international society a body of rules or a *modus vivendi* for the conduct of its members. Westlake points out that a claim by one state against another for a breach of this *modus vivendi* resembles very much a claim of one individual against another before national courts of justice, for both deal with legal relations. These claims are eminently fitted for arbitration. The action of states, however, is not confined within these legal limits. They must sometimes act under circumstances where there are no rules. A situation of this kind in private life is met by the national legislature enacting new legislation. In the absence of an international legislature or immediate agreement on a rule, states must act for themselves, and it is in these spheres that we find what is called the political action of states, or international policy.

The Russian delegates to the First Hague Conference pointed out that the former class, legal claims, being a conflict of rights, may appropriately be made the subject of an arbitration; but that the latter, being a conflict of interests, do not admit of this method of adjustment. The Russian delegates included under such political questions what they called political treaties, transitory arrangements between states which bind the freedom of action of the parties so long as the political conditions which produced them remain without change. Such a question is illustrated in Russia's own history. At the end of the Crimean War Russia, exhausted, was compelled to submit to a treaty in which she engaged to neutralize the Black Sea, and to maintain no fortifications on the coast. In 1871, taking advantage of the disablement of France, she denounced the treaty and proceeded to erect a fortification at Sebastopol. No single power was strong enough to prevent her. As a result a conference was held, a tribute paid to the binding (sic!) character of treaties, and the limitations on Russia removed by consent. Could such a question have been arbitrated? A court could have reached but one conclusion. No state can, by an unilateral act, legally put an end to a stipulation it has signed. Russia, therefore, would never have consented to arbitrate this case. Characterizing it as a political question, Secretary Hay in 1904 considered the Panama question with Colombia unarbitrable. Would we arbitrate our right to fortify the Panama Canal, if the right were brought in question? Such matters as these are embodied in the general reservation of "independence" in treaties of arbitration. Questions of honor can be arbitrated. This is shown by the duel in the German army, where the question of violated honor must first be passed upon by a court of officers before the duel is allowed to be fought. When an enlightened public opinion will induce states to add to the functions of an arbitrator, those of a mediator, even such political questions will, I think, be arbitrated. But first, senseless nationalistic pride must be abandoned, fair dealing and good faith assured by international guaranty, and confidence in arbitrators and mediators strengthened.

Even now where independence or freedom of action is not likely to be affected by an unfavorable decision some states have considered it perfectly safe to conclude arbitration treaties without reservation; as for example, Sweden and Norway, Italy and Holland, Chile and Argentine and other states. The United States and Great Britain are about to undertake a step along this line, which by its example will give an unprecedented stimulus to the cause.

[Those who attended the recent Fisheries Arbitration at The Hague and witnessed the cordial relations between opposing counsel, can easily be convinced that there will never be a war between Great Britain and the United States. It is a matter of temperament and good common sense, which will always predominate to prevent a rupture of friendly relations.]

In the time of the great Empires, the Egyptian, the Assyrian, the Median and the Roman, peace was fairly well maintained by the power of arms of a strong central superior. The Emperor compelled his constituent tribes to refrain from hostilities, and there was comparative peace.

We in the present day are dealing with a different order of international society. We desire to erect another power, an intellectual power, to induce and exercise coercive influence among states to bring about international peace. This intelligence has already created methods to avert war by means other than the fearful expenditures now undertaken in preparation for peace, as some would have it.

First, reason and intelligence have aided in establishing good faith between nations. This alone has placed diplomacy on a higher and more effective plane than ever before in adjusting international differences.

· Secondly, the Congress of Paris of 1856 and The Hague Conferences have succeeded in giving mediation a more potent influence in adjusting disputes than it ever enjoyed before. Formerly regarded as officious intermeddling, it has now secured legal sanction and can no longer be considered an unfriendly act. Where the opportunities for the arbitration of legal differences are now considered as exhausted, mediation has unlimited possibilities in adjusting all kinds of international disputes. In South America on three occasions it has proved its great value.

Disputed questions of fact are recognized as a most dangerous and virulent cause of war. The Hague Conference, thirdly, then created the machinery for settling such questions by Commissions of Inquiry. The use of this instrumentality has already prevented one war (between Russia and Great Britain), and will probably show its usefulness on many other occasions. Had our people exhibited more self-restraint in 1898, it is not unlikely that such a Commission of Inquiry might have prevented the Spanish-American War.

The fourth great agency to prevent war is international arbitration, to which we have already referred. Arbitration in some form is as old as history, and toward its immediate development and improvement every effort should be bent. As the architects of this powerful social institution, The Hague Conferences will have left their immortal justification, both in enlarging the scope of the questions which may be submitted and in improving the machinery.

For its successful operation, confidence in arbitrators is, of course, a condition precedent. But the very fundamental condition on which arbitral justice rests, the most effective means of fostering international peace is education, the education of public sentiment. The resort to arbitration must find its sanction in a compelling public opinion, before it can become positive law. The time is ripe for it. The democratization of the world has taken war out of the hands of kings for the satisfaction of personal and dynastic ambitions, and passed it into the control of peoples. Ignorance, contemptuous conduct, ill-temper, resentment, or fury are now the principal causes of war. Psychotherapeutics constitute the most essential element in the remedy. The education of the people of the world, the people that now pay for battleships, must be aided by an enlightened press which will forego the sensational, and recognize and assume its grave responsibilities in the movement. The force of education when aimed at developing self-control, self-restraint and a habit of thought that will compel a submission of disputes to peaceful settlement, will be the principal factor by which the Peace Movement can achieve the success so earnestly desired.

Every actual instance of arbitration confirms the habit and rivets the bonds of international peace. If people can be brought to realize that this is a better and more equitable method of adjusting their differences than by going to war, the problem of armaments will no longer trouble peoples and statesmen. When enlightened public opinion will compel governments to make use of the improved instrumentalities for removing causes of friction and settling controversies, nations will realize that enormous armies and navies are no longer necessary. It is to prove the existence of conditions which make these vast armaments no longer a necessity that congresses such as this assemble. When this conviction makes its impress on the world we will have reached the goal of international peace.

In the absence of Mr. W. O. Hart, of New Orleans, La., his paper on "Universal Peace Impossible without an International Code" was not read. It is printed herewith as part of the Proceedings.

UNIVERSAL PEACE IMPOSSIBLE WITHOUT AN INTERNATIONAL CODE

W. O. HART

To say that I felt myself highly honored when I received an invitation to read a paper before this distinguished gathering, would be to express my feelings very mildly, but, on the whole, I feel the compliment is due more to my section of the country than to myself as an individual. Be this as it may, however, I feel that I was further honored when I was allowed to choose my own subject, and though for a time I hesitated as to this and asked for suggestions from the Committee in charge of the Congress, on further reflection I concluded not to use any of their suggestions (which, by the way, covered several subjects upon which I have heretofore read papers), but to make my own selection, with the result that the title of my paper is as given above: Universal Peace Impossible without an International Code.

Since selecting this title I have several times felt that I had chosen a subject beyond my powers to properly discuss, but I have done the best possible, and if anything I am able to say may induce others, better fitted than I to discuss the subject, to enter upon a discussion thereof, then I shall feel that my efforts have been amply rewarded.

At the outset, let me say that I approach my chosen subject from the standpoint of a Louisiana lawyer. We lawyers of Louisiana believe that our Civil Code is the greatest book that ever came from the hand of man, for, notwithstanding the criticism that is sometimes made of it, and often by our own lawyers, particularly when the Supreme Court disagrees with them upon the construction to be placed upon some Article of the Code, it is a scientific embodiment of concrete law meeting almost every relation of human life and providing for almost every duty and obligation which a man owes to his family, his fellows, and his State. Every enactment of uniform laws, such as the negotiable instrument law, the uniform warehouse law, the uniform bill of lading law, and others, is a compliment to the law of Louisiana, because these uniform laws are codes, limited, of course, to the subjects of which they treat but, nevertheless, a compilation in connected form, of the best thought of lawyers and judges on the subject. When, two years ago, the American Society of International Law discussed the appointment of a committee to draft an International Code, I took occasion, in speaking to the motion to appoint the committee, to refer to our Civil Code and to show how it was being followed throughout the country, and that the contemplated action of the International Society was on the same lines.

Of course the Code which the International Society will finally prepare, will represent but the voluntary suggestive act of a distinguished body of publicists and International Law students. No government has authorized the preparation of this Code, and no government is bound to consider, much less adopt it; but from the character of the men who are doing the work, and from the character of those who compose the Society, it goes without saying that when the Society is able to send out its Code it will receive careful consideration from the sovereign nations of the world, just as, when the draft of a uniform State law is sent out by the National Conference of Commissioners on Uniform State Laws, it receives consideration from the legislatures of States and Territories and from Congress for the District of Columbia. While several of the uniform laws have been adopted in but few states, the number is increasing gradually, and the negotiable instrument law is the law on that important subject of about four-fifths of this country in extent of territory, about nine-tenths in population, and about ninety-nine hundredths in business transactions.

But my ideas of an international code and the thoughts which I desire to present in this paper are rather of a different, and certainly of a more extended character. I believe that universal peace and the absence of war will be brought about not by arbitration proceedings, not by courts to try cases made up for the purposes of trial, but when the nations are bound together universally, by a code of laws providing in advance for every possible contingency that may arise, and leaving only to the universal court the duty of applying to the particular facts of the case, the principles which have been established 'n advance by the code.

We all know that the present system of courts represents evolution from the most primitive tribunals, and we all know that when courts were first established, crude and simple as they were, an agreement in each case was necessary between the parties as to how the court should proceed. But as civilization and commerce progressed it was found that this was unsatisfactory and inefficient, and gradually laws were established in advance until now every civilized state has a complete system of laws of its own, and almost without exception, the laws of each country, in so far as the proceedings in its courts are concerned, are recognized in every other country. It is an extreme case when a judgment rendered in one country is not given some effect in other countries, if, to put it in force, the courts of other countries must be appealed to.

Now if the leading nations of the world, eight in number, let us say, agree, through a commission or a committee, or even a parliament of the world, to provide for the preparation of an international code which shall fix the relations between countries and the citizens thereof in their sovereign or *quasi*-sovereign capacities, just as the codes and other forms of law regulate individuals of the different states, and this code should be adopted by these countries and the adoption carried with it a provision that no part could be abrogated or amended except by a vote of the majority of the countries represented, and that this code should prohibit a resort to arms for the redress of any grievances, do we not see at once, that the era of universal peace would immediately arrive?

The laws of all civilized countries prohibit a man from taking the law into his own hands, no matter what the provocation or what the character of his complaint. He must resort to the courts of his country, and if he defies the law and attempts to act for himself outside of the law, he at once becomes a criminal and subjects himself to punishment, and so it would be with any of the nations that had agreed to the international code. If any of them should attempt to bring on war or do violence to the citizens or property of another country, all the other countries which had adopted the code would step in and require the recalcitrant country to hold off and submit its cause to the international court, provided by the code. Every country has among its people, whether citizens or sojourners, what is definitely termed the criminal element, as well as the degenerate, the degraded and the irresponsible, and when these attempt to evade the law or to do violence outside the law, the substantial element represented by its law abiding citizens, the courts, the executive officers thereof and of the state, compel all these persons to obey the law or suffer the consequences; and so it would be with an international code and an international court. All countries might not agree to it, but those which do not would be forced to become law abiding or to submit, just as those individuals who attempt to defy the municipal law, or who say there is no law, or who claim to be above the law, are forced to obey the law, or violate it at their peril.

It has been said that universal peace is impossible because many wars are brought about through the inordinate ambition of rulers or military men, and that such conditions cannot be foreseen or provided for in advance, but why can they not? We all know that at one time in many countries, the duel was recognized as a method of settling differences where the honor, so-called, of one of the parties was involved, and no attempt was made to punish the participants in a duel, even though it should result in the death of one of the contestants, but now the civilized world looks with horror upon the duel, and to kill a man in a duel is murder, pure and simple, and while perhaps, owing to the frailty of human nature, punishment as for murder would not be meted out to the successful duellist, he would probably receive some punishment, or, if he did not, would go through the world with the brand of Cain, hated by his fellows, a wanderer upon the face of the earth. So any nation which would not obey the international code, would place itself outside the pale of civilized people and could be punished in such manner as the code provided, by checking intercourse, by stopping diplomatic relations, and, shall we say it, stopping its commerce, so that the money power would come into play, and, if all other means failed, commerce, or perhaps cupidity, would cause the observance of the law.

Territorial aggrandizement is, of course, the cause of many wars, but with an international code in force, the seizure of the territory of another country would be impossible. No man can legally seize a piece of land which his neighbor controls or claims title to, upon the theory that he has a better title, but that issue must be presented to a court for determination. As it is now, almost invariably the question of disputed territory is referred to arbitration and the award of the arbitrators is almost universally accepted. But submitting a matter to arbitration is not the same as having it decided on the basis of an international code, because, as before stated, the code would provide in advance for the rights and obligations of the parties and the method by which conflicting claims should be considered, and, being arranged in advance, it would not be necessary to prepare an agreement to submit the case to the court under the rules then, for the first time, agreed upon; and any nation would be slow to claim the territory of another unless it knew or had good reason to believe that its claims were well founded in law, the law of the international code. The neutrality of many of the small states of Europe, for example, is assured and the inviolability of their territory is preserved because several of the greater nations have gotten together and guaranteed it. If any nation should attempt, for instance, to seize a part of Switzerland, whether that was one of the nations which had guaranteed its integrity or not, the other nations would speedily prevent the attacking nation from doing anything except giving up the attack; and if this can be done by the agreement of several nations as to a particular country it could be done universally through an international code.

Questions of honor, so-called, between nations which are excluded sometimes from an agreement to arbitrate, would cease to exist, in large measure, if there were an international code, just as the so-called code of honor resulting in the duel no longer exists. The code could provide for all conditions, and, so providing, nations not party to it, would be forced to observe the law as laid down in the code.

The power and influence of the larger nations grouped together would be insurmountable, just as the word of the United States calling into effect the Monroe doctrine, prevents any nation of Europe or Asia acquiring territory on the western hemisphere; and if one nation, though the greatest on the earth, is powerful enough against the rest of the world to prevent territorial aggrandizement at the expense of weaker nations, why would not a combination of eight or more of the greatest nations of the world compel the weaker nations to observe the law, just as the weaker individual in the state must observe the law made by those in authority? It is all very well to say that universal peace is the idea of dreamers, but why should it be necessary in order to preserve the rights of a country, that it should kill as many as possible of the inhabitants of another country? Might is not always right, and the successful country in a war does not always have right on its side. The waste of militarism is awful in its extent. The soldier produces nothing and adds nothing to the wealth of the country, but is only a consumer, and while it is all very well to say that the principal guarantee of peace is to be always ready for war, if there is to be no war, necessarily there must be peace, and the reign of law binding upon the nations will put an end to war and bring about the era of universal peace. No words can add to the horrors of war, and its uselessness is understood by all.

It is said that opposition to tyrants is obedience to God, and that war is sometimes necessary to enable a country to throw off the tyrant's yoke. This may have been the case in times past, but there are no longer tyrants.   There is no country in the world today, that is not, in theory, well governed, and if there were a universal code and a universal court, a despotic, tyrannical, or even an unjust ruler, might be removed, just as a president or a governor, or a king is removed today, without bloodshed and without war.

A practice of nearly thirty-four years at the bar has brought me to the conclusion, (though we are all frequently disappointed in the final judgments of courts upon cases which we have in charge), that careful study and reflection will convince us that, in the long run, the courts do substantial justice in all cases. Of course there are exceptions to that rule, and there may be some cases where the final decision represents a miscarriage of justice, but they are few and far between, and only exist because no human institution can be perfect; and an international code by which all the great nations shall be bound, and an international court working under the code, the decrees of which all nations shall respect, will, in the end, do substantial justice to all, and not one man would have to be killed to carry out the decrees of the court.

I may be an enthusiast, but I am one of those who believe the world is better today than it was yesterday, and is going to be still better tomorrow, and such meetings as this will redound to the credit of all connected therewith. We may not see the results this year or the next; we may not live to see them, but every meeting in the interest of peace, every speech on the subject and every publication, hastens the day when peace shall be universal. How it will come, no man can say. My ideas I know are faulty and may be impossible of execution, but I think no one will gainsay me when I give the opinion that if they could be carried into effect, the result that we are striving for would not be far off.

To show that I am not alone in my ideas, I beg to close this paper with a review of a recent book by the well-known author, Mons. E. Duplessis, entitled, *International Organization*. This review I had not seen (and I have never seen the book) until the foregoing had been written. The reviewer says:

"This book is a commentary upon a preceding work in which the author developed the idea of the formation of an association among all the civilized communities, ruled by a common code. In this new book, after having set forth the causes of the development of internationalism and its results with respect to the progress of industry and of intellectual property, he indicates its ruling ideas; the international association should have for its object, necessity, justice, and certain interests of intellectual and economic order. It should guarantee to each state, its territory and should prevent its dismemberment. With respect to justice there should be something better than the tribunal of arbitration, such as operates at present; the present institution furnishes no guarantee to government, each state selecting its arbitrator from a list prepared in advance, from among those which it supposes would be favorable to it; the umpire, who acts in case of a tie, is independent, but his responsibility is too great. The arbitrators are guided by no law; temporary judges, they are unable to establish a jurisprudence; their jurisdiction does not attach to those who refuse to appear before them; they cannot execute their decrees. Therefore there should be instituted an international court, whose organization should be preceded by the elaboration of a law concerning international relations. The members of this tribunal should be supplied in equitable proportion by all the states composing the association of nations; they should be chosen from experts in international law and not from diplomats and politicians; they should be numerous; they should hold their offices permanently, and should reside where the tribunal is held; finally, their decisions should be obligatory upon all nations. The sanctions of their decisions should be moral, such as admonition, censure, restitution, moral and pecuniary reparation, exclusion from the association; and coercitive, such as economic blockade, intervention of the international police. The establishment of an international police would have as its corollary general disarmament."

After various notices, Chairman Remsen announced, "On this copy of the program which was handed to me I find the words, in familiar handwriting, "Discussion, if time therefor." I declare this meeting adjourned, as the hour is late.

THIRD SESSION

The Third Session of the Third American Peace Congress was called to order Thursday morning, May 4th, at 10 o'clock in McCoy Hall, Johns Hopkins University, by the Presiding Officer, Hon. Huntington Wilson, Assistant Secretary of State.

Chairman Wilson delivered the following address:

ADDRESS OF THE HON. HUNTINGTON WILSON

Gentlemen of the Third American Peace Congress: Those who work in the Department of State and Foreign Service ordinarily do not talk much of peace except when war threatens some other country. I am proud to be connected with an administration which within two years has actually prevented three wars. When the opposing armies of Ecuador and Peru were in sight of each other the telegraphic proposals of the United States brought about the tripartite mediation of the Argentine Republic, Brazil, and the United States. The proposal was well received by Ecuador and Peru and they abstained from war. A few months ago the Dominican Republic and Haiti were at swords' points. The influence of the government of the United States stayed their hands. Also within the last few months the good offices of the United States put an end to civil war in Honduras. Here are three actual achievements of the peace which is your ideal. These things the President and Secretary Knox have done.

Among other practical modes of pursuing the ideal of world's peace is the true meaning of what has been called "Dollar Diplomacy." Of course this term may be applied to commercial diplomacy. Today international commerce is everywhere an important department of diplomacy. In so far as our diplomacy is commercially successful, we are proud of the fact. We are not above being practical and commercial, and, from the less material point of view, commerce means contact; contact means understanding; and if one is worthy enough to be respected and liked, if understood, international commerce conduces powerfully to international sympathy. I say, if one is liked as well as respected. Here, fortunately, the idealist's interest in foreign trade as conducive to peace coïncides with the business man's interest in foreign trade for financial profit. A merchant can be so disagreeable that one prefers to pay higher prices to a pleasanter trader. Roughshod methods are a useless handicap that can only be overcome, if at all, by immense superiorities. The most rudimentary business sense should dictate tact, sympathy, and considerateness in dealing with foreign customers. So, in the broader view, every American business man or traveler, every student in university or school, who is inconsiderate, supercilious, or lacking in sympathetic appreciation of his foreign associate, makes himself a missionary not of good will but of ill will, and so radiates an influence not for peace but for war.

But I use the newly coined phrase of "Dollar Diplomacy" in another sense. It means using the capital of the country in the foreign field in a manner calculated to enhance fixed national policies. It means the substitution of dollars for bullets. It means the creation of a prosperity which will be preferred to predatory strife. It means availing of capital's self-interest in peace. It means taking advantage of the interest in peace of those who benefit by the investment of capital. It recognizes that financial soundness is a potent factor in political stability; that prosperity means contentment and contentment means repose.

This thought is at the basis of the policy of the United States in Central America and the zone of the Caribbean. There this policy is one of special helpfulness in a neighborhood where peace and progress are especially important to the United States, and where, moreover, they are due the aspirations and the splendid resources of the peoples of those neighboring republics.

In China the same principle has been invoked to enable the United States to take its share in the material, as it has in the moral and intellectual, development of that great Empire.

To the intellectual and moral development of the progressive Ottoman Empire the United States has contributed the greatest share. There, too, it is hoped that American commerce and material enterprise will also contribute.

So, also, "Dollar Diplomacy" is enabling the United States, through a loan by this country, Great Britain, France, and probably Germany, to give practical effect to its ancient special obligations to Liberia, incidentally removing the causes of friction between that struggling Republic and its powerful neighbors.

The President's aspiration to the ideal of world peace was signalized in more abstract form in the public utterance on the eighteenth of last December of his hope that the two great English-speaking peoples might set a new and higher standard of international self-control by a broader treaty of arbitration. As you know, this task is now the subject of *pourparlers* between the American and British governments, and it is not improbable that diplomacy may gradually solve the extremely difficult problem of finding practicable bases of negotiation.

Governments are the trustees of the nations' international interests. They bear this heavy responsibility and consequently are beset at every turn by considerations of what is practicable, what is practical, what is now and will in future be for the true and enduring benefit of the nations they serve.

Thus, the everyday work of peace through a benevolent and candid diplomacy, as well as the definite working out of the occasional marked advances in international morality, must fall upon governments and upon departments of government expert in the facts of international relations.

In the second category of intrumentalities working for international peace fall the Interparliamentary Union and the work for which Congress has enabled the President to appoint, when opportune, an American Peace Commission. These agencies, although not official in the strict sense nor diplomatic in their functions, still carry special weight through their relations to the representatives of the people in the legislative branch of government.

To the third class belong all those powerful agencies, like the many peace societies here represented, which have been and are doing such a great work in promulgating the ideals of peace and arbitration along with more practical ideas toward their attainment.

While both these classes of instrumentalities must leave to the government its diplomatic work toward peace, they can and do powerfully second that work through their influence and propaganda both at home and abroad.

Great things have been accomplished along certain lines and the criticism that peace propaganda are unpractical has not yet been justified. It may be questioned, however, whether unless new lines of effort are adopted the state of public feeling can be so steadily further improved.

First of all, much can be done by active interest in and intelligent support of the everyday practical policies of government which if looked at otherwise than superficially will be found to be very real measures toward peace. Such is the policy so wonderfully successful in Santo Domingo; such are the broad principles involved in the Honduras loan convention now before the Senate; such is the Lowden bill for the improvement of the foreign service—a service which, charged with all this work, should certainly not be amateurish and untrained. Here are fields for practical effort.

Municipal law confirms and inscribes the high-water mark of the ethics of the majority. International law crystallizes the persuasive value of what powerful nations accept, still with reserve, as the canons, at a given time, of their conduct. Every reasonable man is for peace, just as every man would prefer to go to Heaven; but to secure the one or the other requires something more than aspiration. The millennium will not come for the wishing. Our own nation has a very unenviable record for crimes of violence. Individual self-control has not reached a plane where any peace advocate wishes to have the police force abolished. International peace must depend upon international self-control and sense of justice, and, the spirit of a nation being but that of a collection of individuals, one comes straight back to the schoolhouse, the factory, the farm, and the newspaper. There must be self-controlled and patriotic and enlightened citizenship if there are to be peace-loving, strong nations and governments able to remain at peace. As George Ade states the moral of one of his fables in slang, "In uplifting, get underneath."

It is almost to state a syllogism to say that next to national character the greatest factor toward peace is true international understanding, and that, after diplomacy, the newspapers play the most important part in bringing about or retarding such true understanding. In the case of the United States, the true understanding of the American people and of the true ideals and policies of their government is horribly hampered by the fact that, in the Far East, for example, and still more in Latin America, almost everything bad and nothing good of us is reported in some section of the newspapers of most countries. Every lynching and scandal, every discreditable thing, which it is our unique custom to air so energetically, is repeated in its worst version by a section of the press of most of these countries. In the case of many countries which have important colonies engaged in business—for example, in Brazil, in Peru, in China—their nationals support locally their own organs, which, probably often subsidized, carry on a patriotic service of their country.

Thinking of Mr. Carnegie's munificent gift, it occurs to me that the establishment and subsidy of four or five newspapers in Latin America and the Far East, with means to give adequate and respectable telegraphic news service and with a nonpartisan and patriotic guidance of their policy by trustees who should be disassociated from the government and independently representative of patriotic American citizenship, would be a splendid and proper means to that international true understanding which must be at the basis of peace.

To go back to the root of the matter—that is, to national character and a clear and true outlook on the part of the individual citizen—it has often been pointed out that more care is given the evolution and physical condition of cattle, which enter into commerce, than is given the physical condition of humanity since it lost its commercial value with the abolition of slavery. In these days when we honor the soul and the mind more than the body and when the world is regulated by moral and intellectual rather than physical forces, is it not still more strikingly important (to speak only of the cause of peace) that the minds of the people should be fed and not poisoned in reference to international affairs?

It is quite natural that in countries where dangerous frontiers or other weaknesses make a fight for national existence a familiar possibility to the people, foreign relations should be of vital interest. In such countries the man in the street takes a shrewd interest in his country's foreign relations. Much space is given them in the press. To write of them is familiar and they are a reality. With us it is less so, and consequently when a certain section of the press gives rein to its imagination our public, less compelled to a vital interest, is the more easily misled. When one newspaper promulgates an interesting story of impending war, one can hardly blame its more conservative contemporary for giving the story for what it may be worth. The harm is done by those very few newspapers and seemingly from one of the three following motives: First, because the impression caused by the story will subserve some separate purpose which the newspaper honestly believes for the public good; second, the story is used by an opposition journal to attack the administration; or, third, the story is printed for purely commercial purposes as a "penny dreadful" for the debauchery of the seeker after sensations. Of course the last should be suppressed, like the purveyor of injurious drugs. The partisan newspaper might, one would think, understand that while to attack a government's domestic policy or vigorously to join issue in case of a sincere difference of opinion upon foreign policy is legitimate, nevertheless indiscriminately to embarrass the diplomacy of the country through frivolous misrepresentation or malicious attack is not to assail any administration, but is to attack the country itself among the nations of the world—something for which there is an ugly name, and as to which there should be something beyond the present statute. I am happy to say that I have in mind isolated instances only, and that I believe the American press, as a whole, is already beginning to respond to its patriotic and moral obligations so increased since the United States entered on its destined position as a great world power.

What our press says in the Capital or elsewhere is echoed around the world as the composite speech of America. Thus, irresponsible speech on international affairs carries the double tragedy of misleading the minds which are the ultimate power of our own country and embittering the minds of half-forgotten multitudes around the world.

The subjects of peace and of armaments are usually associated, —sometimes in the sense that disarmament is the object of peace; sometimes even as if disarmament were a means to peace. Sometimes, and more truly I think, it is pointed out that ample armament is the best safeguard of peace. Some nations have what they want. It is not unnatural that these should have an idea as to the best moment to stop the war game different from the idea of those nations which have not what they want. Former President Roosevelt recently pointed out that to be prepared for war no more meant an unpeaceable disposition than to carry fire insurance meant a special expectation of fire; that both meant merely a common-sense safeguard against an off-chance, the off-chance being always that it takes two to insure peace as well as to precipitate war.

I am sure the American people are protagonists of peace for a higher reason than the economy of disarmament. If ever a country could afford armaments it is ours. As a business proposition it would save, in the unfortunate event of war, the appalling loss of life and money involved in headlong hasty preparations and also the time necessary to make a people already warlike also military. As a burden it could hardly exceed what is wholesome to bear, and the effort would focus the national spirit. And undoubtedly the most practicable step toward the desired international spirit of humanity is to begin with the right national spirit. Some people even think that a large army and a system of military training would do more toward peace through instilling patriotic solidarity and discipline than it would for war through the temptation of having weapons handy.

We have laws against carrying concealed weapons because a violent man with a concealed weapon is more dangerous than a muscular Christian fully armed. Is a warlike nation, not fond of discipline and possessed of vast resources, less dangerous than one openly carrying its olive branch and also its arrows and thunderbolt? War springs from the human heart, not from the arsenal; and the human heart, rather than the archives of diplomatic engagements, is still the only ultimate sure abode of peace.

The nation which can do most to secure international peace must be the nation with the highest ideals plus the greatest military efficiency. It is such nations that in striving for and realizing their own advantage contribute the most toward advantaging their neighbors and the world.

In the absence of Professor John H. Latané, due to illness, his address was not read before the Peace Congress. It is printed herewith as part of the Proceedings:

THE PANAMA CANAL IN RELATION TO THE PEACE MOVEMENT

JOHN H. LATANÉ

When President Roosevelt in defiance of all precedent wrested Panama from Columbia, he felt it necessary to coin a new phrase in order to explain his extraordinary action. He declared that he was acting in the interest of "collective civilization," that Colombia had no right "to bar the transit of the world's traffic across the isthmus." Now that our seizure of the canal zone has been generally acquiesced in as an accomplished fact, we coolly assert that the canal is purely an American question and that the rest of the world has nothing to do with it. No longer regarding the canal as a great commercial highway to be managed by us in trust for the benefit of mankind, we give notice to the world that it is to be treated primarily as a military asset of the United States, that it is a part of our general scheme of naval defence, that it is to be used as a naval base and therefore must be fortified. If, in seizing the zone, we acted as the agent of collective civilization, then we assume certain responsibilities to the world at large which we have no right now to ignore.

When the Senate rejected the first draft of the Hay-Pauncefote treaty and forced Mr. Hay to strike out the clause inviting the concurrence of the great civilized powers in the neutralization of the canal, we were told that the principle of neutralization was retained, but under the guaranty of the United States alone, that the guaranty of the other powers was not necessary for its protection and was objectionable from the standpoint of the Monroe Doctrine. Now we are informed that the Hay-Pauncefote treaty means nothing, that the word neutralization was retained merely out of deference to the feelings of England, and that in reality England gave us a free hand to fortify the canal if we should so desire.

Ten years ago General Peter C. Hains, one of the most distinguished engineers of the United States army, said:

"An adequate defence of a fortified isthmian canal can be made in no other way than by providing a navy of sufficient power to control the seas at either terminus. With such a navy at our command, the canal needs no fortifications."

About the same time Admiral Dewey said:

"Fortifications? Why, of course not. As I understand it, the canal is to be, and should be, a neutralized commercial pathway between two great oceans. To fortify it would simply result in making it a battleground in case of war. Fortifications would be enormously expensive and ought not to be erected. Our fleets will be a sufficient guaranty of the neutrality and safety of the canal in time of war as well as in time of peace."

Now it is contended that a navy alone cannot adequately safeguard the canal and that huge fortifications at either end are the only means of protecting it. Two months ago, at the urgent suggestion of the President, the Congress of the United States appropriated $3,000,000 to begin the work of fortification, and the measure encountered very little opposition. Why this change of front on a question so vital to the cause of peace? The answer is to be found in psychological conditions similar to those which have impelled a liberal British ministry to adopt the most extensive naval programme that England has ever known. The American people, notwithstanding the fact that they occupy the most impregnable position on earth, are obsessed with the war scare almost as completely as the people of Europe.

In view of the fact that Congress has already adopted the policy of fortification it may be deemed by some a task wholly gratuitous to undertake at this time to question the wisdom of that policy. But it is not too late to correct the mistake if public opinion can be properly informed on the question. The original policy of our government was for a neutralized canal. Long before the Suez Canal was constructed or even planned, the Clayton-Bulwer treaty signed by the United States and England in 1850 adopted the general policy of neutralization for any canal that might be built across the isthmus. Article I, provided that neither party would ever erect or maintain any fortifications commanding the canal or in the vicinity thereof, and Article II provided that

"Vessels of the United States or Great Britain, traversing the said canal, shall, in case of war between the contracting parties, be exempted from blockade, detention or capture, by either of the belligerents; and this provision shall extend to such a distance from the two ends of the said canal, as may hereafter be found expedient to establish."

At the suggestion of Great Britain the same principles were applied to the Suez Canal and set forth at length in definite rules in the Constantinople Convention of October 29, 1888.

In order to appreciate fully the merits of a neutralized canal as distinguished from a fortified canal, it is necessary to arrive at a clear conception of the term "neutralization." The term itself is comparatively new and its exact significance in international law is not always clearly grasped by those who use it. While the principle was recognized as long ago as the Congress of Vienna, the word itself has until comparatively recently been avoided by diplomatists and publicists. Probably the earliest definition of the term by a writer of recognized merit is given by Holland in an article on The International Position of the Suez Canal in the *Fortnightly Review* for July, 1883. He says:

"States have been permanently neutralized by convention. Not only is it preordained that such states are to abstain from taking part in a war into which their neighbors may enter, but it is also prearranged that such states are not to become principals in a war. By way of compensation for this restriction on their freedom of action, their immunity from attack is guaranteed by their neighbors, for whose collective interests such an arrangement is perceived to be on the whole expedient."

In this sense Switzerland was neutralized by agreement between the powers in 1815, Belgium in 1839, the Ionian Islands in 1864, and Luxembourg in 1867. The Geneva Convention of 1864 extended the principle of neutralization to persons and things, exempting from attack or capture surgeons, nurses, ambulances, and field hospitals. By the Second Hague Convention the same principle was extended to hospital ships, which are exempt from capture provided that they comply with certain specified conditions.

From a study of these familiar cases it will be seen that neutralization implies: (1) A formal act or agreement; it is a matter of convention constituting an obligation, not a mere declaration revocable at will. (2) It implies a sufficiently large number of parties to the act to make the guaranty effective. (3) It implies the absence of fortifications. The mere existence of fortifications would impeach the good faith of the parties to the agreement. (4) It implies certain limitations of sovereignty over the territory neutralized, ordinary neutrality is purely voluntary on the part of the state exercising the same, while neutralization imposes a status of obligatory neutrality not terminable by the volition of the state which accepts it or on which it is imposed. (5) It implies a more or less permanent condition. In this it differs from ordinary treaty stipulations terminated by war between the contracting parties. A treaty establishing neutralization is brought into full operation by war.

When we come to extend the principle of neutralization to waterways, we find the conditions to be somewhat different. The first and most fundamental is that states have acquired by international usage and prescription the right of innocent passage through the territorial waters of other states which they have no claim to exercise in respect to land. Secondly, armies and implements of war are absolutely excluded from the territory of neutralized states, while neutralized waterways are by design open to the innocent passage of war ships not only in time of peace but also in time of war. Thirdly, the warfare of the future will in all probability be confined more and more to the sea, thus enhancing the strategical value of waterways and canals which are adjuncts to the high seas, as well as increasing the temptation to appropriate them for national purposes. It is true that war ships are excluded by international agreement from the Black Sea, but this state of affairs grew out of the "ancient rule of the Ottoman Empire." Until 1774 it was the practice of the Porte to exclude all ships from the Black Sea. After 1774 war ships only were excluded. This restriction has been recognized and continued by the treaties of 1840, 1856, 1871 and 1878, all signed by the great powers of Europe. The Black Sea, however, has never been regarded as an open sea and the Bosporus therefore offers no analogy to a canal connecting two oceans.

When we come to the consideration of maritime canals, the Suez and the Panama stand alone. The analogy between them is very striking. (1) Each is of the nature of an artificial strait connecting two seas. (2) The Suez is at the end of the Mediterranean Sea and the Panama is at the end of the Caribbean Sea, the American Mediterranean. (3) Each lies wholly within the territory of one power. (4) In each case the territorial power is too weak to finance or protect the canal. (5) In each case foreign capital has had to undertake the work of construction. (6) In each case foreign guaranties have been sought and conventions entered into for the control of the respective canals, thus giving them an international character. (7) In the Suez case the peculiar position of Great Britain in Egypt gives her practically a much greater voice in the control of the canal than any other power, while in the case of the Panama Canal, the United States by virtue of the Monroe Doctrine claims a dominating influence.

In view of this analogy no discussion of the Panama Canal would be complete which did not take into consideration England's policy with regard to the Suez Canal. Although constructed by French engineers and mainly with French capital, the canal passed at an early date under the commercial control of England. In 1875 more than three-fourths of the commerce that passed through the canal was British. Disraeli was therefore quick to take advantage of the financial embarrassment of the Khedive and purchase the shares held by him, thus giving England a controlling voice in the management of the canal. The outbreak of Arabi's revolt in 1882 was the occasion of the intervention of England in Egypt and the military occupation of the line of the canal.

In a circular note addressed to the powers, January 3, 1883, Earl Granville explained that the military occupation of Egypt was only temporary and suggested as a permanent arrangement to secure the freedom of the canal that it be placed under international control. Although undisputed mistress of the situation, England continued to advocate this policy and it was finally embodied in a formal treaty which was signed by the powers at Constantinople in October, 1888. This treaty provided that the canal should always be "free and open, in time of war as in time of peace, to every vessel of commerce or of war, without distinction of flag;" that the canal should never be blockaded and that no act of hostility should be committed in the canal or in its ports of access or within a radius of three marine miles from these ports. The terms of this convention were all that the advocates of neutralization could desire. Unfortunately the British government in signing the treaty made a general reservation which raised some doubt as to the practical operation of the agreement during her occupation of Egypt. This reservation seems to have generally been lost sight of until the British government called attention to it again during the war between Spain and the United States. In July, 1898, Mr. Curzon, Under-Secretary for Foreign Affairs, made the following statement on the floor of the House of Commons:

"The convention in question is certainly in existence, but, as I informed the honorable member in answer to a question some days ago, has not been brought into practical operation. This is owing to the reserves made on behalf of Her Majesty's government by the British delegates at the Suez Canal Commission in 1885, which were renewed by Lord Salisbury and communicated to the powers in 1887."

Notwithstanding this loophole, the British government has not deemed it necessary to fortify the Suez Canal, although she keeps it thoroughly policed.

When we come to consider the numerous agreements in regard to an American canal we find that they all provide, or profess to provide, for a neutralized canal. This principle was the most conspicuous feature of the Clayton-Bulwer treaty of 1850 to which reference has already been made. The organization of the French Panama company led to a change of policy announced by President Hayes in 1880 who declared that any canal that might be constructed between the Atlantic and Pacific oceans should be under American control, and that the line of such canal should be considered "a part of the coast line of the United States." Secretaries Blaine and Frelinghuysen tried hard to secure a modification of the Clayton-Bulwer treaty in line with the new policy, but their arguments made little impression on the British government, and when President Cleveland came into office in 1885 he reverted to the policy of a neutralized canal under international guaranty. In his first message to Congress he made the following declaration:

"Whatever highway may be constructed across the barrier dividing the two greatest maritime areas of the world must be for the world's benefit, a trust for mankind, to be removed from the chance of domination by any single power, nor become a point of invitation for hostilities or a prize for warlike ambition."

The original draft of the Hay-Pauncefote treaty, February 5, 1900, provided for a neutralized canal and adopted rules substantially in accord with the Constantinople Convention of 1888. It also provided for the adherence of other powers so as to put the canal under international protection. It further left the United States free to construct the canal as a government enterprise which was not permitted by the Clayton-Bulwer treaty.

The principle of neutralization remained unchanged. The Senate, however, amended the treaty in three important particulars: (1) it declared the Clayton-Bulwer convention "superseded." (2) A paragraph was inserted declaring that the restrictions and regulations governing the use of the canal should not "apply to measures which the United States may find it necessary to take for securing by its own forces the defense of the United States and the maintenance of public order." (3) The article providing for the adherence of other powers is cut out entirely. In an article in the *Cosmopolitan* for April, Mr. James Creelman makes the boast that he and William Randolph Hearst defeated Mr. Hay's plans and forced the Senate to reject the first draft of his treaty. Mr. Hay, he informs us, had a sentimental regard for England and was in the habit of lunching frequently with Lord Pauncefote.

The British government at first refused to accept the Senate amendments and a year elapsed before an agreement was reached. The revised treaty which was ratified by the Senate, December 16, 1901, was to a certain extent a compromise between the original draft and the Senate amendments, though the latter had the greater weight. Article I abrogates the Clayton-Bulwer treaty. Article II provides that the canal may be constructed under the auspices of the United States and shall be under its exclusive management. Article III declares that "the United States adopts" as the basis of neutralization substantially the rules of the Constantinople Convention. It omits from these rules, however, the clause "in time of war as in time of peace" and the entire rule forbidding fortifications. The article inviting the adherence of other powers is likewise omitted.

It is evident that the Hay-Pauncefote treaty does not establish the neutralization that it professes. In the first place all the other treaties effecting neutralization are placed under the collective guaranty of a number of powers, while the Hay-Pauncefote treaty places the neutralization of the Panama Canal under the sole guaranty of the United States. Secondly, this declaration establishes an obligation to England alone. No other power has the right to demand the observance of the rules, further than equality of treatment. In the third place, the fact that a clause forbidding fortifications was inserted in the first draft and after full discussion deliberately omitted from the revised treaty leaves the United States free, by implication certainly, to fortify the canal. This view of the case was in fact admitted by Lord Lansdowne in a memorandum which was communicated to the American government, August 3, 1901. In the fourth place, the omission of the clause, "in time of war as in time of peace," leaves the United States free, by implication at least, to modify or suspend in time of war the rules governing the use of the canal.

In the above consideration of the Constantinople Convention and the Hay-Pauncefote treaty we are again struck with the analogy between the Suez and Panama Canals. In the Suez Canal agreement Great Britain has a loophole through which she can escape in case the provisions of the convention threaten to embarrass her movements, while the Hay-Pauncefote treaty is so full of holes that the United States will have no difficulty in evading any of its provisions if she so desires. Both conventions lay down certain ideals which it behoves the advocates of international peace to uphold. While England proposed the neutralization of the Suez Canal, and while the United States professes to have neutralized the Panama Canal, as a matter of fact neither country has quite the courage of its convictions. England's good faith and good intentions are evidenced by the fact that she has refrained from fortifying the Suez Canal, but the United States, whose position on this continent is infinitely stronger than England's position in Egypt, is practically repudiating the principle of neutralization which theoretically she professes to hold by resorting to fortifications.

The opponents of fortification have made the mistake of assuming that the Hay-Pauncefote treaty really neutralized the canal and that in resorting to fortifications the United States is violating that compact. It has been shown above, however, that the Hay-Pauncefote treaty is a slender reed to lean upon. The whole question resolves itself therefore into one of expediency. Will it serve our best interests and the best interests of the world at large to fortify the canal or to neutralize it? President Taft holds that we can do both. But from this proposition I strongly dissent. Neutralization both in principle and in practice is utterly inconsistent with fortifications. President Taft does not appear to distinguish between neutrality and neutralization. Of course the United States can fortify the canal and permit the warships of belligerents in any war to which we are not a party to use the canal on equal terms, just as we permit belligerent warships to enter our territorial waters and ports under certain restrictions. There seems to be little doubt in the mind of any one that the United States can maintain the neutrality of the canal in any war to which we are not a party. But we could do this equally well without fortifications. With our present naval strength neither belligerent in a war in which we remained neutral could afford to molest the canal in any way, for such conduct would draw us into the war against him.

But what will be the status of the canal when we ourselves are engaged in war? The present intention seems to be to close it to the ships of the enemy and use it as a naval base, keeping a large fleet in the canal to dart forth in either direction as occasion may require. Theoretically this is plausible enough, but practically, where is the power that could send two formidable fleets against us at one and the same time, one by way of the Atlantic and one by way of the Pacific? I suppose that this particular policy has been evolved to meet the emergency of a war with England and Japan. Our fleet from its vantage point in the canal could dart out into the Caribbean while the guns on the Pacific are holding Japan at bay, defeat the English fleet, then rush through the canal to the Pacific and overwhelm Japan. If, however, the Japanese fleet should attack San Francisco and the English fleet New York, we would at least have the satisfaction of knowing that our fleet was safe between the locks, a hundred feet above the ocean, midway between the Atlantic and the Pacific, with huge guns at either end to protect it!

But even if such is the use to be made of the canal, it will be just as safe without fortifications as with them. Even in the absence of our fleet do you suppose that an enemy of the United States would try to enter the canal unless it were neutralized?

If he dared try, we could easily blow up or disable his ships in transit. No enemy would risk it unless he had previously taken military possession of the entire Zone. Fortifications at the ends would not prevent an enemy from landing a military force out of range of the guns and making a dash for the locks. This is the real danger, and this could be avoided only by keeping a large military force along the line of the canal.

If we fortify the canal and use it as a naval base, it will be a legitimate object of attack and an enemy would have the right to destroy it if he were able.

If, on the other hand, the canal is neutralized by a general treaty between the great powers of the world, no enemy of the United States would dare to destroy or injure it in violation of such a treaty. Why? Because at the close of the war he would be compelled to indemnify not only the United States for injury to the canal, but all the powers whose commerce had suffered by interruption of traffic. The neutralization scheme thus depends not on the good faith of any nation but on the liability for indemnity that would inevitably attach to the nation that should violate an international compact which so vitally concerned the commerce of the world. If the canal is neutralized by international agreement, it would have to be open to the ships of our enemies if they cared to use it, and our own ships would have to comply with the same rules as the enemy on entering and leaving the canal. On no other conditions would the powers agree to sign a treaty of guaranty. This proposition raises the really vital question, would we consent to allow the ships of an enemy to pass through the canal under any circumstances? Such an idea is to some minds "unthinkable." Why should we allow an enemy to use a canal which has cost us four hundred millions to build? I ask in rejoinder, why not? When you look into the proposition fully, it is not as preposterous as it appears at first sight. Take a concrete case. Suppose we were at war with Japan. I do not share the views of Mr. Hobson, but suppose for the sake of argument that we were, and suppose—another very improbable supposition—that Japan should send a fleet into American waters. If the canal were neutralized, she could not attack or blockade it but she could send her fleet through into the Carribean Sea

if we did not meet her in the Pacific. If she were foolish enough
to pursue this course it would be decidedly to our advantage to
meet her in the Caribbean which is the key to our naval situation.
There is surely no other spot where we would be prepared to meet
her to better advantage and, if she were defeated there, her ships
would stand very little chance of ever getting home.

Suppose on the other hand that we were attacked by England
or Germany. The West Indies would naturally be the scene
of the conflict and neither of these powers would have any occasion to use the canal unless it should defeat us in battle and gain
control of the Caribbean Sea. In the latter event, if the canal
were neutralized we could still send our Pacific Squadron through
and collect it all in the neutral zone on the Atlantic side before
proceeding to an encounter. If, on the other hand, the canal
were not neutralized but fortified, the enemy could blockade the
outlet and our ships would be in the plight that Cervera's ships
were at Santiago. They would have to come out one at a time
exposed to the fire of a whole squadron.

If the canal is fortified and a legitimate object of attack by
the enemy, our fleet will be tied down to very narrow limits, not
only to prevent the canal from being blockaded, but what is even
more important, to prevent an enemy from landing troops out
of range of the guns at the fortified mouth and making a dash for
the locks which are all inland. If, on the other hand, the canal is
neutralized, our fleet would have much greater freedom of action
and would not have to remain at the western end of the Caribbean. In fact it would not be necessary for our fleet to be near
the canal except when it was necessary to convoy ships to the
entrance or to go there to meet ships coming through from the
Pacific.

The cost of fortification will be enormous. It is true that Congress has been asked so far to appropriate only a paltry $3,000,000,
but the object of this appropriation was merely to commit the
country to the policy of fortification. The sum asked for was so
insignificant that it could not well be refused, but this is merely
a beginning. The cost and maintenance of fortifications will
not be the only expense entailed. Fortifications cannot adequately defend the canal for the real danger is not at the ends

where the fortifications will be placed, but inland where the locks are situated. With the most powerful guns in the world at the ends to prevent ships from entering the canal, the locks will still be exposed to attack by a military force, and to ward off this danger it will be necessary in case of war for us to keep a large military force along the line of the canal.

All this expense could be avoided by neutralization, and at what cost? Merely by refraining from using the canal as a naval base and by conceding to other powers the right to use it in time of war as in time of peace, a right which we have shown they would, unless our navy were practically annihilated, have little occasion or desire to exercise.

But the objection is raised that neutralization would be a violation of the Monroe Doctrine. The answer to this is that we were for fifty years committed by a formal treaty agreement to a policy of neutralization and the Monroe Doctrine did not suffer any serious harm during that time. The warmest advocates of the Monroe Doctrine have also been advocates of an internationalized canal. Neutralization would not give the European powers the right to intervene in the internal affairs of any American state. A treaty neutralizing the canal and placing it under international guaranty would, it is true, impose a limitation upon our sovereign right to do what we please with a piece of property which we own; but this same objection may be raised with equal force against a general arbitration treaty such as President Taft is supposed at present to be negotiating with England. Such a treaty imposes certain limitations upon our sovereign freedom of action; it binds us to refrain from acting on our own sense of right and justice and to accept the decision of others on questions that concern even our honor and vital interests.

The time has come when it is right and proper that nations should surrender under voluntary agreements their sovereign freedom of action in matters that concern the peace of the world. I deplore the policy of the President in the matter of the canal just as deeply as I approve his policy of negotiating compulsory arbitration agreements. In appropriating $3,000,000 for the purpose of beginning fortifications and thereby committing the country to the policy of a fortified canal, we have thrown away a great opportunity for promoting the cause of international peace and we have given the stamp of our approval in a more significant way than ever before to the policy of heavy peace armaments. The position of the United States is as nearly impregnable as that of any power on earth. Why should we be so swept off our feet by the modern war scare?

Neutralization does not mean the surrender of our commercial interest or control. We have put up the capital for the canal and we will draw the dividends. But if it is to fill the place that we expect it to fill as a great channel for the world's commerce, then we must administer it with due regard for the interests of the world at large. If, in taking the canal zone, we acted as the agent of collective civilization, then we have a right to ask the civilized powers of the world to unite with us in protecting and neutralizing the canal. Why have we not done so? Why not do so yet? If you doubt the good faith of the civilized nations, remember that the scheme of neutralization does not rest on good faith alone, but on a very material consideration, namely the fear of the damages that would be assessed in case the treaty were violated. This is a point I wish especially to emphasize, for I believe that the fear of having to pay an indemnity would prove an adequate sanction for the guaranty of the canal. We are told, it is true, that we laymen are not competent to express an opinion on this question of fortifying the canal, that we should leave that to military experts. It is not always safe to go to a surgeon whose specialty is appendicitis to consult him as to whether your appendix should be removed. As a matter of fact we do not leave the size of our army or the strength of our navy to the determination of military experts. If we did, we would be laboring under the burden of heavier war taxes than are paid today by the subjects of the German Emperor, and we would have the high seas covered in a few years with dreadnaughts. Fortunately we leave these questions to the common sense of the American people, and that is where we should leave the question of fortifying the Panama Canal.

Chairman Wilson introduced Mr. Edwin D. Mead of Boston, who spoke in part as follows:

THE ANGLO-AMERICAN LEADERSHIP FOR PEACE

Edwin D. Mead of Boston, speaking upon the Anglo-American Leadership for Peace, referred in opening to the impressive Anglo-American arbitration meeting held just a week before in the Guildhall in London. At that great meeting, Mr. Asquith, the Liberal prime minister, and Mr. Balfour, the leader of the opposition in Parliament, had spoken together in welcoming the proposal of the President of the United States in favor of a general treaty of arbitration between this country and Great Britain. The principles of such a treaty, they rightly declared, would not only serve the higher interests of the two nations, but would promote the peace of the world. Seldom in recent history has the feeling of the English people been so profoundly stirred as over this proposed treaty. It has been a feeling transcending all party lines. When Sir Edward Grey, the British foreign minister, two months ago, made the noteworthy speech which met with such acclaim not only in England but in all Europe, his chief supporter also was Mr. Balfour. So will it be in America. Republican and Democrat alike, in the Senate and in the country, will support President Taft in his demand for reference to arbitration or an international court of every dispute whatever between these two great nations not settled by regular diplomatic negotiations. When President Taft made that demand in his memorable speech in Washington, last December, he took the most advanced position ever taken by the responsible head of a great nation; and the ratification of the proposed Anglo-American treaty, settling it that never again shall there be war between these two nations, will be an event significant indeed not alone for these nations but, as the Guildhall resolution last week well declared, for the peace of the world. For it is known that France is ready for such a treaty; it is said that Japan is ready; and the Anglo-American treaty must prove the opening of a new era in the history of arbitration and of the long struggle to supplant the war system of nations by the system of law.

Mr. Mead discussed the Olney-Pauncefote treaty and its unfortunate failure by a few votes in the Senate in 1897, the votes of three states representing a combined population less than the population of Chicago. That failure accused our Senate and accused our people; and public opinion today must be alert to make sure that no such miserable miscarriage is again possible. Great Britain has been ready all these years for such a treaty as now seems likely; we only are to blame because it does not exist. Our own international leaders have unitedly urged it, as the speaker showed by a review of the action of the great Arbitration Conferences in Washington in 1896 and 1904. At last the time seems ripe; and it is for Britain and America to lead the world.

The important contributions of the United States and Great Britain to the arbitration movement were rapidly surveyed. From the time of Jay's treaty to the present time no other nations have sent so many cases to arbitration as these two. Special reference was made to the successful arbitration of the *Alabama* case between the nations themselves, as involving the gravest possible questions of national honor and vital interest. No more serious case between two proud nations was possible.

It was in the United States and England that the peace movement, as an organized movement, began. The New York and Massachusetts Peace Societies of 1815 and the London Society of 1816 were the first in the world; and from these centres the movement has spread until at last it has created The Hague Conferences and an international tribunal and President Taft's unlimited treaty and last week's meeting in the London Guildhall.

In closing, Mr. Mead spoke of the approaching celebration of the century of peace between the United States and Great Britain, and the powerful lesson in disarmament furnished by the unfortified Canadian frontier. Precisely because unguarded that frontier has been for a century the safest frontier in the world; and it remains a standing and salutary enforcement of the truth that what the nations need is simply to act like gentlemen and so be safe.

CHAIRMAN WILSON made the following announcement, We are fortunate in having with us Mr. James Speyer, of Speyer and

Company, Chairman of the New York Chamber of Commerce, and delegate to this Congress. It will be interesting to hear from one of our leading bankers at this time.

MR. JAMES SPEYER delivered the following address, his subject being,

INTERNATIONAL FINANCE: A POWER FOR PEACE

There are some business men who think that when one of their number publicly expresses his opinions on more or less abstract subjects, it is an indication that he has joined the ranks of the theorists. ·Of course we business men have to reckon with facts and figures and realities; but I think you will agree with me that no great success has ever been achieved by men who do not also possess a certain amount of idealism and imagination, and a firm belief in the honest common sense of the American people. This is the foundation for that optimism which is so well justified, in this great country of ours.

I see in this hall a goodly number of clear-headed business men who are seriously working for international peace, and I therefore feel encouraged to submit a few suggestions, actuated by a desire to assist to a slight extent in reaching the goal toward which our efforts are now directed.

We frequently hear the remark that "there always have been and there always will be wars." Other and abler speakers have dwelt on the difference that exists in this respect in modern times with conditions as they formerly were. Great wars of conquest, pure and simple, or wars caused by religious fanaticism, are practically things of the past.

Today we find that the extension of commerce and industry and commercial advantages are the mainspring, the "leitmotif," of the policy of civilized nations. Each nation is desirous of extending its commerce, and only too often does the resulting rivalry lead to customs struggles, international irritation and complications, which become a strong contributory cause if not the real reason for wars.

Such complications and wars are the greatest enemies of commerce, not only by diminishing or stopping the free intercourse between peoples, but also by largely destroying the fruit of commerce and industry—wealth. A great part of the wealth of a nation is represented by the savings and investments of its individual citizens, and we may well ask whether these savings of each nation could not be employed in such manner as to render such disturbances of its commerce less frequent and severe.

So far it has rather been the aim of the governments of rich nations to limit, as far as possible, the investment of the savings of their own citizens to their own national and colonial enterprises and securities—government, railroad and industrial. I need not dwell here on the financial and economic reasons for such artificial limitations. Exceptions have from time to time been made in encouraging investments in the securities of less powerful and less developed countries, in whose advancement foreign capital has played such an important, and I may add, profitable part. Examples will readily occur showing the importance of the financial link uniting such newer countries to their financial godmother, and its power for order and peace, even *within* such foreign countries, exercised, if necessary, by the creditor nation.

The minds of some of our leading men are occupied just now with the consideration of the extent to which the surplus wealth of the United States should be employed in financing Central and South American countries, thereby extending our legitimate sphere of influence. The construction of the Panama Canal and the large investment which the United States have made in that work, have, perhaps more than we realize today, extended our political influence and responsibilities over the whole region north of the canal up to our own border. The logical consequence, it seems to me, of our upholding the Monroe Doctrine, which makes it difficult for foreign creditor nations to collect what is due them in case of default of Central and South American countries, must be that we ourselves assume, in more or less definite form, the task of assisting these creditors to receive what is justly due them and of keeping order in these countries.

But quite apart from the investments made by older countries

in those that are still less developed, and therefore offer greater
chances of profit, should not the few really great World Powers
also make an effort in their own interest to encourage their citizens
to invest their savings in the enterprises and securities of other
first-class nations? If the people of one country are financially
interested in the affairs and enterprises of another country, this
will produce not only more frequent intercourse but substantial
mutual interests and good will. No great nation would readily
go to war with another when the savings of its own citizens would
thus be jeopardized. Is it, for instance, conceivable that France,
which today owns such an immense amount of Russian securities,
would think of going to war with Russia, even if there were no
political alliance or understanding? Certainly not. International financial links, moreover, lead to more accurate knowledge
of the conditions—financial, social, economic and political—of
other nations, and such closer study and more accurate information have the result of explaining many things, showing the other
point of view and other peoples' legitimate aspirations, and of
thus removing misunderstandings which otherwise might have
grave consequences.

While it is not difficult to point out the beneficial results of
interchange of investments amongst the great World Powers, it
is less easy to indicate in a few words a practical way to bring
about this desirable end. There are many factors that enter
into this mattter, quite apart from the question of return on the
investment and profit. There are national prejudices to overcome, and sentiment does play a greater part in business matters
than is often supposed to be the case. It would be necessary, and
I think it would be found expedient, for some nations to do away
with the artificial discrimination which they enforce against
"foreign" investments, such as higher stamp and other taxes
imposed thereon in favor of home securities. The arbitrary
exclusion of foreign securities from the list of funds in which
savings banks and trustees may lawfully invest would have to be
modified, and for nations desiring a wider market for their securities it would be advisable to adapt to some extent their form, as
regards denominations and currencies, to the customs of the peo-

ple who are to buy them, just as the merchants and great manufacturers adapt their goods to the market which they seek.   The
value of foreign markets and exports might, at times, prove just
as great for securities as for iron and steel and manufactured
goods.

So much for the influence of international investments in times
of peace.

What should and could be done in times of war by first-class
powers?

There surely will occur periods in a nation's history when no
financial investment will, or perhaps should, prevent a nation
from taking up arms, until, of course, some other way is found
and established to settle their differences.   The wars of all times,
and especially of the last century, have shown what tremendous
financial burdens these conflicts impose, even on the victorious
nation, and financial considerations play a greater part in modern
times than they did of old.   One frequently sees the statement
in the papers that "the bankers could prevent wars," but I have
so far not seen any practical way suggested whereby the banks
and bankers really could, if necessary, be made to forego their
own profits, and thus make war if not impossible at least less frequent and shorter.

While in the excitement of the moment, patriotic feeling may
carry a nation into a war, relying on its own resources, history
shows that but very few nations in modern times can carry on any
prolonged foreign war with their own resources only.   How long,
for instance, would the war between Russia and Japan have
lasted, or how soon would it have ended, if neither of the belligerents, had received financial assistance from so-called "neutral"
Powers.   Indeed, it might be asked whether Japan would have
embarked in this war if her statesmen had not known that they
could rely on the financial assistance of England.   These Great
Powers, France and England, who so scrupulously preserved
neutrality as laid down by international law, and who saw to it
that such neutrality was maintained by their citizens, did not
hesitate to assist the belligerents in the most efficient way to carry
on the conflict—with money.   Money enables the belligerents

to buy powder and shells and all they need to carry on war, and it certainly does not seem logical that neutral Powers should be allowed to send money when international agreements will not allow them to send the ships and war materials which their money buys.

We find today in Europe that in *times of peace* certain governments will not allow their bankers to take and place foreign loans in the home market unless the purposes for which the loan is to be used are known and approved, and at least part of the proceeds are used by the borrowing nation for expenditures in such home markets for the benefit of the lending nation.

I do not believe that it is generally known in this country to what extent such supervision by the French and German governments, for instance, goes, and as an illustration I would like to cite from memory what happened last year when the young Turk party wanted to place abroad a loan of the Ottoman Empire. They went to Paris as the cheapest money market, but when they applied to France, the French government, which supervises the listing, or official quotation of securities on the Paris Bourse, wanted to know for what purpose the loan was to be raised, and, if ships, *et cetera*, were to be bought, whether they were to be bought from the lending nation. The Turkish finance minister did not want to submit to any conditions, and, according to the newspapers, negotiations were begun with a prominent English financier, who seemed to be willing to make the loan. The French government called the attention of the British government to the so-called *entente cordiale* between France and England, and intimated in a more or less direct way that they would consider English bankers making a loan which France had declined as a rather unfriendly act. The English government thereupon notified the financier and English banks generally that they would not like the loan to Turkey made by them, and it was not made by them. The Turkish government finally obtained the loan from Germany and Austria on terms satisfactory to the governments of these nations.

Now, if such supervision and control of the bankers already exists in time of peace, it does not seem a wide flight of imagination to suggest that the Great Powers might agree to exercise such control in *times of war* between third parties and to maintain, in future, what, for want of a better term, might be called "Financial Neutrality." In case two nations went to war without first submitting their grievances and differences to arbitration or judicial settlement at The Hague, why should the other neutral Powers not bind themselves not to assist either of the belligerents financially, but to see to it that real neutrality was observed by their banks and bankers. There is little doubt that this could be done. If no financial assistance could be obtained from the outside, few nations would, in the face of this most effective neutrality of the other Powers, incur the peril of bankruptcy. Some wars would probably not take place at all, and those that could not be avoided, would certainly last a much shorter time.

These suggestions may seem Utopian and more difficult of practical accomplishment than they really are. I wish to apologize for the very incomplete manner in which they are presented.

In all financial matters of importance, one should only move slowly and with great caution, but I do believe that in the course of time measures substantially on the lines I have suggested will be approved and demanded by public opinion of the great nations, and will then be carried into effect.

We in the United States are proud of being called a business people. Uninterrupted peace is of more importance to business than the tariff reform, free trade, or currency reform, or even reciprocity with Canada. It is a business question, and we business men of the United States should insist on international agreements making for peace.

We are indeed fortunate to have at the head of our government a man who, without giving way to false and dangerous sentiment, or ignoring existing conditions, continuing the policy of his predecessor, is courageously leading in this world movement. We should make it *our* business, as it is our duty, to back up President Taft. Chairman Wilson made the following announcement

The next address will be on the subject of "Universal Arbitration," and will be by a man whose name is more intimately associated with the practical work toward peace through the Inter-Parliamentary Union extending all over the world than, I think, any other American citizen. His name is associated, indeed, with all practical movements toward peace. I have the honor to present the Hon. Richard Bartholdt, member of Congress from Missouri.

PEACE AND ARBITRATION

HON. RICHARD BARTHOLDT

Mr. Chairman, Ladies and Gentlemen: It is not so very long ago when those who arranged and attended peace meetings were looked upon as harmless cranks. What a change, my countrymen! Today the leading men of the country are vying with each other to lend their presence and voice to such gatherings, and to my mind nothing demonstrates more clearly the triumphant force of the ideas which underlie the peace movement. It is true that even today a Congress of the picked men of the nation such as this is not fully appreciated by all the people, but surely the time is not far distant when the American people will realize that the men who made this Congress possible are really human benefactors and that the City of Baltimore, by extending her hospitality to us, has added a proud, if not the proudest page to her interesting history.

There is something about the peace movement which is a peculiarity of its own. The objects of all great progressive movements of which history tells us—and in our country there has not been one, except the question of the abolition of slavery, which could compare in transcendent importance with the movement to found our peace and the world's peace upon the imperishable rock of law—the objects, I say, of nearly all great movements were either favored or opposed, that is, favored by one side and opposed by the other. The goal, however, toward which the modern advocates of peace strive, seems to have the hearty approval of all. Every good man and woman wants to see the country's peace preserved, and even the most incarnate militarist whose profession is war, does not dare openly to advocate it. This is true to such an extent that modern militarism is actually on the defensive and apologizes for the existence of armaments and for the demands for their increase on the ground that they are necessary, not for the conduct of war, but for the preservation of peace. It appears, therefore, as I said, that as to the ultimate object, namely the necessity of maintaining peace, we are all in accord, and the only difference of opinions as to the method of attaining that object, by armaments or by arbitration. The difference, I admit, is a radical and fundamental one, but while the civilized world still clings to the old plan of coercion, intimidation and force through armament, which is plainly a relic of barbarism, evolution points with unerring finger to a new and better method to maintain peace, namely to a system of international justice through arbitration. And this is the proposition I was invited to discuss.

I assume it to be unnecessary before an audience as intelligent as this, to dwell on the theory of arbitration and its vast advantages as a method of settling disputes, over force and war. Suffice it to say that arbitration, in the accepted sense, means judicial decisions in accordance with recognized principles of justice, while war never has settled and never will settle a question of right and wrong. Arbitration is for nations what our courts are for individuals, so that it signifies merely an extension of the reign of law to international relations. Armaments are a preparation for war and often incite war, arbitration is an assurance of peace. War and the state of preparedness for it sap the life blood of the nation, while the machinery of arbitration will not cost as much as the armor plate for a single battleship, and as against the positive loss to civilization caused by the sacrifice of life and treasure, the suffering, the brutalizing effect and the moral damage of war, we find the positive gain, through arbitration, of an increased sense of justice and humaneness and of continued tranquillity, prosperity and peace. Naturally such comparisons are odious to the militarist, but the odium of it is that the human family has not emerged, hundreds of years ago, from the barbarism of the throat-cutting business.

Now, I may be an optimist, but I can hear distinctly the sound of the clock striking the hour of emancipation from the old order of things and the inauguration of the new. Only we must not expect immediate disarmament.   The transition must needs be gradual, and for a while the world will continue to maintain its armies and navies, as the new system is put to a test.   In considering the practical side of arbitration we find that hundreds of controversies have been peaceably settled by resort to it, but its application heretofore has been a very limited one, the treaties extending only to questions of a judicial nature and expressly exempting all questions of vital interest, independence and honor as well as those concerning third parties.   It was left to an American President to propose—and this should swell every American heart with pride—that all questions without exception, should be subject to arbitration.   President Taft has made such a proposition to Great Britain, and the latter country is gladly and enthusiastically grasping the outstretched hand.   I wonder if the people realize the significance of this act?   To my mind, there has not been since Abraham Lincoln's proclamation of freedom to the slave, a more important step taken on the human stage, and I would not hesitate to brand as an enemy of mankind the man who would dare, from whatever motive, to throw obstacles in the way of our President's great design.   Far from being an alliance, the proposed pact does not concern third parties except as a good example for all civilized nations to emulate, and the two nations, by renouncing the arbitrary power to draw the sword against each other thus remove the possibility of war and become the mutual beneficiaries of the blessings of perpetual peace under an enlightened system of law and justice.   It is a beginning and who will doubt but that the other great nations will soon be drawn into the circle, attracted by the irresistible magnetism of right and reason?   The establishment of the permanent Court of Arbitral Justice, already agreed upon in principle, will follow as a matter of course.

It is proper to ask what the possible objections could be on the part of any nation to join the British-American agreement.   I will tell you.   Universal arbitration would render a large part of the world's armaments unnecessary, and some of the great European governments are averse to surrendering any part of their military power.   Naturally, they do not say so, but base their objections on the ground that submission to an international court involves the surrender of sovereignty which they say they are not disposed to make. This objection looks serious when we remember how jealously all monarchieal rulers are guarding their sovereign power. Nevertheless I predict that sooner or later they will have to make this concession to human progress. Where sovereign power and the true interests of the people conflict, the former is bound to give way, and in this case it would be a sacrifice in the interest of what is or should be the highest aim of all governments, namely the securing of the peace and happiness of the people and the avoidance of the sacrifices for war. And there is one other consideration which, when advanced by me at the last Interparliamentary Conference at Brussels, was hailed with applause by the six hundred or more delegates present, all of them members of national legislative bodies. It is this: When the great rulers of Europe in case of a dispute surrender the arbitrary power of immediately deciding on hostilities, they surely make a sacrifice of authority, but there is on the other hand a gain which more than evens up the loss. They become part and parcel of a higher, an international power which, in a judicial sense, rules the world and sits in judgment on all causes of the nations assenting to the compact. In other words, these sovereigns, in return for whatever authority they yield up to the common good, are made to share in the great world organization created to administer justice between the nations. And is not this plan patterned after the social order prevailing in civilized society? If every individual claimed the right to assert his sovereignty, there would be anarchy, but instead on entering society he gives up his natural rights and in return is guaranteed only such liberty of action as will enable his neighbor to enjoy the same liberty, but both enjoy the protection to life, liberty and property, guaranteed by the consent of all. As long as a nation remains isolated and alone, its government can exercise unrestricted sovereignty, but the moment it enters an agreement with another nation its sovereign authority is circumscribed by the terms of such an agreement. Each government has already bound itself in this manner in many instances, consequently it cannot rightfully fall back upon the assertion of its sovereignty as against a proposed compact, more important than all others, one which will insure to the people as an alternative for war the blessings of a lasting peace. And it makes no difference whether sovereigns rule by "divine right" or by "the consent of the governed" because the happiness of the people must be their first concern. It is an obligation in the one case moral, in the other actual, but in each case absolutely binding.

There may be objections, too, on the part of some powers to the proposition to arbitrate all disputes including those heretofore excepted, namely questions of honor, vital interest and independence. President Taft's courageous position has reminded the world that questions of honor are really the easiest to arbitrate. In the first place no nation will intentionally insult another in this day and time, but, furthermore, the conduct of each government toward all other governments is supposed to be honorable, and if it is, it need never fear the judgment of an impartial tribunal. And as to the other questions I would suggest that in all arbitration treaties, even in that between this country and Great Britain, there be inserted a preamble by which the contracting parties proceed to guarantee to each other at the outset, territorial integrity and absolute sovereignty in domestic affairs. The rest is easy. Such a stipulation would undoubtedly be an incentive for such powers which still entertain scruples against joining the agreement.

The all-absorbing question at this juncture is: Will the United States Senate ratify the Anglo-American agreement? But for past experience it would be an insult to the Senate to ask such a question. It has been suggested that the Senate might insist on being consulted in each particular case that may come up and, consequently, deny to the Executive the wholesale authority so essential in such matters. Let us hope that our lawmakers may not take such a stand. If arbitration is to be made possible, it must in each case be resorted to without much delay, that is, before the popular passion is aroused. If you allow the apple of discord to be thrown into the arena and by heated discussions in the Senate stir the fighting blood of the people, you render arbitration much more difficult, if not altogether impossible, and the benefit of a peaceable adjustment of a controversy would probably be lost. The Senate, in my judgment, cannot afford to thus nullify and negative the efforts authorized by beneficent laws at maintaining the people's peace. Its constitutional prerogatives are satisfied, it seems, by passing upon the treaty which gives the President the needed authority, and certainly there can be no danger in conferring power which can only be exercised for the benefit and never to the disadvantage of the American people.

As Americans let us rejoice in President Taft's wise statesmanship and in the great initiative he has just taken, to add a new meaning to our flag and new honor and prestige to this nation. It is a message which will be hailed with joy by all the people of the earth and reads: "America leads the world in peace."

CHAIRMAN WILSON: I next have the honor and the pleasure to call upon Professor E. H. Griffin, the Dean of the Johns Hopkins University, whose address will be "An Argument from Hobbes' *Leviathan*."

AN ARGUMENT FROM HOBBES' *LEVIATHAN*

E. H. GRIFFIN

I wish to illustrate the nature and functions of the proposed court of arbitral justice by reference to a seventeenth century classic of political and ethical speculation—the *Leviathan* of Thomas Hobbes. This famous work offers so many interesting and salient features that one is tempted to linger upon them, but without any such preliminaries, let me ask your attention to four propositions maintained in the treatise, the truth of which cannot— if we are granted a little liberty of interpretation—be denied, and which constitute a quite conclusive argument for the international tribunal which we desire.

I. As is well known, Hobbes conceives the natural condition of mankind to be one of warfare. The differences, bodily and mental, between individuals are not so great as to enable any

one to claim benefits to which another may not aspire as well as
he.   The powers of men are substantially equal, and hence their
ambitions tend to be the same.   "If any two men desire the same
thing, which nevertheless they cannot both enjoy, they become
enemies" (part I, Chapter XIII).   "Nature thus dissociates
men, and renders them apt to invade and destroy one another."
Hobbes is too clear-sighted not to perceive that these divisive and
hostile impulses are subject to counteraction.   The necessities
of self-preservation compel coöperation, even in the lowest savagery, and tend to bring about a more or less settled and regular
order of life.   Quite independently of the operation of benevolent
and sympathetic feelings, a certain degree of social organization
must inevitably arise.   And so he suggests a doubt: "It may peradventure be thought that there never was such a time and
conditions of war as this."   But in the case of the aggregates of individuals which we call nations, there is no such interdependence;
one nation may dispense with the coöperation of others.   Hence
the original state of war, which cannot be verified in regard to
individuals, is indisputable, so far as nations are concerned.
"Though there had never been any time wherein particular men
were in a condition of war one against another; yet in all times
kings and persons of sovereign authority, because of their inde-
pendency, are in continual jealousies, and in the state and posture of gladiators."   The natural attitude of nations toward
one another is that of hostility, because the disintegrating tendencies of selfishness, which within the limits of the community
are partially counteracted through the dependence of each upon
the others, are not thus held in check outside the limits of the
community.   This is Hobbes' explanation of the fact that the
standards of morality between states are so different from those
which prevail in individual life.

The characterizations of the "state of nature" in *The Leviathan* apply with painful accuracy to the civilised nations of modern
Christendom.   They are "in the state and posture of gladiators,
having their weapons pointing and their eyes fixed on one
another."   Overt hostilities are not, indeed, always in progress,
but "war consisteth not in battle only, or the act of fighting, but

in a tract of time wherein the will to contend by battle is sufficiently known; as the nature of foul weather lieth not in a shower
or two of rain, but in an inclination thereto of many days together."
As to the causes producing this state of things, "we find in the
nature of man three principal causes of quarrel. First, competition; second, diffidence; thirdly, glory. The first maketh men
invade for gain; the second, for safety; and the third for reputation." We may thankfully admit that the last named of these is
less operative now than two and a half centuries ago. With the
increasing power of the people, and the limitation of royal prerogative, wars of mere ambition, undertaken for dynastic aggrandisement, are not so likely to occur. But have the other causes
lost anything of their potency? Most modern conflicts, economic
in origin, are "for gain." The underlying motive is desire to obtain
possession of the natural resources of the earth, to control the
world's markets. It is this which makes Africa, and China, and
the states of southeastern Europe, and the ocean whose name may
some day become an irony, storm centres. One would like to
think that "diffidence"—jealous dislike and distrust—is disappearing from diplomacy and international intercourse, but
when one recalls the relations between France and Germany for
the past forty years, and observes the state of public opinion at
the present time in England toward Germany and in Germany
toward England, and considers the readiness with which we ourselves give credence to wild and sinister rumors and surmises in
regard to Japan, this comfortable belief is not a little disturbed.
In fact, the most disquieting and discouraging feature of the moral
and political life of our time is the profound distrust with which
the leading nations of the world regard one another. There is
no lack of ceremonious courtesy, of profuse assurances of friendship; there are treaty obligations and recognized principles
governing international relations; but one is shocked to find,
from time to time, in the most reputable journals, expressions of
opinion and feeling such as the following: "We must cease to
play and toy with this urgent problem of the independence and
integrity of the smaller states of Europe in time of war. A dozen
years ago, there was reasonable hope that the neutrality of the

small countries bordering upon France and Germany would be respected in case of a Franco-German war, but no one today any longer believes it . . . . It is also possible that Switzerland may no longer stand outside the area of conflagration, and it is probable that in case of an Anglo-German war the conservation of the neutrality of the Netherlands will not remain an absorbing interest to German strategists." In other words, in the event of war the most solemn engagements of honor and good faith would be disregarded. When a well known writer, in a paper like *The London Times*, expresses such a belief, and thousands of intelligent and sensible people concur in it, one feels that a condition not far from chaos discloses itself.

Hobbes's state of war, unhappily, is not a fantasy, or a thing of the distant past, long left behind in the advance of civilization; it is actually realised in the international relations of the twentieth century.

II. According to the author of *The Leviathan*, the inconveniences and dangers of this state of war are so intolerable that men are compelled to seek some means of escape. "In such condition . . . . the life of man is solitary, poor, nasty, brutish, and short."

The ten years from 1895 to 1905 were the most warlike decade since Waterloo. Within that period occurred the war between Japan and China in 1894–95, that between Turkey and Greece in 1897, our own conflict with Spain in 1898, the war between Great Britain and the South African Republics, 1899–1902, and the gigantic struggle between Russia and Japan in 1904–05. The financial cost of these world-embracing hostilities was inconceivably great, England spent nearly a billion and a half of dollars on the Boer War. The direct expenditures for the maintenance of armies and navies, in these five contests, the property destroyed in the course of military operations, the losses incident to the withdrawal of so many hundreds of thousands of men from productive industries, make up a total of economic waste, which no figures can adequately express. As to the ghastly aggregate of human suffering involved, this cannot be imagined— the tortures of the battlefield, the misery of ruined homes and broken hearts. One visiting the English churches is deeply moved by the pathos of the tablets in memory of those who perished in the South African war. These are even more numerous than those which commemorate the Crimea, and they are tragic evidence of the price at which this triumph was won.

One might have hoped that, after this decade of strife, such a revulsion of feeling would have set in that the world would turn away, in weariness and disgust, from such pursuits to apply itself to the arts of peace. On the contrary, hostile preparations have been pushed forward during the past half dozen years with a feverish energy never before known. The naval expenditures of Great Britain in 1910 were precisely double what they were in 1897—the year before our war with Spain, *i.e.*, forty million pounds as against twenty million; our own naval expenditures in 1910 were nearly four times greater than in 1897, *i.e.*, one hundred and thirty-five million dollars as against thirty-five million. All the great nations furnish a similar record.

The ruinous burdens imposed by these increasing armaments are better appreciated when we consider the enormous increase of taxation which they necessitate; and when we consider how much these vast sums might accomplish toward the solving of the terrible problems of our civilization—the problems of poverty, of disease, of ignorance, and of crime; and when we note the extraordinary fact that more than one of the nations indulging in these lavish outlays is actually borrowing money to meet deficits in the annual budget.

The apprehension with which responsible statesmen have long regarded the situation is well expressed in these warning words uttered in Parliament by Sir Edward Grey, Secretary for Foreign Affairs:—"Unless the mischief is brought home to men's feelings as well as to their minds, the growth of armaments must in the long run break down civilization. You are having this great burden piled up in times of peace, and if it goes on increasing by leaps and bounds as it has done in the last generation, it will become intolerable. There are those who think that it will lead to war precisely because it is already becoming intolerable. I think it much more likely that the burden will be dissipated by an

internal revolution, by a revolt of the masses of men against taxation." What will happen when one of the great states of Europe
ceases to pay the interest on its national debt?

Our generation is abundantly experiencing the truth of Hobbes'
assertion that the evils of the state of war are unendurable.

III. Deliverance from these anxieties and dangers is obtained,
according to the account given in the *Leviathan*, by means of a
compact, in which men mutually agree, for the sake of peace, to
renounce certain of their rights, retaining such only as they are
willing that all others should enjoy; and in which they agree also
to erect a common power, a "sovereign," or "commonwealth,"
such as may be "able to defend them from the invasion of
foreigners and the injuries of one another."

"It is necessary for all men that seek peace to lay down certain
rights of nature; that is to say, not to have liberty to do all they
list." . . . . "And it is necessary for them to reduce all
their wills, by plurality of voices, to one will; which is as much as
to say, to appoint one man, or assembly of men, to bear their
person; . . . . . as if every man should say to every
man, 'I authorise and give up my right of governing myself to
this man, or to this assembly of men, on this conditions that thou
give up thy right to him, and authorise all his actions in like
manner.' This done, the multitude so united in one person is
called a 'Commonwealth.'"

As an explanation of the origin of the state, this contract theory,
which seemed so satisfactory to most of the political thinkers of
the seventeenth and eighteenth centuries, is, of course, long since
discredited, but as an explanation of a particular form of government, existing at a given time and place, it is a sufficiently accurate account. When the present constitution of the United States,
framed by a convention and submitted to the people, was finally
accepted by all the states, a contract was entered into between the
several states. When, in 1871, a parliament of all Germany
ratified the present constitution of the German Empire, a similar
relationship was established between the constituent elements of
the Empire. The Swiss Confederation, and the Dominion of
Canada are additional examples. All federal states may be said
to rest upon contract.

While the author of the *Leviathan* was, then, mistaken in supposing that the contract idea expresses the proper relation of the individual to the state—since that relation is not a voluntary one—he was quite right in emphasising its importance, since it is the idea which underlies governments having the form of confederations, and it is the idea which enters into all transactions between independent sovereignties. It is through some wisely conceived application of this idea—let us say, in an international court—that the peace of nations is to be safeguarded.

It is interesting to see, in recent discussions, the tendency to remove the restrictions of jurisdiction which it has so often been thought necessary to impose upon such a tribunal. The words of President Taft, a year or more ago, furnish a leadership for which the friends of peace cannot be too grateful. "Personally, I do not see any more reason why matters of national honor should not be referred to a court of arbitration than matters of property, or matters of national proprietorship." Obviously, if territorial questions, or questions assumed to involve "vital interests," or "national honor" are to be reserved, little could be accomplished. On this point, the case of the "*Alabama* claims" is most instructive; Earl Russell declared that these could never be arbitrated because the national honor was involved, but the more dispassionate judgment of a later time thought them a proper subject of adjudication. As long ago as 1890, the first conference of all the independent countries of the Western hemispheres, held in Washington, declared: "The sole question which any nation is not at liberty to arbitrate is a question which might imperil its independence." This is just the point at which Hobbes limits the authority of the sovereign—an authority which he makes almost limitless; the sovereign may not deprive the subject of the right to defend himself. It would certainly seem reasonable to say that, as a man may not contract himself into slavery, so a nation may not submit to any tribunal the question of its own existence.

But, with this qualification, why may not the jurisdiction of an international court be as comprehensive as the interests for the sake of which it is constituted?

The way out of the embarrassments and dangers of the state
of war is that suggested in the *Leviathan*—a contract of mutual
renunciation.

IV.   Hobbes was severely censured in his day—and the censure is still sometimes repeated—for saying that justice and
injustice, right and wrong, are subsequent to the institution of
society, that they do not exist until after the covenant which
brings the state into being has been entered into.   "When no
covenant hath preceded, then hath no right been transferred, and
every man has a right to everything; and consequently no action
can be unjust."   But when a covenant is made, then to break it
is unjust.   He has been supposed to mean that the obligations of
morality are not inherently binding, but are the mere product of
convention and external enactment.   That this is not his meaning is entirely clear; he expressly explains that he is speaking, not
of the internal recognition of laws of conduct, but of the external
embodiment of them in act.   "The laws of nature oblige *in foro
interno*, that is to say, they bind to a desire they should take
place; but *in foro externo*, that is to the putting them in act,
not always."   The distinction of just and unjust is not created
by society, but the opportunity of acting in conformity to the
distinction is so created.

The reasons why the state must exist before morality can be
externally realised are, as stated by Hobbes, two.

1.   No one can tell what particular outward acts are to be
considered just or unjust until some competent authority has
provided definitions.   "To the Sovereignty is annexed the whole
power of presenting the rules whereby every man may know what
goods he may enjoy, and what actions he may do, without being
molested by any of his fellow subjects."   "As for example, of
what is to be called right, what good, what virtue, what much,
what little, what *meum* and *tuum*, what a pound, what a quart,
etc."

2.   No one can venture to act in accordance with the abstract
principles of which he may be aware until he has reason to believe
that others also will do so.   "It suits not with reason that any man
should perform first, if it be not likely that the other will make

good his promise after." "Therefore before the names of just and unjust can have place there must be some coercive power to compel men equally to the performance of their covenants; . . . . and such power there is none before the erection of a Commonwealth."

For two reasons, then, the social compact, the sovereign commonwealth, is a precedent condition of justice; its authority is needed, first, to define what justice is, and, second, to ensure objective fulfilment of it.

In each of these particulars the analogy which we are tracing holds good.

The establishment of an international court would provide facilities for determining questions of justice and injustice in international relations such as the world has not hitherto known. As we all understand, international law has, up to the present time, developed in a desultory and unscientific manner. Accepted usages, treaties at the close of wars, Congresses such as those of Vienna and Berlin, and of late The Hague Conferences, have furnished its materials. The decisions reached have often, as some one has said, been of the nature of a *post-mortem*; they have had no preventive value. Nor is it possible to procure a prompt settlement of any acute and threatening question that may suddenly arise. The advantages of a permanent and authoritative tribunal to which questions endangering the peace of nations could be immediately submitted are too obvious to call for insistence. Justice and injustice, so far as international relations are concerned, would take on a new meaning, and would have a potency hitherto undreamed of, if they could thus be defined, whenever occasion should arise, in regular process of law.

Whether express provision would be needed to compel the acquiescence of interested parties in the decisions that might be rendered, is a question about which there may be difference of view. It would seem proper that such provision should be made. But it is difficult to believe that, in the case of self-respecting nations, any coercion, other than the moral constraint of enlightened public opinion, would be required.

These are the points which I have endeavored to illustrate by reference to Hobbes's *Leviathan*.

1. The present attitude of the civilized nations toward one another is essentially that of war.

2. The evils of such a condition are so grievous and terrible as to threaten the very fabric of our civilization.

3. The remedy is in an international agreement providing for the peaceful settlement of disputes.

4. A tribunal constituted for this purpose would ensure:— first, the determination of the rights and duties of nations, in such a manner as to give to the principles and rules governing international intercourse a definiteness and consistency not as yet attained; second, the carrying of these obligations into effect, through the constraint of the public sentiment of mankind.

The great historian of the *Decline and Fall of the Roman Empire* has extolled the period of the Flavian and Antonine emperors as one of unexampled felicity. "If a man were called to fix the period in the history of the world during which the condition of the human race was most happy and prosperous, he would, without hesitation, name that which elapsed from the death of Domitian to the accession of Commodus." This was the period of the Pax Romana, when, as another historian has said, "within the sacred limits of the Roman Terminus, the repose of the empire was calm, passive, and almost deathlike. The shores of the mighty ocean might still resound with the murmurs of the eternal conflict of servitude and freedom, but the depths of its central abysses were unmoved alike by winds and currents." But this peace of the empire extended only over lands actually occupied by the Roman legions, and it was, at best, only a breathing space—a brief interval of less than a hundred years. If the endeavors of those who seek to bring about the establishment of a high court of arbitral justice should be crowned with success, we may hope that peace would be inaugurated far more benign and far more enduring—not a Pax Romana, the Roman peace, but a Pax Humana, the peace of the human race.

CHAIRMAN WILSON: The next address will be on the "Relation of the United to other American Governments, as They Are and as They Should Be," by Hon. James L. Slayden, Member of Congress, from Texas. I take great pleasure in presenting Hon. James L. Slayden.

THE RELATIONS OF THE UNITED STATES TO OTHER AMERICAN GOVERNMENTS

JAMES L. SLAYDEN

The relations of the United States to the other American states are unique and of the highest political importance.

Of consequence originally because they were parts of the same continent the relationship now has other and vastly greater reasons for this importance.

Before the development in steam transportation made them neighbors they were separated by almost impossible distances. Today the journey from Buenos Aires, Santiago or Rio, that was once remarkable and the achievement in travel of a lifetime, is a mere commonplace. No part of America is remote from any other part. The sanitation of any one city or country is a matter of grave concern to every other; the political quiet and the unimpeded flow of trade in each touches more or less the life of all others. Population and commerce have grown in the most extraordinary way. The Americas have become a big part of the world and the adjustment of purely American affairs among the American governments is of proportionate importance. We ought to deal justly with all governments everywhere, we ought to live on terms of amity with the whole world, but it is peculiarly our duty, as it is specially our interest, to live on just and friendly terms with our neighbors.

In 1823 a British premier in a private letter to the diplomatic representative of his country in Spain while referring to the United States and another country on this continent said: "They are too neighborly to be friends."

That cynicism, I regret to say, was founded in a knowledge of history and the passions of men.

Is it as true today as it was then that mere proximity makes enmity between men? If it is, the world has not moved towards higher and better things as I had hoped, and we are in contempt of the greatest authority that ever tried to regulate the affairs of men by refusing to obey the injunction "love thy neighbor as thyself."

There is every reason why the United States should be on terms of affectionate political intimacy with the other governments of this continent. They profess the same political faith that we hold; they have flattered us by modeling their governments on ours and it cannot be truthfully said that any one of them has ever menaced us in our territory or sovereignty. As we set out to walk so have they also undertaken to travel. We gave them a set of political principles and now it is our duty to leave them an opportunity to develop along the lines that may seem best to them.

OUR GOVERNMENT THE MODEL

In the eighteenth century effort to transfer power from church and king to the people, the English colonies in America were leaders. It was the success of the movement that they led and the setting up of a government by the people that was safe and conservative, while it also protected life and property, that at once commanded the attention of the world. In royal circles it caused apprehension; among the people whose contributions kept lustre in the purple of the kings it developed high hopes that justified the fears of their masters.

Among the supporters of kings the methods of the young republic were sneered at and its quick collapse predicted. Instead of crumbling it waxed strong and its fame spread the length and breadth of this vast continent. It became an exemplar for all liberty loving American communities.

Information of what was done by Washington, Franklin, Adams and Jefferson spread from the St. Lawrence to the River Plate. It crossed the Andes and forced its way through tropical jungles, carrying light and hope to the oppressed sons of men everywhere, alike on the mountain tops and by the sea at the equator.

Kings who saw the menace to their system of personal government in the new movement pointed to the violent and unreasonable outburst in France as evidence of the incapacity of men to govern themselves. It did bring discredit to the republican system for a while,—but for a brief while only.

The conspicuous success of the American republic had a liberalizing effect on governments of the old world and became an example and inspiration for the new.

INFLUENCE IN SPANISH AMERICA

Under these circumstances it is small wonder that Spain's American colonies rapidly, one by one, asserted their own independence and set up republics similar to that in North America.

At that time Europe was either too much occupied with the Napoleonic wars or too exhausted as a consequence of them to give much attention to American affairs. The Spanish-American population was not large and aside from the output of gold and silver the colonies were not important commercially. It was not interest in the people of the colonies or the commerce of South and Central America that finally stirred Europe to action but the alarming spread of the republican idea.

Just as soon after the passing of Napoleon Bonaparte and the organization of the Holy Alliance as Europe could catch its breath preparations were made to deal with America.

The "Holy Alliance" determined "to put an end to the system of representative government" and to "destroy the liberty of the press."

Originally the Prince Regent of England had given his adhesion to the schemes of the allied monarchs but their reactionary program was not to the taste of the British government and it was withdrawn. The hostile spirit that grew out of the difference of opinion between constitutional England and Continental Europe subsequently had a marked influence on the history of our own country, particularly as our affairs touch those of other American governments.

By the time the royal allies were ready to begin the execution
of their program in America the United States had grown largely
in wealth and population.   The second war with England was
ten years to the rear and "the call of the blood" which, after all,
is stronger and will endure longer than any political exigency,
had made friends of the two great English speaking countries.

Great Britain did not look with favor on the project of the royal
allies to use their combined resources in an effort to reëstablish
Spanish authority in America and of course it encountered a hostile spirit in the United States.

At that very time, when our interests and those of England were
happily concurrent, George Canning, the English foreign minister,
advised Mr. Rush, the American minister, that his government
did not sympathize with the effort of the European allies to force
Spain's revolted American colonies to renew their allegiance to
the mother country.

Rush promptly communicated the important message to the
President, James Monroe.   Mr. Monroe consulted Thomas
Jefferson and James Madison, both of whom were in retirement
in Virginia, and chiefly on the advice of Thomas Jefferson the
President put into his message of December 2, 1823, the language
that gave us what has ever since been known as the Monroe
Doctrine.

WHAT IT IS

This much talked of and generally misunderstood doctrine,
that is, without doubt, the most important of all our foreign policies, was conceived solely as a measure of defense.   That Mr.
Monroe himself so regarded it is clealy deducible from the language in his letter to Mr. Jefferson written on the seventeenth
of October, 1823, the same letter in which he sent the dispatches
from Minister Rush that contained the Canning suggestion.   He
said: "My own impression is that we should meet the proposal
of the British government, and to make it our own, that we should
view an interference on the part of the European powers and especially an attack on the colonies as an attack on ourselves, presum-
ing that if they succeed with them they would extend it to us."

If any student of this question will take the trouble to read Jefferson's letter to the President, written in October 1823, and the message of December 2, he need not remain in doubt as to the precise meaning of the policy that bears the name of Monroe.

It does not set up a protectorate over the other American governments. It does not confer upon the United States the right to censor or regulate the internal affairs of any other country. It does not give us the right to intervene when their domestic affairs are in turmoil nor between them and any other country when they have unsettled questions.

It does not give us, as many Americans seem to think, the right to collect debts by force of arms.

It does not even assert the right of this government to control the form of government that other American countries may have. Under it we have no right to protest if every country on the continent from Mexico to Chile should exchange the republican form of government for an autocracy. We might find some other reason for doing so but certainly we could not under such circumstances interfere because of the rule laid down by James Monroe. It does not seek to protect any country against just punishment for the breaking of treaties or wrongs to the citizens of another government. Now let us see what it really does.

Disputed passages of the Holy Scripture that worry the commentators are often cleared up by reading the bible itself. Just so with the Monroe Doctrine. Even a casual examination of the authorities discloses the fact that after all it is a simple, easily understood matter.

Mr. Jefferson in his letter of October, 1823, that outlined to Mr. Monroe what in his judgment should be our policy said: "We aim not at the acquisition of any of these possessions . . . . but we will oppose with all our means the forcible [interposition of any other power . . . and most especially their transfer to any power by conquest, cession or acquisition in any other way."

That letter supplemented by Monroe's message made the "doctrine."

Here is Monroe's own language: "The occasion has been judged proper for asserting as a principle in which the rights and interests of the United States are involved, that the American continents, by the free and independent station which they have assumed and maintain, are henceforth not to be considered as subjects for future colonizing by any European power."

Of course the President meant political colonies.

Again he says: "We owe it, therefore, to candor and to the amicable relations existing between the United States and those powers to declare that we should consider any attempt on their part to extend their system to any portion of this hemisphere as dangerous to our peace and safety" and . . . . "we could not view any interposition for the purpose of oppressing them, or controlling in any other manner their destiny, by any European power, in any other light than as the manifestation of an unfriendly disposition towards the United States."

Jefferson's letter and the message of President Monroe should be conclusive as to the meaning of the Monroe Doctrine. But the views of our great statesmen may be more convincing to some. Daniel Webster said of it in 1826: "The amount of it was that this government could not look with indifference on any combination among other powers to assist Spain in her war against the South American States; that we could not but consider any such combination as dangerous or unfriendly to us." In another speech in the same year he said, "it did not commit us to take up arms on any indication of hostile feeling by the powers of Europe towards South America."

Richard Olney of Massachusetts, secretary of state in the administration of Grover Cleveland also defined the Monroe Doctrine in a letter of instructions that he sent Minister Bayard during the consideration of the Venezuelan boundary question. He said "It does not establish a general protectorate by the United States over other American states. It does not relieve any American state from its obligations as fixed by international law nor prevent any European power directly interested from enforcing such obligations or from inflicting merited punishment for the breach of them. It does not contemplate any interference in the internal affairs of any American state or in the relations

between it and other American states. . . . . The rule
in question (the Monroe Doctrine) has but a single purpose and
object. It is that no European power or combination of European powers shall forcibly deprive an American state of the right
and power of self-government and of shaping for itself its own
political fortunes."

That dispatach of the secretary of state is a clear and complete
definition of what was meant by Mr. Monroe in his famous message. It so clearly and positively defines the limitations of the
Monroe Doctrine that there has never been any reason since its
publication why there should be doubt as to its meaning. The
positive assertion that it did "not contemplate any interference
in the internal affairs of any American state" is particularly pertinent now when so many thoughtless people are urging interference in the affairs of Mexico and invoking the rule called the Monroe Doctrine as authority for the unwarranted and trouble breeding course they propose.

General John W. Foster of Washington, formerly secretary of
state, an eminent international lawyer and with a broader experience in diplomatic service than any living American, concurs
heartily in the opinion so ably presented by Mr. Olney.

DOES NOT PROTECT DEFAULTING GOVERNMENTS

The impression of many people that the Monroe Doctrine
is an aegis that will protect every government on this hemisphere
against merited punishment for its evil deeds or laches is altogether wrong. Even the former President of the United States
whose strongest claim to the attention of posterity is associated
with a club and threats of violence said as much in his message
to Congress in December, 1901.

Whatever we may think of Mr. Roosevelt personally and of
his policies it can not be denied that he always expressed himself
in clear, strong language.

He said "We do not guarantee any state against punishment
if it misconducts itself, provided that punishment does not take
the form of acquisition of territory by any non-American power."

Mr. Roosevelt in that same message gave his definition of the doctrine, and the correct one, let me say. He wrote: "The Monroe Doctrine is a declaration that there must be no territorial aggrandizement by any non-American power on American soil." That from the head of the tribe of Jingos ought to be conclusive as to its meaning even among those who repudiate the teachings of Jefferson, Monroe, Webster, Olney and Foster.

Some people may be wicked enough to observe that the inhibition of the ex-president applies only to non-American powers, although the makers of the policy disavowed any such design on our part also.

DOES NOT MAKE THE UNITED STATES A BAD DEBT COLLECTOR

Senator Rayner has lately shown eloquently and clearly, that the Monroe Doctrine did not make us an agent to collect doubtful loans made by European usurers. He has indicated with scorching wit what would be the consequences of a policy that would drive us into stock jobbers' and money lenders' wars.

A great deal of needless confusion seems to exist in the public mind as to the extent to which a nation may interfere in order to protect the business of its citizens as against the foreign nations of their residence. The belief seems to be deliberately encouraged in some quarters that wherever American citizens or American owned property may be subject to attack it is the duty of the United States to constitute itself their defender even to the extent of sending armed bodies of troops upon foreign soil. No more mischievous conception could be entertained. It is a negation of the true functions of government that are well expressed in the preamble of the Constitution of the United States:

"We, the people of the United States, in order to form a more perfect Union, establish justice, insure domestic tranquility, provide for the common defense, promote the general welfare and secure the blessings of liberty to ourselves and our posterity, do ordain and establish this Constitution for the United States of America."

Not a word is said about the furtherance of American investments upon foreign soil. Not one syllable is uttered with regard to creating for Americans when abroad a better situation than is enjoyed by the citizens or subjects of the foreign country. We were engaged in forming such a government as would "secure the blessings of liberty to ourselves and our posterity." Our prime duty was and is to insure justice at home, not to enforce our own methods and ideas upon unwilling nations, or to pass, as it were, judicial decrees of injunction against foreign nations, and ourselves put into execution upon foreign soil the decrees we might so pass.

The man who goes abroad does not take with him the liberties he enjoys at home, nor does he carry on his back what we consider the blessings of the common law. When he plants his foot upon foreign soil he accepts the conditions there existing. If the forms of law are more rigorous than are known at home; if their manner of execution be more severe; if the government be less able than his own to insure him the blessings of liberty, there is only to be said to him that he has chosen the bed and in it he must lie.

All this is not to say that the foreign government may, without, redress, execute upon him and his property lawless acts, or to say that it may permit its citizens to injure or destroy the American or the property of the American who dwells among them. But it is to say that he has accepted the chances of revolution or disorder in the country of such government, equally with its citizens or subjects, and that equally with them he has accepted the customary application of its laws.

Many times in the past it has happened that Americans abroad have been the object of peculiar attack because they were Americans, and often has it been the case that Americans have been subjected to especial injustice at the hands of foreign courts. Again national governments have broken faith with them. In many of these instances the friendly offices of our government have been sought to insure for our citizens, not special but just treatment. Often without hesitation relief has been freely accorded and in some instances when not so accorded by agreement between the two countries the matters in dispute have been referred to a competent tribunal for adjudication, the results of whose work have been, as a matter of course and without protest, accepted by both parties. This line of conduct has internationally hardened into a custom that has become a rule of international law.

The course pursued by us is that also followed by other countries. In the winter of 1902–03 the combined fleets of England and Germany, joined later by Italy, created what was known as the Pacific Blockade of certain Venezuelan ports. Prior thereto English and German subjects had been, through the action of the Venezuelan government, or its officials, plundered or wrongfully killed, contracts with them had been broken and in other ways they had suffered. The complaining nations might have required their citizens to seek relief in the national courts of Venezuela, but internationally they were not compelled to do so, the more so because such relief as might have been accorded foreigners before the Venezuelan courts in making such complaints was hedged around with peculiar difficulties, causing a foreigner justly to hesitate in making an appeal to the local judiciary. In this state of affairs England and Germany applied not once but many times to the Venezuelan government for relief for wrongs inflicted upon their subjects, Venezuela sheltering herself behind the provisions of the Constitution that undertakes to limit foreigners to such redress as Venezuelan citizens might receive upon recourse to the local courts, and refused arbitration. The blockade only took place after continued refusals, and its result was the reference of the claims in dispute to three arbitral tribunals that granted appropriate relief.

Internationally the course of the great powers enumerated was strictly correct. They did not take the law in their own hands until Venezuela had persistently refused to afford or accord them the relief it was internationally her duty to afford.

Let us, in the light of the foregoing, consider the extent to which the United States may proceed in the direction of protecting the rights of its citizens abroad. It may call the attention of the foreign offices of other countries to abuses perpetrated against Americans, or violations of governmental contracts by which they have been sufferers. It may insist that resort be had to arbitration if no settlement be effected. Upon the conclusion of the arbitration it may require compliance with the award of the arbitrators. All this is proposed with regard to contract debts in the following provision of the Hague Convention respecting the limitation of the employment of force for their recovery.

Article 1:

"The contracting powers agree not to have recourse to armed force for the recovery of contract debts claimed from the government of another country as being due to its nationals. This undertaking is, however, not applicable where the debtor's state refuses or neglects to reply to an offer of arbitration, or, after accepting the offer, prevents any *compromise* from being agreed on, or, after the arbitration, fails to submit to the award."

ITS IMPORTANCE HAS PASSED

The rule laid down by Mr. Monroe served a good purpose one time but the necessity for it passed long ago. When announced it was a means of defense for a weak country.

Once an asset of value it is now an obligation. In the popular view it has the effect of making us politically responsible where no compensating advantage is to be found. Personally I can see no harm to come from its frank abandonment, at least so far as it is supposed to interdict colonization.

One can not be very proud of those timid Americans who tremble with fright because a few score thousands of Germans, men of our own race and blood, have settled in Brazil.

A SOUTH AMERICAN VIEW

So far as I am advised the people of South America do not want us to protect them against the settlement of white Europeans on their unoccupied lands. They do not believe that we have the right to assert a policy that will retard the development of their resources and I must own that I think their position is well taken.

In a recent issue of the *Century Magazine* Mr. J. D. Whelpley who wrote from Buenos Aires quoted a prominent Argentino as asking: "What do Americans want here? We know you want trade—that is natural—and when you send us capital and take our produce you can have it.   But what else do you want?   Why this enthusiasm for the Pan-American idea?   We are afraid of you because we do not understand.   Do you want to control our foreign relations?   That is what we fear and we resent it, we do not like to be patronized and we resent it.   We are a great nation and we can take care of ourselves."

Mr. Whelpley calls attention to the fact that in South America the traveler finds no fear of England or Germany in the matter of territorial aggrandizement, or undue influence in the field of South American politics.   Such fear as exists is, he says, directed entirely towards the United States and, here I quote Mr. Whelpley's words, "more distrust of the Monroe Doctrine is encountered among the people whom it was designed to protect than among those in Europe against whom it was directed."

IMPROPER INTERFERENCE WITH OTHER GOVERNMENTS

The danger in the policy is that it may lead to an improper interference in the affairs of other countries.   There is never an internal row in some of those countries that are inclined to rows that certain "yellow" newspapers and excitable people do not set up a clamor for intervention.   It is a constantly recurring danger and it takes calm judgment and clear heads in the administration to keep out of a situation that holds nothing but trouble for the meddler.   The danger of intervention is recognized by other American governments and no matter how much we may try to hide the ugly fact behind the polite phrases of diplomacy it has begotten a feeling of suspicion and hostility.

Spanish-American countries deny our right to act as censor of their affairs.   They say that they are free, independent and sovereign states and as such entitled to the same degree of respect and consideration that is shown the most powerful government on earth.

They admit no degrees of sovereignty but hold with Vattel that "nations inherit from nature the same obligations and rights, and that power and weakness could not, in this respect, produce any difference, the smallest republic being no less a sovereign than the most powerful kingdom."

John Marshall, our eminent Chief Justice, who it will be admitted had almost as much knowledge of law and the rights of sovereignty as the editors and their clients who clamor for intervention in Mexico, held and strongly expressed the view of the perfect equality of nations.

How much it would contribute to political calm and to the maintenance of peace if the amateur diplomats and long range warriors who for some time have been clamoring for the dispatch of an army to a neighboring country to interfere in a purely family quarrel could only be persuaded to concur in the views of Marshall, Olney, Adams and Jefferson!

OUR DUTY TO OTHER AMERICAN STATES

Primarily our duty to other American states is to let them alone, to give them an opportunity to develop along those lines that seem best to themselves, only holding them to a strict respect for the obligations of international law, an obligation, by the way, which is mutual.

They have a right to demand that we shall treat them as we would have them treat us if conditions were reversed, if, in other words, they were strong and we were weak. We preach this doctrine of the Golden Rule as the only proper line of conduct for individual men in their relations with each other.

Will the time ever come when we shall see it applied to governments? I hope so, but I am afraid it is a long way off. It is a curious and shameful fact that while individual honesty appears to be the rule among men there seems to be no real national integrity. People with a true perspective of morals are often painfully shocked to hear men of good standing, men who in their personal affairs are scrupulously honest and gentle, violently support the propaganda of war and national theft. Without knowing anything about the real situation, scorning the doctrine of the Golden Rule and of common honesty, they vehemently demand that the government shall adopt a policy that means war and conquest. Now, war and conquest means the killing of other of God's creatures who have as good a right to live as we have, and conquest means the taking from them of something to which they have a good title, at least a recognized title, and we have none at all.

The recent noisy and unjustified demand for intervention by our government in the internal affairs of Mexico is a case in point. The government of Mexico is not the government that we would like. Nor is that of France, or Germany, or Great Britain. But it is the sort of government that the Mexicans have set up for themselves and its form and facts are not our concern so long as international obligations are discharged. That was the view of Thomas Jefferson and it is the correct view today.

For years we have been trying to remove the suspicion with which Spanish America views this government and its policies. The hostility that grows out of that suspicion impedes the development of international trade and so it is economically hurtful. The best efforts of the President, acting for all the people, and of wise and just men everywhere who neither want to kill nor rob their neighbors are largely neutralized by the thoughtless and wilfully criminal.

There is the soldier of fortune about whose activities we have heard so much lately. He is a grotesque and unattractive survival of the least worthy period of knight errantry. Perhaps it would be more accurate to say that he is a descendant of the robber hordes that infested Germany after the Thirty Years War. There is no reason for his existence. He is a criminal anachronism and if he should figure in the list of casualties we would be easily reconciled. He respects no laws. His purpose in life is to overthrow government and to substitute chaos for order, turbulence for peace, and for all that unworthy work he holds himself for hire.

INADEQUATE NEUTRALITY LAWS

One of the best ways in the world of maintaining peace is to have a good code of neutrality and to enforce it. Ours, I am sorry to say, has been shown to be shamefully inadequate.

For some time civil war has been raging in Mexico. It is notorious that the insurrectos, so called, have been equipped from the United States both with men and arms. Everybody has known it but the agents of the Department of Justice. The newspapers have heralded the expeditions and from day to day have given circumstantially the movements of the filibusters. They have usually gone out as advertised in the schedule and with rare exceptions have connected with the insurrectos whom they were proposing to aid.

In the *San Antonio Express*, of April 11, there appeared as an ordinary item of news a statement "more arms and ammunition for the revolutionists have gone Westward." It also said that United States officials there were advised of the movement but could do nothing.

The same issue of the San Antonio paper had several items telling of the activities of the filibusters. We have been expected to sympathize with anarchists and socialists from California and graduates of American colleges who were burning railroad bridges and lifting cattle from such ranches as had the misfortune to fall within the sphere of their activity.

Indeed it appears that we have done nearly everything possible to arouse the hostility of the mass of the Mexican people and to cause all Spanish Americans to think that we are trying to develop an excuse for intervention and conquest.

I can not trespass on your attention to argue the unwisdom of political association with people who speak a different language and who have different ideas of government. About that many convincing things might be said. I shall content myself with calling to the attention of this great Peace Congress a resolution that I first offered in the late Congress and which was promptly and unanimously reported with the recommendation that it be passed. It was first proposed in a great convention of business men and unanimously approved.

It briefly outlines an American policy that will make for peace. It is, in my judgment, a natural and proper supplement to the Monroe Doctrine. It will renew the waning confidence of the Central and South American people in that doctrine, for it will be a pledge of honesty and fair dealing. It merely proposes that the various American governments shall mutually agree that hereafter no territory shall be transferred from one to the other as a consequence of war. It proposes a treaty that will simply say that the American governments in the future shall not steal territory from each other. It will be mightily helped along if you will formally approve it here. I will read the resolution, which is brief and for which I earnestly ask the exercise of your influence.

"WHEREAS, in the opinion of the Trans-Mississippi Commercial Congress, now in convention, the peace and the commercial development of the American Continent would be more certainly and speedily secured if the various South, Central, and North American governments were reasonably assured against the forced permanent loss of territory as a consequence of war or otherwise; Therefore be it

"RESOLVED, That the President of the United States be requested to enter into negotiations for the making of a treaty that will forever quiet the territorial titles of the various American states."

Let the doctrine of that resolution be accepted by the whole of America and it will be a long step towards world wide peace. There is nothing strange in the suggestion. It has been adopted by Germany, Denmark, France, Great Britain, The Netherlands and Sweden in a formal and mutual guaranty of the territorial integrity of the countries bordering on the Baltic, which is epochal in its importance.

Under the wise direction of such bodies as yours and with the policy suggested in this resolution we may hope to have the western world, at least, looking for reasons to keep the peace and not for causes of war.

CHAIRMAN WILSON: I am sure that all must have listened with great interest to the able address of Mr. Slayden, who speaks as a man in business, a man in politics, and a man who has time also to be an idealist.

Before introducing the next speaker, however, I feel it my duty to interpolate a very few words. As this is a national and not an international Peace Conference, we are speaking of our own government and I share Mr. Slayden's views of the injurious effect of sometimes false expressions of opinion by what he referred to as "amatuer diplomatists," and having been fourteen years in the government's service as professional diplomatist, I want to say that I do not share Mr. Slayden's pessimism as to governmental integrity in diplomacy. I think if he will come to Pennsylvania Avenue and Seventeenth Street we can show him a Foreign Office which boasts of complete candor and sincerity.

Only one other word as to neutrality laws and filibustering. It is unfortunately true since the very beginning, that whenever an American Republic had any sort of war, on both sides they have endeavored to draw American citizens into their ranks, and there have been some brilliant soldiers of fortune from the great State of Texas many years ago, and the filibustering habit grew to a deplorable stage, where certain sections of our population cease to regard un-neutral acts as wrong. I think the stand of President Taft in the Honduras case and in case of the exceedingly thorough measures taken to enforce the neutrality laws throughout a long frontier through military policing, as well as the machinery of three or four different parts of the government, have been admitted as entirely satisfactory by the Federal government of Mexico, and I think should be viewed with confidence by the American people.

I have the pleasure now of introducing Prof. F. W. Boatwright, President of Richmond College, who will speak on "The College and Arbitration."

THE COLLEGE AND ARBITRATION

F. W. BOATWRIGHT

Among the vital institutions of our age the college holds high rank. While character is formed continuously throughout childhood and adolescence, it crystalizes most rapidly during the college period. Special interests consume the time and energy of the graduate student, but the undergraduate of a standard college ranges widely for mental food. He opens his heart to many causes, and more or less consciously reflects upon the great motives and appeals of life. He is an idealist, ready to believe in the good, and to espouse noble causes. Hard contact with the world has not yet chilled his faith or his ardor. He believes in men and in his own powers.

To such youth the glamour of war has always strongly appealed. The first call to arms has changed the American College campus into a drill ground and the college into an armed camp. This was preëminently true in the Civil War, and was repeated even in our brief war with Spain. As in other vocations, so in the business of war the colleges have furnished leaders.

When, therefore, men come together to consider how nations may adjust their differences without resort to war, it is becoming to inquire what may be done to direct the thought of college men and women into new and nobler channels, and how we may marshall the colleges under the banners of international peace. Other national and international organizations have not been unmindful of the possibilities of the college. The International Y. M. C. A. recruits its forces from the college. The student volunteer movement which has sent its ambassadors of peace into the remotest parts of the earth has drawn its secretaries and organizers from the colleges. The great foreign mission societies of the various churches, with their wide outlook and their statesmanlike grasp of the future not only seek their missionaries chiefly among college graduates but they have recently employed their ablest speakers to go as traveling lecturers from college to college in order that the needs of less advantaged peoples may be presented to young men and women about to choose their vocations. Several national Sunday School Boards have yet more recently undertaken a similar task, and their well equipped lecturers are finding ready hearing in both the denominational and the tax-supported colleges of America. Why should not the college be the forum in which shall be discussed all causes which appeal to the higher sentiments of men? The colleges seek more and more to carry knowledge and inspiration to all the people. Why should not the leaders of great popular causes plead before the choice youth gathered today in the halls of our American colleges? It may well be that traveling professors shall become far more common than they are today, and the local faculty be supplemented by experts sent out by great central boards. The General Education Board and the Carnegie Foundation have mightily strengthened the colleges in special ways, and the facts just cited show a growing tendency to reinforce the local faculties of our American colleges. Suppose our distinguished publicist, Dr. Lyman Abbott, should give ten lectures on peace topics before one of our colleges, and that this course, open to all students and the public, should be maintained for ten years by lecturers of similar ability; what, think you, would be the attitude toward peace of the graduates of such a favored college? Suppose fifty men and women, such as the membership of this Congress can supply, should accept traveling lectureships, each to twenty schools with courses of ten lectures in every school? We would reach one thousand schools, with ten thousand addresses, heard by not less than a million potential leaders of the nation. Repeat the process for a decade, and estimate if you can the tremendous harvest of goodwill made effective by this seed sowing.

Some such comprehensive plan may well contribute to the great cause of universal arbitration. Either by means of funds already established or upon foundations yet to be created, scholarly, inspirational men and women must be sent into our colleges to teach our future moulders of opinion the criminal wastes of war and the reasonableness of universal arbitration. The cold facts now condemn war beyond the need of further words. But war does not cease. Nor do we not expect war to disappear until it is banished by the enlightened sentiment of the nations. Then we should lose no time in sowing the seeds of peace in our seminaries for youth. In the college period, hope is at floodtide, ideals are forming that will dominate life, the ties of fellowship and brotherhood are sweetest. It is the dream time, and yet the time when the impulses harden into life purposes. At such a time let the peace advocate come, not himself a sentimentalist, though he must have caught a vision of the age "when men shall beat their swords into plowshares, their spears into pruning hooks, and shall learn war no more." Let him come around with facts and figures, and, standing on the firm ground of knowledge, make his appeal to the unselfish sentiments of youth. Thus, it seems may a volume of public opinion be created which will soon be irresistible. Some declare that already peace sentiment grows rapidly. When we think only of the obstacles, the national habits of centuries and the vast armaments of the present, this seems to be true. But on the other hand when we consider the accumulated fund of human experience hostile to war, of the intercourse of nations in trade and travel, of the disregard of boundaries wrought by steam and electricity, of the mighty power of the press and the printed page, we wonder at the tardiness and apathy of the nations to this noble cause. Reflection convinces us that while more men think than ever before, nevetheless men follow their leaders now much as Frenchmen followed Peter the Hermit. Leaders with hearts fired by moral earnestness command the fealty of their fellow men today as in the past. Such advocates of peace must be found not only in every great city or at every capital, but in small towns and in country communities. Why do our American peace societies, and I speak particularly of my own State, languish and fail to command public interest? Because our nation does not intend to wage aggressive war and fears no invader? In part, yes. But if our country is to fulfil her evident duty and to grasp the honorable opportunity that is hers, she must feel the oppression that weighs heavily on old world nations, must realize something of how they are bound hand and foot by tradition and hoary precedent, and America must awake to action. The awakening will come most quickly by winning the hearts and voices of the high hearted youth of our country gathered in the various seminaries of learning from high school to university.

Certain essences poured into streams near their sources will tinge their waters even after they chafe against distant shores, and the ideas for which this Congress stands will carry farthest when introduced into the higher schools. The fertile soil is ready in every seat of learning, and seed sown now may in less than a generation bring forth fruit which shall be for the healing of the nations.

CHAIRMAN WILSON: Inasmuch as the afternoon session begins at two o'clock, and many of you are desiring to return, there is very little time left for discussion, but the President of the Congress has called my attention to the fact that these meetings were intended to give the freest opportunity for discussion and suggested that any short remarks would be very desirable.

DR. BENJAMIN F. TRUEBLOOD: I rise to call attention to the fact that the afternoon program is a long one, and the regular meeting of the American Peace Society is called for four o'clock this afternoon. We hope you will all be here at two o'clock promptly, so that we can get through the regular program of the Congress by four o'clock. I want to say that we hope to see every member of the American Peace Society present, and while this is a meeting of the members of that Society, if there are any other persons here who feel conscience-smitten that they have not already joined, they will be welcome to attend, and after they have become members they can take part in the meeting. We hope that all the members of the Society will remain, as the meeting is a very important one. The meeting is supposed to be held in this room immediately following the close of the Congress.

(Upon motion duly made, seconded and passed, the meeting was adjourned until two o'clock).

ADJOURNED.

FOURTH SESSION

Hon. Theodore E. Burton, Presiding Officer

CHAIRMAN BURTON: The particular object of today's gathering is to secure among numerous organizations efficient coöperation in efforts for the promotion of peace and to avoid collision or duplication of the respective branches of work. It is impracticable to unite in one central body all the societies which are laboring for this end. At the outset we are confronted with marked diversities of opinion represented in peace and arbitration societies in the United States. Some favor the expansion of our navy and the fortification of the Panama Canal. There are few, if any, advocates of absolute disarmament. The desirability of a sufficient naval force which man for man and gun for gun shall be as efficient as any in the world is very generally recognized. There are wide differences of opinion, however, as to what constitutes a sufficient force. There are among us earnest advocates of an abatement of the present naval program of battleship construction. Our views are based not upon any idealistic anticipation that wars have passed, but upon the exceptional position of our country. We enjoy a magnificent isolation. It is not necessary to maintain frowning fortresses upon our borders. For example, we are about to celebrate the one-hundredth anniversary of an arrangement with Canada under which we have lived in peace with an unprecedented freedom of communication and of neutral intercourse. In the broad field of foreign relations, we have settled numerous perplexing and irritating disputes by arbitration and have taken a front rank among the nations advocating this method for the settlement of controversies.

It is not assuming too much to say that other nations vouchsafe to our sense of international justice an exceptional confidence.

The advocates of an abatement in our naval program think we can largely rely upon the growth of a rational public opinion and the development of a cosmopolitan civilization which is more and more extending beyond national boundaries and creating a solidarity of interests which every year renders war more nearly impossible.

There are, however, opinions in which all the advocates of peace are in accord. All will agree that the rapidly growing burden of military and naval expenditures, now amounting to nearly two billions per year, is causing economic disturbances and an increase of taxation which in some nations is well nigh intolerable. Again, moral and intellectual forces were never more potently arrayed against war than today. All again are agreed that the ultimate solution must be the development of judicial tribunals for the settlement of controversies and the maintenance of order among the nations similar to those which prevail within the nations. All will unite in laying increased emphasis upon the imperfection of a civilization in which quarrels between nations are settled by the slaughter of human beings. The time is ripe for the accomplishment of the most beneficent results. To secure these results there must be an education of public opinion which is the all prevailing force in our country. The public needs a more vivid realization of the great facts which confront us at the beginning of the second decade of the twentieth century—the enormous growth of naval armaments, the greatly increased cost of armed peace, the increasing interference with orderly and helpful material development which these cause, the continuance of ideals and methods which do not appeal to the most refined spirit of the age, such as fondness for military conflict and the arbitrament of disputes by the sword.

It is especially important that arguments which are presented should be popular in their nature, that moral and intellectual reasons for peace should be reinforced by portraying the waste of the world's resources and by pointing out how helpful these great expenditures would be in ameliorating the condition of the unfortunate and the weak. All this involves no disparagement of the military or naval heroes of the past or any disrespect for the armies and navies of the present. No doubt in earlier periods there were standards of self-sacrifice and maybe of patriotism infinitely in advance of those of the present day. But conditions in these times were characterized by a cruder civilization in which the necessity for defense was pressing and there was an absence of orderly means for the settlement of disputes.

In the education of the people public speaking and the dissemination of appropriate literature are primary requisites. It is desirable that the membership of peace societies should be increased and that efficient preparation to do something should manifest itself among all of them. Organizations should include churches, schools and colleges. The advantages of peace should be forcibly brought to the attention of the commercial bodies of the country and to the innumerable army of toilers. A well organized body can make its influence felt with Congress in obtaining helpful legislation. It is impossible to overstate the benefits which have been accomplished by peace societies and by the great meeting held in the cause of peace, including the National Peace Congess at New York in 1907 and at Chicago in 1909, and the International Congress at Boston in 1904. The American Branch of the Interparliamentary Union has done its work in the international field. Other societies have labored for the organization of judicial tribunals as suggested at the two Hague Conferences of 1899 and 1907 and the perfection of the details of organization, so that these tribunals may command confidence and be ready for the prompt and satisfactory disposition of controversies. The codification of the body of international law, as contemplated by one of of the socieites in the United States, is altogether desirable, so that from the rather confused mass of agreements and decisions in international controversies a body of harmonious comprehensive regulations may be obtained and conflicting decisions may be harmonized if possible.

The question of immediate importance before the country today is the proposed arbitration treaty with Great Britain. Let this be once adopted and the greatest benefit in the cause of peace which has been accomplished for many decades will have been gained. If ratified, other nations will recognize its benefits and follow after.

The world will turn aside from thoughts of conflict to thoughts of peace. Let us fervently hope that the year will not pass without the presentation of such a treaty and its ratification by the Senate.

Auspicious omens greet us. Those who gather in 1911 for this conference at Baltimore may have a serene confidence that they are laboring in a cause which, so sure as the future is marked by progress, is bound to triumph. More than ever before, those who have hoped and toiled for the dawn of peace are inspired to labor on with the thought that success is near. The reproach that efforts for the prevention of warfare are visionary may yet be succeeded by the general admission that these efforts have been intensely practical and of the greatest benefit not only to our common country but to the great family of nations.

Ladies and Gentlemen, there is a considerable number of speakers this afternoon and I am told that the time is necessarily limited to ten minutes for each speaker. I am glad to introduce Hon. John Barrett of the Pan-American Union.

THE PAN-AMERICAN UNION

JOHN BARRETT

Mr. Chairman, Ladies and Gentlemen: I am not going to discuss peace itself, because I believe that subject has been mentioned once or twice in the last two or three days, but I am going to say just a word about an organization that, by its work, is perhaps the greatest organization in this country for the development of peace. The underlying principle of peace among men and women, among towns and cities and countries is mutual acquaintance. The Pan-American Union, of which I have the honor of being the chief executive officer, is the only institution of its kind in the wide world supported by a group of nations and devoted absolutely to the purpose of the development of commerce, friendship and peace among the twenty-one nations of the western hemisphere. That is a common cause which appeals to every practical man and woman of America, whether he be of the United States or of the countries to the south of us. The Pan-American Union was organized some twenty years ago under the guiding influence of Mr. James G. Blaine, and then it started upon its work of informing the United States about the twenty republics lying to the south of us and informing the twenty republics to the south of us about the United States.   It led a dignified and honorable existence for nearly sixteen years, but in the great material rush of progress of our country, it was almost forgotten, when there came as the head of the State Department one of the greatest secretaries of state that this country has ever produced, one of the greatest living statesmen, Elihu Root of New York.

And he recognized the fact that it was absolutely necessary, if this country was going to occupy its proper position in the world, and also among the nations of the world, for peace and commerce, that it should secure the coöperation of the other twenty countries and they should work for the good of all.   He made his wonderful journey through South America, a journey unprecedented in the history of the world, and he was received, in every capital of Latin America visited, with as much acclaim and enthusiasm as if he had been the crowned monarch of some European land.   With the coöperation of the ambassadors and ministers of the twenty countries, who are credited to the nation, at Washintgon, the Pan-American Union was reorganized upon a new basis of activity, and since then it has been going forward with an acceleration of speed and influence and of power, until today it has resulted in its becoming the most active agency for the development of peace throughout the world. The Pan-American Union is controlled by a governing board made up of the ambassadors and ministers representing the twenty republics of Latin America, and the Secretary of State of the United States, who is chairman ex officio inasmuch as the office is located in Washington.   This governing Board in turn elects the director-general and the assistant director, which are its executive officers, and they therefore are international officers, and it is a great privilege, as I stand before you today, to be not merely an officer of the United States, but an officer of Cuba, Mexico, Argentine, Chile and all the other sister republics to the south of us.

We, as executive officers, are assisted by a large staff of international experts, statisticians, lawyers, clerks and stenographers, librarians and others, who are conducting the work of correspondence and dissemination of knowledge and information of which only those who investigate our work can have a true appreciation.

If I would enumerate to you all the activities this afternoon of the Pan-American Union, you would say, "Why is it that I in my busy life have not realized that there was this organization in Washington carrying on this work and trying to make these countries familiar with each other." Our correspondence has grown in four years from eight hundred letters to over six thousand a month; our distribution of printed matter in regard to these countries has grown in these four years from about sixty thousand pieces of printed matter in a year to about nearly one million. Four years ago only about 10 per cent of the members of Congress in any way, shape or form, used the Pan-American Union. This year 97½ per cent of the total membership took advantage and made use of this organization. A few years ago only a very few of the American nations made use of it; last year every nation upon the face of the earth through some of its officials sent to us for information and received information from us. Four years ago there was no way of tracing the work of the Pan-American Union. Since that time we have been responsible by direct efforts for over one hundred and fifty million dollars of new commerce and trade between North and South America. We were responsible for the International Peace Conference of the Central American Republics. We have been continually exercising an influence throughout Latin America for peace and better understanding and friendship among these nations.

I wish I could picture to you our new building which was erected through the beneficence and munificence of Mr. Andrew Carnegie. Four years ago we were in a little house on the corner of Lafayette Square and Pennsylvania Avenue. Now we occupy a building which a great French architect has stated to be the most beautiful in the world. The latchstring of this beautiful building is loose to every man of North and South America who may be interested in knowing more about the commerce existing between these sister Republics. Tomorrow afternoon at three o'clock the twenty-one nations of the western hemisphere, represented by their ambassadors and ministers and the Secretary of State of the United States, assisted by the President of the United States, will present to Mr. Carnegie in that hall a unique medal, a proceeding unprecedented in the history of the people of all America, as a recognition of what he has done for international peace and good will, and especially in recognition of his gift of $750,000 for the erection of that structure which will stand for all times as a monument, which will make nations better acquainted, and which will promote peace and better understanding among them.   I wish almost that this Conference might adjourn so that all of you could go there and join in this tribute that will be made to that great citizen of all the world.   It is remarkable that at the Buenos-Ayres Conference, held in the capital of Argentina, last year, the representatives of all the American nations unanimously passed a resolution to the effect that this medal should be presented to Mr. Carnegie, a gold medal, on one side of which should be the words, "Benefactor of Humanity," and on the other side, "The American Republics to Andrew Carnegie."   He is so proud of it that he says he regards it as the greatest honor that has ever been conferred upon him in his life.

Ladies and ·Gentlemen, I have only one word more to add; that is in regard to the field of the Pan-American Union.   I want to see the men and women of this country, while paying due attention to Europe, due attention to Asia, to remember at the same time that to the south of us are twenty Republics, ambitious, with the same problems to solve as we have before us, looking to our country, looking to our sense of public spirit, looking to our men and women for direction and leadership as no other group of nations in the world are doing; looking to us for sympathy, looking to us for coöperation which will enable them to solve their problems and grow stronger and stronger.

Ladies and Gentlemen, let us not flirt with Europe and Asia alone.   Let us not sit in cozy corners with Italy and Germany and France and China, but let us gather the sisters of our own family to the South about us and show them the way to peace and better understanding among nations.   Let us not think merely of the great arbitration treaty with England but let us think of an arbitration treaty to which all the American Republics will be signers and then we will have a peace that is potent, unrivalled and unequalled in the history of the world.

Yes, Ladies and Gentlemen, let us be friendly with these twenty nations to the south of us, everyone of them having their constitution framed upon ours; everyone of their leaders who won their independence for them took their example and their inspiration from George Washington; everyone today is trying to solve this problem and to perform its mission of being a successful, independent republic, by profiting by our experience. Be not misled by some of the reports that come to you of revolutions and internal troubles as there has been no revolution in two-thirds of Latin America for the last fifteen years. The trouble in Mexico today is only, as it were, the darkness before the dawn of a progress in development in that Republic which will astonish the world. It was fortunate indeed that we heard those words yesterday from President Taft which mean so much to Latin America. We must remember that every Latin American nation has its sovereignty just as much as we have ours, and we must respect their rights of independence. Those words that President Taft spoke in this city yesterday have been flashed over the wires and today every great newspaper in Latin America is repeating and the people of those countries are rejoicing at the words of President Taft that we care not for territorial aggrandizement and care not for an annexation of other countries.

As you go over those areas, I ask you to stop one instant and let your vision be broadened beyond that of our own land, beyond that of Europe and Asia and other parts of the world and remember that there are seventy millions of men and women with red corpuscles in their blood just like yours who look to you to help them, to fraternize with them and advise them in solving the great problems of the western hemisphere.

CHAIRMAN BURTON: I now take pleasure in introducing Mr. A. D. Call, of the Connecticut Peace Society.

THE CONNECTICUT PEACE SOCIETY

ARTHUR DEERIN CALL

I have but a short and simple tale. I come from the little State of Connecticut, which, some of you may remember, is in the northeastern part of our country, a State unjustly and erroneously

described as "the land of the wooden nutmeg," a State called with
equal injustice and error I confess "the land of steady habits."
Fresh from the New England Arbitration and Peace Congress of
but a year ago, I bring from the Connecticut Peace Society and
many Connecticut friends of peace heartiest greetings and congratulations to this splendid national peace congress.

Connecticut's faith in the ultimate cessation of war is an ancient
faith.   We of that tight little New England Commonwealth are
proud members of the ancient and honorable artillery of the soldiers of peace.   Our faith harks back at least to the year 1814,
the year of the Hartford Convention, and of Noah Worcester's
Solemn Review of the Custom of War begging for a publisher.   As
early as 1835 there were three peace societies with headquarters
in Hartford, Connecticut.   Inspired by William Ladd and organized as an auxiliary of the American Peace Society in 1828, there
was the Hartford County Peace Society with an initial membership
of one hundred and two persons.   There was also the Connecticut
Peace Society which had been organized in 1831.   At the second
annual meeting of the Connecticut Peace Society, held in the meeting house owned by the worshiping descendants of Thomas Hooker,
there were nearly fifteen hundred persons present.   We have
records of this society sending out at that early date thousands of
pamphlets in the interest of peace.   It was this society which started,
in 1834, *The Advocate of Peace*, still the greatest official advocate
of peace in the English language..   In 1834 this same Connecticut
Peace Society presented a plea for a "supreme tribunal," and
offered one thousand dollars for the best essay on that subject.
One of our recent periodicals says of Mr. Norman Angell's noteworthy book, *The Great Illusion*, that it is the one oyster in the literary stew over international disarmament and universal peace.
In what President Taft evidently considers the overflowing plate
of peace organizations, there are many fine morsels.   The Connecticut Peace Society aspires to the dignity of being one such, but
adjures all kinship with the raw or underdone.   Besides the Hartford County Peace Society and the Connecticut Peace Society,
there was also in Hartford, Connecticut in the year 1835 the American Peace Society.   At that time this Society had eight directors,

six of whom were Hartford men. I repeat, Connecticut's interest and faith in the ultimate abolition of war are an ancient interest, and an ancient faith.

Connecticut is interested in her past, but she is also interested in her present and in her future. Connecticut's recent interest and faith in the substitution of law for force between the nations has been an outgrowth from the fine enthusiasms of such rare spirits as Edwin D. Mead, Mrs. Lucia Ames Mead, and others, an enthusiasm and faith founded directly in the teaching of that broad-shouldered Quaker giant, respected dean of America's faculty of prefessors of peace, I am constrained to add, the noblest Roman of them all, the fearless and indefatigable secretary of the American Peace Society, Benjamin F. Trueblood.

Since 1906 our society has been especially active and most agreeably encouraged. In matter of size we rank today second only to the Chicago Peace Society among the branches of the American Peace Society. Among our typical activities may be mentioned many addresses in various places of the State, frequent circularizing of the public schools, the encouragement of school debates, the popularisation of Peace Sunday in December and of Peace Day upon the eighteenth of May, circularizing the press, various clubs, ministers, bankers, and other public persons, correspondence with congressmen and senators, and various other forms of coöperation with those agencies which make for a closer friendship and a better mutual understanding between the nations.

Sir Edward Grey, England's Secretary of Foreign Affairs, recently remarked about Mr. Angell's book: "True as the statement in that book may be, it does not become an operative motive in the minds and conduct of nations until they have become convinced of its truth and it has become a commonplace to them." The Connecticut Peace Society would do its little share in making the fundamental and enduring principles of peace a commonplace in the minds and wills of the American people.

CHAIRMAN BURTON: I now take pleasure in introducing to you Mr. M. Hunda, of the Japan Peace Society of New York. Every time a war scare is threatened, we hear something about Japan, so you will no doubt be interested in hearing from him.

THE JAPAN PEACE SOCIETY

M. HUNDA

The Japan Society of New York was organized some four
years ago for the purpose of promoting friendly relations between
the United States and Japan, as also for the diffusing of a
more accurate knowledge of the people of Japan—their aims,
ideals, arts, sciences, industries and economic conditions, among
the American people. What the Society lacks in the way of venerable history is more than made up by the notable fact that it
came into existence at the very psychological time when a need for
a better understanding of each other began to be comprehended
by the two neighbors who dwelt on the opposite shores of the Pacific Ocean. As it is essentially an American institution, the Japanese ambassador being its honorary president, it becomes a privilege
for a Japanese member to have this opportunity of reporting to
the National Peace Congress of the United States as to what the
Japan Society of New York has been doing as a factor in the great
cause of international amity and good will. The American
ambassador to Japan, the Japanese ambassador to the United
States, and a number of distinguished visitors from Japan have
been entertained by the Society at dinner or luncheon, each occasion of this kind proving a decided contribution to the conforma-
tion of the traditional friendship between the two nations represented by our Society. Lectures, illustrated or otherwise, have
also been given that a thorough knowledge of the people of Japan
may be diffused; and at this moment a loan exhibition of rare color
prints is being held and is attracting crowds of admiring spectators
to its rooms in a central location of the Metropolis.

If one has a wish to learn, he can derive many valuable lessons in
universal peace even from Japanese pictures. A few of the color
prints now on view in New York depict dramatic characters in
long divided skirt or trousers, and this at once takes us back to the
time of Japan's fuedal régime, which secured two centuries and a
half of profound peace to the land after four centuries of constant
warfare. At the Overlord's Court, the *daimyos* were compelled
to wear those long trousers, part of which must be kept between
the toes in order to throw forward three or four feet of the super-

flous ends of the dress that the wearer might walk in a dignified manner. This was, of course, to prevent the rulers of different feudatories from attacking each other. Thus, we of the twentieth century should be so enshrouded-in and tied by our garments of international courtesy and morality, that a physical violence by one nation upon another would be both unthinkable and impossible.

Another feudal device for the securing of peace was to arrange the territories of three hundred lords in such a way as to place a buffer state between two rivals, and something similar to this is aimed at by the modern network of international alliances and conventions. Still another method of securing peace in feudal Japan was to oblige the territorial lords to offer expensive gifts to temples or to undertake costly public works, so that they might have no money left for rebelling against the central authorities or for attacking their neighbors. The heavy burden of war and armaments has convinced Japan, at least, of the undesirability of fighting.

China has accomplished a peaceful conquest of the entire civilized world with her tea-drinking institution, and Japan first took it up as an aid to religious contemplation and then, toward the end of her dark ages, as an ethico-esthetic culture to discipline men-at-arms in self control and politeness. A great military leader, called the Napoleon of Japan, initiated the fashion among his followers and vassals of sitting over a cup of ceremonial tea in a special small room, before entering which, both high and low removed their swords. In the midst of feudalism was thus created a republic of tea-ism, where dignified equipoise and art appreciation reigned supreme. The philosophic tea-master of this esthetic statesman once tested his great pupil's attainment of virtue by purposely upsetting the hot water kettle and raising a storm of ashes and steam in a four-and-a-half-mats room. Should any ripple show itself on the calm sea of one's composure, he was not considered as being a member of the cult of the soothing beverage. A constant effort at genuine enjoyment of what is beautiful and good in other peoples and races is sure to lead us up to that height of human nobility where a sordid strife over worldly possessions is not only distasteful but positively inconceivable.

It is, therefore, a cause of keen delight to all lovers of peace that the Japan Society of New York, and an ever increasing number of clubs and schools are studying Japan and her conditions with sympathetic interest. If, as a result of such investigations, the Japanese can hear fair criticism of themselves from their American friends, then not only Japan but the whole world will gain in more ways than one, for all the children of men can learn from one another to the everlasting good of all.

CHAIRMAN BURTON: We all recognize the potent service woman has performed for the cause of peace. I now introduce to you Mrs. Belva A. Lockwood who has labored for a long while in the cause of peace.

WHAT ARE THE ACTIVITIES, THE OBJECT AND AIMS OF THE NATIONAL ARBITRATION SOCIETY

BELVA A. LOCKWOOD, LL.D.

First: The total abolition of war, and the settlement of all difficulties that cannot be amicably adjusted or compromised, by juridical methods.

Second: The gradual and simultaneous limitation of armaments by civilized powers; the reduction of the army and the navy; and the cessation of the building of enormous battleships, dreadnoughts.

Third: The settlement of all difficulties between nations that cannot be arbitrated by juridical methods, including national honor, *a la Taft*.

Fourth: The education of the people and especially of the children of the public schools, by educating the teachers, distributing peace literature, and inaugurating school peace leagues, after the methods recently introduced by Mrs. Fanny Fern Andrews, and her co-workers.

Fifth: No attempt at hostilities until every effort of amicable adjustment has failed, and then at least one month's delay.

METHODS

Our methods have been in drafting bills and resolutions and getting them introduced into Congress; referred to a Committee

and then a sub-committee if practical; converting the committee;
writing articles for the public press; discussing the question in
public places; making public speeches before churches, schools,
and clubs, and having handy typed copies of speeches for the
reporters; sending peace literature to the Committees of Congress
on War, Navy, Appropriations, and Foreign Relations; and asking
the President to decry war in his message to Congress, and recommend the reduction of armaments; and in trying to enlist our
friends in the movement; getting our most intelligent members
to attend peace congresses both at home and abroad, humanitarian
and prison congresses, press associations, Women's Christian
Temperance Union Conventions, great gatherings of the Epworth
League, national councils of women and large church organizations; and persuading them to embody in their resolutions a resolution on peace and arbitration, and commit their organizations
to the sentiment; and not to forget it when we are called upon for
a toast, for, like the members of the Methodist Church, we are
bound to speak the principles we cherish on any and all occasions.

ABOLISHING THE ARMY AND NAVY

It was my privilege to perform this duty not long since
while standing before an audience in a crowded Opera House,
between two one-legged brigadier generals of the United States,
and preaching peace; and at another time not long ago, while
sitting beside the governor of Bermuda at the head of five-hundred
distinguished dinner guests, including sixty-five members of the
Press Association, and a dozen officers of the English army, who
were quite thrown into consternation by my suggestions, that the
United States and Great Britain combined could keep the peace
of the world, and abolish the army and navy, and asked what I
would do with the army and navy officers, with army and navy
abolished. Ah! Mr. President, my dear brother and sisters,
"there's the rub!" "That is what makes calamity of so long life."
It is the great question. What is to become of the graduates of
West Point and Annapolis?—the young men who are straining
every nerve to distinguish themselves with their military prowess.

So long as the government educates men for the army and navy, it must supply something for them to do. So long as it teaches them to shoot to kill, it will find some enemy to attack.

We have some very nice people who tell us that the total abolition of war is only the dream of fanatics. I am proud to be one of those fanatics. I believe that the principle of love, of kindness, of humanity, of human brotherhood is stronger in the hearts of people of civilized countries, than the cat nature—the love of slaughter, and the desire to kill; and that children are especially susceptible to such instruction; and young men and women to such examples. To educate the public, Miss Lucy S. Patrick secured a peace symposium in the *Sentinel* of January 29, 1911, and distributed it freely.

We do not expect to abolish at once the habit of centuries, but nations can certainly agree upon a gradual reduction of armaments, instead of keeping up this monstrous increase which must necessarily lead in the near future to national bankruptcy.

NEEDS NO ARGUMENT

That international difficulties can be settled juridically needs no argument. Our own country has already settled either by arbitration or The Hague Court, almost every class of case that usually leads to war. Besides war settles nothing. It kills innocent men for the guilty, engenders hatred that it takes centuries to eradicate, and as the war is ended, the difficulty is settled by a Commission composed of persons from both contending parties, and perhaps a neutral. The expense of arbitration, although it may be great, is only about one-tenth of the cost of a war.

DISTRIBUTES LITERATURE

For the last eighteen years our Society has distributed gratuitously peace literature, consisting of books, pamphlets, magazines, leaflets and papers, to all persons who have called for them in our vicinage, or who have written for them from other States or from abroad, and we have kept in touch with all peace societies in this country and in Europe.

THE CLERGY

For the last eight or ten years it has been our custom to write two or three weeks before Christmas to every minister of the Gospel, priest, or rabbi in and around Washington, asking them to preach a peace sermon during the holidays. There are about three hundred of them. We now have this custom so well established that a notice in the daily papers before that time seems to answer the purpose.

THE TEACHERS

Ever since the establishment of The Hague Court, February 1900, and its proclamation, November 1, 1901, we have been accustomed to ask the trustees of the public schools of Washington, for leave to send to our seventeen hundred teachers, peace literature, and to request them to observe the eighteenth of May, the day on which its accomplishment was finally agreed upon, as a Peace Day, and it has been done, until the day has been well established in our public schools.

Last year Miss Lucy S. Patrick, one of our helpers, got all of the teachers of our public schools called together in the Central High School, through the courtesy of Superintendent Stuart, and Hon. Richard Bartholdt of Missouri made them a most admirable peace address, which was seconded by the superintendent, and the next day repeated in the Armstrong High School to the seven hundred colored teachers, no audience room being spacious enough to accommodate them all at once.

This year Mrs. Fanny Fern Andrews has sent some very nicely arranged literature for peace day in the schools, which we have already distributed, not only to our own schools, but have sent to several cities outside, notably Lockport, Buffalo, Tonawanda, etc., and your speaker had the privilege of addressing at the National Hotel in Washington, April 19, last, two hundred of their teachers on this point.

We do not study and carry out fixed plans for our own amusement and entertainment, as we all have our regular business, and no fund for peacemakers, but do whatever we see to do in season and out of season, with a will.

THE ASSOCIATION'S BEST WORK

We believe just now that our best work was a series of resolutions and peace literature sent to the House Committee on Foreign Relations by us, February 22, 1910, which culminated, as we believe, in a joint resolution that was not only admirably but favorably recommended to the House by that body; the report headed "For Universal Peace," but which passed Congress and was approved June 25, 1910, known as Public Resolution No. 47,—H. J. R. 223.

"Joint Resolution, To Authorize the Appointment of a Commission in relation to universal peace"

Resolved by the Senate and House of Representatives of the United States of America in Congress Assembled:

"That a commission of five members be appointed by the President of the United States, to consider the expediency of utilizing existing international agencies for the purpose of limiting the armaments of the nations of the world by international agreement, and by constituting the combined navies of the world an international force for the preservation of universal peace, and to consider and report upon any other means to diminish the expenditures of government for military purposes, and to lessen the probabilities of war; Provided, that the total expense authorized by this joint resolution shall not exceed the sum of ten thousand dollars and that the said Commission shall be required to make final report within two years from the date of the passage of this resolution."

COMMISSION NOT APPOINTED

We are very proud of the resolution but chagrined by the fact that the President has not yet appointed the commission, although the time is limited to two years from its passage, and Italy, Austria, France, England, Holland, Belgium, Denmark and Norway have signified their willingness to appoint similar commissions, and meet us on common ground. The internecine war with Mexico seems to have unsettled the calm repose of the executive and created a distrust in his mind of international agreements, but we still hope.

CHAIRMAN BURTON: I take pleasure in introducing to you Mr. Alfred H. Love, an old patriot in the cause of peace. He has responded to the request that he give us an idea of the aims and activities of his organization, the Universal Peace Union of Philadelphia.

HOW TO AVOID AND PREVENT WAR AND HOW TO SECURE AND MAINTAIN PEACE

ALFRED H. LOVE

Responding to the request that I give the aims and activities of our organization, I shall have to condense the nearly half century work and refer briefly to the following:

We were brought to the front by the Civil War. Men of confirmed principles had been drafted, who from conscientious convictions could not enter the army or comply with the provisions of the conscription act. We felt, however, there were obligations to remove the causes and abolish the customs of war, improve the conditions and promulgate the principles of peace.

It was in 1865 that meetings were held in Boston and elsewhere, aided by such persons, among many others, as Joshua P. Blanchard, Lucretia Mott, George Thompson of England, Judge Carter, Amasa Walker, Julia Ward Howe, Charles Perry, William Lloyd Garrison, Adin Ballou, Thomas Garrett, Frederic Passy of France, Henry C. Wright, E. H. Heywood, the Whipples of Connecticut, James M. Peebles, George W. Taylor, Elizabeth B. Chace, Levi Joslin and Charles Sumner; all but two of whom have passed on to merited rewards.

The Universal Peace Union was organized in 1866 and incorporated in 1888. The first call which showed the aims of the organization was:

"The experiment of 6000 years to establish peace by deadly force has failed, and the record is written in blood! Millions of lives have been sacrificed and treasures beyond computation have been wasted. Believing that legalized man killing is inexpedient, inhuman, unchristian and barbarous, is it not time to try some better plan? We are convinced that the causes of war, as well as war itself, must surrender to the principles of the inviolability of human life, absolute justice, equal rights, human brotherhood and world-wide philanthropy."

This involved persistent daily work from that early date to the present, so that the "activities" of the Universal Peace Union would cover volumes. In all modesty, I select the following.

Soon after the American Rebellion, we petitioned for a peaceable solution of the Mason and Slidell case with Great Britain, and succeeded.

Then came the *Alabama* question. We applied for consultation and gained the treaty of Washington. Through the Joint High Commission we urged an international system and tribunal of arbitration, and a reduction of the army to 20,000 men; which was successful.

We were instrumental in averting a repetition of the *Alabama* troubles, by preventing filibustering vessels of war leaving our ports for Cuba against Spain (with whom our government was on friendly terms) and by visiting Madrid and by appealing to the insurgents of Cuba.

We recommended Grant's "Peace Policy" with the Indians and succeeded in preventing a war between several tribes, and aided in the establishment of Indian schools.

We started over forty branch peace societies in the United States and as many more in Europe and elsewhere, and aided in the organization of the Peace Bureau at Berne and the Berlin Council.

In 1874 we presented to Congress the following, which was adopted:

"That the President is hereby authorized and requested to negotiate with all civilized powers, who may be willing to enter into such negotiations, for the establishment of an international system, whereby matters in dispute between governments agreeing thereto may be adjusted by arbitration and, if possible, without recourse to war."

During the centennial year of American Independence we held, for five days, a large peace convention in Carpenters' Hall, where the first Continental Congress had assembled one hundred years before and had declared war against Great Britain. We sent forth a declaration of peace to the world.

Several swords were presented by army officers who had carried them in battles. They were turned into a plow and pruning hooks and sent to the Paris Exposition of 1878 and afterwards presented to the city of Geneva, and the plow now rests on a dais in the immortal hall where the *Alabama* question was settled.

Interviews have been had with all our Presidents and all the secretaries of state have aided us. Secretary Evarts especially did so in our efforts to adjust the complications between Peru, Bolivia and Chili.

We gave ex-President Grant the memorable reception in 1879 in Philadelphia, when he pronounced the great truths of peace, his hatred of war and his recommendations for arbitration.

Three times we sent Conrad F. Stollmeyer as our peace envoy to Europe with credentials of Secretary Blaine.

In 1886, when a war between Mexico and the United States was imminent, in the Cutting case, President Diaz acted upon our suggestion, accepting indemnity for reparation of losses, and there was no war.

We have been represented in all the peace congresses here and abroad.

The peace flag has had official recognition, being the national colors of every nation bordered with white, and at the Rome Peace Congress it was exhibited by Rowland B. Howard, and by Mrs. Ormsby at the time of the New Orleans massacre of Italians, and it had much to do with preventing a war.

For the Armenians, the Jews, the Chinese, the oppressed everywhere, we have interceded and brought about more peaceful conditions.

In 1891 we built the first Peace Temple, on our own grounds of over ten acres, at Mystic, Connecticut.

From Toronto to New Orleans, from St. Louis to Chicago and to Atlanta and nearly all the principal cities our anniversaries have been held and generally with exhibits of peace propaganda.

We took the liveliest interest in the Alsace and Lorraine question and in the Japanese and Russian war, suggesting at Portsmouth and St. Petersburg terms that were evenutally accepted to terminate the war.

For the Suez Canal being neutral we conferred with Ferdinand Lesseps and with success.

We gained from Spain five concessions to prevent the recent war and would have secured the independence of Cuba, as Minister Woodford and Senator Edmonds assured us, had not Congress declared war.

Since then we have been even more active in aiding the adjustment of political, social, industrial strikes and war-like troubles. At present we are laboring with President Diaz and the insurgents for concessions that will bring about peace. But these recent activities are known through the *Peacemaker* and publications we have issued all these years.

The gratifying coöperation of our present administration and our Congressmen and others who are on our list of members and officers greatly encourages our faith and hope.

The independence of man is a birthright. The Creator never would have inspired His created with the ideals of peace without giving the power to realize the blessing. What man creates man can abolish. All possibilities are in his hands.

To avoid war is to give no occasion for war. If a "soft answer turneth away wrath," the word or act that does not wound or stir up strife will require no "soft answer." If we are just, honest and charitable to all, we will provoke no war, and by being determined, under all circumstances to keep out of it, it can be avoided.

How to prevent war! This comes as a natural sequence to avoiding war. We have to look at the possibilities of the side not converted to our standpoint rising in rebellion. What then? If a fire is burning, do not add fuel to it; quench it by antidote of water or chemicals. War being wrong, a diseased, ignorant and perverted condition, no human authority can force mankind to commit a wrong; hence, *educate* public opinion.

We can prevent war by the substitution of friendly and peaceable intervention, by "pouring oil upon troubled waters," by arbitration and conciliation, by a patient investigation of the causes of a conflict before the clash of arms, and by urging concessions.

It can be prevented by remaining neutral and refusing to loan money or giving aid to either belligerent.

It can be done by not relegating to any man or any set of men the power to declare war, amending the Constitution by taking out the war clauses and substituting "Congress shall have power o. to declare arbitration."

If appropriations will go on for the army and battle ships, make them useless, except, perhaps, as a police force to arrest and hand over to the courts.

To secure peace, recognize peace as a recompense for righteousness, the result of pacific conditions—Peace within ourselves, self-cotrol, love, justice, equal rights, charity, fraternity, humanity, a world-wide philanthropy and the brotherhood of man, remembering that peace must be deserved to be secured.

Live the conditions of peace; perfect the network and peace agencies of our civilization. Friendship is cheaper than cannon and good-will a better insurance policy than all the dreadnoughts and fortifications in the world; put more faith in The Hague Peace Tribunal and urge an international permanent court of justice and arbitration and, not waiting for the Third Conference at The Hague, look to the children as the new administration and introduce into the curriculum of the schools the study of the principles of peace and the drilling of the scholars in arbitrating disputes among themselves, thus educating them to be competent as arbitrators for the coming demand.

To maintain peace, scrupulously observe treaties by more of good faith, more sincerity in the manifestoes of a Czar and The Hague Court. It is an easy thing to sign a parchment peace treaty, but quite another to observe its requirements. There was to be no bombardment of unfortified towns or cities. This, if kept in good faith, would dismantle forts and turn them into repair shops, hospitals and asylums and prevent any need to fortify, even the Panama Canal. Broken treaties are peace-breakers and preparations for war is a menace and an incubator of war.

If there must be naval voyages let them be of merchantmen,

showing our constructive ability and tendering peaceable, unarmed
courtesies by friendly visitation.

More of reciprocity and less of selfishness; more of freedom of
trade,—not necessarily free trade; more of coöperation and less
of competition; more of common welfare and less of egotism;
for these comprehend "Love one another," "Do unto others as
you would have others do unto you."

Standing in the midst of this gathering of wealth and wisdom,
of highest aspirations and divine inspirations, we can see through
the mistakes that have been made and that we have all the peace
we deserve, but not all the peace it is possible to obtain. We
rejoice in the courageous utterances of President Taft as to honor
and arbitration, clinched by the response of Sir Edward Gray.
No wonder the die is cast for an unlimited arbitration treaty between the United States and Great Britain, and no doubt can be
entertained that "the kindred drops will mingle into one" when our
eminent statesman Secretary of State Knox and Ambassador Bryce
submit a treaty that will be accepted and be an example for other
nations to "go and do likewise."

> "Oh, make Thou us, through centuries long,
> In peace secure, in justice strong;
> Around our gift of freedom draw
> The safeguards of Thy righteous law,
> And cast in some diviner mould,
> Let the new cycle shame the old!"
> —*Whittier*.

CHAIRMAN BURTON: Mr. Robert Stein is the next speaker on
the program. I take great pleasure in introducing him.

CAN A NATION BE A GENTLEMAN?

ROBERT STEIN

Mr. Carnegie and Colonel Roosevelt disagree on a number of
points, but they agree on one point: that assured peace is not possible without an international police. consisting of the combined
armies and navies of the strongest, most enlightened and humane

nations, best prepared by identity of ideals to trust each other, and least likely to abuse the police power.

If Britain, France, Germany, and the United States would enter into an agreement for mutual benefit, the international police would exist *ipso facto*.

Britain, France and Germany cannot come to an agreement without mutual concessions. ,

The best way to advocate the policy of mutual concessions is by example.

That is my story in a nutshell, and I might just as well sit down and let these maps speak for themselves. However, I assume that you would like to hear a few details.

The wisest man in England, Sir Harry H. Johnston, in an article entitled "German Views of an Anglo-German Understanding," in the *Nineteenth Century* for December, 1910, shows that an Anglo-German agreement on the basis of mutual concessions is practicable and imminent. A straw thrown in the balance may tip it in the right direction.

The United States can throw that straw. Our nation is universally regarded as the natural leader in the peace movement. If we deem it our duty to accept that leadership, we can not shirk the duty of setting the example in that policy of mutual concessions which is the only avenue to permanent peace. Now we have at this moment a unique, incomparable, God-sent opportunity to show to other nations how a concession is made. To our neighbor, Canada, whose friendship we are just now so anxious to cultivate, we can make a concession which may just suffice, through the force of example, to supply the slight additional impulse needed to decide Britain and Germany to make the two vital mutual concessions pointed out by the wisest man in England. An Anglo-German agreement would inevitably be followed by a Franco-German agreement, also on the basis of mutual concessions, and then the international police would be complete, for everybody knows that the United States would instantly join it. Our duty to set this example is all the more manifest and imperative because the proposed concession to Canada involves no sacrifice; it is simply a question of putting an end to an absurdity.

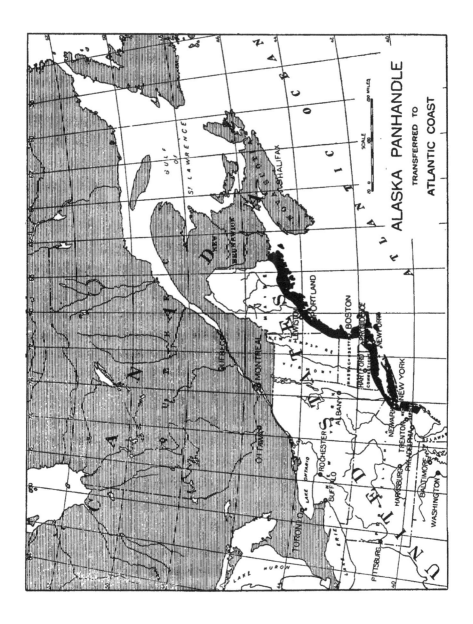

ALASKA PANHANDLE
TRANSFERRED TO
ATLANTIC COAST

You have before you the map of Alaska. You see that Alaska consists of two parts: the main body and the Panhandle, this strip of coast running southeastward to the parallel of 54° 40' a mere ribbon, 536 miles long, 8 to 35 miles wide, shutting off the northern half of British Columbia and the entire Yukon Territory from free access to the Pacific. How large, do you think, is this Canadian territory thus deprived of its natural seaboard? It measures some 600,000 square miles, three times as much as Germany, more than ten times as much as England and Wales together. It has the same climate as Europe in the same latitude. In Europe, north of the parallel 54° 40', you find a slice of Ireland, a slice of England, all Scotland, all Denmark, Sweden, and Norway, all Finland, a slice of Germany; and the richest part of Russia; great cities like St. Petersburg, with 1,700,000 inhabitants; Glasgow, with 900,000; Copenhagen, with 500,000. An equal area in Europe in the same latitude contains 25,000,000 inhabitants.

This Canadian country has immense resources in timber, agricultural and mineral lands. The wealth of all countries is mainly concentrated in their ports—Boston, New York, Philadelphia, Baltimore—but it is derived from the commerce of the country behind them. The wealth of this Canadian country will necessarily be concentrated in its ports—on American territory. This entire slope is drenched with rain and possesses tremendous water power. The factories to be driven by that power will necessarily be on tide water—in American territory; but the reservoirs furnishing that power will be on Canadian ground. The 25,000,000 Canadians who will eventually live behind this Panhandle will constantly be forced to contribute to the enrichment of half a dozen American cities, while these cities will not contribute a cent toward Canadian taxes. What a permanent and evergrowing source of irritation!

The only gentlemanly course, the only manly course open to us is to say to the Canadians: "We are willing to let you have this coast strip; what will you give us for it?" And if I had time I could show you that in exchange for it we could very likely get something far more useful to us than this absurd Panhandle, while the Panhandle itself, in Canadian hands, would be more useful to us than it now is.

Reverse the situation and see how we should like it. Imagine that our northeastern States were cut off from the Atlantic by a similar Panhandle, a Canadian sidewalk running from eastern Maine down nearly to Philadelphia; that all the great cities on that seaboard, Boston, Providence, Newport, New York, Jersey City, were Canadian cities, deriving their wealth from the American country behind them, yet contributing not a cent toward American taxes; that not a pound of freight could be sent from Pittsburg or Buffalo to New York or Boston for export, except in bond! We should long ago have found the situation unendurable.

We should in that case have been greatly vexed if the Canadians had waited in stolid silence till the situation did become unendurable for us, till we were forced to complain. Now you remember what the Model Gentleman said nearly 1900 years ago: "Do unto others as you would they should do unto you." Shall we wait till the situation becomes unendurable to the Canadians? Shall we force them to complain?

If we make the offer of exchange now, of our own free choice, its beneficent effects will be at a maximum. The heart of Canada will be linked to us as with hooks of steel; a noble, generous national deed, more glorious than all our victories, will be inscribed in our annals; our example will be most effective in commanding the policy of mutual concessions to our parent nations. If we delay the concession till the Canadians complain, the memory of the concession will forever be soured by the reflection that we forced them to complain; the effect of our example will be almost nullified.

Suppose that the owner of this Panhandle were an individual. If he made the offer of exchange of his own free choice, we should call him a gentleman; if he waited till his neighbor complained, we should call him a boor, curmudgeon, plebeian, philistine, or some other cacophonous name. The question then arises: Can a nation be a gentleman?

In a letter from the late Prof. Thomas Davidson I found this startling sentence: "Nations are never gentlemen." You may have come across the same statement. One writer even attempts to prove that it is a sociologic law. A nation can not be a gentle-

man, he says.   An individual can afford to be generous, to forego certain rights for the benefit of others; a statesman cannot
do this because the rights which he safeguards are not his own but
those of his fellow-citizens.

What shall we say to this argument? First of all it is not absolutely true that nations are never gentlemen.   The surrender of
the Ionian Islands by Britain to Greece was a gentlemanly act.
The United States, in returning the Chinese indemnity, proved
itself a gentlemanly nation.   In this case our statesmen did not
wait till the Chinese craved our leniency; they did not even wait
for an expression of public opinion in the United States.   They
assumed that the majority of our citizens were gentlemen; that
the foremost right of our citizens, which the statesman are called
upon to safeguard, is the right to be gentlemen not only individually but collectively.   The universal and enthusiastic applause
with which their act was greeted proved that they were not mistaken.

It must be admitted, however, that national deeds like the two
just cited are as rare as comets in the starry heavens.   It would
take a historian a week to find half a dozen national deeds that
could be called gentlemanly.

The reason is very simple.   Most men are willing enough to be
complete gentlemen in their individual conduct, but when it comes
to collective conduct, they split; the positive gentleman breaks
away from the negative gentleman.   For to be a positive gentleman as a member of a political body means to persuade others to
adopt a certain line of action, and this means nearly always a fight.
Now a gentleman, by his very essence, dislikes a fight, because to
fight means to do unto somebody something which that somebody
does not like to be done unto him.   That fraction of the nation
which is not gentlemanly always speaks promptly and loud; the
gentlemen mostly remain silent.   The statesman hears only the
hundred voices of noisy protest; he does not hear the silent approval
of the pacific millions.   That is the reason why nations are so
rarely gentlemen.

Knowing the mosquito that inoculates nations with the malaria
of ungentlemanliness, to wit, the over-pacific nature of the gentle-

man, it is comparatively easy to apply a remedy. If the gentlemen of a nation dislike to fight and yet recognize that they must
fight in order that the nation may be gentlemanly, the natural
thing to do is to look for some means to reduce the fighting to a
minimum. Organization is that means. In union is strength.
An army opposed to a mob has very little fighting to do.

Organization, federation—that is the leading aim of the Washington Peace Society. I confess that in organizing the society
my original object was to gain its support for the proposed concession to Canada. It soon appeared, however, that some of the
most influential men in Washington, while heartily in favor of that
concession, did not think it wise to commit the society to any
specific measures. The discussions at our meetings, however,
brought out an idea of much wider scope, which will accomplish
not only this but many other objects. It is the same idea that was
so vigorously set forth by Mr. John A. Stewart in the *Editorial
Review* for April; that the foremost need of the peace movement is
the unification of all the immense forces available for peace work.
Besides the peace societies, there are the thousands of churches,
the Epworth League, the Christian Endeavor Society, The Chau-
tauqua Societies, the Young Men's Christian Association, the
Federation of Women's Clubs, the American Federation of Labor,
all working for peace. At present their work is scattered, desultory, like that of a mob. Organize them into an army, under a
general and a general staff, and you multiply their force tenfold.
And when this is done, the proposed concession to Canada will
come as a matter of course. When all the ladies and gentlemen
of the land are federated, it will be easy to take a straw vote, an
anticipated referendum, on any question relating to the gentlemanly conduct of the nation. Then we shall no longer have to rely
on those inspired prophets who know precisely what the American
people are willing or not willing to do. At least 90 per cent of the
people whom I did consult—and I consulted perhaps a hundred—
gave ready assent to the proposed concession to Canada, and I
have no doubt that the same proportion would hold throughout
the nation. In other words, our nation is a gentleman, if we will
only take the trouble to find it out.

It was a pleasure to learn that a committee for the unification of peace work is already in existence, having been appointed by the Lake Mohonk Conference through the influence of Mr. Smiley. When finally President Taft and Mr. Carnegie, at the very opening of this Congress, came out strongly in favor of federation, it could no longer be doubted that its success was assured.[1]

Three more suggestions and I am done.

We call ourselves a Christian nation. As such we profess to be guided by the rule which, by the express declaration of its Founder, constitutes the essence of Christianity: "Do unto others as you wish that they should do unto you." Suppose once more that a Canadian Panhandle did shut off our northeastern States from access to the Atlantic, what would we wish the Canadians to do unto us? If we refuse to do likewise unto the Canadians, we may baptize our babies in oceans of water, we may build churches as high as the Eiffel Tower, but we are not a Christian nation. Let us find out whether we are.

In urging that we set the example in the policy of mutual concessions, I only referred to the effect it would have on Britain and Germany. In reality the effect would be far wider. Whoever has the slightest acquaintance with international politics knows that the jealousy and distrust which keep nations armed are due for the most part to unsettled questions, unnatural boundaries, like this Alaska boundary. If European nations are to arrive at that state of mutual confidence and cordiality which will enable them to dispense with armaments, they will first have to make a number of mutual concessions on these questions. We can not tell them what these concessions should be, without running the risk of being called meddlers; but we can urge them by the most persuasive of all methods, that of example. Concessions would quickly become the fashion, for no nation would care to be called ungentlemanly. If we refuse to set this example, and yet continue to preach peace, we must not be astonished to hear the reply: "You Americans are all the time talking about peace and international goodwill, but when it comes to removing the causes of

[1] The movement toward federation came to a successful issue in the resolution, adopted by the Baltimore Peace Congress, May 6, 1911.

international illwill, you are just as regardless of your neighbors' feelings, just as stubborn as any of us in maintaining a geographic absurdity, a geographic atrocity, a thorn in your neighbors' flesh, simply because it is so nominated in the bond. Why beholdest thou the mote that is in thy brother's eye but considerest not the beam that is in thine own eye?"

At present the Canadians are not complaining, because the inconvenience is not serious so long as the country behind the Panhandle is practically uninhabited. But in a year or two the Grand Trunk Railway will be finished, and immigrants will arrive by the thousands. By 1914, when we shall celebrate the 100th anniversary of peace with Great Britain, the inconvenience will have become acute. If we leave this unnatural boundary unchanged, it will hang like a pall over the festivities. The grosteque figure of the Panhandle will sit at the festive board like Banquo's ghost. If we wish to make that celebration a conspicuous landmark in the progress of the peace movement, what better means could we find than to relieve our Canadian neighbors of this night-mare, this thorn in the flesh, this standing discourtesy! What are fair words when the deed is lacking? A body without a soul, a corpse in fine shrouds and flowers. Let us breathe into it an immortal soul, the soul of an immortal national deed. If we wish to have a real joyous feast of good-fellowship in 1914, let us be good fellows. All Canada would come down to get acquainted with the nation that was courteous to her not only in words but in deed. Our parent nations of Europe would gaze across the Atlantic in admiration and envy, and would soon begin to say to one another: "See how gentlemanly the Americans are to the Canadians! Let us go and do likewise."

CHAIRMAN BURTON: The next speaker is Mr. James Brown Scott of the American Society of International Law and the Carnegie Endowment for International Peace. It is with great pleasure that I present him.

THE AMERICAN SOCIETY OF INTERNATIONAL LAW

JAMES BROWN SCOTT

The American Society of International Law is not a peace society in the technical sense of the word. Its object is declared in the second article of its constitution to be "to foster the study of international law and promote the establishment of international relations on the basis of law and justice." It regards international law as an existing system which should be analyzed, expounded and developed scientifically and its chief aim is to promote or to foster the scientific study, expansion and development of the system as a whole.

The founders of the Society felt that an interest could be created in the subject of international law by the organization of a society composed of persons already familiar with its fundamental principles, whether as teachers, lawyers or as diplomats; and that an annual meeting of the members at Washington would not only strengthen the interest, but enlarge and broaden it by an exchange of views upon various questions of international law.

It was also felt that the preparation of papers to be read before the meeting would force the speaker to examine carefully the principles of law and policy underlying the subject chosen for the papers. That the papers read before the Society would spread information among its members; that the discussion of the papers would necessarily involve the consideration of the subject from various points of view, so that the conclusions reached would be not merely enlightening, but would tend to a clear and precise formulation of the principles which either do or should regulate the conduct of nations, considered as members of the family of nations.

It was obvious to the founders that the purpose of the Society would not be fully realized if the papers and discussions were not made a matter of record and placed within the reach of the larger public interested in the questions, but not present at the various meetings. Therefore the Society organized at Lake Mohonk in 1905 determined that the proceedings should be published as soon as possible after the annual meetings, which have been held regularly since 1907. A volume is therefore issued each year which contains the texts of the papers read and the discussions had. The volume is sent to each member of the Society without additional expense and is offered for sale to non-members at a modest price. But it was clear that the organization of the Society and the publication of the proceedings had at the annual meetings would not wholly accomplish the purpose which the founders had in view, for it was not sufficient to bring specialists of international law together for a few days of each year and to exchange views on theoretical and practical questions. The members should have at their disposal a magazine devoted wholly to international law, in which questions of theory and practice could be discussed, as well as questions of the day affecting the family of nations be treated in the light of theory and practice.

No journal existed in the English speaking world wholly devoted to international law; therefore the Society decided to issue a quarretly not only as its mouthpiece, but as a magazine to which publicists might contribute their views on all subjects of an international nature.

In January 1907, the first number of the *American Journal of International Law* was published and it has more than justified its existence; for it is not only the one journal in the English language devoted wholly to international law, but it has taken its place as one of the best and most authoritative journals of its kind.

The founders of the Society, however, were not content to create a Society for the study of international law and an organ for its exposition. The purpose in mind was broader, namely, to "promote the establishment of international relations on the basis of law and justice."

They believed then and now that law and justice are as essential to the family of nations as law and justice are indispensable to the welfare of the individual; that relations which are not based upon law and justice cannot be permanent and that peace between nations is as impossible in the absence of law and justice as peace is impossible among men in the absence of law and justice and their regular and orderly administration.

Civilized nations have their laws and institutions and they are

gradually conforming to the requirements of justice. The family
of nations has its law, but this law, based upon usage and custom
is rudimentary and inadequate to meet international needs. An
agreement upon law based upon just principles is a prerequisite
to its observance. Therefore, the American Society of International Law has taken up the question of the codification of existing principles of international law and devoted much thought and
reflection to the drafting of rules and principles and to their creation where such principles are lacking.

The purpose of the Society is, however, not to codify the law of
nations as a whole, but to formulate international law in time of
peace; that is to say to frame a code, which shall state in clear and
happy wording, principles of law already accepted by nations, and
to devise principles of law which should regulate their peaceable
intercourse. The members of the Society are partisans of the
judicial settlement of international disputes, and the Society
stands for the establishment of a permanent international tribunal
in which controversies between nations may be decided by judges
trained in the law, just as suits between man and man are decided
within national boundaries by judges trained in the law. But
before the law can be administered it must exist or be created and
an agreement upon it reached. An international court could not
render the services expected of it without a system of law to be
administered, unless the judges be invested with power to make
the law which they are called upon to declare and apply.

It is not believed that nations would confer such vast powers
upon an international court. A tribunal can only be called into
being by the action of nations and the progress already made in
the matter of a court of arbitral justice, recommended by the
Second Hague Peace Conference leads to the belief that a truly
permanent court will be established in the very near future. The
present need is to supply the law which this tribunal shall administer, and it seems to the members of the Society that a careful,
thoughtful, conservative statement of the principles of justice
which should regulate the intercourse of nations can be made by
jurists in their private capacity, leaving to the governments in
their wisdom to accept or reject any or all of its proposals.

The nations must create an international court if they are to accept its authority. Private societies and jurists may create the code or at least aid in its creation. Therefore, in the broader aspect of the peace movement the American Society of International Law is a peace society, for it is active in making known the principles of international law which bind and restrain nations, and it is endeavoring to the full extent of its influence to promote the establishment of international relations on the basis of law and justice without which peace cannot be maintained and safeguarded.

CHAIRMAN BURTON: It now gives me great pleasure to present to you Mr. John A. Stewart, of New York.

A CENTURY OF GOOD WILL

JOHN A. STEWART

There is reason for serious thought in the continued controversy in London between the Lord Mayor and the *Morning Post* which has bitterly attacked the proposed arbitration treaty between America and Great Britain. The Lord Mayor, in reply to a recent editorial in the *Post* opposing the Guildhall arbitration meeting, pointed out that arbitration is not a question for the government's politicians, but a question for the nation. He declared that the manner and force of the movement for arbitration is unparalleled in British history. The *Post's* rejoinder argued that the government and not the people was planning arbitration with the United States; that the government and not the people is drafting the treaty, and, in particular, that the presence on the Great Lakes of American training ships is a violation of the Rush-Bagot treaty and a menace to friendship.

Such opposition to an arbitration agreement, the terms of which are even now a matter of negotiation, is yet of service to the extent that it compels consideration of and an answer to this proposition:

Whether it is not fundamentally true that there can be no enduring, binding, arbitration agreement, even among peoples having a language, a literature, and common social and commercial interests, unless such covenant be written not alone on parchment bearing the sign manual of government authority, but, what is of thousand-fold greater weight, into the hearts and consciences of the American and British peoples.

This controversy and this thought have direct relation to the motive which has inspired men and women in the United States, in Great Britain, and in Canada to initiate a movement to bring about the celebration of an event that concerned more directly the peoples of these countries than it did the two governments under which, on Christmas Eve, 1814, there was signed at Ghent, by the respective commissioners of the high contracting parties, a treaty that in 1914, in the mercy of Providence, will have remained for one hundred years a pledge of peace kept in full letter as among English speaking peoples, and a covenant in spirit that there shall never more be war between us and them.

It is true that on occasion there has been bad blood between us; that at several points along the way from the signing of the treaty until today we have felt that the limit of patience had been reached; and at times, too, there has been, with some degree of justice, ill-feeling on the part of Great Britain toward us; yet at no time in the past century has there existed on the part of the whole people of the United States as against all the people of Great Britain any feeling that the day of forbearance had passed and a time come when the matter in dispute could yield only to the arbitrament of armed force.

We, that have associated ourselves together as a committee, to membership in which you are all cordially invited, have felt that the celebration of the one hundredth anniversary of the signing of the Ghent treaty was a matter which concerned primarily the English speaking peoples the world over and not primarily English speaking governments. We would ask the peoples of the world to celebrate this anniversary with us, beginning by a happy coincidence on the eve of that day of all the days of the year which is the day of peace and of the Man of Good Will. The leaders in this popular movement, the men officially identified with our organization, are Theodore Roosevelt, honorary chairman; Andrew

Carnegie, chairman; Albert K. Smiley and Edwin Ginn; former
vice-president Charles W. Fairbanks, honorary chairman, and
Senator Theodore E. Burton, honorary vice-chairman of executive
committee; as vice-presidents all of the governors of the States;
Mr. William Jennings Bryan, Mr. Alton B. Parker, Associate
Justice Day, Associate Justice Lurton, of the United States
Supreme Court; Ambassadors Reid and Dudley, in fact almost the
entire diplomatic establishment of the United States, and representative men from all parts of the Union.

It is our plan and purpose to invite to meet with us this coming
winter representatives of English-speaking peoples everywhere,
that there may be organized to formulate a program and to plan
for helpful interest in the peace cause an International Committee
under whose auspices the celebration in 1914–15 shall take place,
coöperated in by the governments of Great Britain, the United
States, Canada, Australia, New Zealand, and Newfoundland. It
is our intent, so far as it lie within the power of our organization
to bring it about, to make the celebration of the one hundredth
anniversary of peace among English-speaking peoples a peoples'
celebration to be participated in by the peoples of the whole world.

It is in consonance with the will and the spirit of the times that
in organizing to celebrate the continuance for one hundred years
of amity between us and Great Britain, and the nations which are
her off-spring, we recognize the newly awakened interest on the
part of the people in matters which most directly concern themselves. And it is only just and proper that the committee which
has had, in some degree, a part in the initiating of this movement
for the celebration should stand with the people in urging that the
celebration be undertaken by the peoples of the English speaking
world, and that there be invited to join with us in this celebration in
1914-15, the peoples of all the world. For while governments
may exist out of accord with the majority of the people whom they
govern; while nations may, by tradition, be put into the position
of antagonism to other nations, yet everywhere the world over
the common people are united by common interests.

Theirs has been the sacrifice in time of war, and the burden of
taxation theirs when peace comes after war. It is unthinkable

that after having realized in such fullness the blessings of peace for so many years the peoples of the English-speaking world will ever again engage in armed conflict among themselves, for out of this peace has come a partial realization of those hopes and aspirations which have been the dream of the world through all the centuries. It is our belief that such a celebration as we purpose, participated in by all the peoples of the world, will be creative of a popular sentiment so strong for peace as to give encouragement to the hope that some of the ideals of today may be realized tomorrow—at least in the direction of partial disarmament, the establishment of courts of arbitral justice and a broadening of the scope of arbitration agreements. May it not in very truth be said of the whole peace movement of which this proposed celebration is properly a part: The peace cause is the peoples' cause; war their common menace, and their common sacrifice; and the debt of war their common burden. War will end only when the people will that it shall end. The popular celebration of an event of such tremendous importance to all peoples as a peace compact kept for one hundred years would give, through the resultant creation of sentiments of international amity, strength and impetus to every movement that has as its inspiration and ideal the Bethlehem chorus—Glory to God in the Highest! Peace on Earth to men of Good Will!

CHAIRMAN BURTON: The New York Peace Society has accomplished a great deal. I take pleasure in calling on the president of that Society, Mr. W. H. Short.

A POSITIVE INTERNATIONAL PROGRAM

WILLIAM H. SHORT

In one of his last public utterances, the late Justice Brewer said, "There are three great forces in our civilization, each of which voices for international peace. First, the business interests. Nowhere are there more varied and larger business enterprises carried on than in the United States. All these interests look askance

at the prospect of war.   They hate to see the efforts of the brainy
turned away from the furtherance of these interests into devising
additional means of killing and sowing the land with the seeds of
destruction.

"Second, the laborers.   The great mass of the American people
are toilers.   They know that war takes life, that the army is
drawn from their numbers, and that their homes are drained to
fill the cemeteries of the battlefield.   They also realize full well
that the cost of armies and of war is enormous.   We hear from them
already in the declarations of their organized bodies that arbitration must be the rule, that international peace must be the object,
and that military and naval armaments must stop their growth.

"Third, Woman.   No mother nurses her baby boy and rears
him to manhood without dread that his life may in its prime be
cut off by the merciless bullet.   Nowhere in the world is she so
potent a force in public life as in this country, and you may be sure
that that force will be ere long concentrated in steadfast opposition
to war and in favor of the settlement of international disputes
by arbitration."

It can also be asserted, more positively than two years ago, that
the church and organized religion is for international peace.

President Taft, speaking at a public banquet a few months ago,
declared in still more general terms that men in civilized countries
today want peace and not war.   "We are all in favor of virtue,"
he said: we are all in favor of goodness, and we are all in favor of
peace.   .   .   .   We are all opposed to war, because war is hell."
A thousand voices, from all nations, unite in proclaiming that the
world is tired of war and looking longingly towards peace, and who
will deny that much progress has been made when war is branded
as hell, and peace put in the same category as virtue and goodness!

This does not mean, however, that all is won.   There are many
items in the peace program upon which general agreement has not
been reached.   Many demand the immediate reduction of armaments, some going to the length of advocating non-resistance.
Another group, claiming to love peace as much as these, believe
for the present in the maintenance of large armaments, not being
convinced that people of other nations are sincere in their advocacy

of peace. Still another very large class of men, while admitting the desirability and value of peace, fear that after all it is only a sweet dream of impractical minds. But chiefest of all the tasks before us, "the largest proposition ever yet conceived by the mind of man," as General Chittenden has lately declared, is the establishment of the agencies which shall bring us to the desired goal of peace with justice.

This diversity of opinion on matters which, however important, are still secondary, while there is practical agreement on the main points seems to mark this as a time for uniting the forces which favor peace in a supreme effort to obtain their goal. Much of the preliminary work has been done—all honor to the prophets who have taught the world the hideousness of war. It is clearly undesirable for a peace society in any city today to occupy a platform which compels groups of people who would advance the cause of peace to organize separately for the purpose. It is unwise, by insistence on a divisive idea, to compel the organization of a Friends' peace society, a big-armament peace society, an arbitration society, and still another to study and eliminate the causes of war. It seems much better for the advocates of peace to illustrate that unity and spirit of concession which they preach by presenting in one great organization a united front against the spirit of war. Breadth and unity of this kind the New York Peace Society has consistently tried to exemplify, and with some success. "Its platform is a broad one," it declares, "and there is room within its fellowship for men who differ widely as to measures and methods. It includes both those who deny all place to armaments, and those who fear, in the present state of civilization, to abolish large armies and navies. It urges, however, neither non-resistance nor great armaments, but exists to strengthen the forces which are leading toward international goodwill, and the substitution of law for war."

A positive and constructive program is the only one on which all the friends of peace can agree. Advocate disarmament, and voices are immediately raised in question and protest. A society which puts in the forefront of its program the proposal to substitute law for war will find new friends constantly coming to its standard.

A program of this kind, moreover, is the only one that can persuade the skeptical that international peace is obtainable.   It has
besides, the supreme excellence of setting out on a straight road
towards the desired end.

Being situated in a great commercial and manufacturing city,
whose daily life brings it in touch with every quarter of the world,
the New York Peace Society has instinctively felt that it must
stand for positive things.   For over three years no remonstrance
of any kind has gone out from its office.   Every member has felt
free to express his convictions for or against battleships and fortifications.   The Society, however, has believed that its work
could be best done by standing prominently for the building up of
those international institutions which shall give us an organized
world.   It has advocated constantly and consistently the extension
of law into the international sphere, as it has already been extended
from time to time into other realms; at one time putting an end
to private war, later to the duel, and still more recently to war
between the component parts of great nations.   At the time of
the organization of the Society it was declared to be its chief purpose to bring influence to bear for the extension of the principle
of arbitration, the strengthening and exalting of The Hague Tribunal and the erection of The Hague Conferences into a permanent
international congress.   It has from time to time been a strong
advocate of the permanent arbitral court and of all inclusive
arbitration treaties.   With the accomplishment of this international
task as its avowed object, it has been gratifying to see a gradual
change taking place in the attitude towards the society of the general public and the daily press until from one of derision they have
come to show respect and ready coöperation.

A further and essential feature of such a positive program for a
peace society as has been referred to is the practical application
and the practice of the spirit of international goodwill and brotherhood upon which only world organization can be built.   Senator
Elihu Root, speaking to the New York Peace Society two years
ago said, "when public opinion has risen to such height all over
the world, that the peoples of every country treat the peoples of
every other country with the human kindness that binds home

communities together, you will see an end of war—and not until then." On the same occasion he expressed the opinion that an important activity of peace loving men and women ought to be to aid the growth of such a feeling of international brotherhood, "not by great demonstration, but by that quiet, that resistless influence, which among great bodies of men makes up the tendency of mankind, and in the long process of the years moves men from savagery and brutality to peace and brotherhood." Such work the New York Peace Society had been doing, and has continued to do—indeed, it occupies in our great commercial and composite city a place unique among the cities of the whole world for the rendering of such a service.

Among the manifold activities of the society I have the honor to represent, I have thought it eminently fitting to mention two or three which have as their object the expression of international good will.

There are two nations whose complicated home problems, and whose close relation to the United States afford unusual opportunity for friendly helpfulness. One of these is Turkey. For two generations or more American Schools and citizens have been moulding the ideals of her young men and women. At last a heroic effort is being made by her people to redeem their land from the long years of misrule into which stupid tyranny had plunged her. This would seem to be the supreme moment in the relations of these two countries for our enlightened and liberty-loving republic to extend a hand of friendship across the sea. Through the New York Society, several American universities have offered free tuition to groups of Turkish students, and invitation has been sent to the Turkish minister of education inviting acceptance of this offer. The advance has been met with eagerness, and the first delegation of young men from Turkey is studying in Columbia University. An able committee which inspires confidence, both in Turkey and the United States, is making itself responsible for the wise and sympathetic accomplishment of the task.

Last autumn our sister republic to the south was on the verge of revolution. The close commercial relations existing between

the two countries, the large investment of American capital in
Mexico, together with the recollection of past aggression by the
stronger nation agaisnt the weaker, all combined to create a situation where agencies for the cultivation of mutual understanding,
and the expression of friendly feeling, were greatly to be desired.
At this juncture, officers of the New York Peace Society took the
initiative in forming the Mexico Society of New York, and lent
the services of its office for this purpose. A strong and flourishing society composed jointly of Mexican and American citizens
has resulted, already justifying itself by its deeds, and full of promise for future usefulness.

The one other line of activity which I shall mention looks to
the same end—the practical and helpful expression of international
goodwill, and the cultivation of mutual understanding—but is
more general in its scope. From the date of its organization the
New York Peace Society has now and then been the host of important people from abroad. Experience taught the importance and
value of taking advantage of the many occasions of this kind which
the port of New York affords.

A Board of International Hospitality, strongly officered and
with an eminent membership,. has therefore been organized, and
its object announced to be that of extending "proper and adequate
hospitality to high representatives of foreign governments and
other distinguished visitors to our shores, thus aiding the movement
towards international goodwill by the cultivation of personal and
friendly relations." The service of the society in this sphere had
become so generally recognized and valued that its fitness to take
the initiative in this important work seems to have been generally
recognized in the city.

In closing, I will only say that it is the purpose and hope of the
New York Peace Society to be as broad and generous as the subject with which it deals and the city in which it does its work;
while it always remembers that it is organized for the purpose
of hastening by every means within its power the growth of those
world institutions which, by the substitution of law for war, can
alone bring international peace.

CHAIRMAN BURTON: I now take pleasure in introducing Rev.
Gilbert Reid of the International Institute of China.

A CHINESE PEACE SOCIETY

GILBERT REID

I have the honor of representing the International Institute of
China, with headquarters in the city of Shanghai, an organization
where Occidentals and Orientals unite in practical efforts for universal peace, by cultivation of harmonies and friendly relations
between East and West, with better mutual understanding, appreciation and esteem, and through larger recognition of justice,
righteousness and fair-play, especially in the treatment of China
by the other nations of the world.   Hence the aim of this Institute
is summed up in two words, contained in the seal of the incorpo-
ration, "Harmony" and "Truth,"   Realizing the vital bearings
of Far Eastern questions on the large question of international
peace, we center our operations, not so much in Europe and America, as in China—the strategic center of this world-wide movement.
We urge the peace-spirit rather than the war-spirit, not only on
China's leaders, but on the nations of Europe, on Japan, and on the
United States, as they together face the growing, complex problems of China in this new era of progress and development.

In New York you have the American Association of International
Conciliation, consisting only of Americans, and in Paris the French
Association of the same, consisting only of Frenchmen.   Our International Institute might well be called the International Association of International Conciliation, for in the one organization,
devoted to the cultivation of friendliness and concord, Occidental
and Oriental are alike represented.   In our membership, actuated
by the sentiment of cordiality, and operating on the basis of
equality, are Chinese, Manchus and Mongols, Japanese, Austral-
ians, Canadians, and Americans, English, Scotch, Irish and Welsh,
French and German, Spanish and Italians, Belgians and Dutch,
Danes, Swedes and Norwegians, Russians and Austrians—in the
one organization in the one country, meeting together not once

a year or once in two years, but, if they so desire, from week to week. We aim, we plan, we work, for peace that is inter-racial and international—peace between the white race and the yellow race, no yellow peril to the white race, and no white threat to the yellow race—and peace among all the nations gathered together on the other side of the Pacific, with temptation to self-aggrandizement, exploitation, encroachment, but with a divine call to mutual helpfulness, reciprocal obligations and a due regard to the sovereign rights of one another. To consummate so desirable an object, not only is personal influence exerted, but an organization, with full property powers, has been legally incorporated.

To further the objects of universal peace, as dependent on international righteousness, this Institute of China makes definite endeavor to secure harmony and justice between Chinese and persons of other nationalities as participating in the three great interests, commercial, educational and religious. Our Shanghai Committee in the commercial section, consists of eleven Chinese merchants and eleven foreign merchants, namely, two Americans, two British, two Germans, two Japanese, one Frenchman, one Hollander and one Russian, all aiming to secure unanimity of action in improving both Chinese internal trade and her foreign commerce. The Shanghai Committee in the educational section consists of educators and men of scholarship, both in mission schools, in government institutions, and those under private initiative and support, aiming to secure coöperation with economy of energy. The Shanghai Committee in the religious section consists of representative men in the Protestant denominations, in the Roman Catholic Church, in the Hebrew faith, and also in Confucianism, Buddhism, Taoism and Mohammedanism, aiming to secure greater religious toleration, with less persecution, fewer "missionary riots," and a diminishing feeling of bigotry, contempt and schism.

Similar committees, with similar combination for mutual instruction and benefit, are to be formed in all the centres of China, where Chinese leaders and foreign residents sympathize with the objects in view and are willing to be associated together. The scope of the operations directed by this International Institute is limited to no one locality. The whole of China needs to be taught the good policy of being on friendly terms with the "outside world," and to no less a degree the "outside world" needs to be taught the advantage to itself of being on friendly terms with China. Both sides need to follow the path of right and the ways of peace.

What, now, are the methods best suited to the Chinese, in meeting these aims of peace and in carrying out these activities? In brief, the method must be one of conciliation. Specifically, the most appropriate method is the social one. Personal acquaintance, exchange of calls, conversation, afford a medium for bringing ideas to bear in a most natural and effective way on men who stand at the head of affairs. Receptions, luncheons and banquets, add emphasis to the social feature of international intercourse, when large numbers of Occidentals and Orientals come together and inevitably cultivate the spirit of friendliness and esteem, without which no peace can be stable or permanent. A second method is the literary one, publishing in Chinese a monthly periodical devoted to the interests of peace and conciliation, and also publishing and circulating pamphlets and books bearing on these and kindred topics. Such literature prepared in suitable style is a mighty weapon for the cause of peace. A third method, adapted in these later days, is the method of public address and lectures. This method is useful in creating a popular sentiment, especially in resisting agitation for war, boycotts, and other forms of hostility to foreigners and foreign governments. A fourth method is that of conference and committees, where select persons from both East and West, having identity of aims, meet to discuss and to plan problems of international concern. A fifth method is that of class-room instruction, influencing the great student class. A sixth method is the official or semi-official one, wherein memorials are presented to the central and provincial governments, discussing questions bearing on universal peace and the principles of universal righteousness. Fortunately, the International Institute, having been sanctioned by the imperial government, has direct approach to the authorities both in Peking and in the provinces, and needs no introduction or interposition from any legation or any foreign government. For this reason, the arguments presented carry as much weight as they would if pressed on the attention of the Chinese by the diplomats of foreign governments.

From this it can be seen that not only is it important to concentrate on the Orient efforts for peace just as much as on Europe or America, but such efforts are acceptable to the traditional spirit of the Chinese and to the teachings of their great philosophers. It is easy to argue for arbitration, because the method of arbitration has existed in China for thousands of years. No great argument is needed in favor of disarmament, for China at the present time is without a navy, and has no desire to have one, unless forced to have it through pressure from abroad. I am confident that China would be willing to submit to just arbiters every question that may arise between her government and all the other governments of the world. If the other governments can be persuaded to do the same in their relations with China, there is no possibility of collision, of war, or of the increase of army and navy, to the detriment of the principles of peace. This Institute, therefore, does what it can to further these interests, not only with the Chinese, but with the people of other nations having relations with China. It is fittingly called the International Institute of China, and the greetings of both the Chinese and foreign members are extended to this National Peace Congress.

CHAIRMAN BURTON: You all remember that in the month of March President Taft expressed himself to the effect that arbitration treaties should be framed which would provide for the settlement of all disputes without exception. That statement was made before the American Peace and Arbitration League, New York. Its field secretary, Mrs. Elmer E. Black, is here today and will address you. I take pleasure in presenting Mrs. Black.

THE NEW WORLD-CONSCIOUSNESS

MRS. ELMER E. BLACK

In the face of the rapid development of modern civilization we are as those who dream. All, however, is reality. The wonder of our day is—not that we build forty-story houses, or tunnel the Hudson River, or even invent guns that will shoot across the Great Lakes, but that we think under one set of terms one day, and on the next may have risen into a transformed thought-world.

The wonder of our times is that the whole outlook upon man, the entire attitude toward life, changes unconsciously in a day. When we recollect the thought-world in which we ourselves were living only fifteen years ago, do we not seem new beings, or to be living in a new world? As an instance, the word "internationalism," which is everywhere being used, was seldom heard in its wide, modern sense a decade ago.   Nowadays, "international" is one of the commonest words on our lips, a leading word in our newspapers, and the great congresses of all kinds are international.

But there is a far more striking illustrations of this meteorlike rate of evolution, of almost miraculous transformations of the thought habits of years, and it is to this phenomenon I wish to call your attention this afternoon.   I refer to the sudden lifting of the people from national consciousness into world-consciousness.   Is there anything more startling than this—that we who were yesterday thinking in terms of the nation are today thinking in terms of the world?   It seems as though only a night had intervened between the valley of old and the mountain top of new thinking.   After ten years only, our previous national consciousness seems at present provincial, for we think in terms of the world.

This world-consciousness has in a few years advanced far. It is the great promise of the peace movement. Personally, it is to me the basis of my faith in it. Because I see everywhere this new habit of thinking; this growing oneness of humanity; this deepening sense of brotherhood and kinship of soul stronger and more enduring than any mere national distinctions—because of these things, I believe that the promise of world-peace and the reign of law are not only feasible but certain of fulfilment.

The leaders in this movement know and feel this growing world-consciousness. It is becoming clearer from the midst of the chaos of our time to the vision of those whose eyes have been anointed. They hear its music above the earthly discords. The great mass of the people, however, have as yet only begun partially and vaguely to comprehend it.

Herein lies the great task of the peace societies—fostering this world-consciousness; educating the people into it; showing them its inevitableness; interpreting the rapid and confusing processes which take place so fast that they can hardly be fully understood; showing them the manifold signs of its ultimate fruition.

The American Peace and Arbitration League has gladly assumed this task from the beginning. We have felt sure that this new world-spirit was in our very midst. We saw everywhere the greatest minds thinking in world-terms; thinking of humanity as well as of their fellow-citizens; thinking of themselves also as citizens of the world, and not merely of their own nation. We have realized this, and said: "This is for all the people, as well as for the prophets. The prophet simply climbs where all must follow."

We have been trying in the following ways to convince the people that this world-consciousness was an actuality. By showing them how at last all the world has come together at The Hague Conferences, and has been considering the welfare, not of one nation but of all nations. What a symbol of new world-consciousness! The poet's "parliament of man" has come, in these periodic conferences at The Hague.

We have demonstrated how this world-consciousness is expanding incredibly fast by emphasizing the fact that the first ten years of this century witnessed the signing of more than a hundred arbitration treaties. True, we built two battleships in 1908— but, remember, we signed fourteen arbitration treaties during that same year.

We have gone a step further, and proclaimed that world-consciousness must be hastened by making these treaties unlimited. It was at one of our League dinners that the President of the

United States made his world-famous utterance, in which he declared that hereafter arbitration treaties should include all questions whatsoever, even the honor of a country.

We have tried to foster everywhere *the new patriotism*—not the old patriotism which was confined to war, or which was rather hatred of another country than a devoted love of one's own—that spirit which recognizes that to put country above personal gain or comfort at any and all times is true patriotism; above all, that to make one's own country lead the world towards peace is the highest patriotism of all.

In these, and in many other ways—particularly by diplomacy the American Peace and Arbitration League is endeavoring to bring the people to appreciate that which you and I had already seen long since.

I am greatly interested personally in woman's work for peace, and wish in closing, to say one word about it. I believe that woman's opportunities are greater in this than in almost any other field. Her sympathies are naturally broad, and the work of welding nations calls for great, broad, charitable, sympathetic minds.

As she rises from her older status of the silent comforter of man to be a commanding factor in the thought and action of the world, she can, if she will, be equally influential in the great peace cause— as well as find in it a field of endeavor full of interest and charm.

Her battles have always been won by moral force, rather than by arms. Now that man is beginning to see that moral force is more powerful than powder, and is seeking to transfer his battles into the moral fields of Hague Courts and of arbitration, who is more fitting to lead the way than she who has always won her battles by the pure, strong force of reason, love and forbearance?

The American Peace and Arbitration League believes that a common world-consciousness, the sense of citizenship in humanity, the habit of thinking in terms for the whole world, is necessary before permanent world peace can be assured. World unity will lead to international peace!

Let us all rejoice that this world-consciousness has developed so fast in our day!

CHAIRMAN BURTON: The American Peace Society has many branches, among them being one on the Pacific Coast, one in Chicago, and another here in Baltimore. One of the most energetic associations for the promotion of peace is the Chicago Peace Society, and the Rev. Charles E. Beals is largely responsible for its usefulness. I take pleasure in introducing Dr. Beals.

REV. CHARLES E. BEALS: I ask leave to have my address printed, as the hour is growing late.

THE CHICAGO PEACE OFFICE

CHARLES E. BEALS

The story is told of an old time military company which consisted of a dozen officers and one lone private. The private is reported to have said that he could go through the setting-up exercises, the facings, the manual of arms, and the "forward march" movement without difficulty, but that when the order "Deploy as skirmishers" was given, his system was horribly racked if he tried to carry out the command.

If the much-officered private who figured as the hero of this story were alive today, and if he were sufficiently converted from the errors of his ways so that he could be detailed as a peace soldier to man the Chicago peace office, he would think that his former impossible task was as nothing compared with the duties and opportunities of his new warfare. He would find that he would have to "deploy as skirmishers" for almost an entire army, instead of for a single company.

For the Chicago peace office fulfils a double function. It is the seat of the field secretaryship of the oldest and strongest peace organization in America, if not in the world, namely the American Peace Society; it is also the headquarters of the Chicago Peace Society, which is a branch of the American Peace Society.

The duties of the field secretary of the American Peace Society are as follows:

"1. The organization of branch societies, and the visiting and coöperation with the State and other local branches.

2. Attending, and promoting the cause of peace at religious, educational, industrial and other national, state and local conventions.

3. Assisting in the organizing and holding of meetings on arbitration and peace wherever possible.

4. Coöperating with the Intercollegiate Peace Association in work in the universities and colleges.

5. Soliciting legacies, contributions, memberships, etc.

6. Appointment of local agents to take memberships, subscriptions, etc."

It is evident that with the entire United States for a field, a man might well devote his entire time and strength to either one of the six tasks enumerated. But as the treasury does not permit the employment of six traveling workers, the Field Secretary endeavors to do as much as he can along all these lines of activity, being guided largely by the opportunities which open. That is, his plan is to devote himself to the things that seem ripest for results and promise to count the most for the investment of the time and strength and money expended.

Nor is this all. Chicago is almost a world in itself, and when one attempts to do some intensive pacifist work in the local field, he finds between 1000 and 2000 churches, 4500 schools, hundreds of clubs, and other openings without number. Even if a man should confine himself to the purely local work he would need to "spread himself" in the attempt to "deploy as skirmishers."

The present Chicago Peace Society was organized January 4, 1910. It was the outcome of a former Chicago Peace Society and the Second National Peace Congress. In 1902, a society was organized in Chicago as a branch of the American Peace Society. Rev. Hiram W. Thomas, D.D., who for over twenty years was the pastor of the People's Church, was President, and Mrs. E. A. W. Hoswell was Corresponding Secretary. With the breaking down of Dr. Thomas's health, the activities of the organization practically ceased. The last meeting of the Society was held at Hull House some three years ago. At that time it was voted to reorganize whenever the Committee on Reorganization, which was at that time appointed, should deem it advisable.

The Second National Peace Congress was held in Chicago, May 3 to 5, 1909, under the auspices of the American Peace Society. The sum of nearly $12,000 was raised, all bills were paid in full, and a large volume of the Proceedings (containing 524 pages) was published.

This Congress awakened so great an interest that a special meeting of the members of the American Peace Society who were in attendance was called in connection with the Congress, by Hon. Robert Treat Paine, the distinguished president of the American Peace Society. It was voted at this meeting that it was desirable to organize a Chicago branch and to open an office. The Directors of the American Peace Society, at a meeting held in Boston later in the same month (May 25, 1909), voted to transfer the office of the Field Secretary to Chicago, and to allow him to act as Secretary of the proposed branch, provided one should be organized and adequate financial support guaranteed.

After considerable time had been spent in a careful canvass to ascertain what moral and financial support could be relied on, it was decided that the opening of an office seemed warranted. A meeting was therefore called, to which were invited the members of the former Chicago Peace Society, the Chicago members of the American Peace Society, the local delegates to the Second National Peace Congress and other friends of peace. At this meeting (held January 4, 1910, as previously stated), organization of the Chicago Peace Society was effected and the earlier local peace organization, through its Committee on Reorganization (Rev. Jenkin Lloyd Jones, Chairman) merged itself in the new local branch of the American Peace Society.

An office was immediately opened in the Association Building, 153 La Salle Street. This was occupied until April 8, 1911, when the Society moved its office to the Stock Exchange Building, 30 North La Salle Street.

In the sixteen months since the organization of the Chicago Peace Society a membership of 620 has been built up, and about $5500 in cash collected, besides a few unpaid subscriptions amounting to several hundred dollars more. Each month the *Advocate of Peace*, the organ of the American Peace Society, devotes a column to news from the Chicago Society and the work of the Chicago secretary. The Chicago Society pays fifty cents per capita to the parent organization, in order that all members of the Chicago Society may receive the *Advocate* free. Membership in the Chicago Peace Society carries with it membership in the American Peace Society, with right to vote in the annual and special meetings of the parent organization.

The Chicago Peace Society hitherto has been financed almost entirely by means of membership fees. Its Constitution provides for six kinds of membership, namely.

(1) Annual Membership, $2.00 per year; (2) Adhering Membership, $5.00 per year; (3) Sustaining Membership, $10.00 per year; (4) Contributing Membership, $25.00 per year; (5) Life Membership, $100.00 in one payment; (6) Affiliating Organizations, $5.00 per year.

Affiliating Organizations are entitled to representation by two delegates each in the meetings of the society.

The affairs of the Society are carried on by an Executive Committee, which meets monthly at luncheon.

One of the first activities of the Chicago office was to circulate the Proceedings of the last National Peace Congress. Hundreds of copies have been sent to prominent statesmen, educators, and peace workers all over the world. Large cases were shipped to Boston, New York, Philadelphia, Lake Mohonk, Baltimore, the Chinese Students' Conference at Northwestern University, and to Tokyo, Japan. A postal card notice was sent to a thousand colleges and public libraries, offering a presentation copy on receipt of postage. Over three hundred responses were rceived from state, college, and public libraries. By this means, peace literature has been placed within reach of 15,000,000 people, who can have access to this volume without going outside the bounds of their own college or city.

The Chicago office is a depository of literature for the American Peace Society, and all its publications are kept in stock. From all parts of the country requests for literature are constantly being received, to assist in the preparation of papers, addresses and debates. Publications of the various organizations like the

Association for International Conciliation, the Mohonk Conference, the American School Peace League, the World Peace Foundation, the Maryland Peace Society, the Japan Peace Societies, the American Society for Judicial Settlement of International Disputes, the Cosmopolitan· Clubs, etc., are kept on hand. The office is frequently consulted with reference to the intercollegiate oratorical contests and the building of special programs for the larger clubs, etc.

In the office there is a small but valuable working library. The Secretary has loaned his own private peace library for this purpose. Through the courtesy of the Netherlands government a complete set of the official records of the First and Second Hague Conferences has been received. Bloch's great book, which led to the calling of the First Hague Conference, may be found upon the shelves, in the large six-volume French edition issued by the Berne Bureau, and likewise in the abridged English and American editions. A complete set of the *American Journal of International Law* is another valuable reference work. The fourteen large volumes of Moore's *International Arbitrations* and *International Law Digest*, published by the United States government, are also available. Complete sets of Reports of the Universal Peace Congresses, the National Peace Congresses, the Lake Mohonk Arbitration Conferences, and other similar bodies, constitute in themselves a valuable alcove. All the publications of the International School of Peace (now the World Peace Foundation) are provided also, both for reference and for sale. Rare old peace literature, the classics of the subject (like the writings of Erasmus and Grotius), biographies of the earlier and foremost peace workers, and many volumes bearing on the general movement have been gathered together, one by one. The history of diplomacy is represented in an increasing number of volumes. The First and Second Hague Conferences are very fully covered by monographs. The Northwestern University Law School has a special fund for the purchase of publications bearing on international arbitrations and law. As the members of the Peace Society may have access to this collection, which is located in Chicago, the heavy expense of building up a special library is avoided.

The principal peace publications of Europe are received regularly by the Chicago office and may be consulted at any time.

The first president of the present Chicago Peace Society was Hon. George E. Roberts, now Director of the Mint. Upon his removal to Washington the Chicago Association of Commerce joined with the Chicago Peace Society in tendering a farewell luncheon. This was a brilliant and important affair. Mr. Alfred L. Baker succeeded Mr. Roberts. At the annual meeting of the Society, held January 21, 1911, Mr. Leroy A. Goddard was elected president. Mr. Goddard is President of the State Bank of Chicago, President of the Chicago Clearing House, President of the Bankers' Club, Ex-president of the Union League Club, etc., and is a man of many friendships and wide social influence. The complete list of officers for 1911 is as follows:

President: Leroy A. Goddard, President of State Bank of Chicago.

Vice President: Edward M. Skinner, Former President Chicago Association of Commerce.

Secretary: Charles E. Beals, Field Secretary of American Peace Society.

Treasurer: Charles L. Hutchinson, Vice President of Corn Exchange National Bank.

Auditor: Maurice S. Kuhns, Secretary Safeguard Account Company.

Executive Committee: The first four of the above and the following: Miss Jane Addams, Head Resident of Hull House; Richard C. Hall, President of Duck Brand Company and Former President of Chicago Association of Commerce; Hon. Harlow N. Higinbotham, President of World's Columbian Exposition; Prof. Charles Cheney Hyde, Northwestern University Law School; S. W. Lamson, Lamson Brothers and Company; Alexander A. McCormick, Former President of Union League Club; Julius Rosenwald, President of Sears, Roebuck and Company; Albert H. Scherzer, President of the Scherzer Rolling Lift Bridge Company; Sydney Richmond Taber, Attorney and Counsellor at Law; Harry A. Wheeler, Vice President of Union Trust Company and President of Chicago Association of Commerce.

Past Presidents: Hon. George E. Roberts, Director of the Mint; Alfred L. Baker, of Alfred L. Baker and Company.

Honorary Vice Presidents: Hon. Franklin MacVeagh, Secretary of the Treasury; Hon. J. M. Dickinson, Secretary of War; Hon. Walter L. Fisher, Secretary of the Interior; Hon. William J. Calhoun, United States Minister to China.; Hon. Charles S. Deneen, Governor of Illinois; Miss Jane Addams, of Hull House. Bishop Charles P. Anderson, Protestant Episcopal Bishop of Chicago; Judge Edward Osgood Brown, Illinois Appellate Court; Mrs. Joseph T. Bowen; E. J. Buffington, President of Illinois Steel Company; Edward B. Butler, President of Butler Brothers; Charles R. Crane, 1st Vice President of Crane Company; David R. Forgan, President of National City Bank; James B. Forgan, President of First National Bank; President Abram W. Harris, Northwestern University; Mrs. Ellen M. Henrotin, Former President of Federation of Women's Clubs; Rev. Emil G. Hirsch, Minister of Sinai Congregation; Rev. Jenkin Lloyd Jones; Director of Abraham Lincoln Centre; William V. Kelley, President of American Steel Foundries; John R. Lindgren, donor of Lindgren Peace Fund; Bishop William F. McDowell, a Bishop of the Methodist Episcopal Church; President John S. Nollen, Lake Forest College; James A. Patten; Doctor Daniel K. Pearsons; Philanthropist; Archbishop James E. Quigley, Roman Catholic Archbishop of Chicago; Julius Rosenwald, President of Sears, Roebuck and Company; Prof. Graham Taylor, Chicago Commons; Towner K. Webster, President Webster Manufacturing Company; Mrs. Ella Flagg Young, Superintendent of Schools.

The Executive Committee, on November 3, 1910, voted to invite the foreign consuls residing in Chicago to accept honorary membership in the Society. Practically all the consuls have accepted this invitation. Through the courtesy of the Japanese Consul, Hon. K. Yamasaki, several of our officers and members were present on two important occasions, namely, at a luncheon given to Baron Oura, Minister of Agriculture and Commerce of Japan, and at a reception in honor of the birthday of His Majesty the Emperor of Japan.

Since the opening of the Chicago office, valuable service has been rendered by many of our vice presidents and members. Addresses and lectures have been given by Miss Jane Addams, Dr. Jenkin Lloyd Jones, Dr. Hirsch, Professor Hyde, Mr. Morris, Mr. Higinbotham, Mr. Wheeler, Bishop Anderson, President Nollen, Dr. Stolz, Dr. Schanfarber, Mrs. Henrotin and many others. Dr. Jones, on the eighteenth of May, Hague Day, addressed the Cosmopolitan Club of the University of Chicago.

Moreover the Secretary has delivered addresses at the following colleges: Lake Forest (two), Adelbert and Western Reserve in Cleveland, Ohio (three), Purdue University (Lafayette, Indiana), University of Wooster (Wooster, Ohio), Greer College (Hoopeston, Illinois), the Y. M. C. A. of the University of Wisconsin (Madison, Wisconsin), the Case School of Applied Science (Cleveland, Ohio), Wheaton College (Wheaton, Illinois), Grinnell College (Grinnell, Iowa), Garrett Biblical Institute (Evanston, Ill.), and the University of North Dakota (at Grand Forks, North Dakota).

He has also addressed the following schools: New Britain, Connecticut (two), the State Normal School in New Britain, Connecticut, the Evening College of the Chicago Association Institute, Wooster Academy (Wooster, Ohio), the Friends Academy, (Bloomingdale, Illinois), Park Manor School, Chicago, the Medill High School of Chicago, and the Central High School, of Buffalo, New York.

Of his pulpit services, sermons in the following churches may be cited: The First Presbyterian of Lake Forest; the Plymouth Congregational of Cleveland, Ohio; the Superior Avenue Baptist of Cleveland; the Union Park Congregational of Chicago; the Wethersfield Congregational of Hartford, Connecticut; the Prospect Congregational of Cambridge, Massachusetts; All Souls Church of the Abraham Lincoln Centre, Chicago; three times in the First Congregational of Evanston; the Congregational Church of Winnetka; the Ninth Presbyterian of Chicago; the Church of the Redeemer of Chicago; (several times); the Lutheran Church of Wooster, Ohio (union meeting); the First Congregational of Madison, Wisconsin; the First Baptist of Oak Park; the Washington Park Congregational Church, Chicago; the First

Congregational of Fargo, North Dakota; the Universalist Church, Sycamore, Illinois, (four addresses); the Second Congregational Church, Oak Park, Illinois; and (prayer) in the Sunday Evening Club service in Orchestra Hall, Chicago.

The Secretary has also addressed the following clubs: The Hamilton of Chicago; the University, of Lake Forest; the Cosmopolitan of Madison, Wisconsin; the Quadrangle, of Cleveland, the Men's Club of the First Congregational Church of Evanston; the Fellowship Club of Unity Church, Oak Park; the Men's Club of the Glen Ellyn Congregational Church; the Isaiah Woman's Club; the Chicago Congregational Club; the Chicago Woman's Club (three times); the Hawkeye Fellowship Club of Chicago; the Woodlawn Woman's Club of Chicago; the South Side Woman's Club of Chicago; the Park Manor Woman's Club of Chicago; the Men's Club of the Westminster Presbyterian Church of Buffalo; and the Men's Club of the First Unitarian Church of Buffalo.

He has in addition spoken on various occasions and before the following bodies: The Congregational Ministers' Meeting of Cleveland, Ohio; the Woman's Congress at the Tower Hill Summer Encampment, Tower Hill, Wisconsin; the public lecture course of Bloomingdale, Ind.; the Buffalo Chapter of the D. A. R., Buffalo, New York; the Theodore Parker Celebration (three addresses), the Chicago Anthropological Society; a banquet of the Y. P. S. C. E. of the First Congregational Church of Evanston; the Ottawa (Illinois) Business Men's Association's annual banquet; the Maxwell Social Settlement of Chicago; the Fellowship House of Chicago; the annual banquet of the Independent Religious Society of Chicago; the Grand Lectureship of Fargo, North Dakota; the Knights of Columbus of Buffalo; and the United Trade and Labor Council of Buffalo.

An important group meeting of churches was held in the South Congregational Church, Chicago, on December 18, 1910.

The Chicago Congregational Club invited our society to build the program for its November meeting. In like manner we were requested to provide for the January 11, 1911, meeting of the Chicago Woman's Club. More and more we are being recognized and called on for such service.

The Secretary has been present at the following peace gatherings: The New England Peace Congress, in Hartford and New Britain, at which he delivered an address at the labor mass-meeting; the annual meeting of the American Peace Society in Hartford, Connecticut; the Mohonk Arbitration Conference; the annual meeting of the Cleveland Peace Society, at which he delivered the address; a mass meeting in Milwaukee, for the organization of a State Branch, at which Mayor Seidel and the secretary were the speakers; a meeting of the Peace Association of the University of Wooster, Wooster, Ohio; a luncheon of the Executive Committee of the Buffalo Arbitration and Peace Society; the International Congress held in Washington, D. C., under the auspices of the American Society for Judicial Settlement of International Disputes; the Third National Peace Congress, Baltimore, May 3–5, 1911. At the coming Mohonk Conference the Chicago Peace Society will be represented by its President, Mr. Leroy A. Goddard, and the secretary.

Through the courtesy of the International School of Peace, Chicago enjoyed the presence of Rev. Walter Walsh, of Dundee, Scotland, for ten days. Many of the colleges and clubs, which gladly would have extended a hearing to Mr. Walsh, had closed for the season. But we kept our distinguished guest busy during his stay. The newspapers interviewed him and accorded generous space in their columns. The Executive Committee of the Chicago Peace Society, at a luncheon conferred with Mr. Walsh as to the peace situation in Great Britain. The City Club held a luncheon in honor of Mr. Walsh. Mr. David R. Forgan, President of the National City Bank, a fellow countryman of Mr. Walsh, presided and introduced the speaker in a happy manner. Mr. Walsh's theme was "The Military Situation in Europe," and his address was printed in full in the City Club *Bulletin*.

The First Congregational Church of Evanston, through its pastor, Dr. McElveen, and the Hyde Park Presbyterian Church, through Rev. Dr. Joseph A. Vance, pastor, opened their pulpits to Mr. Walsh, and the First Presbyterian Church of Lake Forest, Rev. W. Wray Boyle, D.D., pastor, devoted its prayer meeting to the subject of international peace. The Congregational Ministers' Meeting of Chicago set aside its regular program in order to hear the visiting Scotsman, and special postal card notices were sent out to all the pastors. "Militarism and the Church's Duty" was the theme presented. An animated and enthusiastic discussion followed the formal address, and the parsons agreed that their fellow craftsman from beyond the sea was a "live wire."

The University Club tendered a reception to Mr. Walsh, as did also the Housing Committee of the City Club. He was likewise the guest of the Ways and Means Committee of the Association of Commerce when "New Chicago" was discussed. As a member of the City Council of Dundee, Mr. Walsh heartily appreciated the plans for the betterment of city life and was enthusiastic in his praise of the Chicago plans.

A special meeting of the Chicago Peace Society was held at Hull House. Miss Addams presided in her own inimitable, gracious way, and Mr. Walsh talked on "How the Movement Moves."

During Mr. Walsh's stay in Chicago, a meeting was held at General F. D. Grant's headquarters for the purpose of organizing the Boy Scouts of America. By special invitation Mr. Walsh attended and protested against emphasizing the military features of the movement.

Mrs. Lucia Ames Mead, of Boston, a director of the American Peace Society, made a tour of some of the principal cities of the country, giving her services without charge, except traveling expenses. We were permitted to have ten days of her time, from January 7 to 17, 1911. Mrs. Mead spoke twice before the Chicago Woman's Club. She also addressed the Chicago Normal School, the Northwestern University, Chicago Theological Seminary, Lake Forest College, Lake Forest Academy, Ferry Hall School, Rockford College and the Churches of Rev. Dr. A. B. Francisco and Rabbi Tobias Schanfarber.

The *Chicago Record-Herald* published on Sunday, February 26, a symposium entitled "What Chicago Could Do With Some of Her War Money." The Secretary wrote the introductory article, showing that if the present military and naval budget of the United States is maintained during the next decade, the people of Chicago will pay as Chicago's part of the national expenditures, $41,000,000 *more* for war purposes than in the decade ending with the Spanish War. This sum of $41,000,000 was divided up into four nearly equal parts. Dr. Graham Taylor showed how $10,000,000 could be spent to advantage in Chicago in the next ten years for various civic improvements and social engineering projects; Mr. Frank E. Wing, superintendent of the Tuberculosis Institute, told what $10,000,000 would do in the war against disease; Prof. C. H. Judd put $10,000,000 worth of improvements into the educational system; the remaining $11,000,000 was entrusted to Walter D. Moody, of the Chicago Plan Commission, to help to realize a "Chicago Beautiful."

The Illinois State Intercollegiate Oratorical Contest was held at Northwestern University in the spring. Mr. LaVerne W. Noyes provided the first prize of $75, and one of our beloved honorary vice presidents, Hon. H. N. Higinbotham, donated the second prize of $50.

Mrs. Vandelia Varnum Thomas, widow of Rev. Hiram W. Thomas, D.D., the president of the first Chicago Peace Society, has established a World's Peace Oration in Alfred University, Alfred, New York, and will establish similar prizes in two other colleges in the very near future.

An interesting and important conference of Chinese students was held at Northwestern University in the last week of August. The conference represented the territory of the mid-west. One hundred and twenty students registered in attendance. These students are sent to the United States by the Chinese government, the cost being defrayed out of the indemnity which was returned to China by the United States after the settlement of the Boxer claims. The students are highly intelligent and exceedingly interesting. Within five years most of them will have returned to their native land to be the leaders of the young China which is so rapidly forging to the front. The Secretary was invited to address the students at their Y. M. C. A. session and did so on August 30th. A case of Peace Congress Proceedings was shipped to the conference and a copy presented to each student.

Our office obtained from the State Department certain data for the *Chicago News* and *New York World Almanac*. This material is published in the 1911 editions.

At a suggestion from our office, the Chicago Association of Commerce sent two delegates to the Fourth International Congress of Chambers of Commerce which was held in London in June.

We have coöperated with the other peace societies in the movement for a peace commission. Congress has acted favorably in this matter, and the appointment of the members of the commission is in the hands of President Taft.

We have circulated copies of the report of the 1910 Mohonk Conference, and of the Report of the New England Peace Congress. Congressman Bartholdt has furnished us several thousand copies of an extract from the *Congressional Record* containing several peace addresses, some of which were delivered at the Chicago Peace Congress. Most of these have been mailed out under Mr. Bartholdt's frank.

The Peace Society of the City of New York prepared a "Battleship Circular," showing what might be done with the $12,000,-000 which a modern battleship costs. We have made free use of this and have found it very effective.

Another pamphlet which we have distributed is one containing an extract from the report of the Massachusetts Commission on the High Cost of Living.

It is pleasing to note that Dr. Nightingale, the Superintendent of Schools of Cook County, gave instructions to the teachers of history under him that less time be devoted to the description of battles and military strategem, and more time to the causes and results of wars.

It is gratifying to observe that the great newspapers seem more friendly and less skeptical than a year ago. Certain of our Chicago papers are constantly publishing editorials and articles which cannot help making for a new day in world life. Such papers are the heralds of a new and nobler civilization and deserve our heartiest appreciation.

The Chicago Association of Commerce made preparations for a visit to Japan by over one hundred and fifty delegates. Unfor-

tunately an accident to the ship, which had been specially char-
tered, necessitated the giving up of the original plan. Many
of the delegates went on other ships, however, though the party
could not go in a body. Letters were sent to all the delegates,
giving them the latest information about the peace movement
in Japan. Letters of introduction were also written to many of
the leading peace workers in the Orient.

The Chicago office has sent to the President, members of the
Cabinet, Senators and Representatives of the 62nd Congress,
pamphlets containing an account of the organization of the American Peace Society of Japan.

It has written to one hundred of the leading local clubs asking
them to place the subject of international arbitration and peace
on their programs for the coming year.

Three of the honorary vice presidents of the Chicago Society
are now members of the President's Cabinet.

Our office coöperates in the holding of the Intercollegiate
Oratorical Contests, and is frequently called on to furnish judges.

The work of the past season culminated in the visit of Baron
d'Estournelles de Constant and Hon. William Jennings Bryan
to our city within the past week. Baron d'Estournelles was the
guest of Mr. Cyrus Hall McCormick during his stay in the city.
Mr. McCormick tendered our distinguished guest a luncheon at
The Blackstone on Saturday, noon, April 29, which was attended
by the leading business men of the city. In the evening the
Chicago Peace Society gave a dinner to Baron de Constant,
Mr. Bryan and Hon. George E. Roberts in the Gold Room of the
Congress Hotel. The Sunday Evening Club gave the Baron a
great audience at its service in Orchestra Hall. Monday noon
the distinguished French pacifist was the guest at a luncheon at
the University of Chicago, and in the afternoon he addressed
a great meeting of the faculty and students of the same
institution.

In view of the rapid progress of the peace cause during the
last year, it is easy to believe that we are just on the eve of finish-
ing what Mr. Asquith calls "the greatest of all reforms." In
a very few years we shall see the consummation of the greatest

reform which ever has been effected in all history. No other
generation of the children of men ever has witnessed what we are
permitted to witness in our day and generation. We are far enough
along to see that the substitution of courts for camps, of law for
war, will go down in history as one of the great achievements of
the twentieth century, yes, as the greatest achievement of all the
centuries hitherto. Chicago wishes to do her part in the movement, and proposes to have her society well up towards the head
of the marching column of peace battalions of the various cities
and countries, as they move forward for their last campaign in
the war against war.

CHAIRMAN BURTON: You all know of the Lake Mohonk
Conference on International Arbitration, and I know you will
be pleased to hear from Mr. Daniel Smiley.

THE LAKE MOHONK CONFERENCE ON INTERNATIONAL
ARBITRATION

DANIEL SMILEY

The first Lake Mohonk Conference on International Arbitration
was held sixteen years ago. There was then apparently little
popular interest in urging on the world's peace. A wonderful
gathering like this for such an exalted purpose would then, I
believe, have been impossible. Then a treaty for permanent peace
by judicial adjustment between two great nations was considered—
if considered at all—a dream too unsubstantial to seriously advocate. It is not easy for any of us to realize the great change
which our country has met with and which this notable and splendid Congress assures us is an accomplished fact. Sixteen years
ago it was with much labor that fifty persons could be induced
to attend the first Mohonk Conference. After seven years the
attendance was limited only by the number which could be entertained, and it was necessary to open a conference office with a
permanent secretary.

In establishing the Conference my brother had in mind three
points:

First, that most thinking men already appreciated the horrors of war, and the desirability of avoiding it.

Second, that any movement looking toward the world's peace should be discussed on an international rather than a national basis, and

Third, some sort of arbitral settlement, or, in the primitive New England phrase, "Leaving it out to men" was the simple Quaker method between individuals of avoiding quarrels and litigation. With adaptations it seemed applicable between nations.

Taking this much for granted, the question was one of method. It was quickly proved that on this ground practically all patriotic and earnest men could join in harmonious and profitable discussion to an extent which had not been possible before on any other basis for promoting peace.

To men in all walks of life these propositions began to seem reasonable. We have held in all honor those whose duties led them into the practice of that very profession which we hope to render largely unnecessary. From a great company of men in the army and navy the work of our Conference has had most loyal and wide aid.

From those who make, as well as from those who interpret, our laws there has come advice which experience in public affairs has made particularly practical.

Those who represent this nation abroad no less than the distinguished representatives of other countries also seem to have found no bar to joining on the common ground selected.

To business men, also, in large numbers it particularly appealed —possibly because the methods proposed were on similar lines with usages to which they were long ago accustomed.

Almost from the first, leaders of the conferences, particularly Edward Everett Hale, looked beyond simple arbitration to a real international court of justice—such a court as our government is now earnestly seeking to put into being—and some of the early platforms advocated policies not unlike those that have later given the United States its leading position in the peace movement.

As years passed the representative character of its meetings, the opportunity it afforded for men of widely varying views to

agree on many of the topics discussed, have made it possible
for the Conference to substantially settle some questions and, in
its printed report, to give out its conclusions in such form as to be
widely accepted, for it has been from the first well understood that
the published platform contains only matter to which there is
a substantially unanimous consent. It has been the care of our
Conference to make the annual platform a body of decisions representing the best thought of those who have considered the various questions with care and earnestness, and that too, if possible,
without professional, class or personal bias.

Our purposes have been materially forwarded by a large and
increasing body of correspondents of all classes and countries,
and by nearly two hundred leading chambers of commerce and
boards of trade in the largest cities of the United States and Canada, including many bodies of national scope. These correspondents and business organizations are officially associated with
the Conference and have a large and much appreciated part in its
work.

The Conference has never considered itself adapted for general
propaganda. Hence about the only line it has undertaken has
been among the colleges, which field it entered in 1905 only because a large part of it was then totally neglected. The results
of five years have been gratifying, and we are now glad that with
the recent advances in the peace movement, other and better
equipped agencies will doubtless carry on more effectively the
work which our limitations have only permitted us to begin.

The Conference has recently been drawn into a service it had
not contemplated but gladly assumed—that of promoting coöperation among the leading American peace societies. The Mohonk meetings have been occasions for friendly exchange of views
by the officers of the societies, and for two years a special committee
of the Conference has been working on a plan for a national
arbitration and peace council through which the societies may
coöperate in a business-like manner. I am especially glad that
such a council is sure of early establishment and I hope this Congress, itself an example of coöperation, will give the new council
the stamp of its approval.

A backward glance at the Mohonk Conference indicates that one of its largest services has lain in giving initial impulse to new undertakings. One of its early meetings led to significant action by a committee of the New York Bar Association in drafting an almost prophetic plan for an international court which attracted wide attention in personal and official circles. The American Society of International Law was launched at a Mohonk conference with our hearty endorsement. Some other societies have been kind enough to credit Mohonk with inspiration; and it is needless to say it has given us special pleasure to have a part in bringing about the national council of which I have just spoken.

Finally, will you indulge me in taking the time to express the personal delight which it gives me to realize that this work is no longer left to individual effort or to that of local societies; but that now in this great and singularly attractive City of Baltimore whose hospitality and friendliness are so good to experience a Third National Congress can be held under such favoring auspices and with the sure promise of most beneficent results.

CHAIRMAN BURTON: There are other speakers on the program, but in view of the lateness of the hour and the fact that the American Peace Congress holds its session after our adjournment, they have begged to be excused. That brings this session to a close.

ADJOURNED

FIFTH SESSION

Thursday Evening, May 4, at Eight O'clock

Rev. Lyman Abbott, D.D., Presiding Officer

CHAIRMAN ABBOTT: A criminal judge in England was once asked how long a sermon ought to be. He replied "Twenty minutes, with a leaning to mercy." I suggest that anecdote as a hint to myself and to the speakers who are to follow me. If we eight speakers can each of us keep within twenty minutes we shall keep you here, I calculate, just two hours, and that ought to be enough to satisfy the most hungry for eloquence and perhaps not too much to weary the patience of those who are not so hungry.

There are two objects which I take it we have in this Peace Congress: One is to create public opinion in favor of peace; the other is to define and formulate our own convictions on the subject. As I have been attending the deliberations of this Congress and of previous conventions of this kind, I have come to the conclusion that there are as many creeds of peace in a peace congress as there are creeds of religion in a congress of religion. It is better so. It is well that we should interchange our various views in order that by that interchange we may more clearly understand what is to be the ultimate conclusion of all those who look for peace as a final ideal. I think, as those in a religious congress are all agreed, that faith, hope and love are the essence of religion, but are disagreed as to how religion is to be promoted and expressed, so we here are all in favor of peace as an ultimate end, while we differ in the steps that are to be taken and the order in which they are to be taken.

I have thought that I could do nothing better than to tell you tonight, as clearly and as simply as possible, what is my own creed, although I am sure it will differ in some radical aspects from the creed of others among you.

247

I do not believe that war is always wrong. I do not believe that war is what it was defined last night to be, "collective murder." To believe that war is collective murder would necessarily involve the belief that William of Orange and Cromwell and Garibaldi and Washington and Grant and Lee were the leaders of murderers and themselves murderers, who were entitled to be placed by the history of the world upon the scaffold. And there is no one who believes that. War is not collective murder. It is collective homicide, but homicide is sometimes justifiable and war is sometimes justifiable. Nor is it true that if we could abolish war we should abolish all the cruelties and all the barbarities that come from the use of physical force by wrath and bitterness. The contrary is true. If peace has its victories no less than war; peace has its barbarities and cruelties no less than war. There were more men, women and children killed in the massacres in Turkey at a time when Turkey was absolutely at peace with the rest of the world, than were killed in the Crimean War. There were more men, women and children killed in the Pekin rebellion probably than in the whole Russo-Japanese War, and at the time of the Pekin rebellion, China was not at war. No one knows how many Jews have been killed in Russia when she was not at war, but we know that those massacres were perpetrated and enacted with cruelties and horrors far worse than any that were perpetrated in the Russo-Japanese War. War does not put an end to the barbarities and to the use of phyical force.

These two things let us remember. What we are seeking here, I think—certainly what I desire—is not merely peace, but peace founded on righteousness, peace accompanying justice, peace with law and order as its components. What we are seeking is, first, justice and next peace. "If it be possible, as much as lies in you," says the Apostle, "live peaceably with all men." What we are seeking in this Congress is to find out how far it is possible for us to live in peace with all men, how far it lies within us to bring about that beneficent result.

For this reason disarmament must follow peace, not precede and prepare for it. Disarmament is the result and peace is the cause, not disarmament the cause and peace the result. To take the arms away from those who are under control and leave them in the hands of those who are not under control, to take them away from the police and put them in the hands of the blackhanders, is not the way to peace. To take away armaments from those nations that know how to use them and to leave them in the hands of those nations that do not know the power of self-restraint, that are without the self-control that is necessary to an armed nation, is not the pathway to international peace. To take arms away from the highest, the best and the most cultured nations and leave them in the hands of the least cultured is not to prepare for the Kindgom of God. "The Kingdom of God"—I quote again from that old writer, Paul—and I don't know how far you regard him as an authority, but he is at least a favorite author with me—"the Kingdom of God is righteousness and peace and joy and holiness of spirit." There is no peace not founded on goodwill, and also there is no goodwill not founded on righteousness. Righteousness first, peace next, universal welfare last of all.

So neither do I think that arbitration is the panacea that will cure the world of its woes and put an end to all war. Many wise things have been said at this conference, and some otherwise. None wiser, however, than Mr. Taft's statement at the opening of the Conference, that we must not expect that peace would instantly follow after arbitration. Arbitration was well-defined, if I remember right, by Mr. Holt, who said that it was substituting the appeal to reason for the appeal to force, and when-ever that substitution can be made, it must be made. But, if there is no reason you cannot appeal to it. You cannot appeal to reason when facing a pack of wolves. When dynamiters blow up our raliroads and homes, you cannot appeal to reason, because they haven't got it. You organize the court not to find out whether it is reasonable to blow up houses and bridges, but to find out if it was done. When marauding bands assail private persons in Turkey and the government stands by and looks on without doing anything, then there is no reason there to appeal to. When the Armenian massacres were going on if one nation had brought a man-of-war up the Dardenelles and told them that the massacres must stop, they would have stopped, and it would have been the threatening of war that would have stopped them. For one hundred years appeal was made to Spain by the United States in behalf of Cuba, and made in vain. At least forbearance ceased to be a virtue. After from one-quarter to one-third of Cuba's citizens had been killed, some by secret assassination, some by assault, some by starvation, then this country, having for one hundred years appealed and appealed in vain, appealed by the guns of Sampson's fleet and Cuba was made free.

What we claim—what I claim—is this: First, certain great causes of war have ceased to operate. One of the great causes was religious animosity. When the crescent entered Europe and thundered at the gates of Vienna, Vienna could not submit to arbitration the question of whether the cross should bow to the crescent. When the Duke of Alba ran the plowshare of war through the Netherlands, the Duke of Orange could not submit to arbitration whether the Netherlands should submit to Spain. I hope there is not one of us here who would not fight to the death to prevent his own religious faith from being taken from him and his family and children. I am sure there is not one here who would raise a finger to enforce his religious faith on another. The peril of religious wars is gone forever from Christendom. Other wars have gone. Julius Caesar ran his legions over Gaul to take Gaul for the benefit of the Roman Empire. No Julius Caesar will do that again. I have read an article stating that Germany could put four hundred thousand troops on our Atlantic Coast, and Japan on our Pacific Coast, if we did not have an army and navy to keep them from doing it. But they won't do it. We have found that we can do more with people by trading with them than by conquering them and taxing them. Napoleon went to Italy and conquered Italy and robbed Italy of her art treasures. J. Pierpont Morgan went to Italy, after those treasures had been regained by Italy, and he bought those art treasures, and it did not cost him one-tenth of what it cost Napoleon to rob Italy of them.

It is said that when the rivalry of nations brings them in contact then war ensues. We assert that for years three thousand miles of border land have been left open and unprotected. During all that time England and America have been competing throughout the world. Canada and America come in competition with railroads across the continent. There has been bitter and hot competition between that country and this Republic, and when we take the great step suggested by the President, when this reciprocity treaty goes into effect we hope—I do— that these two great countries will clasp hands in a freer and a more generous trade than they have known in times past. What he proposed that we say to Great Britain, if I interpret it right, is this: We will arbitrate all questions with you, including questions of honor and independence and of vital interest. We know you. You would not, if you could, put a slur upon our honor. You would not, if you could, interfere with our independence. You would not, if you could, disturb our vital interests. And we have no purpose to put a blot upon your honor, or blight your interests, or interfere with your independence. We trust you. Will you trust us, and in that mutual trust and confidence leave all questions that can arise between us to a court of arbitration?

There is not one of us here tonight who would vote to arbitrate our independence. If Great Britain said a hundred and fifty years ago, "You are our colonies and you must return and be our colonies again," we would not leave that to a Hague Tribunal. But it is preposterous to think that England would propose such a thing, and therefore it is preposterous to guard against it. We say to Great Britain, "We trust you, and we leave all questions that can arise between us to a judicial tribunal." And when our country has really said that—when the Senate—for the people of the nation have already said, excuse the Methodist figure, "Amen," to the President's address—I say when the United States Senate, after greater deliberation, says, "Amen," also, we know that Great Britain will make a like response. And when we two nations have done that, then we may well turn to the other nations of the globe, certainly to the other nations of Christendom and say "This is our estimate of modern civilization. Great Britain and America are sufficiently civilized to believe that they can trust each other with all questions of vital interest and honor and independence. Whenever you are sufficiently civilized to take the same stand and repose in us the same trust, we shall like to make the same agreement with you.

I was asked today by a newspaper reporter whether I thought Japan would enter into such an agreement. I told him I did not know. He asked me whether I thought the people of the United States would be willing to enter into such an agreement, and I told him again I did not know. I am not speaking for the people of the United States. But I will say for myself that if Japan, in the spirit of Great Britain and in the spirit of the United States would agree to recognize the integrity of our country, to recognize our independence, to recognize our national honor and to recognize our vital interests, and we would agree to do the same with Japan, and based on that agreement she would agree to leave all questions that might arise between us in the future to arbitration, I would say that we would say, "Do it by all means," and I believe we would have a better protection for the Philippines and the Hawaiians and our own coast than we could ever get by army or by navy.

That is my creed. I got it into twenty-two minutes, and I am going away tomorrow morning and leave it to be riddled by those who do not agree with me, in the subsequent sessions of this Congress.

"The Why, When and How of Disarmament." If Dr. Warfield can tell us why armaments should cost us so much and why they should be abolished, and how we can bring that abolition about, we shall all be delighted. I have the honor of introducing Dr. E. D. Warfield, President of Lafayette College.

REDUCTION OF ARMAMENTS; WHY, WHEN, HOW?

ETHELBERT D. WARFIELD, DD., LL.D.

Emerson has strikingly said: "Every reform was once a private opinion". . . . "Every revolution was first a thought in one man's mind; and when the same thought occurs to another man, it is the key to that era." Judged by this statement the movement for peace and arbitration must have in it a great political possibility. But like so many of Emerson's phrases this looks upon only one side of human history. Every reform, every revolution, was indeed once a private opinion, and remains for us a thought embodied, a dream come true. But there have been many opinions, many dreams, that wailed out their wan lives in the vain quest for bodies in which they might be made flesh. And the question for us today is this. Is the idea of reduction of armaments only a pious opinion, or is it a resolute purpose? Is it merely a dream or is it a determined program of action?

The mind of contemporary thinkers has felt the drift of our age towards philosophical uncertainty, and has sought in pragmatism to regain for conduct its just place in all human thinking. The will to do is being valued to us at its true worth. A civilization rich in bloom, heavy with the odors of a too languid love of beauty and ease, must be stimulated to test all truth by action. And no contemporary movements are more criticised for the disproportion between their ideals and their deeds than those represented in this great gathering.

Of all the subjects under discussion, the man who calls himself practical thinks this of the reduction of armaments the most impractical. I dare to believe the very contrary is true. It presents the problem of a situation that every one will admit to be a crime against society, to which no one has the courage to apply the key. The man for the hour, that and that only is needed. A statesman of large views with a strong nation behind him, possessed of the courage and capacity of leadership, such is the need of the hour. Is it the old receipt for roast hare; first catch your hare? Let us at least see what the situation really is.

WHY SHOULD THERE BE A REDUCTION OF ARMAMENTS?

Let us take the pressing practical argument first. There should be a reduction of armaments because the burden of armed peace *is*—not merely is becoming—intolerable to a considerable number of the great powers, and oppressive to every nation of any

weight in the world's councils.   The time does not permit me to
dwell upon the details which are familiar to this audience.   The
terrible cost in money, in taxes wrung from peoples already oppressed by the unpaid cost of the wars of earlier generations,
is known in every ministry of Europe.   Far more vivid is the
knowledge of this cost in the boards of industrial corporations.
But only the workingman and his household appreciates with
due poignancy the price of national pride and international suspicion.

If this burden were necessary it were the part of patriotism to
bear it with a cheerful spirit.   But if it is only the child of national
vain-glory, the creature of ministerial illusion, the invention of
vampires who suck the blood of nations to enrich themselves, not
only patriotism, but a higher passion for mankind demands that
this burden be lifted from the shoulders of men.

There was a time when our ancestors dwelling in the forest
depths along the Rhine, the Elbe and the Weser saw amid the
shadows of the forests the fearful shapes of were-wolves and other
creatures of their imaginations which filled their days with tremors
and their nights with dread.   An unhappy atavism seems to op-
press the imagination of some of their descendants with uncouth
survivals of ancestral fears so that they see in all other nations

> Brutes that wear our form and face,
> The were-wolves of the human race.

But this burden of taxation is not the highest price that is paid
for armed peace.   The burden of a manhood tribute—three years
of a strong man's life in some countries—and the ever growing
threat of the spread of this plague, is not to be reckoned little.
I need not press this point in this land so accustomed to liberty,
so nobly schooled in the precious freedom, not merely from governmental dictation, but for a self determining manhood.   And to
all those whose minds have risen to the conception of a world-
wide fellowship in the arts of civilization and the aspirations of
religion, nothing could be more hateful than the attitude of international suspicion and distrust which is represented by these
burdensome preparations for a war which seems ever at the gates.

And it is not capable of any kind of proof that these armaments have prevented war, or placated opinion. On the contrary it is easy to show that they have bred distrust and even precipitated war. And even on the commercial side the lack of confidence in them as merely defensive is shown in the lower price and greater fluctuation of the public securities of the nations armed to the teeth as compared with those which are practically without armaments. Compare for example, Belgian 3 per cent at 96 with German at 82; and Norwegian 3½ per cent at 102 and Russian at 81.

The education of the age in a gospel of force instead of one of justice is also to be counted against this delusion. Not only is this a peril to every people ("He that taketh the sword shall perish by the sword" was not written in vain), but new nations are going to school to the old. Has not Japan proved an apt scholar? Let Russia answer. Had the great western powers preached to Japan from the same texts as their scholars and missionaries used, would American jingoes ride the same nightmares they bestride today? Surely in every sin is sowed the seed of its own punishment.

WHEN?

But when? When shall reduction of armament be realized?

No law should be written on the statute books until it has first been written on the hearts of the people.

But who are the people? I once heard Mr. Bryce say under very impressive circumstances, that few realize what a very small body of men really govern every country. Nothing could be more true than this. An efficient majority is not necessarily a numerical majority. Those who are wise after the event are forever pointing out that the great revolutions, the Reformation in England and the American Revolution for example, have been the work, not the of many, but of the determined. The men of force, the men of leadership, in any time of progressive movement bear other men and measures forward by sheer force of will.

But great movements begin with discussion, with the education of the mind and the conscience. Then they are felt to be "in the air." An intellectual and moral contagion is felt. What was a private conviction becomes public opinion. What was dependent upon individual initiative, begins to move in the pulses of the body politic. Then it is that there must be found men of courage and unselfish devotion who are ready to risk their careers for national well being.

The great work of educating the people in the significance of arbitration and kindred methods of replacing international conflicts by international justice, has been carried on with amazing success during the past decade. The dead weight of public indifference has been overcome and a progressive impulse has been imparted to contemporary opinion. The time has come for decisive action.

When Gladstone upon mature and conscientious reflection resolved to throw aside his strongly intrenched prejudices and recommend the submission of the *Alabama* claims to arbitration, he not only astounded the world,—he advanced the world's civilization by a century's mark.

When Roosevelt flung precedent to the winds and gripped with a brave man's iron grasp a great opportunity, he not only made peace between Russia and Japan, but he showed how progress is to be made possible.

HOW?

How is the reduction of armaments to be begun? How else than by those to whom the high trust of governing nations has been committed breaking away from mere convention and acting with the courage of high conviction?

Every statesman, every cabinet, every ruler, is beset by phantoms of the past, by half defined perils of the present, by self seeking politicians and manufacturers of warlike materials. Not many could act if they would; still fewer would act if they could. But it is for us who believe in lifting this burden, not only from our country, but from all mankind; for us who believe that the time is ripe for Christian civilization to reap the fruits of centuries of growth, to beat upon the dull ears of legislators and stir the cold hearts of executives, until the thoughts of the wisest statesmen are translated into action. Today is ours. We know not what the future has in store. It is for us to act now while it is called today—for us as individuals, and for us as great bodies of men and women informed and inspired by a great cause.

Abraham Lincoln in his address in Independence Hall, Philadelphia, February 22, 1861, spoke of "that sentiment in the Declaration of Independence which gave liberty—not alone to the people of this country, but hope to all the world for all future time. It was that which gave promise that in due time the burden should be lifted from the shoulders of all men."

That promise will be fulfilled in great measure when governments shall be content to seek the happiness and welfare of their own people within their own territory, neither greedy for the land of others nor jealous of their prosperity, strong in conscious rectitude of purpose, and united in international bonds which shall make it at once the duty and interest of each nation to seek and maintain the integrity and freedom of every other.

CHAIRMAN ABBOTT: "What are We Doing for Peace in the Far East?" I am very glad to introduce to you now one who needs no introduction to the readers in America, Mr. Price Collier, who will give us some answers to that question.

WHAT ARE WE DOING FOR PEACE IN THE FAR EAST?

PRICE COLLIER

Mr. President, Ladies and Gentlemen: Six months ago I returned from a year of travel in the Far East. I visited India, Burma, the Straits Settlements, China, Japan, Korea, Manchuria, Siberia and Russia. I have been asked here to speak on the subject of "What we are doing for Peace in the Far East" and I propose to add to that "What more can be done in America and by Americans" in that direction.

More, far more, than half the distrust of one another, of the nations of the earth is due to nothing more mysterious than just plain, complete and indifferent ignorance. We can do much for peace therefore by knowing one another better. The prejudiced and superficial talker, and the scare-head loving press, do more, to quote a line from Macbeth, "to pour the sweet milk of Concord into Hell," than all other agencies combined. A purposeless curiosity that cares nothing for truth, pampered each day with highly seasoned misinformation, is far more dangerous to peace than any peril now existing on the horizon of international affairs, whether it be yellow, black, or brown. The greatest peril to peace today is not brown, nor yellow; it is white! It is white ignorance, white prejudice, and the sheltered snobbery of the suburban sectarianism of the white man! I am no orator, no seeker after the precarious popularity which comes to him who fondles the mob with deceitful words: "those windy attorneys of client woes, those poor breathing orators of miseries!"

I return to my country to hear much of sedition in India; and even more, of the aggressive preparations for war on the part of Japan and I am astonished at the ignorance of my countrymen on both subjects.

India has a population of 320,000,000 and an area in square miles equal to the whole of Europe less Russia. India for the two thousand years that history has known her, has been rent and torn and mauled by foreign conquerors and raiders from without; and by fierce jealousies of race and creed and caste from within. India is governed today by the British and for the first time in the life of India there have been peace, security and equal opportunity there, greater security to life and property than in the streets of New York, unless you belong to a Teamsters' Union, or are a protegé of Tammany Hall! The governing of India by the British is the most splendid service ever rendered to one nation by another. India is no more fit for self-government at this moment than the inmates of a menagerie. There is a society of white men in this country sending money and literature into India to stir up sedition there. Mr. President, if I had the power I would arbitrate those white seditionists, with their headquarters in America, out of existence! The civil service of the British in India is above either reproach or suspicion, *candor non laeditur auro.* Fortunately for India and for peace in the East, sedition, unrest, disloyalty in India are helpless. Of themselves they can no more throw off British rule, than this audience can add another hue to the rainbow, or wave aside a Cape Cod fog with fans.

Wendell Phillips once remarked that the Puritans believed Hell was a place where every man would be obliged to mind his own business. We Americans can do something for peace by minding our own business, and letting the British mind theirs in India; even though some of my meddling fellow-countrymen find the heat of such non-interference in other people's affairs, oppressive.

We are just recovering from a fever of excitement about Japan. Japan has a population of 50,000,000 with compulsory education and compulsory military service. She is able to put 850,000 fighting men into the field at a moment's notice. She has 191 war vessels aggregating 495,000 tons. She has spent on her navy during the last four years $134,000,000. She has 5000 miles of railway, and more are building, and her export and import trade amounts to about $450,000,000 per annum; our exports and imports of domestic merchandise, amounted in 1908 to over $3,000,-000,000. Her expenditures in 1910 amounted to $267,000,000; her taxes in the same year amounted to $160,000,000, and her national debt stands today at $1,151,000,000. The total area of Japan, whose national debt is larger than ours, is 147,651 square miles, a little smaller than the State of California. So mountainous, and barren and difficult, is the land of Japan, that even these people of ant-like industry can only bring one-sixth of the total area under cultivation; there are therefore only 24,608 square miles which can be cultivated at all, and one-half of this is given over to the raising of rice! The farm area of the State of Missouri alone, is twice the extent of the whole available farm area of Japan.

The Russian War, an inconclusive war, cost the Japanese 85,000 killed; 600,000 casualties and $1,000,000,000. Do not be discouraged by these figures. They are part of an interesting picture, and with all the chatter one hears about Japan it is worth your while to know the facts of the case, when the Japanese peril is being dealt with in the *lingua Hobsoniana.* In 1895 Japan took from China the island of Formosa, of some 13,000 square miles in area, with a population of 3,000,000. Only the other day she annexed Korea with an area of 71,000 square miles and 10,000,000 inhabitants; and after the Russian War she occupied the Liao-tung peninsula and controls part of southern Manchuria. This pyramid of recent conquests is built upon 24,000 square miles of cultivated area, one-half of which is given over to the raising of rice; and upon a population just emerged from feudalism, worshipping the ancestors of a puppet king, and with a national debt larger than that of the United States. If the English and American bankers attempted to sell the Japanese bonds they hold at this present moment, Japan would be bankrupt in a month.

I traveled through Japan, crossed to Korea, traveled through Korea, crossed the Yalu River in a Chinese junk—there is no bridge as yet—and then on the crazy little 30-inch gauge railway, which General Kuroki laid down for the transportation of troops and supplies during the Russian-Japanese war, I traveled through Manchuria to Mukden. It is a tortuous, tiresome, and even dangerous journey, but there lies the heart of the whole Eastern question. Japan is building bridges, building a broad-gauge railway from the Yalu River to Mukden, and using every effort to push Japanese settlers into that country. Japan will then have direct communication over a well-built railway, from Tokio to Peking and Shanghai; from Tokio to Moscow, St. Petersburgh, Berlin, Paris and London. She will then pour her cotton goods into China and tap the rich coal and ore fields of Manchuria and Middle China, for her factories at Osaka and elsewhere. The open door to China will be a wide open door with custom house officers, with police, and soldiers on both sides of it; and they will all wear Japanese uniforms. But only twenty-five miles of the new railway between Mukden and the Yalu River are completed, the bridge over that river is only just begun. There are from three to five years' work at least, ahead of them, and hard work at that, for part of the railway line is through mountainous and difficult country. As I have just come from that country, you will forgive me, if I smile at the mass of lurid misinformation to which you in America have been treated. The paramount and imperative interests of Japan, for some years at least are in Formosa, in Korea and in Manchuria. I will prove it to you. In the year 1908, 9544 Japanese were admitted into the United States (exclusive of Hawaii); while during the year 1909 only 2432 Japanese came to this country, and this includes all Japanese whether laborers or not. In the year 1910, only 705 Japanese came, and they were all without exception returning laborers, or parents, wives or children, of domiciled laborers. The immigration of Japanese into Hawaii from 1908–1909 decreased 83 per cent and from 1909–1910 more Japanese left Hawaii than entered. I am willing to admit all the selfishness and aggressiveness of the Japanese, but having seen their struggles and difficulties in consolidating their power in Formosa and Korea, having seen the feverish activity in Manchuria, I beg to submit to the bellicose orators, and to the epicene warriors whose titles are derived from prancing in uniform behind a civilian governor, that Japan has her work cut out for some years to come; to pay her bills, to gain and hold and control her new territory; and that bankruptcy not battle is her chief concern.

There is no country in the world with such a large proportion of people who can read and write, but who do not think, who have a passion for the disconnected, as in this country. With a few exceptions our press is irresponsible, flippant and uninformed; and it panders to the purposeless curiosity of this great number of intellectually dissipated readers. This mass of undigested news ferments in the body politic for its own undoing.

Nothing is more aggravating than parochial ignorance, nothing more opinionated than racial prejucide, nothing more difficult to deal with than that narrow uprightness which so often expresses itself in downrightness. I take it that one object of this National Peace Congress is to triumph over such obstacles; to give battle to the suburban sages who pretend to rule this country, and who by their stiff self-satisfaction, and their profound ignorance and contempt for any basis for society except their own, make amicable relations between this and other countries doubly difficult.

In the past we were internationally speaking a negligible quantity. A small boy with a wooden sword, and his hat cocked over his eyes, parades the streets, shouting that he is a Robin Hood, and nobody cares. A grown man with a bowie-knife in his belt and a revolver in his hand steps into the street and every citizen denounces him. There was no danger from our complacent ignorance in the past, our self-righteous ineptitude was safe, though ridiculous. I bring you the message that this is no longer the case.

There is no immediate danger, as I believe I have shown you; but if we do not take a hand in educating the American out of his newspaper-bred bumptiousness, and his complacent conceit, and the scornful dominance of a depressing mediocrity there will be trouble.

This platform is no place for party politics, and I am not here to introduce controversy; and I place myself, and I hope you also, outside of party for the moment, to mention two opportunities for the furtherance of good fellowship between nations which I hope this country will not neglect. One is the reciprocity treaty with Canada, and the other, some form of arbitration treaty between this country and Great Britain. Is it possible that any section of this country is willing to proclaim that its own selfish interests must outweigh the good of the whole? Are there farmers who will fight this plan for commercial intercourse, and hence for friendlier feeling between Canada and the United States on any such ground as that? It may surprise you to know, that I have a farm in this very State of Maryland, and that my forbears for more than two centuries have lived in this State, and were that farm worth a thousand times what it is, I would sow it with salt, rather than that anyone should say, he pitted the products of his farm against his country's reputation for friendliness and fair-dealing. "My Maryland, My Maryland," but not at the price of branding my country as a nation of pedlars.

If we make impossible a treaty of arbitration with Great Britain we shirk a duty and a high one. If Europe were relieved of the enormous burden of armament, if that colossal statue of Mars built of steel and iron which weighs like suffocation upon the workers of Europe and Japan were removed, we should give every man seeking the religious and political freedom we enjoy, a better chance to win them. Are we to hug our privileges to ourselves? Is this the ideal of democracy? Is this our vaunted love of liberty? Is this our championship of the downtrodden of other lands? This is Liberty turning her back upon the world! This is Prowess cowering in its prosperity and refusing to abide by its own baptism! This is Freedom in a shroud! We proclaim ourselves the chosen people. The lately elected Speaker of the House of Representatives in his opening speech spoke of us as "the hope of the world!" Well, here is our chance to prove it. Here is an opportunity blazoned before the eyes of all other nations, to translate some of our sickening Fourth-of-July bombast into deeds; to subordinate our sectional grievances, our petty party cries, our acidulous political jealousies to the welfare of the world! When we Americans decline to take part in arbitration treaties we are far more guilty than other nations. For our very excuse for being as a nation, our very political ideal, the very democracy in which we pretend to believe; these all imply equality, liberty, opportunity for us, and for all men to whom we can extend them. The Germans, the Russians, the Japanese may be wrong when the they decline arbitration, but we Americans are traitors to our trust, and hypocrites besides.

We are already suspected of hypocrisy by other nations. They claim and not without reason, that we are fierce and not always fair competitors for trade, but that is too hazy an accusation to discuss. But I do agree that we are making a bad impression by our drummer diplomacy. Our ministers and ambassadors abroad should of course protect to the utmost our trade and commerce, and see to it that we have equal privileges with our rivals. We are now-a-days—and a woeful blunder it is—permitting our diplomatic representatives to take active part in the selling of goods and the getting of contracts. It is considered a feather in a diplomat's cap if he succeeds in getting the contract for the building of a gun-boat. I consider such activity a disgrace to him, and a disgrace to the country that employs him. Is democracy to be sent abroad to play its part among other nations in the gabardine of Shylock? Is the sole ideal we have to represent, say

to the South American Republics, that of a pedlar? May I
claim for you that such a man does not represent you? I certainly claim that he.docs not represent me. I deny that all the
activities of this country, its education, its striving for equality
and liberty and the opportunity for distinction, are best set forth
in the person of a mere bargain hunter. No wonder other nations
distrust us, if we are to be thus represented. It is a very cheap
invitation to friendliness and confidence and arbitration to begin
by attempting to sell something! We want trade, yes, and let
every honest trader receive full protection; but we want the world
to know and to see the best products of democracy; its scholarship, its magnanimity, its gentleness, its good breeding, its friendliness, its love of peace. We win some renown for our country
when we are represented by a Hay, a James Russell Lowell, a
Bayard, a Choate, a Reid, a Rockhill; but when we send the toady
of a political party or a smart salesman, we give the lie to our ideals
and other nations are quick to sneer.

> You call me misbeliever, cut-throat dog,
> And spit upon my Jewish gabardine

and well they may, if we are to permit this drummer diplomacy.
We gain more of appreciation and belief in our good intentions
abroad, through four years of a Hay, a Choate or a Bayard or a
Reid than by contracts for forty gun-boats. It is a fatal blunder
we are making in South America to give them the impression that
what we want from them is their trade; and to send them drummer diplomats. What we should say to them is: We want your
friendliness, your fellowship, your coöperation in building and
maintaining democratic institutions, and let trade follow if it
will.

I say this much of reciprocity, of arbitration, of drummer diplomacy, because I distrust thinking that finds no vent in action;
I believe it to be mentally and morally debilitating to listen merely
out of curiosity; I believe it weakens a man, a society or a nation,
to have purposes that find no plans. I do not believe that any
great object of public policy can be attained by congresses, conferences or subsidies alone! But we can all take a hand in these

matters. We can protest by voice and pen and at the ballot-box and in the newspapers against sectional selfishness; against the mean nationalism that fears to take its share of responsibility in keeping the peace; and above all we can protest loud and long against drummer diplomacy. We can all do something toward cutting out the canker of buncombe, which eats away at our intellectual sincerity whether political, moral or international. We can all shout buncombe at the man who proclaims that we are the light of the world, and then proceeds to so shade its beams that they only fall upon his own constituency, his own party, his own political advancement.

I was talking not long ago with a hungry office-seeker in Washington, who lectured me upon the value of having a constituency to back your begging for office. He was pleased with his own efforts in courting and nursing a constituency, which he proposed to use to back his claims. He said that he proposed to join a church, that the American people liked a man to be a church member! I do not believe that the American people are so degraded, so easily humbugged that they have no use for a man whose only constituency is his own soul. On the contrary, I believe that we are coming more and more to see that such men are a necessity; that such a society as this for example where men meet to lay aside the rancor of party in order to promote the welfare of all, is invaluable. But even here we must not lose ourselves in any hazy sentimentality. We writers and speakers get into the bad habit of mistaking the problems of the world. We think that these problems are a maze of words; in reality these problems are masses of men! The reformer of all men should be tough not tender-minded. I have always believed, and my experience of the Far East has strengthened that belief, that a strong man, that a strong nation are best adapted to bring peace.

Duelling ceased—Why? Because men whose honor and courage and physical ability were unimpeachable, said that duelling was ridiculous. If weak men refuse to fight they are called cowards; but when strong men refuse to fight, fighting ceases.

I suppose no intelligent man believes in war *qua* war; neither can he possibly believe that the settlement of boundary claims, of matters of national sensitiveness is best arrived at by the slaughter of thousands of men and the spending of millions of money. Our only differences are questions as to how to avoid such deplorable and childish methods.

In the present state of the world, I can see no alternative, but that the peace-loving nations should keep themselves strong enough to maintain peace. Gentlemen dropped wearing rapiers when they found that law and public opinion were strong enough to protect them. If I marched upon this platform with a rapier by my side, I should be ridiculed. When nations and the strong nations prove to the world that they can live in peace, other nations will lay aside their swords, because to wear them will be absurd.

That most peaceable of men, the poet of the church, George Herbert, wrote: "You cannot get beyond danger without danger." I defy any American to show me how he can get beyond the danger of the Monroe Doctrine, for example, without the danger of a fortified canal, and a powerful navy. Not even Yankee ingenuity can get beyond danger without danger! Our selfish, thoroughly unchristian, and topsy-turvy logic which preaches peace in India, China, Japan and Korea and then threatens dire punishment upon any one who attempts to share with us the opportunities of the golden west, needs a powerful force behind it, until we can solve such problems among ourselves.

I admit, I have admitted, not only the horrors of war but its lunacy among civilized peoples, but I will be no party to a policy of defencelessness. The ambassadors of peace should not be sent with the halters of powerlessness dangling from their necks. Teaching and training our boys and youths rough sports does not make them bellicose. And a nation prepared to fight if necessary, but holding out stoutly for peace is our best policy till the world laughs at its past of quarrelsomeness and lays aside the sword, belt and bayonet.

In short, I believe every man ought to know how to fight, and be trained to physical toughness and then do everything in his power to prevent fighting. A proud and powerful people which proves that it can live and prosper without war is the best apostle of peace. "By the peace among our people let men know we serve the Lord."

CHAIRMAN ABBOTT: It now gives me great pleasure to call upon Mrs. Fannie Fern Andrews, who will address you on the subject of "Education and International Peace."

EDUCATION AND INTERNATIONAL PEACE

FANNIE FERN ANDREWS

All that has been accomplished in the international peace movement has been done through the process of education. The development of constructive peace machinery has progressed just so far as public opinion has supported the specific measures. No convention was adopted by the delegates at The Hague Conferences, and no progressive steps in international agreements have been taken since that time without the sanction of international public opinion. This obviously has shaped its decisions according to the knowledge possessed by the people of international affairs. The international peace movement is today, as it has always been, an educational campaign. The peace societies, the national peace congresses, the international peace congresses and all other efforts aiming to create a sentiment which will demand advanced steps in international politics are all a part of this world-wide education. We have indeed witnessed a great change in the world's viewpoint, as was evidenced yesterday by the significant address of the President of the United States. The burden is to disseminate the spirit of justice and reason throughout the length and breadth of the whole world, so to habituate the nations into thinking in terms of peace.

This is one phase of the educational campaign; but there is another, more far-reaching and fundamental, which must proceed simultaneously. If law is to be substituted for war it must be chiefly through the children of the present generation and their successors who must carry out those constructive measures begun at the present time. It rests upon future generations to perfect the great plan of world organization, a task larger and more complex than man has yet been called upon to perform.

Since the school is the most thoroughly organized agency of education, it is to the teacher that we must look for the inculcation in the minds of the youth of these new ideas which are demanding new responsibilities for the citizen. It was in recognition of this function of the schools that the French minister of public instruction prescribed the teaching of international arbitration, humanity and brotherhood in the primary, secondary and normal schools of France.

Fancy the universal teaching of these principles! How long before the spirit of justice and peace would be ingrained in the lives of the future citizens. Indeed, the teacher has the power to reweave the whole fabric of human thought.

An organized body of teachers, therefore, formed for the purpose of inculcating the spirit of justice and equity in the minds of the growing youth is a vital element in the international peace movement. It is of such a body of teachers that I shall speak this evening. The American School-Peace League, organized in 1908, aims to secure the support of the teaching force in the development of the international peace movement. Through summer schools, educational conventions, and teachers' institutes, through the educational press of the country, and through the distribution of literature which especially relates the international movement to the teachers' work, the League has secured the active coöperation of thousands of teachers. There are, however, nearly five hundred thousand teachers in this country, and the League counts its work incomplete until the information has been passed to each one of them.

In order, however, to reach the teachers with the greatest directness and therefore with the greatest economy, the League has organized State branches to the number of twenty-one, which have assumed the responsibility of interesting each and every teacher in their respective States. Some of these branches have made invaluable contributions to the propaganda of the international idea, notable among which are the Arkansas and the Massachusetts branches. The former has published a play, called "Arbitration," which it is sending out to the teachers of the State. The play will be used this year for Peace Day and commencement exercises. The Massachusetts branch has just completed an outline course of study on what it has termed "Goodwill." This is a graded course covering the first eight grades of school, and develops in an interesting, practical fashion the principles of internationalism. The subject for Grade I is, Good will to Pets and Playmates; in Grade II, The Ties of Home Life; Grade III, Those of School and Play-time; Grades IV and V, The Ties to the City or Town; in Grade VI the course reaches out to the nation as a whole, associating the work with history and geography; in Grade VII, the course accents month by month the helpful characteristics of the many nationalities who mould American life; Grade VIII, teaches the need of fighting together, a united army of many nations, against disease, corruption, and in defense of civic ideals. The Committee which have constructed this course have designated the method of using it, as illustrated in the following explanatory statement:

"The plan here suggested can be used by each teacher in the way best suited to the needs and opportunities of the school. When there are no definite periods planned for moral training, the topics can be made the subject of morning exercises or can be brought out through classes in literature. In many instances the work can be associated with history or civics.

"Ethical lessons for little children should not be more than ten or fifteen minutes in length. With advanced children thirty or forty minutes may be profitably spent. Lessons should be frequent enough to make a lasting impression.

"There is no better way of securing a permanent impression than by weaving the lessons in Goodwill into the very fabric of school life and associating them with simple progressive forms of social service.

"Thus even the youngest children can learn from the lessons on kindness that they should refrain from rudeness to the Chinese laundryman or the Italian organ-grinder; in the primary grades they can practise respect for the laws of the country and the police. Before long they can form Junior Citizens' Clubs and keep the

neighorhood in good order, and through every year they can be
led to exercise their loyalty, open mindnedess, and goodwill."

As soon as the League was organized, it recognized that the
greatest opportunity for teaching justice is through the teaching
of history, and it moreover recognized that much of the present
teaching of this subject developed just the opposite idea which
the League was aiming to stimulate. The Committee on the
Teaching of History instituted an investigation. It found that
"in some school systems much time is devoted to the study of
(1) Such useless details as unimportant dates and statistical matter; (2) the complex principles underlying the organization and
evolution of political parties; and (3) battles and military campaigns." The report further states that "by far the greatest
waste in history teaching results from the excessive and dispro-
portionate amount of time which is spent in the study of wars.
While, of course, wars should be studied and should receive much
attention on account of the important part they have played in
both racial and national evolution, they should not involve the
teaching of the military minutae of campaigns and battles."
And finally the Committee says, "When we learn to keep in mind
the right perspective in teaching the national biography of such
a peace-loving people as we have been from the beginning of our
history, we shall devote to the arts of peace and to the social and
industrial conditions of life that large measure of attention which
is their due."

Twenty thousand copies of this report have been distributed
all over the country and in Europe, and many conferences have
been held to discuss the next steps which our Committee might
follow to bring about a better balanced teaching of history. The
writing of history text-books is a most important element in this
discussion.

The Amercian School Peace League believes most strongly that
the teachers of the whole world should work together in this movement, so that the coming generations of all nations may be trained
simultaneously to recognize the efficiency of judicial and legislative measures in the constantly increasing relations among the
nations of the world.

To develop this plan, the secretary of the League spent three months in Europe last year studying possible methods of approach. After numerous conferences in Sweden, Denmark, Holland, Belgium, France, Germany and England, where the most cordial response was given to the idea, the secretary found that certain lines of organization were necessary for any complete development of international coöperation among the educational forces of the world.

In the first place, there is needed in every country some national organization, similar to the American School Peace League, through which a knowledge of the international movement can be extended to the teachers, and by means of which common action can be obtained among the educators of the world. The League, therefore, recommends the formation of national leagues.

Secondly: Several educational publications bearing on internationalism, which are in use in different countries, might with great benefit be translated for the teachers of other countries. As an example, one might mention *Cours D'Enseignement Pacifiste* by A. Seve, a book which received one of the three first prizes offered by the International Peace Bureau for the best course on internationalism for the use of teachers. This book has been placed in the hands of many French teachers during the past year. Many parts of this book, as well as parts of the two other winning books, might with equal profit be read by teachers of all countries. Some of the publications in England, Belgium, Italy, Sweden, Germany, and the United States ought to be made accessible to readers in other countries. Moreover, to develop common international sentiment among educators, it is highly desirable to build up a body of literature which can be used by educators all over the world. There could be, for example, a set of international school readers, stories and plays treating of incidents which develop broad and generous ideas about other nations.

Moreover, a very important consideration of the matter of publications should be the systematic effort to place such literature in the libraries throughout the world.

Thirdly: As the educational magazines of the United States have proved an effective agency for spreading the knowledge of

international events, so the educational magazines of every country could be enlisted for this purpose.   The secretary of the American School Peace League has been asked to write articles by
the editors of several European educational journals, and has responded as far as time permitted.   To do this work systematically
and thoroughly, as its importance would justify, direct concentrated effort should be given to reaching the educational magazines of the world. '

It was suggested to the secretary in Europe that an international
educational magazine would fill an important need.   The creation of this as well as the specific methods of enlisting the magazines, would depend on the future development of the general
plan.   In some countries, however, other journals might also prove
of great use in spreading the international idea.   Mr. John Barrett, for example, director of the Pan American Union, generously consented to print in the *Bulletin* of the Pan American Union
an article on the American School Peace League, this article to be
printed in Spanish as well as in English.   It would probably
require only a request to have similar articles printed in the
educational journals of Central and South America, which are for
the most part issued by the government.

Fourthly: Many activities are now carried on in the educational field which tend to bring about international acquaintance.
The exchange of university professors and public school teachers
is one of the most far-reaching devices for developing international
friendliness and goodwill.   The exchange of pupils, carried on
by a strong organization having offices in France, Germany and
England, is another method of promoting the same object; and
if the plans of Dr. Ernst Richard in this country are carried out,
we shall have a pupil exchange between this country and Germany.
International correspondence among school children has already
proved its value, not only as instruction in language but also in
cementing international friendships.   The writing of international
prize essays, relating to phases of internationalism, carried on
under the auspices of the American School Peace League, which
has opened the contest to the pupils of the United States and
Europe, can have but the effect of instilling into the minds of the
young contestants a feeling of equality and common responsibility.

All these activities should be stimulated and promoted by a central organizing force.

Fifthly: In the course of a year, numerous educational international congresses are held, attended by large numbers of educators from different countries. At many of these congresses, a discussion of international coöperation would not only be consistent but welcome. The difficulty in placing this subject on the program lies in the lack of appropriate speakers, or in the inaccessibility of getting such to take part in the discussion. To take advantage of reaching at one time many teachers of different nationalities, a list of speakers should be arranged and plans made to secure their services.

Sixthly: To promote international standards in education has long been one of the objects of advanced educators, as is illustrated by the holding of international educational congresses. The appointment by the National Education Association of the Committee on Coöperation with Educational Organizations in Other Countries represents a significant endeavor to study the matter of international standards; and it is to be hoped that this Committee will report on its work at the coming convention of the Association.

The most important subject, however, for teaching international solidarity, and one which admits of treatment, according to uniform underlying principles, is the subject of history. So much depends on the interpretation of human action and the lessons gained thereby, that no time should be lost in making an effort to bring about an international standard in the teaching of history. Through this subject alone, common sentiment can be developed among the coming generations of all nations, which will recognize the efficiency of judicial and legislative measures in international relations.

To develop all these activities, some central international organization should be formed with regularly established departments, each of which to be responsible for one of the six lines of work described above.

The American School Peace League has taken the initial steps in the organization of an International Council, to be composed

of two representatives of each nation, which shall have full charge
of the work of the six departments.   The plan of the League involves the naming of two members of the Council to represent
the United States, and the selection of two representatives from
each of the other nations.   One Councillor from each nation shall
be selected for one year and the other for two years.   Thereafter
all Councillors shall serve for two years and shall be elected by the
Council itself.   The Councillors shall elect from among themselves
a President, Secretary, Treasurer, and an Executive Committee
of five, including the President, Secretary, and Treasurer, which
shall appoint the heads of each of the six departments.   As soon
as Councillors representing six nations have been secured, the International Council shall be declared constituted and shall proceed to its own organization.   Until this time, one of the Councillors from the United States shall act as temporary secretary.

The response from Europe has been most favorable.   Already
we may count on France, Germany, England, Sweden, Austria,
Belgium, Italy, and probably Holland, Switzerland, Denmark,
Russia, and Japan; while it all probability, many of the Central
and South American countries will join the Council.

Through the departments of Speakers, Press, and Publications
the work of the State branches should be stimulated and unified.
These branches, however, must maintain their own organization,
and the Secretary should be provided with adequate funds to
pay for printing, postage, expressage, clerical services and traveling expenses.   At the present time, there are twenty-one secretaries who have volunteered their services for this work.

Moreover, there is work of a specific technical character which
should be undertaken by the League at an early date.   The work
of the History Committee should be continued, a model course
of study developed, and a text-book of United States history
written which will lay emphasis on the constructive factors in the
development of our country, and these factors will include the
social and industrial life of our people.

The League is organized on the supposition that every teacher,
upon enrolling as a member, becomes a volunteer worker, and
extends the influence of the League in his immediate sphere.   No

membership dues are, therefore, exacted from the teachers, so that the work of the League must be carried forward through the income of an endowment or annual subsidies. I wish these were large enough to enlist the interest and encourage the efforts of this vast army of unpaid peace workers, who have the power of instilling the principle of goodwill into the very warp and woof of life.

CHAIRMAN ABBOTT: I now have the pleasure of calling on Prof. William I. Hull. The subject of his paper is "The Abolition of Trial by Battle."

THE ABOLITION OF TRIAL BY BATTLE

WILLIAM I. HULL

When Clio, Muse of History, shall take up her pen to record the story of the new peace movement which is the glory of our twentieth century, she will write that this story, like that of the development of law within nations, is a story of the substitution of organized reason and right for anarchic violence and might. Her eyes, farther-seeing than ours, will discern a series of remarkable resemblances between the abolition of trial by battle and the substitution of law *within* nations, and the abolition of trial by battle and the substitution of law *between* nations. Even now, in the midst of this evolution, complex and of absorbing interest as it is, we may discern a number of those resemblances; and, since we have no surer light for the pathway of the future than that which shines from the lamp of experience in the past, it will be the attempt of this brief paper to signalize some of them. May they, like light-houses along some rock bound coast, send forth their beams to guide and cheer those mariners on the world's ships of state who are voyaging in search of assured international peace and justice.

1. Those French philosophers of the eighteenth century who sought to prove that mankind's golden age lies in remote antiquity were grievously mistaken. All history and all science are against this assumption, and show us that man's true golden age is with us

now and stretches on before us to the illimitable horizon of human progress. Early man lived a miserable, fearful and brutish life. *Faustrecht,* fist-right, the law of the strong arm and the big stick, ruled in the affairs of men. This was true of our Teutonic ancestors when history first dawns upon them in their forest homes in Germany. Their fount of justice was the judgment and deed of each individual; every freeman or free-necked man,"whose long hair floated over a neck that had never bent to a lord," was the "weaponed man," who possessed the right of private war and exercised that right in the avenging of his wrongs.

The nations of the earth, until quite recent times, were like primitive men in their relations with each other. Every free and independent nation, which had never abdicated its sovereignty to an international court, which girt itself round with armaments on land and sea, possessed the equal right of doing battle with its neighbors and, rejecting the wisdom and justice of mere man, appealed to the justice of Mars or Odin for the settlement of its differences.

2. When human life became valuable to someone other than its possessor, the right of private warfare to the death was restricted by the law of retaliation (*Lex talionis*), which permitted only "an eye for an eye, and a tooth for a tooth," and thus stopped the course of the blood feud this side of death.

It is rare for a victorious nation to exact as the spoils of a successful war only those territories, goods or chattels which served as the original cause of the war, or to take from the vanquished only that which the victor claimed it had lost. But in the eighteenth century the theory of the balance of power arose to prevent the utter annihilation of the vanquished state; and through the processes known as retorsion, reprisal, and pacific blockade, international law has sought to modify the blood feud between nations by a species of international *lex talionis*.

3. In primitive times, when blood relationship was the basis of state and church and social life, every outrage was held to have been done by all who were linked by blood to the doer of it, and every crime to all who were related to its victim. Hence, entire communities and successive generations were involved in the com-

mon ruin resulting from the evil deed of a single doer. When the territorial tie superseded that of kinship in Anglo-Saxon England, the custom of Frankpledge, or *Frithborh*, enforced collective responsibility for the crimes committed by an individual.

Modern governments in their strife with each other have appealed to the tie of common citizenship and summoned forth the workers from counting-house, field and workshop, to be offered up as "food for powder" in many a valley of death, where it was not theirs to reason why, theirs but to do and die, in a quarrel not of their own making, but the result of another's crime or blunder.

4. When the family grew into the tribe, responsibility for crime and its punishment was taken out of the hands of the family, as family responsibility had superseded that of the individual, and the tribal law replaced, in theory, both family feud and private warfare. The lives and limbs of warriors became too valuable in intertribal warfare to be wasted in strife within the tribe; hence, a system of money compensation, instead of death and retaliation, was enforced as the punishment of crime within the tribe. A tribal code of morality arose, which taught that while fraud and violence were legitimate and praiseworthy weapons against other tribesmen, honesty and justice should be practised towards one's fellows.

Modern nations advanced to the stage of compensation and tribal morality in their dealings with each other, and agreed that while money damages should be offered to some nations, and treaties of arbitration and arbitral courts should be entered into with those same nations, "defiance fell and bloody war" were alone possible or desirable with others.

5. When the tribe grew into the nation, under the growing influence of mutual interests, it came to be recognized that a wrong done to an individual was something in which the entire community had a common interest, and was really a crime committed against the State. The king's peace, and with the growth of democracy, the peace of the commonwealth, became a reality which was not to be broken with impunity by individual's attack upon individual, or even by an individual's or family's attempt to punish such attack. Public guardians of the peace were ap-

pointed to preserve the peace which was the public's due, and the public itself punished or redressed private wrongs.

With a growing perception of the solidarity of nations, and a realization that benefits and injuries experienced by one member of the family of nations are shared in common by the others, there is a growing belief that the true motto for international relations should be "All for each, and each for all." Already, the ban of international law has been placed on treaties which promise intervention on the part of one state in the domestic difficulties of another; and treaties of offensive and defensive alliance which couple the nations together to give chase in pairs or triplets against the "enemy" are being denounced by twentieth century Washingtons who condemn such entangling alliances on grounds both of national welfare and of international solidarity.

6. The evolution from the individual's right to avenge his wrongs by his own right arm, to the duty of the state to preserve the peace and administer justice by peaceful means, was long and slow; for the old freeman's fistright was hard to down. The state compromised with it, admitted it in certain cases, threw formalities around it, and dignified it with the name of "trial" by battle. When their crude means of securing evidence had been used without avail, the mediaeval men, in despair of reaching a practical conclusion by judicial means, reverted to the barbarism which lay just beneath their skins and resorted to the primitive law of force. This descent was softened by the sophistry which underlay the ordeals of fire and water, namely, that God would intervene and send victory in the combat to perch upon the banner of the innocent. In the edict of Gundobald of Burgundy, which established trial by battle among the Burgundians in 501 A.D., this philosophy was implied in the questions: "Is it not true that the event both of national wars and of private combats is directed by the judgment of God? And does not Providence award the victory to the juster cause?"

Even ecclesiastical courts preferred this appeal to Mars rather than one to the Prince of Peace, and clung to their right of trial by battle. In a monastic charter of 1008 A.D., we find the words: "We give to God and St. Denis the law of the duel." About the same time, in Spain, two knightly champions fought out for their clerical clients the question as to which of two rituals was acceptable to God. Two and a half centuries later, when St. Louis prohibited trial by battle within his own domains, the prior of one of his own monasteries protested against this violation of vested interests.

This convenient device and its plausible justification were applied in the relations between nations, and are only now being effectually ousted in theory and practice. When the Albigensian Crusaders stood before the walls of Beziers, in the first half of the thirteenth century, their ecclesiastical leader urged them to the slaughter of the heretics with the words: "Slay on, slay on God will know his own." At the siege of Damascus, during the Second Crusade against the Saracens, a lofty crucifix was erected at the principal gate of the city, and the bishop, attended by his clergy, laid a copy of the New Testament before the image of Jesus Christ and prayed that the Son of God would defend his servants and vindicate his truth. When the Holy Sepulchre was conquered amidst streams of human blood, and the Kingdom of Jerusalem established, trial by battle became one of the corner stones of its system of injustice. Six centuries later, Sir William Blackstone, the great historian of English jurisprudence, declared that "war is an appeal to the God of hosts to punish such infractions of public faith as are committed by one independent people against another." In the next century, Prince Bismarck declared repeatedly his belief in a God of battles who decides international disputes by casting his iron dice;" and down into this twentieth century of enlightenment, even civilized nations have acted on the dictum of that early Berserker who declared that it "is much fitter to contend with swords than with words." The efficacy of the ballot has not yet destroyed the nations' reliance upon the bullet; courts must still struggle for survival with the cutlass; and international Justice must still sometimes be portrayed as grasping the sword *without* the bandage or the scales.

There are those who, still championing "the right divine of kings to govern wrong," are champions still of the divine right of war to perpetuate the wrong. General von Deimling, of Germany, for example, is reported recently to have said: "Perpetual peace and the movement in favor of its establishment constitute a genuine danger. Nobody fights now for the pleasure of fighting, but for honor's sake. When an affair of honor has to be settled, it is the sword in the last analysis, which must decide the matter. We must therefore oppose the idea of peace, for it is a thing that would enervate the nations." While from the land of Ambassador Bryce and Sir Edward Grey has later come the strangely discordant Berseker wail: "It is still true, as it was a century ago, that, take it all in all a ship of the line is the most honorable thing which man as a gregarious animal has produced." Truly some twentieth century Cervantes is sorely needed to launch a new *Don Quixote* with its all-conquering laughter against the outworn chivalry of barbarous days which has revived in these grotesque forms of barrack philosophy and dreadnoughtitis.

Sir William Blackstone's excuse for his definition of war was much like the mediaeval man's justification of trial by battle, namely, that "neither state has any superior jurisdiction to resort to upon earth for justice." But now, thank God, since the First Hague Conference that lamentable fact is no longer true, and international justice is moving rapidly along the same path which enabled national justice to abolish trial by battle between individual citizens.

7. In the early administration of trial by battle within the nation, the two parties to a dispute were themselves called to the combat, the theory in its logical conclusion being that neither weakness nor age could count against the innocent, since God was on their side. But gradually the custom of securing champions for the feeble arose and developed into the shameless employment of professional pugilists from men who made a profession of letting them out for hire. To the victor went the spoils of the vanquished; hence these champions went abroad in quest of combats which would bring them fortune as well as fame.

In the international administration of trial by battle, it has been by no means unusual for a standing army of professional soldiers to take the place of volunteer "defenders of the right," and even for mercenary troops from foreign lands, such as the free lances in

European wars and the Hessians in our own Revolution, to be brought in to sustain a declining faith in the intervening justice of the God of battles. It would seem, too, that the present eager competition in the building of dreadnoughts and super-dreadnoughts is in line with reliance upon sturdy champions rather than on the justice of one's cause, and is indeed a practical application of the familiar though not all too trustful motto, "Trust in God— but keep your powder dry."

8. To our English ancestors of the eleventh and twelfth centuries however, there was something alien and dangerous in the favorite Norman device of trial by battle. It is probable that their Teutonic ancestors had used it, but the church and advancing civilization had abolished it in England, and when the Norman conquest introduced it they denounced it as a "barbarous foreign custom devised for the purposes of tyranny. William I, to conciliate the English, permitted them to decline trial by battle and to choose an ordeal of fire or water; and he and his successors hedged in the judicial combat by so many rules and formalities that it required an able-minded, as well as an able-bodied, man to appeal to it successfully.

When the Hague Conferences restricted warfare on land and sea by a great code of regulations, thus "canalizing" the activities of belligerents in defense of peaceful neutrals, a great cry of indignation went up from the military and naval delegates, that in future wars they would be so cribbed, cabined, and confined by rules and regulations that they would have left but little space or time in which to *fight*. It is instructive also to note that when the Second Hague Conference provided that no future wars should begin without a previous declaration of war, a Chinese delegate arose and blandly inquired what would happen in case the nation against whom the declaration had been launched should refuse to accept the challenge. Of course his inquiry was greeted by inextinguishable laughter; but that Chinaman not only recalled the concession which the English exacted from William the Conqueror, but he became the prophet of the future when war drums throb no longer and battle flags are furled in the jury box of nations, the tribunal of the world.

9. The Conqueror's successors did not continue to grant to all their English subjects exemption from trial by battle; but the growth of peaceful industry within the towns brought with it increasing wealth and political power, and during the twelfth century they purchased from their Norman lords the coveted exemption from trial by battle, and decided their disputes by means of the old English trial by oath, or compurgation.

The marvelous growth of economic internationalism, with its commercial, financial, and industrial ties that bind the world together, has caused international trial by battle to be increasingly frowned upon in our modern time, and has given great impulse to mediation and international commissions of inquiry which may be regarded as The Hague Conferences' equivalents for the old compurgation.

10. The rural tenants of the Norman lords looked with longing eyes upon the exemption from trial by battle which had been won by their English fellows within the city walls. At last a farmer by the name of Kebel was subjected to trial by battle, and, although notoriously guiltless of the crime with which he was charged, the combat went against him and he was hung just outside the gate of St. Edmondsbury. The taunts of the townsmen looking on from the walls aroused the victim's fellow farmers to a realizing sense of their condition. "Had Kebel been a dweller within the borough," said the burgesses, "he would have got his acquittal from the oaths of his neighbors as our liberty is." Thereupon the farmers demanded the same liberty and received it from their lord, the abbott; and the farmers throughout England slowly followed their example.

We have seen in our own day how, when nineteen members of the family of nations, indifferently absent from The Hague Conference of 1899, were given the chance to attend the Conference of 1907, they eagerly adhered to its "liberty" of avoiding trial by battle. We have seen also how infectious has been the fever of negotiating treaties of arbitration, 133 of these pacific agencies for settling disputes having been agreed upon since 1899; and we have seen how, within nine years, nine cases have been settled by the Permanent Court of Arbitration established at The Hague—

Great Britain, Germany, France, Italy, Japan, Norway, Sweden, Mexico, Guatemala, and Venezuela, having followed the beneficent example of our own Republic in submitting disputes to that more than imperial tribunal.

11. The Norman lords continued for a time with "sword and lance to arbitrate the swelling difference of their settled hate;" but gradually the kings began to "hate the dire aspect of civil wounds ploughed up with neighbors swords," and greatly reduced the Norman custom of trial by battle, lest it should "wake our peace, which in our country's cradle draws the sweet infant breath of gentle sleep." It was retained for certain classes of crimes and disputes; for example, it was considered the only honorable method of answering the accusation of felony, the worst and basest of crimes; and it was applied to debtors who disobeyed the sheriff's order to pay their debts.

We have seen how, in recent years, the sovereigns of the world have begun to hate the dire aspect of international war, and to fear the growing burden of preparation for trial by battle; how they have met at The Hague to devise peaceful means of settling their disputes; and how they have negotiated numerous treaties of arbitration and submitted a growing number of disputes to arbitral tribunals. In 1889, it was thought that only "judicial" questions could be successfully submitted to arbitration; in 1907, it was thought that questions of "national honor" should still be submitted to the Norman knighthood's "honorable" trial by battle, while the Porter proposition—great step in advance though it was—still recognized trial by battle as an ultimate means of collecting contractual indebtedness in case arbitration should fail.

12. During the reign of King Stephen, when England underwent a reaction in many phases of her life to the violence and brutalities of fuedal anarchy, the barons by the might of their mailed fist beat down wherever they could the nascent forms of civil justice, and restored trial by battle. Although the miseries of the time—as recorded in the *Anglo-Saxon Chronicle* which comes to a despairing end in lamenting the terrible evils it records—must have been grievous indeed for that generation of Englishmen to

endure, they served as a most useful object lesson and proved a great incentive to the adoption of the great legal and pacific means of settling disputes which Henry II was soon to usher in.

The Spanish-American, the Boer, and the Russo-Japanese wars were a sad surprise to the world which had witnessed the rise of the First Hague Conference; but they were at least a revelation of the imminence of warfare in the most advanced of nations, and a reminder of the ferocity and futility of trial by battle as practiced even by the most civilized of nations. They doubtless gave impetus, too, to the progress in the amicable settlement of international disputes which has made the last few years so illustrious.

13. The reign of Henry II witnessed the rise of trial by jury, that unrivalled palladium of English liberty—unrivalled, for it is older than Parliament itself, and bears within it the principle of representative government as well as the bulwark of civil liberty. It began with the jury of inquest, which was designed merely to procure information; developed into the jury of accusation or presentments, or grand jury, as we call it, whose function it was to present criminals for trial; and ended with the jury *par excellence*, the trial jury, or the petty jury as it is, apparently, unworthily called. This great juristic invention had existed in early times among the Franks and other Teutons on the Continent, but it had been overwhelmed by the spread of the Roman and Canon Law, and had practically disappeared from the German Fatherland. In England, however, it rose again and became one of England's choicest gifts to the civilization of the world.

The rise of jury trial on the international stage vividly recalls many incidents connected with its rise within the nations. The Anglo-American people have had most to do with laying the foundation of the international jury trial, even as the English gave the trial jury to the municipal jurisprudence of the nations. International commissions of inquiry may find their prototype in the jury of inquest. The international jury of presentment has not yet been evolved, but Professor de Martens' proposition at the Second Hague Conference that commissions of inquiry shall not only seek the truth about a controversy and publish it to the world, but shall also fix the responsibility upon the blameworthy nation, may yet develop into a grand jury, which shall bring guilty nations to the bar of international justice.   The arbitral character of the early jury, impanneling as it did an equal number of representatives of each litigant, together with others to act as umpires, has been preserved in the equivalent features of the Permanent Court of Arbitration.   The early jury was composed of both witnesses and judges, their value depending largely on their knowledge of the question in dispute, hence their verdict was both a partial and a compromising one; the final separation of witnesses and jurors is reflected in the American attempt at the Second Hague Conference—an attempt which is soon bound to succeed to establish a genuinely permanent, impartial and judicial tribunal.

Back of the national jury lay the royal power of the king, as opposed to the independent and disintegrating privileges of the feudal barons, while the jury itself represented the "country" and expressed the "country's" verdict; back of the international jury lies the power of the family of nations, as opposed to the exclusive sovereignty of independent states, while behind its awards there lies the greatest power in all this world—the power of international public opinion.   The first parties to jury trial within the nation were probably those powers which were almost coördinate in the time of Henry II and Thomas Becket, namely, the English church and the English state; it seems eminently proper that modern states, of equal sovereignty, but refusing in the interest of justice to be judges in their own cause, should submit their disputes to the international jury.   The first class of disputes regularly submitted to the national jury had to do with the ownership of land; disputes over international boundary lines have been among the first to be submitted to special arbitration and to the Permanent Court as well, while there is fair promise that the new Anglo-American arbitration treaty and the Third Hague Conference will assign territorial disputes invariably to an international jury.   The Constitution of the United States, growing out of the fruitful soil of English law, provided for the trial by jury of all criminal cases, but neglected at first to provide the same guarantee for civil cases; this omission nearly caused the rejection of the Constitution in the Virginia Convention, and an amendment was adopted which provided for the jury trial of all civil cases of the value of twenty dollars or more; with this English and American precedent to reénforce the Monroe Doctrine and the Porter Proposition, the American government has induced The Hague Conference to require all claims of contractual indebtedness to be brought into the international court.

Jury trial, like Parliament, was not popular at first with the richer freeholders of England, and they purchased immunity from its jurisdiction in considerable numbers, while many poorer freeholders groaned under its operation until its virtues appeared undoubted and supreme; some of the great powers of our time, notably Germany, have needed to become convinced of the efficacy of the international jury, while some of the smaller powers do not even yet yield unquestioned allegiance to this sure shield of their weakness. But it is growing more and more to be realized that, like the national jury, the international jury also is a protection of the rights of the weak against the tyranny of the strong; and that, as the national jury is a protection of national justice against the violence and vindictiveness of individuals or mobs, so is the international jury a protection of international justice against the ignorance, jealousy and prejudice of nation towards nation.

14. The year 1215 was an ever memorable one in world history for it saw the signing of Magna Charta and the meeting of the Fourth Lateran Council. The first guaranteed, among other liberties, the great liberty of trial by jury; and the second prohibited the church from lending divine sanction to trial by ordeals, thus making the choice a necessary one between trial by jury and trial by battle, and discrediting the Christianized Odin or Thor who was supposed to preside over trial by battle and trials by ordeal alike.

The Hague Conferences of 1899 and 1907 have discredited international trial by battle by denouncing warfare, in the words of Baron d'Estournelles de Constant, as a conflagration and commissioning every responsible statesman with the prime duty of preventing its spread and of putting it out. The year 1915 will also be marked by two ever memorable events, the meeting of the Third Hague Conference, and the celebration of a century of peace between the United States and Great Britain and their mutual disarmament on three thousand miles of border-line. May these events, like those of seven centuries ago, mark a great advance in the permanent and universal substitution of international peace and justice for the iniquitous and unjust trial by battle.

15. Among the priceless gifts that our Republic owes to the Motherland of Great Britain, there is none fairer than jury trial and the courts of justice in which it is enshrined. These are imbedded in the constitution of every State and of the Union itself, and are rightly regarded as the bulwark of justice, the palladium of our liberties. The time came, a century and a quarter ago, when our forefathers felt that they could no longer dwell beneath the imperial sway of the British Parliament and of King George the Third; but when they broke the political ties which bound them to their kinsman beyond the sea, they carried into their new constitution Old England's juristic triumph of trial by jury.

In view of this great historic fact, it was most appropriate that in the early infancy of our Republic, in the year 1794, the United States, negotiating the Jay treaty, with its arbitral provisions, inaugurated with Great Britain that series of international jury trials, which in the form of arbitration, have made the succeeding century supremely illustrious.

In this coronation year of King George the Fifth, when the nations are sending to the new sovereign their varied tokens of goodwill, no fairer gift can be sent to him by our Republic than that of a treaty of arbitration which shall apply to *every* dispute which may arise between our nations that principle of peace and justice which, received from England's law, has been enthroned within our American courts for many generations, and is now being crowned within the courts of nations. No fairer gift can be made to Britain's people and the world than such a bar, which shall forever close the doors of the Temple of Janus and forever open those of the Palace of Peace at The Hague.

In these days of great and increasing armaments, when Horror sits plumed upon the crests of nations, and when dreadful deeds may well ensue—"nor only Paradise, in this commotion, but the starry cope of Heaven perhaps, or all the elements at least may go to wrack, disturbed and torn with violence of this conflict"—we may well give thanks that "The Eternal, to prevent such horrid fray, hangs forth in Heaven his golden scales;" and that the fiend of trial by battle, looking up, beholds these golden scales of justice, and murmuring flees, while with him flee the shades of Night.

CHAIRMAN ABBOTT: Mr. Milton Fairchild has been carrying on for some time the moral instruction of our youth, and he will speak upon "Law and Order and International Peace."

LAW AND ORDER AND INTERNATIONAL PEACE

MILTON FAIRCHILD

Many a strong word is being spoken in favor of popular education in the cause of international peace. To my mind it is essential that this education deal chiefly with the youth of the nations, because it is in youth that the personal disposition is fixed for life by experiences and by the ideals that fascinate the mind. The spirit of the fighting bullying boy persists through manhood, and war appeals to such a man as heroic and as having the elements of largeness and greatness. Men of this fighting-hero type are more numerous throughout the world than those who love peace when indignation is aroused, and good red blood rushes to the head and the muscles become tense with anger. The natural man, uneducated in the cause of a world peace, his character fixed in youth and early manhood, is the unit of public opinion. This uneducated public opinion will force the hands of any government, and compel war when serious disputes arise between the nations. It is intelligent distrust of public opinion that restrains the world from international arbitration as a permanent and fixed policy. If Germany, fully prepared for war with England, should say "you shall not do what you intend and plan to do," would the British nation be capable of self-control? Not at all. The peace cry would fall upon deaf ears. The boy scouts would all turn soldiers. The God of war would be the controlling spirit of the nation, and the heroes of both nations would be the victors in the bloody battles of the war. It is folly to under-estimate the native instinct in the men of any nation to use violence and brute force as the final arbiter of serious differences between nations. This instinct of the beast must be educated out of them. The boys must be brought up right, and educated to believe that war is an ignoble and unintelligent mode of settling international disputes and of upholding the national honor. We must do our duty by our American youth by furnishing an adequate education in law and order and international peace.

The extreme importance of the work done by the American School Peace League is the strongest possible argument for strengthening the work along these lines.

Granted that education of the youth of the nation in the benefits of international peace is of prime importance to the cause, how is that enlightenment to be given? It is this work of national education of boys and girls in "law and order and International peace" that the National Institution for Moral Instruction wants to help do as its service to the cause. We have found a way in which these greater national interests can be presented to youth with telling effect. Our experiments have proved that there is a way to teach in our American public schools the truth about the serious side of life.

If the facts of human experience are presented in photographic lantern slides from reality, and made vivid, realistic, instinct with human interest and importance, then the boys and girls are intensely interested to interpret and understand these facts of the real world. If morals are presented as the "wisdom of experience," and the experience itself given as the fact basis, then morals can be taught effectively in public schools.

The best way to present the facts of life is in photographs from reality. Why not make up, with extreme care and at an expense of about $5000, an illustrated lesson in morals on the title "Law and Order and International Peace?" Why not introduce this stereopticon lesson into the regular moral instruction of public schools throughout the nation? The plan is feasible and practical. Within the last two months fifty-five grammar schools of Chicago have used the "Illustrated Lesson in Morals" which I hold in my hand, entitled "What I am going to do when I am grown up," the total audience being about 22,000 boys and girls. Good morals will be taught during April and May of this year to fully 50,000 boys and girls in American schools by means of these illustrated lessons which we furnished in lantern slides and texts. It is possible to educate the boys and girls in every high school throughout the United States in the good morals of law and order and international peace, by preparing a stereopticon lesson on this topic, duplicating it in many sets of lantern slides, and circulating it among the schools. It is the purpose of the National Institution for Moral Instruction to do this, and your moral and financial support is asked that this purpose may be carried out. There might be extensive coöperation with the School Peace League.

What should be the scope of this stereopticon lesson? It should traverse, with a wealth of detail, the simple argument that law and order based on justice are essential to well being and achievement in the school, in the city and country and the state, in fact throughout the nation as a unit. Then it should reach out to the moral obligation upon all to support law and order based on justice throughout the world that human beings of all nations may have their rights, and the brotherhood of man become a reality.

I submit the following outline in detail, and beg your help in carrying out this plan of peace education in the schools.

The Red Cross has promised to coöperate in furnishing photographs. The War College will loan the use of the Brady photographs of the Civil War. The National Geographical Society will help by supplying such photographs as it has bearing on the world conditions. The peace societies can help with photographs and ideas. Many special photographs can be taken, and the whole text prepared with great care for the education of youth in the ideal of world peace.

OUTLINE FOR ILLUSTRATED LESSON IN MORALS ON TITLE "LAW
AND ORDER AND INTERNATIONAL PEACE" BY NATIONAL INSTI-
TUTION FOR MORAL INSTRUCTION

Law and Order in Schools

Assignment of seats is made in school so that each can have
his own things ready for use.

The preservation of personal property rights has to be looked
to in school.

Protection of public property from defacement is necessary.

Quiet must be preserved so that each can have a chance to study.

Classes are called according to an orderly plan, so that each
has its discussion of the lesson.

All these regulations are carried out for the common good, that
each boy and girl may have a chance to learn the things he needs
to know.

The teacher is in authority to see that this law and this order
of the school are preserved.

The Board of Education establishes regulations for the teacher
to carry out.

Disputes among scholars are settled on the basis of personal
rights and justice.

The law and order and peace of the school is preserved for the
benefit of all.

Law and Order in the City

Above the city is the State law, the State constitution, the
national law and the national constitution.

City authorities must abide by these and enforce them.

There are city ordinances, for health, for fire protection, for
boulevards and parks, for good morals and for all matters of common good.

The Common Council creates these ordinances.

The City officials direct their carrying out and enforce them.

Means of preserving law and order: The officials, the police,
the citizens, the State militia, the national army.

Result: People have confidence to work, to build homes and stores and manufacturing plants, to be out at night, and to provide for a happy life.

All disputed points are settled by the courts, or by judges and officials, and the rights of each are preserved under the law, and according to what is natural and just.

Law and Order in the County

The county is the unit of organization. National and State laws are supreme in county. County officials and courts exist.

Adequate means of preserving law and order are provided.

Results: People live in peace, work their farms, have their rights preserved even in isolated places, and are free to provide for a happy life.

Law and Order in the State

The national Constitution and laws take first place—State constitutions have to conform. State legislatures make laws within the limits of the Constitution. State officials direct affairs and enforce laws. State courts decide disputes. State militia preserve order. The national authority is back of all.

Law and Order in the Nation

The National Constitution. Congress makes the national laws. National officials carry them out and enforce them. National courts decide disputes. National army preserves obedience and peace. Interstate war is at once suppressed.

Result: people are at peace and have their rights throughout the nation.

Law and Order throughout the World

In times of peace the rights of all are preserved even outside the limits of the nation.

In times of peace there are international agreements and treaties which the governments uphold.

But there is no provision for preserving the "peace of the world," and nations declare war, and fight, to reach a settlement· of serious disputes by force.

War sets aside justice and human rights as the basis of the settlement. Even when both sides are convinced their cause is righteous, it is force, not reason, that decides the issue.

International law should provide a court of justice for disputes between nations, because the common welfare demands this. (a) War is wasteful; (b) War is heart breaking; (c) War is degenerating; (d) War is unworthy of human beings.

The Peace Movement

The international consultations held.

The peace societies at work.

The peace foundations endowed.

The world-wide business and friendships established.

The increasing inclusiveness of treaties.

The great "Red Cross" for the alleviation of suffering.

The nations seem to be approaching a World League for the peaceful settlement of all disputes.

If this can be established it will be dishonorable for a nation to go to war for any cause, and a new and better era will be achieved.

All this mass of experience can be shown in photographs that will make it real and convincing to boys and girls. They can see for themselves the better way, and grow up intelligent in this the most important of world topics, prepared in times of popular excitement to exercise due self-control, that justice and not force may have its way throughout the world. It is this education of youth in the reasonableness and morality of international courts of justice that seems to me fundamental, and there is a way to give it universally throughout all nations with adequate thoroughness by means of a carefully prepared "Illustrated Lesson in Morals" on the general topic of "Law and Order and International Peace."

If the necessary financial and moral support can be arranged, about $5000 and the backing of the Peace Societies secured, a national work of education in the world peace ideal can be achieved.

ADJOURNED.

SIXTH SESSION

Eugene A. Noble, Presiding Officer

CHAIRMAN NOBLE: The function of a presiding officer at a meeting of this kind is to state in a single sentence, or, at most, two sentences, the essential facts connected with each speaker. That is, the presiding officer is to be an abbreviated "Who's Who," in relation to the speakers. I confess that it is a misfortune for me to be compelled to state so briefly the unusual and extensive qualifications of the eminent persons who are to address you. They are worthy of most elaborate introduction. That Scriptural phrase, "By their fruits shall ye know them," would suggest at least a description of "the fruits," but the necessities of the hour require that the "fruits" shall be canned, preserved, concentrated, reduced to a mere extract, and my hope is that this necessary process may increase in sweetness what it minifies in substance.

Before, however, introducing any of the speakers, I should like to say a word or two in connection with one aspect of this general peace question.

Among the agitators for peace from the beginning have been well-known disinterested thinkers, teachers in the highest sense, men and women of intellectual independence, penetration, and power of expression. The prophetic function of clear seeing, of appropriate exposition, of frank declaration is exhibited by such teachers most clearly, and when the last word of peace agitation has been spoken, if that ideal condition is ever reached, "when the war drum throbs no longer," and stable equilibrium is universally kept on the basis of reason, justice, fraternity and sane good-will, it will be found that such teachers have contributed to this desirable end.

In the pamphlet entitled, "The literature of the Peace Movement," Mr. Edwin D. Mead, of Boston, has called the roll of many of those who have spoken vigorously about peace. There are, however, some necessary omissions in Mr. Mead's pamphlet. I wish to mention two. One of the sanest statements ever made in connection with the peace agitation is the statement of that eminent humanist, Erasmus, who says:

"Nature hath given unto man alone the commodity of speech and reasoning: the which things verily may specially both get and nourish benevolence, so that nothing at all should be done among men by violence."

I never think of Erasmus as other than a teacher—a man so benign and placid and well-balanced that he could not be disturbed from any of those sure convictions which he calmly announced with the equanimity which is essential to humanism. He believed what he knew, and his knowledge has the quality which makes for universal truth. Therefore, he was undisturbed, and waited patiently but with assurance for the truth to make its way.

The other teacher who deserves unusual recognition because of what he says and how he felt on the question of the world's peace is one of the bravest and truest American teachers we have had. I refer to Mr. Emerson, superb in his mental equipment and superior in his moral discernment. There are a few pregnant words spoken by Ralph Waldo Emerson that ought to ring clear in every peace meeting, and I desire to submit them as a kind of keynote for the meeting we are holding this morning.

"Everything great must be done in the spirit of greatness. The manhood that has been in war must be transferred to the cause of peace before war can lose its charm, and peace be venerable to men. . . . If peace is to be maintained, it must be by brave men . . . . men who have, by their intellectual insight or else by their moral elevation attained such a perception of their own intrinsic worth, that they do not think property or their own body a sufficient good to be saved by such dereliction of principle as treating a man like a sheep."

But if Mr. Mead has left out of his pamphlet a few of the persons whom I regard as notabilities in the cause of peace, he has

mentioned some others who will some day wear as their highest
honor the praise of a peaceful world.   One of these, I now have
the pleasure of introducing.   When Mr. Carnegie devoted ten
millions of dollars—only temporarily, however—to the cause of
the world's peace, with the expectation that it would be realized
sooner than pessimists concede, and would then be devoted to
curing the next of the pressing grievous ills which afflict the world,
it was necessary to find a man of distinction to give practical direction to Mr. Carnegie's munificence.   The man so selected was
Mr. James Brown Scott, whose personal contributions to the
question of the peace of the world have given him a foremost
place among those who think and speak upon this question.   He
lives in one of the attractive suburbs of Baltimore, the City of
Washington, and I am pleased to present him to you as the first
speaker at this session.

THE POSSIBILITIES OF THE CARNEGIE ENDOWMENT FOR INTERNATIONAL PEACE

JAMES BROWN SCOTT

On the fourteenth day of December, 1910, Mr. Carnegie gave
to the trustees of the Carnegie Endowment for International
Peace the sum of $10,000,000, the income of which is to be ad-
ministered, to quote Mr. Carnegie, "to hasten the abolition of
international war, the foulest blot upon our civilization."

Mr. Carnegie left the trustees of his choice a free hand, saying
in his deed of trust that "lines of future action cannot be wisely
laid down.   Many may have to be tried, and having full confidence in my trustees I leave to them the widest discretion as to
the measures and policy they shall from time to time adopt,
only premising that the one end they shall keep unceasingly in
view until it is attained, is the speedy abolition of international
war between so-called civilized nations."

The income from the vast fund with which he has endowed the
cause of peace is to be expended until such time as war shall cease,
which the generous donor believes possible because he states in

his letter of trust that when "war is discarded as disgraceful to civilized man . . . . the trustees will then consider what is the next most degrading remaining evil or evils whose banishment—or what new elevating element or elements if introduced or fostered, or both combined—would most advance the progress, elevation and happiness of man, and so on from century to century without end, my trustees of each age shall determine how they can best aid man in his upward march to higher and higher stages of development unceasingly."

If the income of the endowment were to be devoted to procure the abolition of war, the institution created for this purpose would indeed be long-lived, but Mr. Carnegie means it to be perpetual because, when war shall have ceased to perplex nations and to block the path of civilization, the trustees are to devote the income to the eradication of the greatest existing evil in order, as Mr. Carnegie says, to "help man in his glorious ascent onward and upward and to this end devote this fund."

The trustees mentioned in Mr. Carnegie's letter accepted the fund generously vested in them by Mr. Carnegie, have created headquarters at Washington and organized permanently in order to carry out the purposes of the trust. At the meeting of the trustees held on the ninth day of March, 1911, the following statement of the objects and purpose of the endowment was unanimously adopted: "To advance the cause of peace among nations, to hasten the abolition of international war, and to encourage and promote the pacific settlement of international differences." Following this general statement, the trustees enumerated in a series of paragraphs the specific purposes of the endowment and the means and instrumentalities by which the purposes of the trust will be effected:

(a) To promote a thorough and scientific investigation and study of the causes of war and of the practical methods to prevent and avoid it.

(b) To aid in the development of international law, and a general agreement on the rules thereof, and the acceptance of the same among nations.

(c) To diffuse information, and to educate public opinion regarding the causes, nature and effects of war, and means for its prevention and avoidance.

(*d*)   To establish a better understanding of international rights and duties and a more perfect sense of international justice among the inhabitants of civilized countries.

(*e*)   To cultivate friendly feelings between the inhabitants of different countries, and to increase the knowledge and understanding of each other by the several nations.

(*f*)   To promote a general acceptance of peaceable methods in the settlement of international disputes.

(*g*)   To maintain, promote, and assist such establishments, organizations, associations, and agencies as shall be deemed necessary or useful in the accomplishment of the purposes of the corporation, or any of them.

(*h*)   To take and hold such property, real or personal, and to invest and keep invested and receive and apply the income of such funds, and to construct and maintain such buildings or establishments, as shall be deemed necessary to prosecute and develop the purposes of the corporation, or any of them.

(*i*)   To do and perform all lawful acts or things necessary or proper in the judgment of the trustees to promote the objects of the corporation.

An examination of the various activities of the endowment set forth in the paragraphs above quoted shows that they fall within three general groups: First, a careful study of the principles of international law involved in peace and its maintenance (*b*, *d* and *f*); second, a purely scientific study and investigation of the causes of war, for if war is to be avoided, the causes which have led to it must be studied and analyzed in all their aspects in order to determine "the practical methods to prevent and avoid it" (*a*); third, the propaganda to be undertaken by the endowment in order to realize the purposes for which it was created (*c*, *e*, *g*).   Paragraph (*i*) confers power upon the trustees generally to take action other than that specified in the preceding paragraphs in order to promote the objects of the endowment.

From the general statement of the objects of the endowment and the enumeration of the powers specifically conferred upon the trustees, it is evident that the scope of the endowment is very wide and that its usefulness will be very great, if the fund be wisely and conservatively administered. The presidency of Mr. Root is both a guaranty and a hope.

It is not my present purpose to outline the policy which the endowment will pursue in the immediate future, other than to say broadly and generally that the endowment does not intend to supplant existing agencies but intends to assist and strengthen them, so that the movement toward peace may be rendered more effective, and the goal which is ever before our eyes may seem less distant, even although unaided vision may fail to discover it.

The endowment may find it advisable to supplement societies and agencies already existing, but will only take this step when its necessity is clearly demonstrated, for the endowment has come to strengthen, not supplant, to broaden the movement, not to control it or limit it, but to add fresh life and vigor, not to deaden or paralyze existing activities.

Without entering into details or attempting to define the work which the endowment may undertake, I pass to the possibilities which the wise and conservative, yet progressive, application of the fund may reasonably suggest. In the first place, Mr. Carnegie's generosity has made it possible to study carefully and exhaustively the principles of international law which are necessarily or properly involved in peace and the peaceable settlement of international differences. For example, one of the specific purposes of the endowment is to "promote a general acceptance of peaceable methods in the settlement of international disputes." This naturally requires an examination of the methods by which international disputes may be peaceably settled, and it may be that the wisdom of mankind directed to this object may devise methods hitherto unsuspected, and develop those which are imperfect or susceptible of a larger and more generous application. Diplomacy may be affected, good offices enlarged, mediation rendered more frequent, commissions of inquiry and the resort to arbitration popularized, and the judicial settlement of international disputes promoted by the establishment of a permanent international tribunal in whose decisions the nations of the world

will have confidence, because its decisions are based upon the
passionless application of well-known and recognized principles
of law and justice.   But obedience to law is impossible if there be
no law, and the endowment may well take up seriously the problem of codifying existing usage and custom, which we call international law, and supplement it by principles of law and of justice
of which the nations stand in need.   This can be done on
an international scale by interesting in the undertaking specialists in various countries, so that the result of their labors may be
a law international in its application because devised by the
enlightened of various countries, and for the same reason calculated
to meet the needs of nations.

In the next place a scientific study and investigation of the
causes of war is now possible, for political economy, history and
sociology can be drafted into service and an analysis be had of the
causes of war, and a clear and accurate statement made of its effect,
not merely upon the parties to it, but upon the world at large,
viewed from the standpoint of history, economics, and sociology.
We can and we must do, to quote Mr. Root, "what the scientific
men do, we must strive to reach some deeper insight into the cause
of the diseases, of which war is a symptom, than can be obtained
by casual and occasional consideration.   That deeper insight can
be attained only by long and faithful and continuous study and
investigation.   We have it in our power now to employ the men
who may be the investigators in our behalf, but the method that
we shall follow is something to be evolved by the most careful
consideration."

What the results of this investigation will be, I may not attempt
to predict, but any examination of the causes of war will show the
thoughtlessness and folly which drove nations to arms and plunged
their peoples into the depths of sorrow and despair.   The investigation will fail of its purpose if it does not show how easily most
of the wars might have been prevented if there had existed, ready
at hand, agencies and institutions to which nations could have
resorted for the settlement of their disputes without sacrificing
what they regard as higher than their welfare—national honor.

Again, the economic effects of war, which are known to be great, will be shown to influence not merely the actual combatants but neutral nations as well, so that the evil and loss inseparably connected with armed conflict are spread, like a mildew, over the uttermost parts of the earth.

And finally, the sociological effects of war will be made clear. What we have seen as in a glass darkly, we shall see face to face, and the actual reality will be such as to give us pause. For general statements, there will be substituted precise, detailed information, and the causes and consequences of war will be worked out with the precision of science. Facts are stubborn things, and when proved beyond a peradventure, they cannot be wiped out of existence or defied with impunity by the strong men and the masses of men which we call nations. Just as the physician recognizes the symptom and eradicates the disease, so we, treating war as a symptom of a diseased condition, will press beneath the surface to those causes which have made war possible, paralyzing, if not utterly destroying, the body politic.

But the results achieved by investigation and science would be of little value if they were not brought home to the people, if they were not popularized, so that he who runs may read. The Endowment can scatter broadcast the results which patient investigation have achieved and make them a part of the life and thought of every man in every country, and unite the efforts of humanity in the great crusade against what Mr. Carnegie rightly calls the "foulest blot upon our civilization." The press may be furnished reliable and readable information, reviews and magazines can be utilized, and leaflets distributed, so that in the fulness of knowledge, we may press forward in the great movement which has for its aim and ultimate goal, the honorable and just settlement of international disputes by those means and instrumentalities which men, within national lines, have found productive of law and order and a condition of permanent equilibrium and peace.

Our methods must be largely educational, and while we must not exclude the present, our hopes must be set upon the future. I do not say that the present is lost, because that would be an exaggeration and at best a half-truth. It is evident, however, that the present has made up its mind and can be changed only with difficulty.   We must seek to influence the young lives which will make and control the future.   We must go to the schools, the colleges and the universities and impress upon youth in the formative periods of their lives those principles of law and justice which, if observed and applied, will make their children's heritage a heritage of peace and justice.   The past has its lessons, but they are largely lost on the present generation.   The history of the United States is not, as our school books would lead one to believe, an endless series of conflicts.   The colonists engaged in war, to be sure, but they converted a wilderness into the safe and sure abodes of strong men and brave women.   The Revolution united the colonies and made us a nation, and from the Declaration of Independence until the present day, we have grown in strength, in power and influence, carrying the doctrines of the Declaration and our beneficent institutions into unsuspected and undiscovered worlds.   A history which chronicles wars and descends into the details of the battlefield may satisfy the needs of the professional soldier—it gives the layman no adequate idea of the growth of America, of the origin of American institutions, and of the civilization which we have planted and are diligently developing in this new world of ours.   I would not eliminate wars from our history, for otherwise it would be a false statement of American life and growth, but I would lay stress upon the essentials, not upon the accidentals, of national growth and life.

Greece and Rome are only dead in the sense that they have ceased to exist as nations.   Their art and philosophy, their literature and science are immortal. ' The institutions which each country created to meet its needs, the federation of Greece, the world law of Rome, and the instances of arbitration with which Greek history sparkles, are unknown to the younger student.   It is only in after years that he appreciates the heavy debt we owe them.   The head is full and turned with endless wars and rumors of war, leagues and alliances, whereas very great contributions in the realms of thought and the problems which they met and solved are lost upon the student in his formative days, when he is most likely to be influenced by example.   The civilization of the ancient world disappears, as it were, in a sea of blood.   School books could be prepared and introduced into our schools, colleges and universities which would reanimate the past and make its lessons safe and sure guides to an enlightened, and, we hope, a better future.

Political economy which Mr. Carlyle perversely called "the dismal science" is taught as the science of wealth, but its principles are studied as in a vacuum. The influence of war upon production and distribution, exchange and consumption, is disregarded. A proper text should examine the effect of war upon the principles of political economy, and by so doing would broaden the subject and be, in no small sense of the word, an inducement to peace, for wealth is created in peace, it flourishes in peace, and it has its highest development in peace.

Lest this enumeration grow tiresome, I shall call your attention merely to international law which is generally treated as dealing with the rights and duties of nations in peace and war. This classification which dates from Grotius and which was accurate enough in his day, is inadequate in our more enlightened generation. The rights and duties of nations should be studied and expounded in systematic form. The means by which rights are preserved and wrongs redressed should constitute procedure, and in this procedure stress should be laid upon the peaceful means of settling international controversies. Just as self-redress between man and man gave way to private arbitration, and just as private arbitration resulted in the establishment of permanent tribunals, so war, which is self-redress, is yielding to public arbitration between nations which will, just as in private law, produce as the final flower of our international civilization, a truly permanent court in which nation may sue nation as easily, as peaceably as man sues man in national courts of justice. A proper text can and should be prepared, setting forth these views, so that the students of our colleges and universities will understand the rights and duties of nations, the peaceable means by which they are preserved, and which will frankly treat war as an extra legal remedy, as certain to be discarded in the future as self-redress is non-existent in all civilized communities.

If the past is full of regrets, if the present is out of joint, the future is full of measureless promise. May the Carnegie endowment for international peace rise to its mission and be a factor as Mr. Root has happily phrased it, in the substitution of the rule of law for the rule of man.

CHAIRMAN NOBLE: There are one or two matters to which I now desire to call your attention. You will note in your programs that there is to be a debate held in this hall this evening, and I have been requested to announce that all contestants are to meet Professor Rogers here immediately after this session.

There are a few persons, agitators by profession, who would have us believe every once in a while that a war is imminent between this country and Japan. Those persons, it seems to some of us, have almost proved that there can be motion without energy. They are endorsed, at times, by newspapers which might be described as polychromatous newspapers, who would have it appear that we are on the verge of a great eruption of war between the United States and Japan. None of these things move us. We do not believe in such impending war for a very good reason, because there is too much intelligence in Japan to permit that to come to pass. And the intelligence in Japan, I am pleased to believe, has been produced in some measure, by the educational practices of the United States. Japanese students in this country understand very well what our position is on this question, and we believe there will be no such war.

One of these Japanese educated and trained men is to be the next speaker, Dr. T. Iyenaga, a graduate of this University, and if I may speak for this University let me say that the Johns Hopkins welcomes him here this morning as well as the members of' this Congress. I have great honor and pleasure in now presenting Dr. T. Iyenaga.

PEACE IN ASIA

T. IYENAGA

The Far East has been for the past few decades the storm center of the world. Often has the tranquility of the Occident been ruffled by the disturbances in the Orient. So unstable still is

the political status, and so vast and often conflicting are the interests of the Powers involved, in the Far and Near East, that they
are factors potent enough to set at any time the world ablaze.
For the cause of peace nothing is, therefore, more urgent than to
ensure it in Asia. The wisest statesmanship and all the forces
of propagandism for peace will do well to be enlisted for its promotion in the old continent.

The humanitarian idea of peace is, however, nothing new to
the Asiatic. "Pity for all living creatures," "The Brotherhood
of man the four seas over,"—these messages were given to Asia
by the Indian and Chinese sages long before the names of Ind and
Sinim first fell from the lips of a Hebrew prophet. Europe too
has seen nineteen centuries since it first accepted the gospel of
love for its guide. Neither Europe nor Asia has, however, ever
obeyed the mandate of its master. Their history is the story
of war and bloodshed. This is conspicuously true of Europe.
Since modern nations have reared their political structures upon
the ruins of Rome, the dominant note of their existence has been
and still is militarism. To join their ranks, the best passport is
martial prowess. This assertion is strikingly proved by the manner
in which Japan was at last admitted into the list of modern Powers
For half a century Japan assiduously applied herself to the recon-
struction of the arts of peace. She remodelled her educational
system, codified her laws, brought the administration of justice
to the modern standard, consecrated her energy to the cultivation
of Western science and literature, created the commercial and
industrial middle class, opened a Parliament, and proclaimed the
freedom of speech, press, and faith—in short, she completely reorganized her political and social fabric upon the model of the
West. Did this progress of Japan in the arts of peace, however,
succeed in placing her on an equal footing with the Western
nations? No. Unpleasant as it may sound to you, the position
which Japan coveted in the family of nations was gained only
after she had unwittingly demonstrated her skill in the game of
war. When in defense of her national honor and interests she
fought her great neighbor, and won the battles of Phyong-Yang
and the Yalu, Japan discovered to her surprise that her prestige

in the eyes of the West had become suddenly enhanced.   And it was only after another terrible war, waged with fear and trembling for her national security, that the frank recognition of the Insular Kingdom as a great Power was given by the world.   This is forsooth a sad commentary on the militarism of the West.

That the militant spirit is not yet dead receives a strong confirmation by the recent utterance before the Reichstag of so high an authority as the German Chancellor that "a nation must maintain its sea and land forces at such a point as shall correspond with its national strength," for otherwise, "it would run the risk of forfeiting its present place among the Powers to some stronger nation that is willing to take it."   Is there, then, any wonder that the conviction of the dire necessity for guarding herself by efficient armament has sunk deep into the heart of Japan?   This conviction it is that makes the Japanese people bear without murmur the heavy burden of maintaining their army and navy—a burden that costs them yearly 120 million yen, equal to 35 per cent of their total national revenue.   What a relief to them if they could be assured that their national safety and vital interests were safeguarded without these costly engines of war!   How welcome to them the thought that these enormous expenditures for the instruments of destruction might be turned to the beneficent purposes of enlightenment and economic well-being!   To imagine that Japan's armament is for aggression is to confess an ignorance of her history and to forget the kindly disposition and artistic temperament of her people.   Japan is in essence a peace-loving nation.   Her pursuance of a policy of peace is further dictated by the consideration of her true welfare.   She has a population of sixty millions.   It is increasing at the rate of 600,000 yearly.   It is crowded into a territory not larger than that of Texas.   This represents the entire extent of the Japanese Empire, including Korea, Formosa, and Southern Saghalien. Moreover, as you are aware, her laboring class is not welcomed in the lands of the white peoples.   In these circumstances, Japan's salvation lies in commercial and industrial expansion on the continent of Asia.   As the delicate plants of trade and industry best thrive on peaceful soil, peace is the first requisite of Japan's prosperity. She wants peace within her borders. She wants peace in Asia. She wants peace in the world. Every measure that makes for peace is, consequently, most welcome to her.

What vitally concerns Japan is the continuation of peace in Asia. To further that end, therefore, no stone has been left unturned, so far as lies in her power. Among such means the most efficient is the Anglo-Japanese alliance. A cursory examination of the cause and nature of the treaty will prove to us that its primary object is the preservation of peace in Asia, resting as it does upon the maintenance of China's integrity and of the "open door" policy. The first Anglo-Japanese alliance was formed in 1902. The decade preceding the compact was one of the most critical in the annals of the Far East. The China-Japan war had resulted in an easy victory for Japan, and by the treaty of Shimonoseki China had ceded to the victor the Liao-tung Penninsula. The moment the peace terms were known, however, Japan was confronted by the powerful coalition of Russia, France and Germany, and the best fruits of her victory were wrested from her. England had looked with the strongest disapproval upon these proceedings, but she chose to stand aloof. This vacillating policy produced the inevitable result. England and Japan each found itself completely isolated, and were helpless before the strong combination of three European Powers. The policy of aggression won the day. Within a few years the Russian eagles were flying on the fortress of Port Arthur, Germany had seized Kiaochou, and France had secured Kwang Chow Wan. In addition to these seizures of territory there was inaugurated an era of a wild scramble for railways and mining concessions from China. And the audacity of the Powers knew no bound. They even mapped out among themselves the huge Chinese Empire into what they were pleased to call "spheres of influence." While the partition of China was thus imminent, these high-handed actions of the Powers had so roused the ire of the Chinese people that it at last burst forth into the strangest crusade this weary earth after an experience of tens of centuries has ever known—the Boxer uprising.

During that trouble and its settlement, the concert of Powers was barely maintained. Peace in Asia was seemingly restored, but that it was only a short respite and that a terrific storm was approaching was evident from the ugly clouds which lowered over the Manchurian sky. These developments and past experiences were sufficient to convince England and Japan that, unless a strong combination be effected, it would be impossible to stem the tide of European aggression in China, and uphold their common policy of peace in Asia. Herein is the genesis of the Anglo-Japanese alliance.

The first treaty failed to avert the outbreak of the Russo-Japanese War; but there are strong grounds for believing that the salient provision of the treaty that the British Empire would come to the aid of Japan, if any other Power than Russia were to enter the field, prevented the war from becoming a world-conflagration. To that extent, then, the first Anglo-Japanese treaty was an instrument that made for peace. In 1905 the treaty was renewed, framed on a much broader basis, and designed to preserve peace in Asia in a more effective way. It is often called an offensive and defensive alliance, but it implies no aggression whatever. It is purely an instrument of peace. The alliance has fully justified its existence. It has proved to be not only the most powerful instrument for the preservation of peace in Asia, but the foundation-stone upon which have been framed the later international agreements that maintain the balance of power and peace in the world.

Will this strong guarantee of peace come to an end at the expiration of the term of the treaty in 1915? We hope not. The cause of peace in Asia, the security of China, and the imperial policy of Japan and Great Britain loudly call for the continuance of the alliance. If it is broken, who can assure us that the old days of western depredation in Asia, bringing in their train an era of carnage will not again be ushered in? There are of course some pessimists, whose broodings over creations of their fancy make them nervous about this alliance, lest it embroil England in a war between Japan and America. To say the least, such a fear is as silly as it is absurd, for, logically, the alliance must rather act as a strong check upon the realization of the fear. Japan, on her part, will do everything in her power to prevent the occurrence of such a calamity as hideous to her ally as to herself. No! the war between the two nations on the opposite shores of the Pacific is as unthinkable as that between the two English speaking peoples. The Japanese ambassador, Baron Uchida, has lately put it before the American Asiatic Association in these happy words: "There have been wars of the Cross and the Crescent, of the Red Rose and the White, but the sun and the stars have never quarrelled in their courses—neither shall the two flags which bear these celestial emblems ever be carried at the head of hostile armies. It is unthinkable, impossible." This war talk, I know I need not assure you, is nothing but either the product of a disordered mind, or the machination of an evil genius. No more signal proof of the long standing friendship between America and Japan can be given than by the new treaty concluded a few months ago. In truth, all the precious sentiments the past goodness of America toward us has stored in our memory, all the goodwill our pleasant association with you in school and in social life has cultivated, the vital interests of our commerce, in which America distinguishes herself as our best customer, and the sound and good common sense of the American people, which has never failed to make them understand us rightly—these form the solid foundation for our friendship with you, which neither a few attacks upon us by the ignorant rabble nor the campaign of falsehood and misrepresentation so ingeniously prosecuted to estrange us can shake or undermine.

This firm friendship between America and Japan is another guarantee of peace in Asia. Their coöperation is not only the herald of peace, but the sponsor of Anglo-American civilization in Asia. You will not charge me with egotism or self-conceit, when I say to you that the influence of Great Britain, America, and Japan is now paramount over great portions of Asia. This means that Asiatic development is molded on the model of Anglo-American civilization. This is of the deepest significance to the future of the great Asiatic continent. I have of course no cause whatever to say anything derogatory of the German, the Russian, or any other type of European civilization. Each has its greatness. But we may be pardoned if we take just pride in the heritage our fathers have bequeathed to us, and in cherishing and perpetuating it. And not for a moment do I hesitate to say that the salient features of the civilization of modern Japan have been cast in the Anglo-American mold. This was inevitable from the time the Samurai, who wielded the power of pen and sword in the old days, merged themselves with the common people and took up their cause. Shall we, of Japan, then, be blamed for wishing our Asiatic neighbors to enjoy the same blessings, the principles of Liberty, Equality, Justice, and Order, that rule the Anglo-American-Japanese world? Peace in Asia and the future civilization of the Orient must, then, depend much upon whether the coöperation of America, England and Japan, in perpetuating their present influence, will continue or not.

CHAIRMAN NOBLE: Before introducing the next speaker, I want to say a frank word to those in the audience who are not Baltimoreans. Baltimore is hospitable to strangers, and we rejoice when you assume our ways. Now, tomorrow morning when you ask for a copy of one of our leading papers, don't ask for a copy of the *Baltimore Sun*, but ask for a copy of the *"Sun paper."* That is a localism here. The *"Sun paper"* is a mighty good paper. I doubt if there is any city in this country whose newspapers are more intelligently edited than the newspapers of Baltimore, and I doubt if there are any papers in the country which give more attention to all good movements. We are very proud of our newspapers.

I am pleased now to introduce an editor of one of them, Mr. Allen S. Will, of the *Baltimore Sun.*

POPULAR INTELLIGENCE ONE OF THE BEST PRE-VENTIVES OF WAR

ALLEN S. WILL

A political change of far-reaching importance to us who believe that war is preventable has been taking place in the last hundred years. This is the gradual transfer of the power of making war from those who reap its rewards to those who bear its burdens.

The change has come through the development of that giant, public opinion, whose smile every prince and statesman must now court and before whose frown thrones shake and politicians sink into obscurity. The diffusion of intelligence is awakening the man who fights in the ranks to a sense of his real responsibility for the hazard of his own life; his inquiries are stretching beyond the rudimentary stage indicated by Little Peterkin's question: "But what good came of it at last?"

That was a striking remark by Governor Woodrow Wilson the other day, when he said that a reaction had set in against government by the "superior people," and that the change would gradually become more pronounced until the masses would be "their own masters and arbiters." For centuries men were willing to offer themselves to be shot at for no stronger reason than that a person superior in birth wished them to do so. The dawn of popular intelligence shattered this atrocious system and the conscience of the world long ago revolted at wars of succession. The people remained willing to go to war at the behest of persons of superior position in their governmental structures whom they trusted as leaders to such an extent that they were ready to leave their wives widows and their children fatherless for a cause which in their own judgment did not justify such a sublime sacrifice.

So strong was their habit of being led that they were easily deceived by the threadbare trick of titled or untitled politicians who sought to confound patriotism with the war feeling. Fanatical or unscrupulous men found a ready means of prolonging and increasing their power and affluence by inciting a storm of popular passion under cover of which their own selfish schemes might be worked out. Their motives in many cases were not higher than those of the pickpocket who suddenly diverts the attention of his victim by some apparition of danger and then deftly steals a watch. When every heart has leaped to the cry "The country is in danger" politicians have known that they were free to huckster men's lives and plunge their greedy hands deep into the public treasury.

How many of the world's wars have been, as Tennyson says, broad-based upon the people's will? If war is for the benefit of ambitious princes, politicians, agitators and other harpies who usually dominate at a time when organized conflict is impending, it may well be that the decision should be left to them; but if it is for the benefit of the nation—and this is always the guise in which it is presented—is it not just that the judgment of the people should approve the necessity for such a tragic enterprise before they embark on it? The peril of present conditions lies in the willingness of the people, from long-established custom, to be led. If a politician who helped to bring on an unnecessary war knew that instead of being rewarded by his constituents, he would be swept out of office by a torrent of indignation at such a crime against humanity, his habit of steering by the compass of popular favor would guide the ship of his ambition in a different direction.

So recent is the institution of popular education that the average man feels that he is not yet sufficiently equipped to decide the question of war or peace for himself. He has an impression that he is not in a position to know the facts and that if he did know them he is probably not qualified to reach a proper conclusion. His duty, as it appears to him after centuries of habit, is to abide to the uttermost by the judgment of the public officers in whom rests the power of making war. If the war is long and particularly if it is disastrous to his personal interests, he is apt, if he survives, to express sorrow later that it was fought; but coupled with this is usually a belief that it was unavoidable, that some sweep of events which he could not control brought it about, and that he was a helpless unit in the whole business. If he had a dispute with a neighbor in which a corresponding cause of difference was involved, probably he would not have resorted to blows, but would have found some other method of adjustment which would have been fully as satisfactory; yet he knows that the restraints of justice and moderation which obtain among individuals do not yet apply to nations, which are too willing, when moved by selfishness, not only to dissemble their love for the golden rule, but actually to kick it downstairs.

Under these circumstances, one of our strongest appeals must be to the masses of the people. Let in the light and their own sound sense will make it impossible for their delegated representatives to embark them on an unjust war. The greatest multiplication of newspapers, magazines and books which deal with international problems is desirable. If there is a war, reports of its horrors from day to day will help to prevent another one; if there is a rumor of war, those who read of it will have time to sift the question for themselves and realize how absurd it would be to take 10,000 or 100,000 lives to settle a question which can be better adjusted without the loss of any. Here and there some incendiary will print a "war extra" or some valiant stay-at-home will call on the people to rise with arms in their hands. In the long run, this will serve to awaken the intelligent to the real danger—not the other nations which may be involved, but the alarmist at home. It will quicken the public sense of peril from the stage thunders of demagogues and teach men to be resolute in deciding vital questions for themselves.

We know that war is the fruit of an illusion and the best way to drive away the clouds which have obscured the subject so long is to help the people to arrive at a knowledge of the truth. The literature on the subject of peace which is springing up throughout the civilized world is a potent help. But a small minority of people is willing to engage in war for the pure love of it. The only excuse for an international conflict is the belief that it is necessary—that, calamity though it be, it must be endured at times because humanity has never found a way to avoid such things. As popular intelligence spreads, the citizen will learn that war can be and ought to be prevented; that it is just as honorable to settle a difference by resort to a tribunal of just men as to a gamble of bloodshed on the field of battle; that a nation can make preparation for an act of unauthorized or unintentional injustice with better grace than an individual; that even an apology under the decree of an impartial court is far less humiliating than the bitterness of defeat in armed conflict.

The economic waste of war is the soundest argument against it and one that is bound to prevail in the end as intelligence spreads. The man and woman who have built a home and are rearing a family will be more than willing to pause and ask "Is war worth the sacrifice of these things?"   And then, in time, will come a realization that the present vast expenditure for armies and navies is a reckless waste of their resources.   They will see that it is much better for them to add a room to their cottage or to educate a son or daughter than to pay their share of taxes for the war budget.   They protect their children from small-pox by means of vaccination and strive to ward off the curse of typhoid fever. Will they not learn in time to guard them from the scourge of war, which can be more deadly than either?   With the more general diffusion of intelligence will come a deeper interest in the affairs of other nations.   Education clears the international mystery and brings about a real sense of the brotherhood of man. The time is past when the inhabitants of the world can be divided into Greeks and barbarians.   Education and invention have brought us in touch with the antipodes and we no longer dread another people as being so fierce and dangerous that, like the Romans, we must always keep the treasure in the temple to defend ourselves against the Gauls.

These are the fallacies upon which the war feeling has been fed. Deprive it of its sustenance, and it will die of starvation.

Truth is the prime corrective under a system of popular government.   We need not greatly concern ourselves because the pages of history are so filled with the deeds of the soldier that there is scant room for anything else.   This lack of proportion is already disappearing in the newer historical works and the accomplishments of peoples in the arts of peace are now engaging the general attention of scholars.   Awakening intelligence refuses to believe that the nations of antiquity did nothing but make war on each other; that the knight and the archer performed the principal constructive work of medieval days.

We reprehend the "pistol-toter" and outlaw his offense as menace to the community; are we to continue to permit the family of nations to be a family of "pistol-toters?"   Each of them professes to be guided by lofty impulses of humanity, yet bristles with cannon, rifles, bayonets and battleships and some of them even now are seeking to use the airship in the business of taking life.   Popular education will disclose the absurdity of this double standard to the citizen who controls by his ballot the ultimate destiny of a free people. He will penetrate the thin disguises of diplomacy and detect with unerring analysis the piratical instinct which still lurks in the policy of one nation toward another. Catch phrases and cunning appeals to the war feeling masked under the name of patriotism will no longer lead him to abdicate his reason and forsake his prosperous home to perish of camp fever in a damp trench. He will be no less ready than before to serve his country—perhaps he will be readier, for there is patriotic work to do besides echoing the mouthings of the fanatic and the international schemer.

A danger to be avoided at all hazards is the stirring up of popular passion based on an appeal to ignorance. Formerly the hope of plunder could be held out as an inducement to men who bore the cross-bow or the musket to risk their lives in a conflict of nations. Even before the spread of education public opinion rendered impossible the sacking of cities and the holding in servitude of men who had been captured in war. With this resource exhausted, the promoters of strife hit upon the expedient of craftily producing a sort of national "brainstorm" which swept them forward to the fruition of their designs. This form of hysterics is akin in its psychological manifestations to the phenomenon of panic. Persons in the rear of a crowd trapped in a burning theatre feel all the madness of those in front before they know that a fire has broken out, or that there is any cause for alarm. With the wider diffusion of intelligence reason will be able to hold her seat against the assaults of public tumult. Men will see the folly of submitting to a capital operation for the cure of a slight illness. Someone will cry "peace" and the intelligent will hearken to him more readily than to the shrieks of the war advocate. Men who have the capacity to understand will demand to be informed why they should give up every stake they hold in the game of life in order to shoot at other men whom they have never seen and offer themselves as targets in turn. They will ask why when their neighbors commit an aggression they go to court but when a nation attempts the same thing they must go to war.

The highest function of government is the promotion of the

happiness and prosperity of a people and there is enough in this task to call forth all the devotion and intelligence of every citizen.   Teach him to know—place the means of sound education within his reach and you will find that he will soon learn to see things as they are.

The great number of newspapers and magazines which reason soberly will awaken his perception to a point where he cannot be deluded by an occasional "war extra" or alarmist article.   He will be adamant to an appeal for revenge against a whole people and will be ready to rebuke at the polls the trickster who would fan the flames of public excitement.   He will perceive that the peace movement does not mean that disputes between nations shall remain unsettled, or that injustice by one nation to another shall be permitted, but that its real object is that methods for the orderly adjustment of differences among individuals which have long been practiced shall be applied to nations; and that the rule of justice instead of the rule of force shall be the standard of governments everywhere.

CHAIRMAN NOBLE: Peculiarities of cities are described, as you know, in phrases.   Baltimore is the "Monumental City" and the other cities of the country have words or phrases that describe them.   If my friends from other cities will not object, I should like to characterize Boston as the "City of Philanthropic Mind," and that mind finds expression in the great deeds of certain men.   It will be my privilege now to introduce a distinguished citizen of Boston, who, more than a year before Mr. Carnegie made provision for his great endowment of $10.000,000, saw what was coming and did what was timely.   Mr. Edwin Ginn, of Boston, provided for a great gift of $1,000,000, and is contributing $50,000 a year, for the propagation of the peace idea.   That is not all that Mr. Ginn is doing.   It would perhaps be a longer story than I should tell if I were to repeat some of the things which he has made possible.   I would like to say that through his generosity certain books are being published in a peace library and sold at scarcely the cost of publication.   Books that should be sold at a dollar and one dollar and a half are being sold

at fifty and seventy-five cents.   Mr. Ginn is responsible for this.
He is a man who is widely known and loved.   I now have the
pleasure of introducing Mr. Edwin Ginn of Boston.

THE WORLD PEACE FOUNDATION

EDWIN GINN

The limited time at my disposal does not permit me to go over
as fully as I would like the plans of the World Peace Foundation
and I will therefore proceed at once to the discussion of what I
consider the most important part of our work in the immediate
future; namely, the problem of disarmament.

This is a difficult matter to handle.   Men do not throw away
their lives or property carelessly.   They believe that the present
system is necessary.   If we would attack it effectively, we must
substitute a force that will protect the people in all their rights
at less expense in blood and treasure.   When the different countries were widely separated with imperfect means of communication, when each had to solve its problems independently and rarely
felt the presence of the others unless by contact in war, this system became firmly entrenched and has gradually strengthened
until it has become a most serious menace to civilization.   Conditions have now entirely changed.   Steam and electricity have
brought the nations into such close relations that an injury to
one is almost immediately felt by the others.   The world is fast
ignoring border lines.   It does not ask whether you are German,
French, American or English, but what can you do for your fellows in overcoming the ravages of tuberculosis, for instance, or for
the development of mankind along any humanitarian line.   This
coming together of the nations is shown in various international
organizations which are considering the well-being of all without
regard to nationality, such as the International Institute of
Agriculture, the International Medical Association against Warfare, the Permanent Committee of the International Congress
of Chambers of Commerce, the International Congress of the
Press, International Congresses of Science, the Red Cross Society,

and scores of other organizations. The advantages coming from a closer intercourse among the nations cannot be overestimated. A few countries have done something in exchanging professors and in sending to one another representatives of churches, of boards of trade, and the like, but hardly a beginning has been made. A systematic effort should be made in every direction to bring people of like callings in the different nations into association with one another, in order that they may become better acquainted. The governments themselves should lend a hand in this fraternization.

Military control by individual nations is too expensive in human life and property. No nation is strong enough to defend itself from attack from all directions. This system of independent action is producing an intense rivalry between the nations which is leading to bankruptcy.

INTERNATIONAL ARMY

May I venture again to suggest a plan for safeguarding the nations more perfectly than the present method, with a great saving of life and property and without disturbing the existing order of things? It is this: To form an international army along the lines of our national armies, to consist of, say, 10 per cent of the present armament of each nation, and to station portions of this international army in localities where friction is likely to occur. Each nation will be as strong as now, relatively, after it has given up 10 per cent of its armament to an international force. Its military system can be carried on as effectively and as independently of the other nations, as at present. No extra expense will be incurred. The question of the *amount* each nation shall contribute to this army is solved, since each is required to give a certain proportion of its force, be it large or small. The question of organization need not disturb us. We have a precedent for such a force in the Boxer difficulties. It *is* feasible, and, if established, within ten years will prove adequate for the protection of each and all. When this is done the fear and distrust from which the nations are now suffering will disappear and with

it the large armies and navies.   They will no longer be needed.
A plan so simple and practical is certainly worth the trial.

The great step being taken now by England and America—
perhaps by France and Japan—for an arbitration treaty to settle
at The Hague all difficulties that may arise of whatever nature,
is along lines of coöperation.   If a treaty is formed by these four
powers, it will have a great influence upon other nations and
without doubt this movement will spread until all will agree to
settle their difficulties in this way; but we shall always need a small
international force, as we need now a national force, to restrain
the violent and turbulent.

INFLUENCES AGAINST DISARMAMENT

It is only fair for us to recognize that most of those engaged in
militarism are conscientiously performing what they consider to
be their duty, and if we are to educate them to realize their mistake, we must try to understand their point of view.   No one is able
to tell to what degree his opinions are influenced by his surround-
ings.   Those who are profiting yearly by these two thousand
million dollars of contracts for military purposes cannot help
being biased because of them.   It is natural for them to defend
the present military system and to use a portion of the enormous
profits they are receiving for its continuance through the lobbies
in the various parliaments of the world and in every other way
open to them.   We can readily see what a tremendous influence
these selfish interests have upon public opinion; and we have to
reckon with this influence in our endeavor to bring about a change
in the existing order of things.

ORGANIZATION OF WORLD PEACE FOUNDATION

It is with a view of educating the world along these and other
permanent lines that the World Peace Foundation was formed.
The people must be educated to higher ideals of international
life.   This we have been endeavoring to do for the past ten years,
so that our organization is the result of practical experience.   We
have aimed to attack this problem in every effective way—

politically, economically, educationally and morally. Our plan
or organization, as you know, is similar to that of the ordinary
college, calling for a board of trustees, a board of directors corresponding to the faculty, and an advisory council.

In choosing our representatives the first requirement is always
devotion to the cause. One such worker will be more effective
than a hundred who enter the service simply as a means of support. Next, they must be able men, fitted to write and speak
with power on international questions. Our directors are such
men. I need only mention their names to prove this:

President David Starr Jordan of Stanford University, who has
been chosen chief director; Edwin D. Mead, the secretary of the
Foundation; James Brown Scott, long connected with the State
Department, and editor of the *Journal of International Law;*
Rev. Charles R. Brown, recently elected Dean of Yale Theological School; John R. Mott, who has done such effective missionary work in organizing the student bodies in the different
countries to work together; James A. Macdonald, the very efficient
editor of the *Toronto Glove* and an able public speaker; and Hamilton Holt, the well-known editor of the *Independent.* All are men
of large capacity.

Besides our directors, we have several lecturers in the field,
prominent among whom is Miss Eckstein, who has for several
years been laboring for the cause, not only here but in other
countries. Most of you know of the great petition for arbitration which she presented at the last Hague Congress. For the
last two years she has been working very effectively in Germany
and England.

PLAN OF WORK

We intend to carry on this work through organized channels.
We have not the means to employ a thousand and one teachers
in the regularly organized schools, but we can bring these teachers
together in conventions and work through them in every classroom
thus making the teacher an important factor in our organization.

We shall pay special attention to the courses of study in the
schools, in order that we may improve conditions there. In times

past, when fighting was the main busiɳess of the world, literature
consisted largely of the stories of conflicts, and much space and
time were taken up by these descriptions in histories. Fortunately recent histories show a marked improvement in this
respect, though there still remains too much that has a pernicious
influence upon the young. Is it surprising that our children
should receive the impression that war has contributed cardinally
to the development of mankind, when so large a part of our histories and so much of the literature studied in our schools are
devoted to the details of the battlefield and so little to the more
real things of life—the things that are constructively developing
the nations? We desire to have it made very plain to what extent
civilization has been hindered by these misfortunes. The study
of history should dwell largely upon the peaceful pursuits of life—
agriculture, trade, commerce, schools, science. These are the
things to which the children should give their chief attention, and
not the struggles between the nations.

Then there are the preachers, who come in contact with all
classes and conditions of men, young and old, the world over.
Here is a tremendous influence that should be taken into consideration. Our directors will meet these ministers in conventions
and awaken their special interest in these matters so that they
will take up the work with their congregations.

THE PRESS

The press is a most powerful influence and the one that the
world responds to most readily. We mean to keep in touch with
its great leaders, personally and in conventions, and endeavor to
impress upon them the kind of work the cause needs in the magazine, the weekly, and the daily journal. Editors will be urged to
use the greatest care in the selection of material and to eliminate
such matter as would incite the people of one nation against another. Those who write for the newspapers should have a serious
appreciation of their great responsibility. Is it not desirable that
we seek for bright young men who have an aptitude for this profession, and educate them carefully to take up its duties? In

every other branch of educational work the teachers and directors serve a long apprenticeship; but here is one of the greatest
powers on earth for which there is seldom any special training
required.   It seems to me of the utmost importance that means
should be provided for educating young men for this profession—
men of high moral tone, who could not be induced by any consideration to lend their influence to unworthy objects.   I say this with
the fullest and most grateful appreciation of the thorough, conscientious, and effective work being done by so many of our newspapers.

'Not only do we need a director to give his whole time to the
press of the world, keeping in communication with the leading
editors, but we also need to supplement his work by a press bureau
for the collection and distribution of important information bearing upon this subject.

BUSINESS MEN

Another great body of men of great influence are the merchants,
the manufacturers, and the financiers.   They hold within their
grasp the means for carrying on war, and we should see that they
have the fullest information bearing upon this subject, in order
that they should withhold their support from a system that is
exercising such a baneful influence.   Our directors will endeavor
to meet these men in their conventions, as well as individually,
and urge them to shoulder their responsibility in this great cause.

PEACE LITERATURE

We shall continue to publish the best literature on the subject
in our International Library and scatter it broadcast.   Many of
these volumes could be made very important factors in this campaign of education.   *Lay Down Your Arms* by Baroness von Sutt-
ner, also her stirring autobiography, might do for the peace cause
what *Uncle Tom's Cabin* did for the freedom of the slaves.   In
this autobiography she has woven into her own life history the
historical narrative of her work, and others', in the great peace
movement in which she has taken so prominent a part.   But

before people will read extensively their interest must often first be awakened by the spoken word. Earnest men and women who recognize the evils of war must go into the field and exert their personal influence—those who have implanted in them the divine spark, which will kindle a like spirit in others.

The glorious side of war has been too much emphasized—the brilliant charges, the full regiments marching to the front with flying colors to the strains of martial music. The other side of the picture should be as carefully portrayed—the return of these regiments reduced to a tenth of their original number, maimed and feeble, carrying torn and blood-stained battle-flags. A knowledge of that side of the picture is necessary for a full comprehension of what war means. Children should read the account of Napoleon's march into Russia and return, as given by Grote and Segur in *The Two Great Retreats.* The painter Verestchagin going upon the Russian battleship that he might depict more effectively the horrors of war in the great conflict between Japan and Russia, in which nearly the whole fleet of Russia with more than ten thousand seamen was destroyed, by his own death when the ship went down, left a deeper impression upon the world than anything he had previously been able to do. Victor Hugo's description of the dead and dying on the field after the Battle of Waterloo, should be read in all our schools. There is work enough for an army of men and women in properly educating the people.

LATENT INTEREST

At the present time there is a very general feeling against war and in favor of universal peace, but that feeling is inactive. The great mass of people the world over are giving 99 per cent of their thought and time and money to the various enterprises in which they are engaged, with hardly a moment's consideration of this greatest of all problems, affecting as it does every human being in the cost of his food, his clothing, and his housing. We must take steps to awaken this interest to active coöperation.

Some people think that we are very near the solution of this military problem. I am not of their opinion. It will take many millions of dollars to carry this work to a successful issue, and the funds given by a few generous people are wholly inadequate. Moreover, it would not be well for the people to feel that this responsibility had been taken off their shoulders and that the work could be accomplished without their assistance. They must be made to realize that world-wide coöperation is necessary. A person is interested in that in which he has an investment, either in time or money, and it is this investment, this responsibility, that the friends of peace must take upon themselves if this problem is to be solved.

The odds against us are great and we cannot successfully meet them with a few millions. It will take long to overcome the general belief in the necessity for the present system and the selfish interests working for its continuance, but we have a good background on which to rely—the latent sentiment in favor of peace which we must bring into activity by *continuous, persistent* and *personal* effort. We must seek out and employ those who have the spirit of a Burritt, a Phillips, a Garrison, a Godfrey, a Savonarola. Only such a spirit can overcome the tremendous odds against us.

CHAIRMAN NOBLE: The last speaker of the morning is from the "Lone Star State", the State of great territory, the State of big hope, the State of big promise, the State of big performance, the State of big men, and I have the privilege of introducing to you now the President of Baylor University, Waco, Texas, Mr. Samuel P. Brooks.

THE SCHOOLROOM IN THE PEACE PROPAGANDA

S. P. BROOKS

No man knows how long it took the Almighty to build the worlds that make up the Universe. Certain it is He did not do it in a day. No man knows how long civilization has been in the making. Every wise man knows that the Creator did not set up human society as a complete organism, even approximating its completion as now found in its interrelated but manifold parts.

Our ancestors did not know the tricks of the modern tailor, but they did the best they knew. They did not order by telephone refrigerated meats; they went about in the forests hunting for food. In dire distress they sometimes ate each other. Just as soon as they discovered that it was better not to eat prisoners captured in war, they put them as slaves to taming wild animals and to herding them in flocks.

The hunter with crude implements of warfare put to rout the weaker man or race. He nowhere knew about modern rights as exemplified in our courts of law. In the process of time the hunter became the herder. Herding the flocks was impossible without recognition of certain elemental property rights shown by possession. The chief herders became patriarchs. Diplomacy between patriarchs pointed the way to diplomacy between nations.

The tiller of the soil was the successor of the herdsman. The advent of the plow, or agricultural stage of society, introduced new blessings, more than society had ever enjoyed. Discoveries and inventions of merit are rarely ever made unless needed by society. The herder needed less land than the hunter; while the plowman, needing the land, ran dividing lines across the pastures of the herdsman. To the plow we owe our highest expression of law at home or abroad. Without peace among men planted crops are never harvested. The plow is a veritable exponent of peace on earth and good will to all men. The plow introduced homes with every domestic blessing, schools with their far-reaching and ever-increasing advantages, churches the best visible means of keeping alive or propagating the religion of Jehovah. Only the imagination can give rightful honor to this implement of the agricultural stage of society.

The school is a type of, and has developed as a contemporary with, this period of social growth. Jesus of Nazareth was the world's greatest teacher. The very strength of His teaching was its simplicity, to which teachers of the world have been slow to give credence. However, they now know that teaching is done best by him who deals in parables, as did the Son of Man. Parables attract and hold the student, for they have to do with the universal as to time and place. They seem to take one out of

the realm of theory and place him in the field of fact.   Teachers
do not always see this.   They too frequently have hobbled their
instruction by making local applications.   They have sought to
develop the interest of students by an appeal to patriotism, which
patriotism was false in fact for it was based on hatred to what lay
without the field of study.   Throughout the ages men have des-
pised what they were ignorant of and have hated whomsoever
they did not know.   Historical teachers, so-called, have been
synonymous with tyrants.   They have yielded up their ignorance or have taken on new knowledge reluctantly.   They have
punished students who dared to object; have mocked any discovery of new knowledge; have, as if by authority of Heaven,
condemned to perdition the souls of those who would not pro-
nounce with humble reverence and belief the religious formulas
of the ages.

It is a matter of world interest that the teacher of today, the
real teacher, is not a simple pedagogue.   In the evolution of
affairs he shows evidences of growth.   He has come out of the
dark ages and carries a lamp of light; he guides his students into
realms, known and unknown, and encourages them to find their
way out; he loves home and neighbor, language and law, life and
belief.   Having knowledge, he regards himself a citizen of the
world of geography as well as the world of fact.   Getting more
knowledge prepares him for larger living in world thinking.

With the martyr spirit teachers have gone, and are going, to
the uttermost parts of the earth, giving instruction in the ideals
of democracy and western Christian civilization.   To the schools
of Japan thousands of Chinese go annually; to American universities and those of Europe young students of the whole world
are wending their way.   To Oxford the Rhodes Scholars go.
Cosmopolitan ideas and conduct are rapidly supplanting provincialism in all the leading nations.   The interchange of professors,
as has been done in the last few years between American and
European universities, furnishes a fine field for respect rather than
hate.   The world has a choice example of international courtesy
and good will in the return of the Boxer indemnity fund, out of

which now several hundred Chinese men will be educated annually in the universities of America.

The modern teacher can rule the world, let him grip and be
gripped by a faith in some policy, and that policy will become
world-wide in significance and power. There is, therefore, no
propaganda undertaken with much hope of success unless its
truth has entered into the schoolrooms of the world.

National existence in the past has depended on force; national
existence in the future will depend on a square deal. Let the
teacher of history teach it.

As democracy has developed in the light of liberty it has required of each citizen to yield his own rights where they were
subversive to the rights of others. Individual freedom ends
where community interests begin. Let teachers dwell more on
the rights of others.

As nations have grown strong in the out-reach of trade and
influence, they have mutually developed each other into a community of governments. Each has surrendered some right of
local law for the good of the international governments. Let
teachers learn international law and teach the comity of nations.

Governments of the earth will never thrive any more on the
conquests of others; world wisdom in trade and world religion
setting up the protector's care of the weak will not suggest it;
world consciousness will not allow it. Let the schoolrooms
proclaim this wholesome gospel.

There never was a war settled unless by one side yielding to
the other. Record of the fact was made. This record was made
firm in a written treaty signed by the contracting parties. It
does not signifiy that the right prevailed, only that the strong
won. If the perpetuity of the result is guaranteed by the treaty,
might not the war itself have been kept off by a prior treaty or
an arbitration of the troubles? Let teachers show forth the
beauty of life and not so much the glories of the battlefields. Let
teachers lead their students into an appreciation of the heroics
of moral victories in the paths of home and industrial life. Let
them show forth the fact that there can be as much manliness in

keeping the stroke in some productive labor as in keeping the step on the drill ground.

Teachers can win the growing child to the fairness of a game well played. He learns quickly that victory in a game does not destroy the loser. It may help him; not so the war that maims or destroys the vanquished. Out of the schools, colleges and universities, the future statesmen and citizens will go. They should go trained aright. Some of them will have been influenced by the moral quality found in peace and the evangelizing agencies of it, *e.g.*, the Student Volunteer Movement; some of them will be imbued with the spirit of gain in wealth made possible by trade uninterrupted and the saving of unnecessary taxation. Let teachers take advantage of either to point the way to peace.

Civilization will not now stand for some things which were popular with our ancestors. The duelist is banished. So ought the modern manufacturer who not only makes war goods but by flaming head-lines, by paid oratory, and by organized groups of men makes international wars to order.

The schoolroom is no longer the place for the timid soul who fears to smash the images of tradition. Teachers may well learn to teach what ought to be, as well as what has been. Service to country is not opposition to others. Enemies more frequently live within than without. World-wide trade with world-needed articles is a harbinger of peace. The pirate of history can never more be idolized in story. He was a simple robber. School children are now taught it. The licensed privateer on the high seas is little removed from the pirate in the thinking of some of us. All school children should be taught it. Through the wide-spread news agency of the earth there are few state secrets. There needs to be few. Publicity develops knowledge; knowledge develops faith in each other. Public opinion is moulded by the teacher of the young. Education is atmospheric and highly vicarious. Let public opinion and education run in the same channels. Let the constructive character of peace be set over against the destruction of war. Let the embryonic Napoleons of war be transformed into the captains of industry and social development.

It took a greater man to project and build a railroad across the

American continent than to march an army across the Alps. Let the idealism of it grip the student. War has glamor for the officer but for the private mere duty must be enthroned. If the private in the army marches in pride may his energies not be transformed into service of industry with equal fidelity and with greater hopes of reward? Service in the army hinders the making of home, dethrones women and the ideals of her virtues, mocks privacy and hinders individual initiative. Service in industry allows one to remain in home, holds up the true ideals of wife and mother and strengthens initiative.

If we enthrone the ideals of the peace propagandist, we may as William James says: "Inflame the civic temper as past history has inflamed the military temper." Let us follow James. By so doing, we may not bring the millennium, but we are sure to make this old world better.

Let every teacher understand that he deals with worlds in microcosm. Each schoolroom is full of future citizens. Each little one can think thoughts and see facts that are too frequently dallied with by a prattle of words.

The world is a unit knit together by bonds of steel. No longer do walls divide us, nor mountains, nor rivers, nor oceans, nor air.

The political machinery of peace has two parts, federation and arbitration. No teacher in the world ought to be able to see this so easily as the American. He has before him the federation of the original thirteen colonies, bound together by a treaty, or constitution, made up of mutual concessions.

The Monroe Doctrine has never been free of its corollary. It forbids any European government taking territory here. If other nations will not join, surely the United States may without hesitancy propose to the Republics to the South of us that Uncle Sam has no ulterior end in view in the future regarding them, that they may unite with him by treaties for mutual protection and as a guarantee among all nations that they run up the flag of confidence rather than distrust.

Finally, let us teach the parallelism of politics and government, religion and church. Let it be sounded forth in every high school, college and university in the world that politics is to government as religion is to the church, that government is to the peace of the world as the church is to the evangelization of the world, that whatever helps politics helps government, and whatever helps religion helps the church, that whatever helps either at home helps both at home and abroad. Let us teach well the old Latin proverb that "By concord the weakest things grow strong, by discord the strongest totter."

Let us teach the fallacy of the doctrine so widely advocated. that if you wish peace prepare for war. On the contrary, si vis pacem para pacem.

CHAIRMAN NOBLE: The morning session is now adjourned.

ADJOURNED

FRIDAY AFTERNOON, MAY 5, AT TWO-THIRTY O'CLOCK

John W. Foster, Presiding Officer

CHAIRMAN FOSTER: Before introducing the speakers who are to occupy your attention this afternoon, I desire to make a few remarks upon a subject which I regard as quite germane to the objects of the present Congress.

In the intercourse of our country with foreign nations it is our first and most important duty to preserve the peace and cultivate relations of friendship with our coterminous neighbors. And yet within the last few weeks we have seen local disturbances in the northern States of Mexico fanned into the flames of war along the boundary line, and our entire population astounded by the rapid concentration on the frontier of a large portion of our army equipped for hostile operations. Those best informed tell us that this lamentable condition of affairs has been brought about largely by the abuse by foreigners of the contiguous territory of the United States and by the active participation of American citizens. Great quantities of arms and munitions of war, evading our customs houses, have been surreptitiously introduced into Mexico. Large numbers of American citizens, both singly and in bands, accoutered for war, have openly crossed the frontier and joined the forces which are seeking to overthrow a government with which we are at peace; and when worsted in battle have sought a refuge within our borders, only to return at will and take part in a contest in which we should properly be neutral. A so styled "provisional Governor of Chihuahua" has openly established his office at El Paso, Texas, and therefrom issued his orders and carried on warlike correspondence across the frontier; while insurrectionary chiefs in other localities on American territory were actively plotting against the established government of Mexico.

It is not necessary that we should consider the merits of the controversy in Mexico, to pass judgment upon the condition of affairs on our side of the southern border.   Every patriotic American citizen who has regard for the honor of his country and its reputation among the nations of the earth must deplore these events, and inquire whether there is not a remedy for them.   I am satisfied that there has been a sincere desire on the part of the President and his Cabinet to enforce a strict observance of our neutrality laws.   I am not so certain that a similar spirit has existed on the part of the local authorities, either Federal or State, along the frontier, where the popular sentiment seems to be largely on the side of the insurrectionists.   But whether or not the neutrality laws have been strictly enforced, it is plain to any student of our history who has given attention to the subject that they are antiquated and are in great need of revision and enlargement.

Our first neutrality act was passed during Washington's first administration, and were put into their present shape in 1818. At the time of their enactment they marked a great advance in international law and practice, and gained for our country much credit.   But they have proved to be too limited in their scope. At that time our land frontier both on the north and the south was very sparsely settled.   Our intercourse with foreign nations was then almost entirely by sea, and an examination of our neutrality code shows that it applies chiefly to maritime matters. The great development of our population both on the Mexican and Canadian border requires a reëxamination of the neutrality laws by our legislative and executive departments.   .

The attention of Congress has been repeatedly called to this subject, and that body has been urged to the adoption of stricter measures to enable the Executive to more fully discharge its international duties of neutrality.   Following the embarrassments on our southern frontier attending the independence of Texas, and on our northern border by the Canadian rebellion, in 1838 President VanBuren in a special message laid before Congress the defective character of our neutrality laws, and asked that these laws be thoroughly revised and enlarged in order "to vest in the Executive full power to prevent injuries being inflicted upon neighboring nations by the unauthorized and unlawful acts of the citizens of the United States or other persons who may be within our jurisdiction and subject to our control." And later in his administration he repeated these recommendations. The Fenian plotting in our territory and the raids into Canada led President Arthur in 1884 to urge again upon Congress "the prompt and thorough treatment of the question, which" he said, "intimately concerns the national honor."

Notwithstanding these urgent appeals to Congress, the neutrality laws of 1818 remain unaltered with all the defects pointed out by successive presidents. The fact that defective legislation does not relieve or excuse a nation from discharging its international obligations was made very clear after our Civil War, when our government announced to that of Great Britain that "no sovereign power can rightfully plead the defects of its own domestic penal statutes as justification or extenuation of an international wrong to another sovereign power" and the Geneva Arbitration Tribunal confirmed this principle by inflicting upon Great Britain a penalty of $15,500,000 because of its defective legislation and neglect of its international duty. Great Britain recognized the justice of our complaint, made a thorough revision of her laws, and now stands at the front of the nations in her neutrality legislation. Unless we follow her example, we shall continue to expose ourselves to the just complaints and reclamations of Mexico and Canada.

The time at my disposal will not allow me to enter into a full discussion of the changes called for by our defective neutrality laws, but I venture to suggest briefly three modifications.

First, Some restriction should be placed upon the free commerce as a mercantile commodity of arms and munitions of war; and power should be conferred upon the President to limit or suspend, in his discretion, their export across the border in time of disturbance or insurrection.

Second, It should be made unlawful for Americans to enter the military service of any power or chief at war with a nation with

which we are at peace.   It was the personal aid of Americans that
gave strength to the Canadian rebellion in 1838, to the late insurrection in Mexico, and to the recent civil wars in Nicaragua and
Honduras.   In this respect the laws of Great Britain, France, and
other countries are in advance of ours.   The British Foreign
Enlistment Act of 1870 makes it unlawful for any British subject
to enter the military service of any power at war with a nation
with which its government is at peace; and it subjects them to
heavy fines and imprisonment.   In all its neutrality proclamations
on the breaking out of hostilities in other nations, the British
government notifies its subjects of the penalties they will incur
under their own laws, and it further warns them that they will
enter such foreign service at their own peril, in no wise obtain any
protection from their own government, and must suffer such penalties as the enemy may inflict upon them.   We certainly should
do no less than this.

Third, Greater power should be conferred upon the President,
in time of civil disturbance on the frontier, to limit or prohibit
intercourse across the border, to prevent the abuse of our territory by foreign conspirators, and in his discretion to enforce martial law on our soil within the zone of disturbance.

We had a foretaste during our Civil War of what an unfriendly
neutrality may do to aid our domestic enemies.   The conservative government of Mexico allowed the free entrance through
Matamoros and across the Rio Grande of unlimited warlike supplies for the Southern armies.   The Confederate agents in Canada, harbored by a sympathetic government, were enabled to
raid and burn towns, loot banks, seize and destroy steamers on
the Great Lakes, and threaten the destruction of New York and
Chicago.   Should internal strife again unhappily visit our fair
land, the recent occurrences on the Mexican frontier suggest what
an imperfect neutrality might allow to be inflicted upon us.   Is
it not time we set our own house in order, as we exhort other nations to international peace and good will?

I will now introduce Prof. Samuel T. Dutton, of Columbia
University, who has been for many years well known for his services in he cause of education and of late a prominent factor in
the peace movement in New York.

THE NEWER PROPAGANDA FOR PEACE

SAMUEL T. DUTTON

It is generally considered that the growth of civil government is favorable for world peace. As education becomes more universal and more free, and as the people participate more fully in public affairs, there is an increased capacity for understanding and appreciating what peace means. But even in the most intelligent nations there is still so much apathy and so much ignorance that the masses can hardly be counted upon in civic affairs at home, much less in world politics. Hence in democratic communities we often see wrongs committed and injustice and greed winning easy victories. Under such conditions the attitude of men toward international affairs is likely to be one of indifference. You can hardly expect people who do not exert themselves on the side of honesty and fair-dealing in local and State affairs to be alert or enthusiastic respecting those problems which call for an intelligence and a patriotism transcending the bounds of State or nation. Neither can you expect to find an active public sentiment which in times of great moment will exert a commanding influence in the halls of legislation. When in 1897 a general arbitration treaty had been arranged between the United States and England and the supreme moment had arrived when the United States Senate was called upon to vote "Yes" or "No," what evidence have we that Senators were influenced to any considerable extent by the opinion of their constituents or that the country as a whole was alive to the importance of the question at issue? We have had two world conferences at The Hague in which important conventions were arranged and forward steps were taken toward the establishment of international justice but there is no evidence that the delegates from England or Germany or the United States were stimulated or urged forward by any strong volume of public opinion. They had their instructions from their several governments and to carry these out faithfully was considered enough. Several important matters affecting the international movement are now pending, such as the Peace

Commission already provided for by Congress; the unlimited arbitration treaty with England which is likely soon to go again before our Senate; the degree of coöperation which other nations will be permitted and expected to share in the use and protection of the Panama Canal.   Then there is the great problem of organizing the program for the Third Hague Conference and the possibility of discovering some way of tempering international suspicions so that the frightful burden involved in the increase of armaments may be lifted.

The press, it must be admitted, and it certainly is cause for rejoicing, has shown during the past five years an increasing readiness to aid in peace propaganda.   This is a distinct gain and an augury of success.   The press is a mighty force and ought to lead and assist in the education of the people but we must not deceive ourselves as to the extent to which the masses are awakened to the necessity of standing for international friendship and of resisting every suggestion pointing in the other direction.   The average man reads about the things in which he is interested and as far as my personal acquaintance goes his preference for peace rather than war is not pronounced.   I do not believe that one in a hundred of the voters in the United States has at this moment any adequate knowledge of that hundred-year old controversy over the Newfoundland Fisheries which was so amicably and so satisfactorily settled last year.   The fact is that people of this country and of all countries need education.   There must be propaganda carefully organized and directed and persistently applied until the body politic is charged with a new spirit.   The Russian revolutionist more than any other propagandist at the present time appreciates the need of continuous and vigorous preaching and teaching of the ideas to which he is committed. He knows that the only hope of success lies in the enlightenment and the quickening of the sluggish minds of his fellow-citizens to feeling and a faith in the new régimé.   In the same way our fellow-citizens need to be aroused respecting the moral, economic, and political phases of international relations.   They need to be impressed with the moral grandeur of a world united in seeking the good of mankind and of governments honestly, sincerely, devoutly striving to establish justice and abolish forever the thought of violence.

It is evident that the hour has arrived when the gospel of peace must be widely and earnestly preached. Some may think that diplomacy may be equal to the task of binding the nations together; others may believe that money applied in the scientific study of war and its causes will reveal a remedy. Both of these things are important but will be entirely inadequate. Mr. Norman Angell thinks that the economic relations of nations instead of inviting war are tending to make it impossible and in case war occurs, the victor can gain no advantage which is not more than offset by his losses. If this is true or even partly true, the news ought to be carried to every hamlet in the country so that when the next war scare comes the people may intelligently resist its insidious and seductive influence.

Doubtless many influences are working for the establishment of perpetual peace. Human progress and the growth of the institutions of civilization are charged with that altruism and with that sense of solidarity which are fundamental in the peace movement. Men and women the world over must apprehend and appreciate these things. Hence the tremendous need that clergymen, publicists, social reformers, jurists, educators, as well as men of science and leaders of commerce should declare the gospel of peace so that everywhere, in church, in State, and school, and in civic assembly, the public mind and the public conscience are summoned to action.

The five hundred peace societies of the world are doing much but their work as yet lacks organization and direction. Those who are able to finance the peace cause may justly insist that the peace forces in this country should be federated upon a basis of equality and coöperation that the whole land may be covered and that such a wise, constructive and educative program of propaganda be organized as will give the United States distinction and enable her to take a place of leadership along the new path.

Assuming that this may be brought about, what shall be the nature of the propaganda which in the pulpit, on the platform, through the press by means of books and tracts is to be presented?

In the light of what I have said it must appear that the old propaganda — moral, economic, humanitarian, are always new until
the mind and the heart of men have grasped their deeper meaning.
To most people it will come as a new idea that the age of war has
passed, that as we can see in Europe today vast museums full of
ancient and mediaeval weapons kept as souvenirs of the barbaric
past, so it may be predicted that a few years hence the horrid
engines of destruction which modern genius and science are constructing will be objects of historic interest rather than of practical
use.

There will be, unless all signs fail, no more racial wars.   The
great Congress of Races to be held for the first time in London in
July at which fifty nations are to be represented gives promise
that in time race prejudice, especially the sort that has caused
war, will be absolutely eliminated from the world.   Even in the
Turkish Empire which has been for hundreds of years a melting-
pot for all peoples there is, under the new régime, a good degree
of racial peace and friendship.   Again, there are to be no more
religious wars.   Religious toleration is universal except in Russia
and it is worth noticing that that nation has earned the disapproval of other nations for the racial injustice which it practices.

Wars of races and religion having passed, it can be shown that
nothing remains to cause war except national cupidity or some
fancied insult of national honor.   Thus it can be shown that war
has no place in a system of modern justice and that the time is
rapidly approaching when the conscience and reason of the world
will demand that every dispute whatsoever shall be settled in a
court of arbitral justice.   As the gospel of world redemption is
always new, so the doctrine of peace on earth, good will to men,
will never lose its vitalizing and uplifting power.

All propaganda respecting the desired reduction of armies and
navies should never overlook the peculiar conditions of central
Europe.   The historic position of the military establishments in
their social and political relations constitutes a most difficult
phase of our problem.   Such institutions so deeply rooted in the
national life must be treated with a degree of respect and even if
military men are slow to recognize the victories of peace, let us

give them the consideration which they deserve. In our zeal to see the world organized upon the plane of honor and justice, we forget that in times past we have had to defend the integrity of the nation and have helped to control disorders elsewhere. It is only just to say that many of highest rank in both army and navy are opposed to war and are among the most outspoken lovers of peace. I was sorry to see in the *Army and Navy Journal* of August 20th an editorial which attacked very strongly the work undertaken by the School Peace League of teaching the children and youth of the land those things which make for good will toward those of other lands. Some may be overzealous and unwise in the use of such propaganda but the general plan of emphasizing in the teaching of history those factors which relate to the economic, civic, and social welfare of the nation and the minimizing of war as a factor in human progress, will, I am sure, receive the commendation of all thoughtful people. The new propaganda should discriminate clearly between that large number of officers of the army and navy who recognize that the world is being changed to a condition where war is unnecessary and rejoice in it and the few who deride and impugn the motives and methods of peace workers. The new propaganda will interpret and enforce the idea of a league of peace so often urged by Mr. Carnegie and clearly stated by Mr. Roosevelt in his Christiania address. The idea is not new except to large numbers who have given it no thought whatever. Reduced to its simplest terms it means that while nations may employ force to suppress disorders within their own borders, unlawful conduct on the part of any nation affecting other nations shall be taken in hand by an international force under the direction of the league.

The propagandist may show the diminishing importance of physical force in the world as compared with that of moral force. It is moral power that is lifting up the backward peoples and making some of the great nations that have long been dormant arouse themselves for new action. In China, Turkey, Cuba, Porto Rico, and the Philippines we see this moral awakening.

The United States can do nothing better than to help China in every possible way to establish representative government.

She needs this help and deserves it. She is a peaceful nation. The civilized world should frown upon any procedure which compels China to waste her substance in defending her territory from aggression or in maintaining her self-respect. The same kind of sympathy and support should go out to the Young Turks who are trying to join together the heterogeneous elements of which the Empire is composed on a basis of toleration and civic coöperation. All attempts to cheat them, to extort territory or unjust concessions or otherwise to exploit them for selfish ends should be condemned by international public sentiment.

Another theme which has not received the attention it deserves is the moral and social influence of conscription. It is not difficult to show that it is out of harmony with the doctrine of individual liberty; it does not encourage but suppresses true patriotism, it partakes of the nature of slavery, which the Christian world has abolished.

Some are deeply concerned regarding the destiny of military and naval officers if war is made impossible. There is no need of alarm, for such officers have received a scientific training. There will always be strenuous work for all such. The conservation of natural resources, the construction of great public works, the national and international control and uplifting of backward peoples, scientific work in battling with famine and pestilence— these offer a field large enough for all competent men. While schools of military and naval science would need to change their curriculum somewhat, they may still go on training men for constructive, humanitarian work.

Among the newer propaganda is the possibility of extending the principle of the neutralization of territory to keep pace with the advancement of public opinion in the direction of world unity and coöperation. Few know that Switzerland, the Suez Canal, and various other portions of the world have long been neutralized and that there never has been any serious difficulty arising in regard to this arrangement. The neutralization of the Philippines is well worth considering as a possibility. In short, it may be thus possible to neutralize all the oceans and waterways of the world. This idea is certainly worth our study and discussion.

While there can probably be no immediate limitation of armaments in Europe, the United States may well set an example and while there is little danger of war, the danger of increasing poverty and human suffering because of the economic waste now incurred calls for energetic appeal and protest. A nation may commit national suicide as Spain and Portugal have done, but that is not the worst of it. Men, women and children live in ignorance, squalor, and abject hopelessness. This condition is the heritage of the warlike past. It is to be seen not merely in southern Europe, but to a considerable extent in Great Britain and central Europe. The propagandist may not be able to prove that rifles and cannon are unnecessary, but he can revive that ancient cry of a condemned soul, "Am I my brother's keeper?"—or that lawyer's question—"Who is my neighbor?"—and that universal answer of the Prince of Peace who showed that all enmity is to be brushed aside to make way for deeds of mercy and of helpfulness. In struggle and striving the world is gradually yielding to the greatest of all commandments, "Thou shalt love thy neighbor as thyself."

In closing I will briefly suggest some of the topics about which the masses are to be instructed, to wit:

The relation of Christianity to peace.

The duty of all churches and the clergy.

The philanthropic aspects of progress toward peace.

A comparison of the twentieth century with the seventeenth, eighteenth, and nineteenth as to war and its decadence.

Ancient and modern forms of heroism and the fallacies regarding the necessity of war as a moral tonic.

The financial, economic, and educational restraints upon the war spirit.

The relation of war scares to original sin and pure cussedness.

The justification of wage-earners and socialists in demanding that governments agree to the judicial settlement of all disputes.

The need of peace commissions in every country working separately and collectively to arrange the new order.

The need of a thorough re-organization of the peace forces of the United States under the advice of a representative national council.

The propriety of asking the United States government, which spent in the year 1910 $443,000,000 for war and pensions, to appropriate annually $1,000,000 for peace, to be expended by a commission appointed by the President.

This is only adding the touch of practicality and of sincerity to those memorable words spoken by Mr. Roosevelt at Christiania, and with these I will close this paper:

"Granted sincerity of purpose, the great Powers of the world should find no insurmountable difficulty in reaching an agreement which would put an end to the present costly and growing extravagance of expenditure on naval armaments and it would be a master stroke if those great Powers honestly bent on peace would form a League of Peace."

CHAIRMAN FOSTER: Reverend Frederick Lynch, of New York, desires to mention an important matter.

REV. FREDERICK LYNCH: I was asked by the officers of the Conference if I would not do what it seems eminently fitting we should do on this occasion, just to bear our testimony to one of the greatest friends of peace who has passed away while this Congress was in session. I refer to Mr. Paulson, of the Heckla Iron Works of Brooklyn, New York. Mr. Ginn led the way toward helping this great movement and Mr. Carnegie followed. Mr. Paulson got the idea from him, and said that he wanted to leave several hundreds of thousands of dollars to establish closer and better relations between the countries of the world. He came here from Denmark some sixty years ago and has built up a great fortune, and I think you will hear that practically all of that vast fortune is to be used to bring students from Scandinavia and Norway to America and give them the best that the United States has to give, and when they go back they will be permanent friends of the United States in Europe, and thus will be established closer and more intimate bonds between the two nations.   I think it is fitting that we should recognize this great man's name here.   I wish we could pass resolutions for his family, but he has no family, none in this country anyhow, and it is a

beautiful thing that as he dies he leaves his money to this great
cause, which is the cause of the twentieth century, and I want to
put this Conference on record as showing its gratitude and
appreciation of this great act.

CHAIRMAN FOSTER: I am again instructed to interrupt the
printed program by the announcement that the Hon. Henry
Clews, a delegate from the New York Chamber of Commerce
has arrived in this city, but must return this afternoon to New
York, and it is desirous that he be heard for a few minutes. Mr.
Clews negotiated the sale of the first Civil War bonds in 1861
by a commission direct from Abraham Lincoln. He is now negotiating for peace under President Taft. He has been for fifty
years a banker in New York. You had yesterday the scheme of
another New York banker to stop wars, which looked to me to be
very feasible. I expect Mr. Clews might endorse such a proposition. Permit me to introduce him.

ADDRESS OF MR. HENRY CLEWS

Last week we celebrated the birthday of him who immortal-
ized himself in what, to those who fought on both sides of it,
seemed to be a righteous war; yet the four words which will always
be most closely associated with his memory—"Let us have peace!"
will outrank in importance all his utterances as general, and later
as President, and even his ablest state papers.

I wish that General Grant might have lived long enough to
know that a commission of the English-speaking nations is uniting in an effort to secure an enduring peace, and an amicable
settlement of all disputes of nations by arbitration. His hand
which grasped the sword, and so ably directed the forces engaged
in deadly strife, would gladly wield the pen in favor of peace with
honor.

As highly as I value universal peace, and as much as I hope for
its consummation, I do not think it advisable to stop the building of warships, or the fortifying of any weak spots on our coasts

until we have our treaties signed and our fond hopes are positive certainties. The best preventive of war, under existing circumstances, is being ready for war. When the Panama Canal is finished a foothold in the vicinity of the Isthmus will be a tempting bait to some of the great Powers, and I favor the building of impregnable forts to guard this gateway between the oceans. The canal will belong to us and we should make it stronger than Gibraltar, and I believe that in their hearts all the statesmen of Europe would think it folly if we did not take these precautions. As a man takes out a fire insurance policy hoping and believing that he will never have to collect it, so we should fortify our ports as insurance against the unexpected.

I do not expect that anyone will be robbed or assaulted in the block where I reside, but I am willing to be taxed proportionately to have a policeman on that beat, and I certainly want to know that one is there.

It is but a few short years since organized effort was made to unite with other countries in favor of arbitration and the abolition of war. If it had been suggested by the weaker nations it might have been attributed to cowardice; but when the United States and Great Britain join hands in proposing a treaty in furtherance of this great cause, it is courageous action which will meet the approval in time of all righteous people in every country. Just think of a congress of nations banded together to abolish war! When the project becomes a fact, think of the internal improvements for the comfort of citizens that can be paid for with the money now used in the support of armies and navies. Socialists talk of the abolition of poverty. Certainly the monies spent to sustain a war footing would go far towards relieving the poor. Good roads, pure water and public parks would yield more in comfort to our fellow men than dreadnoughts and 12-inch guns. All of this is but a dream at present, but the foundation has been laid for lasting peace; and while some of us may not live to see the end of our work, our children and their children will be proud to say that they are descendants of those who were instrumental in promoting peace on earth and goodwill towards men by settling disputes about national questions by argument, rather than by bullets and bayonets.

Just at this time the civil strife in Mexico recalls to our mind very vividly the horrors of war and the necessity of settling disputes by peaceful methods. It is fitting that the influence of our wise President should be thrown in favor of a settlement of the Mexican troubles. The sending of our troops to the border line to protect our own territory from outlaw raiders, and also to enforce the neutrality laws, as well as to be in readiness for drastic action in case of the necessity of protecting the lives and property interests of our own citizens or innocent foreigners, is an exemplification of the wisdom of the Monroe Doctrine, and should be considered by the people of both nations as a guarantee of continued peace. Hence our army, being strewn all along the dividing line of both countries, instead of proving a menace, is really exactly the reverse.

If President Taft had stood idly by and allowed matters to take their course until some actual breaking of the neutrality laws had been reported, it is possible that some European Power would have landed troops on Mexican soil, and might have demanded a slice of territory for a coaling station or a base for supplies before they withdrew their troops. A case of this kind would have led to serious complications, in which the United States would unwillingly have had to adopt drastic measures to conserve the letter of the Monroe Doctrine.

The wonderful feeling of confidence that the people of the United States have in the judgment of President Taft is exemplified by the fact that his order mobilizing troops near the Mexican line, while it caused feelings of wonderment and surprise, did not meet with adverse criticism from any source.

Fortunately, we are not actuated by a desire for territorial extension. We are willing to live and let live. The peace organizations of the United States are respected all over the world, and the closer we bind ourselves together in our work the more our influence will be felt for good. Whoever may be at the head of our organization proper, he will bow in respect to the great man in the White House who is entitled to a part of the credit for any good we may accomplish.

There is one thing very sure—that the millennium which

almost everybody expects will be realized some day upon the earth, can never be achieved by humanity until we first get what this Convention is earnestly and ardently striving for—international peace! That is the only real and substantial basis on which we can repeat the angelic song "Peace on earth and good-will towards men"—not for a day, not for a season, but for all time; and this is what the millennium absolutely means. Let us hasten the coming of that era of universal peace by every means within our power.

CHAIRMAN FOSTER: The trouble with us is that we live too long, and when Brother Clews and I get to talking we are apt to think of the times in the Civil War when we had a pretty pugnacious disposition. I have gotten over mine. But there is one thing which he said that we will all agree upon, that was his commendation of that great man who did a great lot of fighting, but had a wonderful influence upon the peace of the world, Ulysses S. Grant. He made the ablest and greatest arbitration treaty that was ever made, which resulted in the Geneva decision. Let me say that President Taft denied that he had any patent on this treaty that is likely to be made submitting all questions, without exception or reservation, that might arise between Great Britain and the United States through arbitration. Thirty-four years ago President Grant in writing declared himself in favor of submitting all questions of every character that could not be decided by diplomacy, to arbitration, so that if we have any patent on it, we can go back that far to the inventor. What could we have done without George Fox for all these generations? We have with us now President Sharpless of Haverford College, of the Society of Friends. I take pleasure in calling on President Sharpless.

THE EDUCATION OF PEACE MEN

ISAAC SHARPLESS

The best way to secure a result is not always to aim directly at it. The astronomer can sometimes see a faint star by indirection when he fails if he looks towards it. He who concludes to turn all his energies to finding happiness pretty certainly does not find it. He who finds it, finds it by forgetting it. The man who succeeds in solving the problems that are worth solving, in doing the difficult things that are worth doing and which he much desires to do, gets happiness as a by-product. Scholarship comes not necessarily to the man who always has that end in view. It comes through the mastery of intellectual difficulties of a certain kind, in which the man becomes so absorbed that he forgets all else until he wakens up some morning and finds that he has formed certain intellectual habits and tastes and is, almost unknown to himself, a scholar. He who starts life with a purpose to make a character for himself may not succeed, but he who approaches the duties of every day with a conscience which makes him meet them fairly and faithfully, who never shirks a responsibility and never quails before a danger is making character all the time, though it may be farthest from his thoughts.

There is often a close and unknown relation between acts and tendencies which are seemingly far remote from each other.

The reports of the Rhodes Scholars betray a striking difference in the character of English and American education, a difference not hitherto unknown, but perhaps never before so strikingly evident.

In the new country there is an abounding enthusiasm, both individual and collective. This brings about much popular knowledge, much general diffusion of educational ideas and theories, much interest in study, much ambition for advancement. It is stimulated by the easy conditions of entrance to many schools and colleges which the popular numerical standard of success constantly accentuates. As our friend Mr. Dooley, who so often catches the spirit of American tendencies, tells us, the admission to college is not a great bugbear. "The President takes the boy into his Turkish room, offers him a cigarette and says, 'Now me dear boy you are admitted. What brand of larnin' do ye wish studied for you by me competent professors.'"

When we wish an educational justification for all this vigor and enthusiasm we point to Froebel and the kindergarten or to Her-

bart and his doctrine of interest, or to the college elective system
and the arguments for it, all of which we misapply or pervert.
We reap the product, a generous, agreeable, progressive, well-
informed youth, full of a solid belief in America and himself, full
of the spirit of abundant life and energy, rather careless of methods
and judging success by tangible results.

In England interest does not count and enthusiasm is below
par. The boy studies his lessons because he must. If he does
not like them today he surely attends to them tomorrow. His
early work is kept down to a few fundamental things and these
are well and thoroughly learned. Slovenliness is the great sin
and superficiality has no defence. What wise men decree as the
proper discipline for the boy, that he takes. He makes a face
but he swallows. . He learns to do unpleasant things. *Grind*
so contemptuously spoken of in America, is his habit, his normal
educational life. At twenty he does not know much about many
things but he can do what lies before him. He has not touched
a great variety of subjects, can not talk interestingly of all sorts
of things, seems lacking in the ardor of conquest and the essence
of progress, but he can sit down to master a problem which will
take hours and days of uninteresting drudgery and has a fund
of thorough knowledge of a few essential things, which makes
such a mastery possible.

Is it a far cry from these educational conditions to certain other
conditions which are the result of adult tendencies in the development of the national life? We need only mention one. Our
municipal government in America is often extravagant, inefficient,
corrupt. In England it is economical, largely efficient, honest,
and the best men work night and day to keep it so. Our negli-
gent habits would not be tolerated at all in many cities. Their
management is thoroughly and carefully attended to—ours is by
slap-dash methods, and crude and careless machinery. The
expenses of two cities of equal population in the two countries may
be in the proportion of 4 to 1 and yet it would not be safe to say
that the quadruple expenditure brought more to our tax payers.

And our people do not seem to care. They are too little interested or too selfish to make the necessary exertion to rescue the

government from evil or weak hands. They will hardly vote, and our most competent men will not take upon themselves the burdens and unpleasantnesses of active political or official life. We believe with a perennial optimism that some day when we have more time we will fix this thing right, and the history of the past will probably justify the belief. If we can keep out of wars with the extravagance and demoralization which they entail we will probably learn our lesson and reform.

But suppose that we could rear a generation of youths who were taught above all things the sacredness of doing things well, who had not held up before them continually the mercenary ideal that education pays in cash, whose athletic morality was not based upon the notion that to win the game was the only thing to strive for, and that methods did not matter, who had developed a conscience which would never allow a slovenly incompetent thing to be done without a protest, and who would spend days and nights in laboring to prevent it; would not such a generation when manhood came to them instinctively refuse to allow government to go awry? Could they see with any degree of tolerance the incapacity, the carelessness, the unrighteousness of our present management, and allow it to go unrebuked? Would not, in the face of such a public opinion, the evils fall of themselves?

There may be a closer connection between the way we require our children to study their lessons in spelling and arithmetic and elementary language, and the resulting character in our men and women than we think of; and it might be better to get habits of honest work through these things, than to have many lectures on civic duty and personal morality over which we may become enthusiastic, which our boys hear with interest and straightway forget, because they are not drilled into them by the steady force of patient self denying discipline.

The application of this to our present question is obvious. Lectures on the iniquity and inexpediency of war in school and college may be useful and somewhat effective. It is not necessary to abate efforts in this direction for there is a place even for superficial interest and influence in the great movement. They reach a class of minds, and create opinion and votes, among people whose judgment is rather immature, but whose intentions are meant to be well directed.   They create something of a contagious atmosphere in which reforms thrive.

But there may be a more sure word to be said, a condition created in which peace will become inevitable and wars impossible.

The indirect method is the way to promote this.   It will come gradually, and its effects may be invisible for a long time, but the final outcome is certain and permanent.

Do we wish to show the nation that war, with its preparation and consequences, is an economic waste?   We will appeal in vain to a people that care nothing about economy, that are accustomed to strew their resources around with a liberal hand, with a confidence that they will be indefinitely renewed, that see the forests and mines, the water power, and public lands given easily away or destroyed or sold for a song.   The children that grow up in this atmosphere will waste their toys, waste their time, waste their pencils and their books, waste their chewing gum and their cigarettes.   Waste will be a virtue rather than a fault as indicating the free generous American spirit.   The schools must enforce ideas of economy and thrift, set themselves strongly against squandering even to the extent if necessary of positive prohibition, even when extending to very little inexpensive things.

Do we want to curb the spirit of pseudo-patriotism, a frequent cause of trouble; the patriotism which always boasts of our country right or wrong and advocates her unlimited uncritical support in every emergency?   There is a lot of this spirit in the schools, sentiment for *our* crowd, our side of a game, our school, our college, a noble sentiment in proper limits.   Anything to win is our battle cry.   To pack our team is a merit if we do not get detected, to disable an opponent when the official can not see, is a very venial fault lapsing into a virtue.   And the men and women on the side lines whose business is not to enjoy fair play but to shout for our team, applaud these things, call them shrewd and commendable methods of winning a victory, worthy of all admiration, and if victory comes by these devices, they light bonfires and carry the captain on their shoulders and perhaps secure an enthusiastic speech of congratulation from the college president or the school principal. A generation reared in this spirit is the same that a few decades later will cheer a smart but indefensible political trick, will cry for a war in an impulse of excitement and howl down a moderate man who questions its propriety.

Do we wish to curb the demand for an unreasonable increase of our territory, the demand which in an American Fourth of July dinner in Paris was voiced by the toast, "To the U. S. To be bounded on the north by the Aurora Borealis, on the south by the Precession of the Equinoxes, on the east by the Primeval Chaos, and on the west by the Day of Judgment?" A demand which many times in many nations has brought on wars. If so we must somewhat revise our standards of greatness. We must have something better to be proud of than square miles of territory, and linear miles of railway, and tons of pig iron and bushels of wheat, indispensable as these things are. We must strive to be able to feel complacent over the quality of our government, of our schools, of our care of dependents and defectives, of our criminal administration, of our intellectual and moral habits of life.

But when we hold up these material standards alone to our children, when we are forever telling them that education pays, and will fit them for business rather than for service, when the spirit of the technical school, which is honestly a preparation for money making, pervades the academic school and college and the value of all education is reckoned by its cash proceeds, we are surely not rearing a race of men who will prefer quality to magnitude, and duty to success. To enlarge our domain will be, at least beneath the surface a sufficient justification for aggression, even though aggression may lead to war.

Do we want to impress on the world the efficiency and sensibleness of arbitration and have a popular backing when treaties come to be ratified, and courts established? The George Junior Republic boys when they grow to be men would inevitably stand for it. They could not help it. But what about the boys in schools with no efficient self-government, whose teachers' laws are the every day authority and whose differences are adjusted by arbitrary power? Is there not a seed of distrust sown for the free play of arbitral courts and a habit of depending on power and position and "arms and the man" for the emergency? Does it not encourage the reliance on the imperious dictator, the show of arms at least to carry a point, and bully a weak power, rather than a gracious surrender when in the wrong, and a willing adherence to a decision against us?

Do we want to apply the highest moral standards to the question of war, to appeal to the best sentiments of our religion, which would impel us to suffer much rather than do a wrong thing, to extend the bonds of fraternity and the obligation of service to all mankind? The nation will hardly get this except through its youth. They must learn that a moral ideal must be sustained even at a sacrifice, that the conquest of an enemy is best made by considerate treatment, that the boy who wants a fight can usually find one, but that it is an unnecessary luxury for the average youth. They must be taught to have faith in a moral law of some sort rather than in the haphazard easily evident suggestions of the moment, they must believe that in the long run the right is the expedient, and that among themselves, love and kindness and courtesy, and honest dealing in examinations, in the disciplinary questions that come up daily, in the games and common intercourse with their fellows, are the real solvents of troubles, the real secret of successful dealing. For it is only a moral basis that in the last extremity will keep a nation true to the cause of peace, and withstand the excited clamor for a fight.

The schools and the national characteristics react upon each other, but the strongest influence is from the schools to the nation, rather than from the nation to the schools. The teacher in a larger sense than we have often understood makes the next generation. The indirect effects of honest teaching, thorough learning, fair playing, and intelligent obedience to rule, show themselves in good government, in the growth of proper sentiments, in the advance of all reasonable moral movements. The boy who honestly works out a problem in arithmetic, may be in a better plight to handle a grave question of right or utility, than the boy who is soaked with moral precepts, or with a sober face listens to pious reflections on human duty. It is the habit of mind which will not endure faulty conditions, which instinctively demands thoroughness everywhere, which stands for a right because it is a matter of conscience, a habit of mind and character inwrought by years of youthful discipline, which is going to reform America. The remedy for our ills in a more complex manner than we have usually conceived, lies within and around the doors of our school houses, and in the homes of that remnant of the American people who still really educate their children.

CHAIRMAN FOSTER: We have seen in these last few days the many evidences of the growth of peace in this country. One of the most notable of these evidences was shown by the action of the American Peace Society, the oldest Peace Society in America, which has a great history behind it and, I am quite sure, has a great history before it. It has heretofore had its headquarters in an ancient and somewhat dilapidated town in the eastern part of the country, which after all its pretentions must be a provincial sort of town. They have recently transferred their headquarters to the capital of the nation at Washington.

Now, I have two motives in making this announcement, one is that I am expected outside of this hall in five minutes by a person whose call I have always learned to obey to keep peace, if not in the nation, in the family. Another reason which I have for vacating the chair is that I want to show you the man who is going to Washington for the American Peace Society. He is going to take my place this afternoon and preside at this meeting. The ladies will say he is a handsome man, but we who know him know that he is just the man fitted for the work which lies before him. Dr. Benjamin Franklin Trueblood will now take my place as chairman.

DR. BENJAMIN F. TRUEBLOOD: Ladies and Gentlemen, this quite takes away my breath. I feel very much tempted to extend the remarks of the presiding officer this afternoon, but I think I will resist the temptation.

I have the pleasure and honor of introducing now Dr. S. C. Mitchell, president of the University of South Carolina.

S. C. MITCHELL

So far from writing the history of America for the past three hundred years from the standpoint of Europe, it is necessary to write the history of Europe during that time from the standpoint of America. That this thesis of Sir John Seeley may not unduly elate your pride, I must hasten to add that he has in mind the fact that most of the wars in Europe had as their cause the scramble of the Spanish, the French, and the English for lands in America. The significance of America during those three centuries was as a war-maker, so the English historian would lead us to believe. Once as I dined in England with the editor of a Norwich paper, I asked him how it was that the English papers had so little news of real value from America. One reason, he replied, was that the difference of six hours in the time is against the English newspapers, our news arriving too late for use that day, unless urgent. Then he added, in an off-hand way: "After all, we are interested only in the *big disasters* in America." He thus expressed a traditional view of our new country; but it is a matter of joy to witness the change throughout the world in men's estimate of America's rôle. Events are multiplying every day to show that America has a moral mission as a world-power.

The task of the nineteenth century was nationality. Each nation, moved by an instinct that was as resistless as it was contagious, desired to set up housekeeping for itself, to live under its own vine and fig tree. Prior to the last century, it was the custom to build states according to dynastic interests, such as the widely extended empire of Charles V, pieced together by inheritance, by marriage, and by conquest. But in our time blood tends to become the sole cement of a state. The only enduring political bonds prove to be ties of kinship. This passionate yearning for nationality remade the map of Europe in the nineteenth century, of which process the unification of Italy and Germany in 1870 is typical. Each race sought to disentangle itself in the skein of peoples, and to live to itself in its own bounds. Such was the work of the nineteenth century.

The task of the twentieth century is to define the relations of these separate nations, and to enable them to live side by side in the spirit of harmony, peace, and mutual helpfulness. While the nations have established their right to live alone, they are not to live unto themselves alone. Given the advantages of nationality, will it not be possible for the nations of the world to enter into a higher union of friendship and coöperation for the largest human ends? In a word, as nationality was the task of the nineteenth century, so internationalism is the task of the twentieth century.

Of this there are many infallible proofs. We have just turned the first decade of the century, and yet two Hague Conferences have been held, a Permanent Court of Arbitration has been established, and also an International Court of Prize, while ninety-six arbitration treaties have already been made. In the beautiful Peace Palace in Washington there gather around the oval table twenty-one American republics to discuss in the spirit of amity their common affairs, thus witnessing to the Union of Pan-America, while there is rising in Central America a Peace Palace for that region; and at The Hague a still more imposing one as the home of all nations. To crown the achievements of this decade in the interest of peace comes the proposal of President Taft to strike with England a treaty of arbitration covering all causes. Sir Edward Grey's response in the House of Commons on March 13 last will doubtless take rank in history with Burke's immortal speeches on American Conciliation, marking as it does the reunion of the English speaking world into a league of peace, destined to be of world import.

While many nations have espoused great causes, there is one post left vacant. It is that of peacemaker. For this task America is singled out by geography and the genius of her people. "Who knoweth whether thou art not come to the kingdom for such a time as this." No clearer call ever came to the Hebrew to be the revealer of religion, or to the Greek to be the exponent of culture, or to the Roman to be law-maker, or to England to be the mother of parliaments, than has come to America to be peacemaker for mankind. Edward Everett Hale, having in mind the

Supreme Court as the arbiter among the forty-six States of our Union, used to say that the United States is the greatest peace society in the world.

This understanding of the unique opportunity of our country to serve a universal cause is held by intelligent thinkers in other lands. Once as I worshipped in historic St. Giles in Edinburgh, the venerable minister made the burden of his prayer a petition for our country, closing with this significant sentence: "God grant that America, as she is eminent in position, so may she ever continue to be in moral power." America's eminence in position and in moral power are felt today as never before in the interest of world-peace. The fulfilment of that prayer in a vast democracy like ours, where public opinion has the force of law, will depend in large measure upon the definiteness with which the rank and file of the citizens of this country are brought to realize the divine purpose that is marked out for our country in the rôle of peacemaker. Dr. Henry S. Pritchett is fond of saying that a man's efficiency in society depends upon his purpose multiplied into his ability to think straight. The same remark applies to nations with equal force. If America, richly endowed with energy of will, springing out of popular sympathy with progressive causes and exhaustless material resources, once gets a vision of the active part it can play in bringing the blessings of peace to peoples weighed down by burdens of arms and iron-clads, it will prove resistless.

The fulness of the blessings resulting from such a course on our part cannot even be forecast by the imagination of man. We have to oppose war, with its carnage and after-horrors. While we Southern people have little love for General Sherman, we have great respect for his veracity—"War is hell!" He really died too soon to know the full meaning of his definition. Only the other day the Southern Commercial Congress met in Atlanta to celebrate the *South's physical recovery*. Think of it! Fifty years after Fort Sumter, Southern men gather to greet one another in the partial recovery of their land from the waste and desolation of war, the ultimate burdens of which will press heavily upon the backs of generations yet unborn. But wars are spasmodic and may be expected to become less and less frequent. The present peril is armed peace, the cost of which is proving ruinous to modern countries. This armed peace is a novel fact. It is a poor compliment to Christianity to record that, while Rome with forty legions preserved profound peace throughout the wide extent of her empire, the Christian nations of Western Europe find it necessary to maintain millions of men in arms to secure like peace.

The vast armaments of the present day in Europe are the heritage of the great wars of the nineteenth century in the interest of nationality. Modern nations such as Italy and Germany, came into being by "blood and iron." To guard their individuality thus attained, they now keep these great standing armies and navies. The purpose now is to beget a spirit of trust and mutual respect between these nationalized states, fresh as are their scars from the struggle for nations' rights.

In the United States 70 per cent of our revenue is spent on wars either past or prospective. President Thwing only yesterday told us, for instance, that the battleship *South Carolina* cost a little more than $6,000,000, whereas the property and endowments of all the colleges and universities in this State amount to only about one-half that sum. However, owing to the enormous resources of our country, this burden is not seriously felt in comparison with the daily strain upon the working people in many European states. At Queen Victoria's diamond jubilee I stood on the Strand in London watching that pageantry of the British Empire, as it swept in procession down the street. As the last of the troops marched by, and the crowd on the sidewalk began to break up, a poor woman near me, with all the marks of hardship in her face and dress, shook her fist at the retreating soldiers, and cried aloud vengefully: "Yes, and every one of you fellows costs us a shilling a day." To me, entranced as I had been by the splendor of the military display, that agonizing voice came like an alarm bell in the night, warning of the workingman's view as to the weight of standing armies and dreadnoughts.

It is needless for me to recount the advantages which America has for promoting peace among mankind. Geographically our situation is unrivalled, with an ocean as bulwark on either side.

Enjoying a territory of vast extent and varied resources, we are without land-hunger and a lust for conquest. On this virgin continent peaceful tasks have engaged our hands—clearing forests, tunnelling mountains, and building cities.

Coming into this new home in the West, we treasure the bonds of blood, common traditions and sympathy that bind us to the peoples in the mother land. The very aloofness of our position quickens in us a response to the progress of mankind in all quarters of the globe, while our detachment of view enables us to discern perhaps more clearly the large facts in diplomacy than nations enmeshed in entangling alliances and conflict of interests, such as Europe presents. Our separation from the old home breeds sympathy with the noblest aspirations of our kin across the sea, and enforces impartiality in our understanding of the difficulties that beset such a country as Germany, which makes a bayonet its boundary.

The commingling of many races and nations on our soil gives us an interest in the well-being of all the countries from which we hail. The ties of affection reach out from America to every civilized land. Who can voice so freely the deepest instincts of Sweden as the Swedes in America? Who can speak out more boldly the purposes of Germany than the Germans in America? Who values more highly the political debt of the world to England than the English in America, in whose veins flow the impulses and ideals of Simon de Montfort, John Hampden, and John Bright?

The genius of democracy is the sense of the brotherhood of mankind. In it there throbs a fellowship that is world-wide. Modern missions, trade-unionism, and socialism are merely indexes of the common sympathies that bind together all struggling peoples in a democratic age like ours. Autocracy makes boundaries for itself, but democracy overleaps bounds and embraces all peoples in a common cause of liberty, progress, and peace. 'Export' is of the very spirit of democracy.

America has uniformly advocated arbitration as a means of settling international disputes, and the Geneva Award of the "*Alabama* Claims" was the most signal instance of arbitration prior to the permanent court at The Hague. As America was the first to bring a case to The Hague, so she has been a party to the greatest causes laid before that tribunal.

By the absence of fortresses on the long Canadian border and of armaments on the Great Lakes since 1817, now nearly a century, America has set an example of the feasibility of peace that is of world import.

The Monroe Doctrine dedicated the western hemisphere to freedom from foreign wars, while the Pan-American Union has shown conclusively how twenty-one republics on these continents can come together in the Peace Palace at Washington to transact international affairs in the spirit of mutual helpfulness. John Hay was fond of saying that the foreign policy of the United States consists of the Monroe Doctrine and the Golden Rule.

The Supreme Court, substituting reason for force in the settlement of all disputes between the forty-six States of the Union, is a concrete model for the forty-six nations of the earth striving at The Hague to erect an International Court of Arbitral Justice. As Hugo Grotius was the father of international law, so John Marshall may come yet to stand as the forerunner of an international court of justice.

There is no time to speak of America's part in inducing Russia and Japan to make peace, nor the moral effect of the return in part of the Chinese indemnity by our government, nor the efforts of the American delegation at the Second Hague Conference for the establishment of a Permanent Court of Arbitral Justice, nor the master stroke of President Taft on December last, at the banquet in Washington, suggesting an arbitration treaty with some great power covering all causes, which event may come to rank as the greatest fact in world history since the meeting of the First Hague Conference.

Considering all of these things, it seems that America is marked out by geography, by the genius of its people, by the spirit of its institutions, and by the dominant purposes in its history to act as peacemaker among mankind.

It should be the aim of the teacher and preacher, of the thinker and the publicist to intensify in our people the consciousness of this moral mission committed to America. The unity of Italy may be dated from the moment when Mazzini, in the dungeon of Savona, conceived his electric message: "Life is a mission." With this idea he inspired the heart of Italy's youth, and as a result she has taken her place among the great nations of the earth in the march of progress and peace. May we have some share in imparting a like inspirational impulse to the youth of America to strive heroically for peace founded upon justice and love of mankind.

CHAIRMAN TRUEBLOOD: One of the most encouraging signs for the peace movement is, I think, the entrance into it of so many of the leading educators of the country. We have just heard a distinguished educator of South Carolina, and now we are to listen to another distinguished educator, formerly the President of the Northwestern University and now Dean of the Yale University Law School. Last year he presided over the New England Peace Conference. I take pleasure in calling upon Prof. Henry Wade Rogers.

THE UNITED STATES AND THE PEACE MOVEMENT

HENRY WADE ROGERS

In 1849 Victor Hugo predicted that a day would come when a cannon ball would be exhibited in public museums just as an instrument of torture is now, and he added that people would be amazed that such a thing as a cannon ball could ever have been.

But Tolstoi having no more use for war than Hugo had no faith that the world would ever be free from it for any great length of time. In his *Kingdom of God is Within You* he says: "The suggestion to governments to desist from violence, and to adjust all differences by arbitration, would be to recommend a suicidal policy, and no government would ever agree to that. Learned men found societies (there are more than one hundred of them), they assemble in Congresses (like those held in London and Paris, and the one which is to be held in Rome), they read essays, hold banquets, make speeches, edit journals devoted to the subject, and by all these means they endeavor to prove that the strain upon nations who are obliged to support millions of soldiers has become so severe that something must be done about it; that this armament is opposed to the character, the aim, and the wishes of the populations; but they seem to think that if they consume a good deal of paper, and devote a good deal of eloquence to the subject, that they may succeed in conciliating opposing parties and conflicting interests, and at last effect the suppression of war."

Peace congresses reminded Tolstoi of a story told him when a child that if he wanted to catch a bird he must put salt on its tail. He took a handful and went in pursuit of the birds. He soon realized however that what he had been told was a joke and that it was as easy to catch the birds as it was to sprinkle salt on their tails. He thought that those who read essays and write works on arbitration must feel much as he did when he realized the truth about putting salt on birds' tails.

This Peace Congress has been convoked by men who have the faith of Hugo and who are not disheartened by the discouraged and despairing Tolstoi. We believe, too, that the government of the United States is to have a great part in the ultimate establishment of the principle that disputes between nations shall be settled in judicial tribunals even as are those which arise between man and man.

A distinguished prelate of the Anglican church, the Bishop of Hereford, on returning to England after a visit to this country emphasized the important contribution which the United States has made to the peace movement. The United States is, in his opinion, the greatest and most influential peace society in the world. It illustrated, he said, the beneficent operation of three great principles, those of interstate trade, an interstate court, and federation. He thought the extension of these principles to international affairs would result in the kind of organized world that is needed. We should then have "The Parliament of Man, the Federation of the World."

In discussing the relation of the United States to the peace movement it may be well to recall that it is not a new idea in this country that some way should be found to abolish war and establish permanent international peace.

In a letter of instruction drafted by Samuel Adams for the General Court of Massachusetts to be forwarded to the Massachusetts delegates in Congress and prior to the adoption of the Federal Constitution it was said:

"You are, therefore, hereby instructed and urged to move the United States in Congress assembled to take into their deep and most serious consideration whether any measures can by them be used, through their influence with each of the nations of Europe with whom they are united by treaties of amity or commerce, that national differences may be settled and determined without the necessity of war, in which the world has too long been deluged, to the destruction of human happiness and the disgrace of human reason and government.

"If, after the most mature deliberation, it shall appear that no measures can be taken at present on this very interesting subject, it is conceived it would redound much to the honor of the United States that it was attended to by their great Representative in Congress, and be accepted as a testimony of gratitude for most signal favors granted to the said states by Him who is the almighty and most gracious Father and Friend of mankind."

From the beginning of our government down to our own times the attitude of some of the most distinguished of American statesmen has been one of pronounced hostility to war.

George Washington said: "My first wish is to see this plague of mankind (war) banished from the earth, and the sons and daughters of this world employed in more pleasing and innocent amusements than in preparing implements and exercising them for the destruction of mankind."

Benjamin Franklin said: "I hope that mankind will at length, as they call themselves reasonable creatures, have reason and sense enough to settle their differences without cutting throats, for in my opinion, there never was a good war or a bad peace.

"All wars are follies, very expensive and very mischievous ones. When will mankind be convinced of this, and agree to settle their differences by arbitration? Were they to do it even by the cast of a die, it would be better than by fighting and destroying each other."

Thomas Jefferson said: "I love peace, and am anxious that we should give the world still another useful lesson, by showing them other modes of punishing injuries than by war, which is as much a punishment to the punisher as to the sufferer.

"I abhor war and view it as the greatest scourge of mankind."

Charles Sumner said: "War crushes with bloody heel all beneficence, all happiness, all justice, all that is godlike in man—suspending every commandment of the Decalogue, setting at naught every principle of the Gospel, and silencing all law, human as well as divine except only that impious code of its own, the *Laws of War.* . . .

"There must be peace which cannot fail, and other nations must show the great possession. To this end must we labor, bearing ever in mind two special objects, complements of each other: first, the Arbitrament of war must end; and secondly, Disarmament must begin."

John Hay said: "War is the most futile and ferocious of human follies."

It is also well to recall that the peace movement as an organized movement originated in the United States, the first peace society in the world having been organized in this country. Peace societies exist today in every part of the world. There are now some six hundred organizations of this character which are seeking to influence the public opinion of their respective countries. The first of these societies, the New York Society, was established in August, 1815, by David Low Dodge. Membership in the Christian church was a condition of membership in that society. And the Massachusetts Peace Society was organized in December of the same year by two Christian ministers, Worcester and Channing. In 1816 the first peace society in England was founded. It must be that the peace societies throughout the world have helped materially in educating public opinion against war.

A peace congress does not need to be told that war in all ages has been a frightful evil. And yet I am disposed to call attention to the fact that serious an evil as war has always been the evil is much more serious in our day than ever before. Herbert Spencer saw that war was in his time approaching an era of development when there could no longer result any compensating advantages for the death, devastation and misery which it would entail and when it would be compelled to give place to a more humane and civilized method of settling the disputes of states. The extraordinary development by modern science of the destructive agencies employed in war has made war an infinitely more heinous crime against humanity than it was in the time of our fathers. The destructive and fearful forces of modern armaments have revolutionized in our own time, the entire art of war and have made its possible horrors so enormous as should make war forever impossible.

Maxim, the inventor of some of the new and terrible agencies of destruction, was told that his genius might be better employed than in devising new weapons of war. His reply was that the inventors of the machinery of annihilation were the most effective of the peacemakers of the world.

The gunpowder our fathers used has been supplanted. Newer explosives of far greater power have taken its place. Each new explosive is far more deadly and more powerful than its predecessor. Rapid-fire guns discharge a thousand bullets a minute. And on the sea great dreadnoughts make antiquated the war ship of a few years ago. They carry guns with ranges of fifteen and more miles. They are fitted with sights that make it possible to train the guns upon objects invisible to the ordinary eye. Submarine boats submerged beneath the waters discharge torpedoes from fourteen to eighteen feet in length, weighing over a thousand pounds, which can propel themselves for more than a mile and blow up the largest war ship afloat. If war was hell in General Sherman's day, what is it to be called in our day?

It was said some years ago, that if an army equipped as in the days of Napoleon, should be confronted by one with equal numbers but with modern guns, the latter would be able to destroy the Napoleonic force before it could even be brought into action. Their infantry arms would carry farther than Napoleon's best artillery. So we need to remember that bad as war was in the days of Washington and Napoleon, and of Sherman and Grant, the advances of science and the progress of invention have multiplied its horrors a hundred fold, and quite beyond the power of language to set forth.

Almost in our own day, has come the steamship, the railroad, the telegraph, the telephone, and now the air ship, facilitating transportation and transmission of intelligence, breaking down the barriers which, in former times, made it easy for nations to lead separate lives and which made them so largely independent of each other. Nations are, today, near neighbors the one of the other and they are in great degree dependent upon one another. Hence a war between two nations is infinitely a more serious matter. It means now "a rupture of arteries of common life-blood, a stoppage of the agencies of common well-being and advancement."

The United States should lead all nations in the movement to abolish war and establish the principle that international differences shall be settled by means of judicial proceedings. This Republic, the richest and strongest among nations, can better afford than any other to lead the advance in this great cause for it is less liable to have imputed to it the motive of fear or of selfish advantage. It would seem as though God destined this nation to assume the leadership in this, the greatest movement of the nations. He planted the United States in this continental stronghold with no powerful neighbors to threaten our borders and make it necessary for us to maintain great armaments on land or sea. He gave us natural protection against attacks by separating us from the source of possible invasion by three thousand miles of ocean on one side and five thousand on the other. The United States is the natural leader in the movement to secure the peace of the world. The cause is worthy the leadership of the greatest nation. Mr Asquith, the present British prime minister says the greatest of all reforms is the movement for the abolition of war and the establishment of permanent peace. The former prime minister, Sir Henry Campbell-Bannerman declared his highest ambition for England to be that she might place herself at the head of a movement to unite the world powers in a league of peace. We covet that leadership for the United States.

If we were to study the relation of the United States to the peace movement, by an examination of its budgets, we should not find much to encourage us.

In 1845, Charles Sumner spoke before the authorities of Boston on the "True Grandeur of Nations." He vigorously denounced what he regarded as the wasteful extravagance of the United States in that day, in its preparations for war in time of peace. He described the appropriations made for that purpose as "a measureless, fathomless, endless river, an Amazon of waste, rolling its prodigal waters turbidly, ruinously, hatefully to the sea." He pronounced the whole thing evil and demanded that it be remedied. There was once a time when this nation was the envy of the world as the one great power which had the priceless privilege of exemption from the oppressive burdens of warlike preparations under which other nations were staggering on to bankruptcy. That distinction and preëminence among nations we can no longer boast.

Figures are not interesting, but they are instructive. If we would understand the subject now under discussion, it seems necessary to give attention to "the serried array of figures" found in the record of the appropriations of Congress.

The Chairman of the House Committee on Appropriations in the Congress preceding the one now in session stated that this government had expended in the past ten years on account of preparation for war the enormous sum of $2,192,036,580. These appropriations had been made to defend a nation against which no nation had ever declared war. Every war this country has been engaged in our own government commenced. These appropriations have been made to prepare against war, when there is not a single power on the face of the globe that can wish or can afford to have war with the United States. And if any European nation or any Asiatic nation should undertake to make war upon us and should send its fleet across the Atlantic or the Pacific oceans, it would present to its rivals the most tempting opportunity they could possibly covet for hostile action.

This country has made these vast appropriations because Congress has been influenced by men with morbid hallucinations who with hysterical cries have contended that England, or Germany, or Japan was making ready to insult our flag, thwart our policies, destroy what commerce we have left, devastate our coasts and perhaps capture our possessions. The activity of these folk has been supplemented by that of the manufacturers of all the diabolical weapons and agencies of warfare who realize perfectly that increased expenditures in the preparation for war enlarge the profits of the business in which they are engaged.

Large as these appropriations have been, these people are now telling us that they are wholly inadequate and that this country today is quite unprepared for war. If they are to be believed the army is almost hopelessly behind the times. The United States, they say, should either have an army, which, for its size, is as well organized and equipped as any other army in the world, or else we should do away with the army altogether. We lack men to man our defenses and lack ammunition for the guns which guard them. Our field artillery is weak. There is not enough of it, and there is not enough artillery ammunition. The existing want of field artillery, guns, carriages and ammunition constitute a grave menace to the public safety. Fortifications have been constructed but there are not enough men to man them, nor enough ammunition to fire the guns so that the guns have no more value than so many dummies. This is their indictment.

According to Captain Hobson, not one city on our coasts is properly fortified. If attacked, little serious resistance could be made and a force attacking in the rear could easily capture any one of them. We must have a great navy. We have now a one ocean navy and we must place it on a two ocean basis. A fleet on the Atlantic is not adequate for the defense of the Pacific coast. Germany is building four battleships a year, while the United States is building only two. In eight years her first line of battle will be almost twice as strong as ours. This is the picture which is held up before us today by these gentlemen at the end of a decade in which we have expended $2,192,036,580 in making preparations for war.

The Revolutionary War cost $370,000,000 and $70,000,000 in pensions.

The War of 1812 cost $82,627,009 and $45,808,676 in pensions.

The Mexican War cost $88,500,208 and $43,956,768 in pensions.

The Civil War cost $5,371,079,748 and $3,837,488,171 have been paid already in pensions.

The Spanish-American War cost $171,326,572 and $30,191,725 have been paid already in pensions.

The Revolutionary War, the War of 1812, the Mexican War, and the Spanish-American War combined, cost this country, not counting pensions, $712,453,789. This amounts to only one-third of what this country has expended in the past ten years in its preparations for war in a time of peace.

The debt of the government of the United States in 1909 amounted to $1,023,362,531. The sum which the government has spent in its preparations for war within the past decade would have paid this debt twice over.

The aggregate debt of all our states, territories, counties, cities, towns and minor public corporations, according to the last compilation of the Bureau of the Census was $1,864,195,826, and the money expended by Congress in the past ten years in its preparations for war would have paid this debt and left a surplus of $328,-840,754.

The total appropriation made by Congress in 1910 for the army, navy, fortifications and military academy amounted to $248,832,-714.

In 1897 the appropriation amounted to but $61,688,477. The appropriation for 1910 therefore exceeded that for 1897 by more than 400 per cent.

The total value of the productive funds of all the universities, colleges and technological schools in the United States in 1909 amounted to only $260,736,256. And the total income of all these institutions, counting tuition fees, income from invested funds, and appropriations from the public treasury amounted to only $65,792,045. The higher institutions of learning in America are spending about one-fourth as much money each year in training men to be useful citizens and in fitting them to become leaders of public opinion as the government of the United States is expending in preparing for war.

In 1910, Congress expended on our navy $123,114,547. The highest annual expenditure for the navy in the Civil War was $123,000,000. The total amount of benefactions in this country in 1910 is stated as having amounted to about $125,000,000. So that the amount given to schools, colleges, asylums, hospitals and to all the other charitable undertakings was much the same in 1910 as what the government expended on the navy alone in the same year.

In 1850 we expended on the navy .... $ 7,904,723
In 1880 we expended on the navy.................. $ 13,536,985
In 1900 we expended on the navy.................. $ 55,953,078
In 1910 we expended on the navy.................. $123,114,547

At present our national expenditures are 72 per cent for past wars and in preparation for future wars, and 28 per cent for all other governmental purposes. The United States is today expending more money for military and naval purposes and pensions, excluding interest on the war debt, than any other nation. The British foreign secretary in speaking of the increased expenditures which all the nations have engaged in during the past ten years says that they constitute a satire upon civilization.

But we are told by Rear Admiral Mahan who believes in a big navy that national wealth is increasing faster than our appropriations so that in reality we are spending less upon the navy than we did in former years. And another writer considering our navy as an insurance against foreign aggression has recently pointed out that this country is spending on the navy only one-tenth of 1 per cent of our total wealth or $3\frac{1}{2}$ per cent on the value of our foreign commerce. And taking, as he says he does, a purely business view of the situation he declares he cannot see anything so very ruinous about it. He must know that the $3\frac{1}{2}$ per cent of which he speaks is about six times the average rate for fire insurance. He must also know that if the navy is to be regarded as so much insurance the army is so much additional insurance and increases the insurance rate to about 7 per cent or twelve times the average rate of fire insurance— and he ought also to know that there are other modes of insuring national prosperity than by armies and navies. Let these unnecessary and wasteful expenditures on the army and navy end, and let the money be expended in a more useful manner.

Statesmen, in imposing these tremendous burdens of taxation for war purposes, are not employing the public money to the best advantage. The demand is each year becoming more urgent at home and abroad for larger and larger output for social betterment. Instead of spending with lavish hand in constructing war ships that in a few years must be thrown to the scrap heap, it would be wisdom to spend it in improving the health, the physique, and the intelligence of the nation. Let the burden of national taxation through Tariff duties and excise taxes, be lessened, and war expenditures decreased, so that the States may, without imposing too heavy charges upon the taxpayer, better the conditions under which men and women live and work.

Why should these ever increasing burdens for military and naval defense be imposed on the United States? And why should they be imposed at a time when all the chief factors in the problem of peace are favorable for the United States? We never before have been as free of difficulties with England as now. This is the day of The Hague Tribunal and when all the nations are agreeing on an Arbitral Court. It would seem as though the need of great spending for war preparations had lessened and not increased. Were our forefathers lacking in sagacity and in political foresight when they thought a small army was sufficient and that it was needed only for purposes of police, that a great navy was a useless expense and that a small one would answer, provided it was large enough to rid the sea of pirates, protect our merchant marine and suppress the slave trade? Sixty-five years ago Charles Sumner spoke of the navy of the United States as "an unnecessary arm of national defense" and declared it was "a vain and expensive toy."

There is another matter in which the action of the United States has been distinctly disappointing to some of the friends of the peace movement. The action of Congress in appropriating money for the fortification of the Panama Canal is one of the sad results of the emotional insanity which has afflicted the people

of the United States ever since the war with Spain.   The victory
of Dewey in Manila Bay seemed to change the attitude of not a
few of the American people.   It caused them to discard the political philosophy of the fathers and consent to assume the burden
of great military armaments.   This they have been induced to
do on the pretext that it is necessary in order to safeguard the
country against a will-o'-the-wisp of a non-existent foreign enemy.
The blood poison of militarism has in some way gotten into the
veins of our people.

I cannot think of this changed condition of the American mind
without recalling Lowell's words in *Hosea Bigelow:*

> We were gettin' on nicely up here to our village,
> With good idees o' wut's right and wut ain't,
> We kind o' thought Christ went agin war and pillage,
> An' thet eppyletts worn't the best mark of a saint;
> But John P.
> Robinson he
> Sez this kind o' thing's an exploded idee.

The President of the United States, a sincere friend of peace,
and one commanding the respect and confidence of his countrymen in an unusual degree, thinks this government ought to fortify the canal and that those who differ with him are influenced
by sentiment and idealism.   Mr. Roosevelt in his speech at
Omaha in October, 1910, declared this country was in honor bound
to fortify it.   He said not to do so would be to incur the contempt
of the world.   That it would involve the surrender of the Monroe
Doctrine.   That it would be in its essence treason to the destiny
of the Republic.   But his predecessor, Mr. McKinley, while
President, sent to the Senate the Hay-Pauncefote treaty of 1900,
which he had negotiated with England, and which contained a
clause which expressly declared "No fortifications shall be erected commanding the canal or the waters adjacent."   A motion
was made in the Senate to strike out that clause.   It was voted
down by a vote of 26 to 44.   If Mr. Roosevelt's statement is to
be accepted, Mr. McKinley and the Senate must have been very
obtuse not to have discovered that what they were approving

was "in its essence treason to the destiny of the Republic." The treaty of 1900 was ratified by the United States but with an amendment and as Great Britain refused to accept it in its amended form that particular treaty failed. Mr. Roosevelt's assertion that non-fortification of the Canal involves the surrender of the Monroe Doctrine is hard to accept. The United States must, if he is correct, have abandoned the Monroe Doctrine as long ago as 1850 when it agreed in the Clayton-Bulwer treaty that it would not fortify the canal. That treaty continued in force for more than fifty years and until it was superseded by the second Hay-Pauncefote treaty of 1902. It was in force in 1895, when Mr. Cleveland sent to Congress his celebrated message in which he stated that the Monroe Doctrine was not obsolete and could not be while our Republic endured. To neutralize the canal by an international agreement does not involve a surrender to European powers of any controlling interest in the western hemisphere. It is not proposed that any European nation shall control either canal zone or the canal itself, but only that the powers shall agree that the canal shall be immune from attack.

The Clayton-Bulwer treaty and the action of the President and Senate concerning the Hay-Pauncefote treaty of 1900 make it incontrovertible that this government conceded the principle as late as 1900 that the canal should not be fortified.

But it is claimed that under the second and existing Hay-Pauncefote treaty of 1902, the United States has the right to fortify. From that treaty there was omitted any clause prohibiting in express terms the canal's fortification. The argument is that because of that omission the right exists. If the omission proves the existence of the right, then by the same process of reasoning the United States has lost the right to police the canal. For the second treaty not only omitted the clause prohibiting fortification but it omitted also the clause authorizing the United States to protect the canal against lawlessness, both of which provisions had been in the Hay-Pauncefote treaty of 1900.

It must be conceded that no treaty now in force in express terms denies to this government the right to fortify the canal. It must, however, be admitted that the existing treaties bind this country in express terms to neutralize it. That makes it necessary to determine whether we can neutralize and fortify at the same time, or whether neutralization and fortification are not absolutely antagonistic in principle.

The treaty of Vienna which provided for the neutralization of Cracow stipulated that no armed forces should be introduced there on any pretense. When the neutrality of Belgium was guaranteed it was deemed necessary to demolish Belgian fortresses. When the Ionian Islands were neutralized, it was stipulated that "as a *necessary consequence* of the neutrality" the fortifications "being purposeless" should be demolished. In the neutralization of Luxemburg, it was provided that it should cease to be fortified as fortifications *were without necessity as well as without object*. A part of Savoy was neutralized in 1815 and when France in 1883 began to fortify it Switzerland protested and France at once discontinued its fortification. The treaty of Paris neutralized the Black Sea and prohibited the Emperor of Russia and the Sultan of Turkey from maintaining any military-maritime arsenals along the coast *the same being unnecessary and purposeless*. And in the neutralization of the Lower Danube it was provided that all fortresses and fortifications on the banks from the Iron Gates to the mouth should be razed and no new ones erected.

There are writers on international law who say that neutralization "implies the absence of fortifications." Latané says "The mere existence of fortifications would impeach the good faith of the parties to the agreement." Professor John Bassett Moore of Columbia, one of the foremost authorities in this country, writes: "The idea of neutrality or of neutralization has usually been deemed incompatible even with the mere maintenance of armed forces and fortifications." But it is not simply a question of whether we have or not a legal right to fortify. The claim the friends of non-fortification make is that the United States should negotiate a convention with the Great Powers of the world similar to the Constantinople Convention of 1888, which guarantees that the Suez Canal shall be immune from attack in time of war, and that it shall not be permanently fortified. To this it is answered that the United States cannot trust the honor of the nations. They tell us that treaties are broken. The answer is that individual treaties have sometimes been broken but that a convention signed by great nations would be kept. One convention neutralizing the Suez Canal has never been broken. The neutralization of Switzerland and of Belgium and of Luxemburg has been kept. If the United States is to fortify the canal, it must defend it against all nations. It is safer unfortified. Under The Hague Convention of 1907 it is contrary to the rules of war to bombard unfortified coasts.

The Panama Canal as a military asset is of questionable value. Rear Admiral Evans is quoted as saying that it cannot be so fortified as to protect a fleet passing through the canal. A hostile fleet at the exits would capture or destroy the war ships as they come out one by one and before they could form in line of battle. Rear Admiral Dewey is also reported as opposed to any policy of fortification. Fortification is unnecessary and worse than useless. Fortifications invite attack. "They draw the lightning of battle," and are not less a safeguard than a danger.

We are told that there was at least one spot in Greece, the small island of Delos, which was dedicated to the gods, and kept at all times sacred from war. It is said that no hostile foot ever pressed its kindly soil. Would that the United States, adhering to its original policy, had dedicated the Panama Canal Zone, ten miles wide and fifty miles long, as a spot to be held henceforth sacred from all the operations of war. Through this artery of commerce uniting the waters of the Atlantic and the Pacific the ships of the world should pass and repass in perfect safety. The Panama Canal, like the Suez, should have remained unfortified and been made immune from attack by agreement of the nations.

The United States throughout its history as an independent nation has thrown the weight of its influence many times in favor of the substitution of reason for force in the adjustment of international disputes found to be impossible of settlement by diplomacy. In the treaty between the United States and Great Britain negotiated in 1794 and known as Jay's treaty, provision was made for the adjustment by arbitration of certain disputes between the two countries. The provision was inserted through the influence of the American negotiator. It was the first time that a provision of this kind was introduced into a treaty between two foreign nations. The Greeks often resorted to arbitration but they only practiced it among themselves and never with foreign nations. Rome never arbitrated her disputes with other states. It would have been regarded as an abasement to have done so.

The United States and Great Britain set a notable example when they agreed not to arm on the Great Lakes. The first suggestion of making the region of the Great Lakes neutral, originated during the administration of Washington, and with the President himself. When Washington sent Jay, in 1794, to negotiate a treaty with Great Britain, he gave him this among the other instructions: "In peace, no troops to be kept within a limited distance from the lakes." Jay did not succeed in embodying this principle in the treaty. The agreement for disarmament was to come twenty-three years afterwards. The close of the War of 1812, left on the waters of the lakes a considerable naval force of both nations. It was found desirable that it should be much reduced or entirely dispensed with. Gallatin had proposed disarmament in 1814. But each of the combatants in the war which had closed was suspicious of the other and the proposition was kept pending. A final agreement was not reached until April 28, 1817. It was then agreed that the two governments would maintain not more than one vessel on Lake Champlain, one on Ontario, and two on the upper lakes, of not more than one hundred tons each, to be armed with one eighteen-pound cannon. It was also stipulated that no other vessel of war should be built or armed on these lakes. This has been construed as a prohibition against any vessels being built for the American navy in the large shipyards on the lakes to be taken through the canals to the sea. Although this has provoked criticism and some remonstrance, it has been adhered to. In 1812, the United States had forty-six forts along its Canadian frontier and Canada had about the same number. But after this arrangement was made, the forts were destroyed and the ships withdrawn. The peace has been maintained between the two countries and neither has

encroached upon the other's frontier.   Disarmament on the Great
Lakes affords an object lesson to all the nations.   This experience
of almost a hundred years shows that it is safe to trust to national
honor.

In view of the fact that many of our ablest public men, including Franklin, John Adams, Seward and Sumner, believed that
the greatest menace to peace between the United States and Great
Britain consisted in the maintenance of a colonial possession on
our northern border, it is significant and impressive that this
arrangement was ever agreed upon and has never been abrogated.

The two countries have not alone refrained from fortifying the
shores of the Great Lakes but the whole boundary line, which
separates the United States and British America, is alike free from
hostile arsenals and frowning armaments.   This boundary line
is the longest between any two countries in the world.   You can
travel from end to end throughout the whole four thousand miles
without seeing a single soldier in uniform on either side of the
line.   It is a profoundly significant fact that it is the one frontier
in the world upon which, as Mr. Mead has pointed out, perfect
peace and order have prevailed.

While Chile and the Argentine Republic settled their differences
and agreed to disarm, they commemorated the event by uplifting on the summit of the Andes, nearly three miles above the
level of the sea, a colossal statue of Christ; the Prince of Peace.
They cast it from the bronze of old cannon left there by the Spaniards at the time of the struggle for Argentine's independence.
They placed on it this inscription: "Sooner shall these mountains crumble into dust than Chileans or Argentines shall break
this peace which, at the feet of Christ the Redeemer, they have
sworn to maintain."   No similar statue has been lifted upon the
border which separates the United States and Canada.   But may
God forbid that the time shall come in the history of these two
countries when the folly of either shall lead it to fortify against
the other, or break the Truce of God which they entered into in
1817.

The United States has been engaged in a number of arbitrations
since those provided for in Jay's treaty.   But the most important

arbitration in which this country has been engaged, and the most impressive and august arbitration in the history of the world, is that which was authorized by the treaty of Washington in 1871. By that treaty the United States and Great Britain submitted to arbitration the *Alabama* Claims. Mr. Gladstone in speaking of the matter in the House of Commons in 1880 said: "Although I may think the sentence was harsh in its extent and unjust in its basis, I regard the fine imposed on this country as dust in the balance compared with the moral value of the example set when these two great nations of England and America, which are the most fiery and the most jealous in the world with regard to anything that touches national honor, went in peace and concord before a judicial tribunal rather than resort to the arbitrament of the sword."

It appears probable that a long step forward in the peace movement is about to be taken and that another great moral example to all nations is about to be set. Unless all indications fail it is again the Anglo-Saxon race which is to take the step and set the example and justify its right to the leadership of the world in the most important cause which today commands the thought of the world.

President Taft in an address delivered on December 17, 1910, said:

"If now we can negotiate and put through a positive agreement with some great nation to abide the adjudication of an international arbitral court in every issue which cannot be settled by negotiation, no matter what it involves, whether honor, territory, or money, we shall have made a long step forward by demonstrating that it is possible for two nations at least to establish as between them the same system of due process of law that exists between individuals under a government."

He has also said:

"Personally I do not see any reason why matters of national honor should not be referred to courts of arbitration as matters of private or national property. I know that is going further than most men are willing to go, but I do not see why questions of honor should not be submitted to tribunals composed of men

of honor who understand questions of national honor, to abide
by their decision as well as in other questions of difference arising
between nations."

These are very notable deliverances coming as they do from the
President of the United States. No man who has filled that high
office with the exception of President Grant has ever before taken
so advanced a position on this subject.

These statements of the President at once commanded the
attention not only of our own people but of the statesmen of
Europe and particularly of Great Britain. The reply which
evoked was fully as remarkable as the appeal itself.

The English secretary of state for foreign affairs, Sir Edward
Grey, speaking for the British government in the House of Commons on March 13, 1910, said:

"Arbitration has been increasing. I should perhaps have
thought it unprofitable to mention arbitration had it not been
for the fact that twice within the last twelve months the President of the United States has sketched out a step in advance
more momentous than any one thing that any statesman in his
position has ventured to say before. His words are pregnant
with very far reaching consequences.

"Mr. Taft recently made the statement that he does not see
personally any reason why matters of national honor should not
be referred to a court of arbitration. He has also expressed the
opinion that if the United States could negotiate a positive agreement with some other nation to abide by the adjudication of an
international arbitral court on every question that could not be
settled by negotiation, no matter what they involve, a long step
forward would be taken. These are bold and courageous words.
We have no proposal before us, and unless public opinion rises
to the height of discussing a proposal of that kind it may not be
carried out. But supposing two of the greatest nations of the
world were to make it clear to the whole world by such an agreement that in no circumstances were they going to war again, I
venture to say that it would have a beneficent effect I
should be delighted to receive such a proposal. I should consider

it so far reaching in its consequences that it would require not only the signatures of both governments but the deliberate sanction of Parliament. That I believe would be obtained.

"The general adoption of such a system might leave some armies and navies still in existence, but they would remain not in rivalry, but as the world's police."

The House of Commons received this speech with enthusiastic cheers.

These sentiments of Sir Edward Grey seem to have been received throughout England with almost universal enthusiasm. The leader of the opposition, Mr. Balfour, announced his hearty concurrence and his most cordial support. The churches, all the various Protestant bodies, the Angelicans and non-conformists alike responded enthusiastically. Almost the entire press of that country the radical and the conservative, the imperialistic and the anti-imperialistic, alike united in commending the negotiation of an Anglo-American treaty of general arbitration along the lines suggested by the remarks of the British secretary of state for foreign affairs.

It is well for the world that the English statesmen led by Sir Edward Grey are today so very far in advance of the opinion held by Lord John Russell, who, while he was foreign secretary, announced that England would never consent to arbitrate the *Alabama* Claims as to do so would be incompatible with national dignity.

We have read many times in the Sacred Book that "he shall judge between the nations, and shall decide concerning many peoples; and they shall beat their swords into plow-shares and their spears into pruning hooks; nation shall not lift up sword against nation, neither shall they learn war any more." The United States is a Christian nation. It should believe in the ultimate fulfillment of the promise. It should not forget that it was also written: "For as the rain cometh down, and the snow from heaven, and returneth not thither, but watereth the earth, and maketh it bring forth and bud, that it may give seed to the sower and bread to the eater.

"So shall my word be that goeth out of my mouth; it shall not return unto me void, but it shall accomplish that which I please, and it shall prosper in the thing whereto I sent it."

Pray God that the day may speedily come when nations shall not learn war any more and when

> "All men's good shall
> Be each man's rule; and universal peace
> Lie like a shaft of light across the land,
> And like a lane of beams across the sea
> Through all the circle of the golden year."

CHAIRMAN TRUEBLOOD: After the next speaker, who is the last on the program, the Committee on Resolutions will present its report. It is hoped that you will all stay to hear the resolutions and to vote on them.

I now have the great pleasure of introducing Rt. Rev. John G. Murray, the Bishop of Maryland.

WORLD-PEACE, PROPER, PRACTICAL AND PROFITABLE

JOHN G. MURRAY

No one can add to the wisdom which has already waited upon the consideration of this good and great subject. The peaceable adjustment of differences between individuals in their private and corporate capacity by the intervention of a third duly constituted and qualified agent has long been an established principle in the conduct of all human affairs. The effectiveness of this principle is universally acknowledged and its permanency assured for all time. Its exercise prevents the disruption of society and the destruction of business by protecting the righteous cause of the weakest and circumventing the unjust endeavor of the most powerful. It maintains the established standard of equity, and might prevails only when it is also right. It proclaims the inability of human nature to duly recognize the rights of others, or rightly divide any word of truth when motives of self interest, prejudice or passion prevail. It operates in and through a tribunal of equity or justice, the very title of which is vocative of the conviction that in no other way can that which is honestly due each of the disputants in a case be impartially ascertained and equitably awarded.

So successful has this principle proven in the affairs of individual life and labor that the strongest minds in the world have given their best thought to the problem of its application to and operation in the affairs of nations in their domestic and foreign relations. The logical conclusion of all this consideration, duly deduced and formulated, is, that what has proven possible to and with the individual is also possible to and with nations of individuals; that what is indispensable to the moral welfare of man and the enjoyment of simple justice in his individual capacity is also necessary for the realization of the same condition in his every reciprocal relationship; that the Supreme Judge of the universe is not going to wink at that in nations which He unqualifiedly condemns and severely punishes in the individuals comprising those nations; and that the same wisdom and learning and invention of man which were competent under God to conceive and construct a tribunal qualified and meet for all requirements in the case of individuals will not be found lacking under that same God, in ability to make proper provision for the needs of a world of nations when those nations, under the inspiration of a mighty impulse to lay hold upon the righteousness and rest of peace, shall stretch out their hands and implore the necessary assistance to supply their needs.

I am in perfect harmony and full accord with these stated conclusions because I believe the idea of world-peace, national and international, is not only perfect in its consistency with the highest ideal of the individual life, but also because I am convinced that the pursuit of this world-peace is in the highest sense proper, practical and profitable.

It is proper because it is patriotic and philanthropic. The true patriot may not hesitate at need to die for his country, and no one here or elsewhere would deny him the glory of his death. But what the world has needed in all ages, and is still crying for today is the service of life, not the sacrifice of death. The necessity for the death of anyone now, thank God, has been abolished forever by the death of One. Man's prerogative is to enjoy life and to enjoy it more abundantly. The abundance of that life is to overflow for the welfare of his fellow man and the glory of his God. And the patriot of this day and time is he who not only enhances the wealth and welfare of his country in constructive occupation of peace, but makes the pursuit of peace with God and fellow man everywhere the chief object of his aim and the supreme end of his every endeavor.

The pursuit of this world-peace is philanthropic, because the office of true philanthropy is not so much the relief of destitution and need, as the prevention or amelioration of the condition producing that destitution and need. The philanthropy of the Red Cross, while it breathes upon the wounded and dying on the scarred and bloody battlefield, the benediction of love, sadly moves on its errand of mercy in the sable garb of mourning and desolation and death. The philanthropy of the olive branch may appeal less to our imagination, and fail to invite to such considerable degree our coöperative sympathy, but it too is on an errand of love, and clothed in garments of light, its movement is full of joy, for its mission is to make real the angelic message, "Peace on Earth, Good will to men," and to banish every battlefield from the face of the earth forever.

The pursuit of this world-peace is practical because it is progressive. It is not the web from which is woven the Utopian dreams of fancy, but the material for garb of forceful fact to clothe universal endeavor with a new power of mighty accomplishment in every sphere of constructive and progressive utility in which man lives and labors and loves. The words, "They shall beat their swords into plowshares, and their spears into pruning hooks; nation shall not lift up sword against nation, neither shall they learn war any more," constitute a declaration of prophecy, the fulfilment of which shall in the day of the accomplishment of the perfect will of God be realized, it is true; but they are also descriptive of conditions with which we are perfectly familiar even now, the destructive desolation of war, the constructive conquests of

peace. In every age and under every sky the history of every
people has been, and is, that Peace is the hand maiden of practical progress and prosperity and that war has been, and is, the
harlot of wanton wickedness and waste. The one walks in the
light of the love and law of God; the other haunts the darkness of
the hatred and lawlessness of Satan. The one is established in
and exists upon the principle of practical progress; the other is
incited by and lives upon the spoils of perfidious plunder.

But my commendation of this cause is most positive in that the
pursuit of world-peace is profitable because it is pious, and in the
end must win. To some of us the end seems near. The action
of our own President in the interest of a court of equity and justice, designed for and adapted to the needs of nations, which action has the support and gratitude of the best citizenship of our
own land, and the unqualified reciprocal approval of the enlightened civilization of all other lands, encourages us in our hope and
sustains us in our conviction. But whether the coming day of the
victory of universal peace has actually dawned, or whether we
have yet to grope through the darkness of another night of war,
the light of amicable adjudication which is to illumine every land
and sea is steadily shooting its shafts into the shadows of strife;
and to every doubter and skeptic here and elsewhere, our message
is that the sun of righteousness in this sphere of Divine provision
for, and supervision over, human affairs has arisen never to set
until God's pious proclamation of peace for man's profit shall
obtain and direct and control all matter, mind, and morals, in the
whole universe of His creation.

And so my word to this Peace Congress is one of commendation
in that its cause vindicates valor in its consistency with right;
is proper in its proclamation of the true principles of patriotism
and philanthropy; is practical in its contribution to the permanent progress of the world in everything that makes for the welfare of the body, the enlightenment of the mind and the uplift
of the soul; and is profitable in its accordance with and obedience
to the pious will of God as revealed in the Divine word which we
are positively assured shall in the end accomplish that where-
unto it is sent.

My attitude is that of willing and hearty coöperation; and my
one word of loving admonition to every advocate of the cause is
that he shall never forget that it is the cause of God and not of
man; that in its activity and accomplishment every agency of
God stands enlisted and engaged; and that in this as in all other
movements that make for the establishment of principles that
are eternal as against the temporary expedient and makeshifts
of time, we are every one ambassadors of that King of Peace to
whom Prophet declared every knee shall bow, and of whom
Apostle affirmed every tongue shall proclaim Him God and Father.

CHAIRMAN TRUEBLOOD: The time has now arrived for us
to hear from the Committee on Resolutions. The success of this
Congress is due to the never-tiring efforts and hard work of Mr.
Theodore Marburg, of Baltimore. I think that a resolution of
thanks should be passed for Mr. Marburg. He has been the moving spirit of this Congress, and he will now read you the Resolutions adopted by the Committee.

MR. THEODORE MARBURG: My services amount to very
little. To arrange a program and a series of meetings such as
this called for earnest coöperation on the part of many men.
The counsel of the president of the Congress, Mr. Hamilton
Holt, was most helpful throughout, notably in connection with
the program and the resolutions. He emphasized particularly
the importance of having the resolutions dwell upon the things
still to be done in preference to recording and lauding past achievements. Then, too, the chairmen and members of the various
committees were thoroughly interested and most generous in
the time they gave to their task. Especially is this true of Mr.
Richard White, chairman of the Finance Committee. But if
there is any one man who has borne the burden of the day more
than another it is the executive secretary, Mr. Tunstall Smith,
and I should like to shift to him this resolution of thanks. No
volume of work has been too big for him, no task too difficult.
From the beginning he has made considerable sacrifices and I
want to say that anyone seeking executive ability will find it there.

In framing the resolutions your committee designedly omitted certain big sides of the peace question, such, for example, as propaganda. Our main object was to raise a little higher the plane of practical institutions which will offer a substitute for war. We feared that if we included these other sides of the movement then the practical things and what you regard as the big things would be lost sight of. They are the big things because if we get institutions which will raise an "international question mark" whenever nations are inclined to war, institutions which will cause the element of pride to drop out from controversies, above all a court which will open its doors and invite the nations of the world to enter, wars will be less frequent. The resolutions read as follows:

RESOLUTIONS

WHEREAS, there is a great and growing sentiment between English-speaking peoples in favor of the settlement of all disputes by means other than war, a sentiment which has found memorable expression in the utterances of President William Howard Taft and of Sir Edward Grey, therefore be it

Resolved, that the Congress records its profound appreciation of the attitude and action of President Taft and Sir Edward Grey on this important subject and expresses its firm conviction that, if the proposed treaty is made, the example thus set by Great Britain and the United States will be followed by other nations.

Resolved, that this Congress notes with satisfaction the zeal and ability with which the Honorable Philander C. Knox, Secretary of State, has been carrying forward the work initiated by his predecessor looking to the establishment of the International Prize Court and of the International Court of Arbitral Justice. It regards both these institutions as of the highest importance in themselves and urges the earliest possible establishment of the Court of Arbitral Justice by such of the powers as are willing to organize it, leaving it open to the adherence of other powers later on and free of access to them in the meantime.

3

WHEREAS, the practice of not including within the scope of so-called general arbitration treaties questions which affect the vital interests or the honor of the contracting states and the interests of third parties greatly diminishes the value of such treaties, be it

Resolved, that this Congress urges upon the United States Government the importance of formulating an all-inclusive arbitration treaty on the lines of the proposed treaty with Great Britain with a view to its adoption jointly by the leading powers.

4

WHEREAS, the treaty relating to pecuniary claims originally adopted by the Second International American Conference, and renewed by the Third and Fourth Conferences, not only definitively binds the High Contracting Parties to submit to arbitration a certain and very large and important class of cases but does this without making qualifications or exceptions that nullify or tend to nullify the force of the engagement, therefore be it

Resolved, that this Congress, following the practical precedent here set, recommends the more general adoption by governments of treaties whereby all claims for pecuniary loss or damage which may be presented by their respective citizens or subjects and which cannot be amicably adjusted through diplomatic channels shall be submitted to The Hague Court.

5

Resolved, that the proposed celebration in 1915 of the one hundredth anniversary of peace among English-speaking peoples is viewed by the Congress with satisfaction, the more especially as

attention will thus be directed to the happy results of the enlightened statesmanship which has refrained from erecting fortifications along the 3700 miles of frontier between Canada and the
United States and has excluded war vessels from the boundary
waters.

6

Resolved, that the Third American Peace Congress records its
satisfaction at the resolution passed by the Congress of the
United States calling upon the President of the United States
to appoint a commission to investigate and report back to the
government the possibilities of an international understanding
with regard to armaments, international coöperation and new
institutions calculated to preserve peace, thereby carrying out
the wish of the Second American Peace Congress expressed by
resolution. The Congress understands this Commission to be a
purely American Commission, not endowed with diplomatic
functions, and entertains the conviction that the Commission
should be appointed at an early day and should begin its labors
without regard to the opinion which other powers may entertain
as to possible results.

7

Resolved, that this Congress urges the government of the United
States to enter upon negotiations with other powers looking to
the formation of a league of peace planned simply to settle by
amicable means all questions of whatever nature which may arise
between the contracting powers, with no idea of the employment
of force to impose the will of the league on any of its members
nor to force any outside power to join the league, nor to force any
outside power to arbitrate a dispute, nor to enforce the decision
of an international tribunal of any character, nor to use force in
any other way. The successful conduct of such a league would be
greatly promoted by annual conventions which would serve the
double purpose of resolving difficulties that may have arisen between members of the league during the year and of formulating
international practice.

8

Resolved, that this Congress congratulates the governments of Great Britain and the United States on the successful settlement by arbitration of the Newfoundland Fisheries dispute, a case which diplomacy had vainly attempted to settle for the greater part of a century; and that the Congress points to this case as a striking example of the usefulness of the Permanent Court of Arbitration at The Hague.

9

WHEREAS, this Congress views with concern the heavy burden imposed on civilized nations by armaments and especially their continued increase despite the growing sentiment in favor of the amicable settlement of international disputes, be it

Resolved, that this Congress favors, not a spasmodic, but a continuous study of the limitation of armaments by official commissions of the various governments interested.

10

Resolved, that this Congress calls attention to the importance of an early determination of the measures to be brought before the Third Hague Conference in order that opportunity may be given for such thorough preliminary study by the governments interested that the delegates to the Conference may come with full knowledge of the subjects to be discussed.

11

Resolved, that this Congress expresses to Mr. Edwin Ginn its profound gratitude for his munificent contributions to the cause of peace.

12

Resolved, that this Congress expresses to Mr. Andrew Carnegie its profound gratitude for his munificent contributions to the cause of peace.

13

WHEREAS, there has been a manifest need for a central representative body which shall serve to coördinate the efforts of all the societies in America devoted to the settlement of international disputes by methods other than war, as emphasized by the President of the United States at the opening session of this Congress, therefore be it

Resolved, that this body of delegates declare that this National Peace Congress shall hereafter be known as the American Peace Congress, that it shall be a permanent institution which shall meet once in two years, and that while the Congress is not in session its Executive Committee shall be charged with all the powers of the Congress, provided that said Executive Committee shall have power to reorganize by enlarging its numbers so as to become representative and after its reorganization shall elect its own chairman. And be it further

Resolved, that said Committee shall adopt a form of organization which will enable it to act as a clearing house for all the societies represented at this Congress.

14

WHEREAS, the demand that our own citizens abroad receive the equal protection of the laws, and that persons guilty of violating their personal or property rights be punished, is weakened by the inability of the Federal government of the United States, under the law, to punish similar offenses against foreigners within its borders, and

WHEREAS, the absence of such power has been a cause of friction in the past and is likely to give rise to difficulties in future, therefore be it

Resolved, that the Third American Peace Congress urges upon the United States Congress early attention to the recommendation of President Taft for the enactment of laws which will confer upon the Federal government the power to fulfil its treaty obligations in this respect.

15

Resolved, that this Congress favors the suggestion that nations should prevent, as far as possible, loans being raised by their subjects or citizens in order to enable foreign nations to carry on war.   And be it further

'   *Resolved,* that the government of the United States be requested to include this question in the program of the Third Hague Conference.

16

WHEREAS, international controversies have frequently arisen out of disputed boundaries, and

WHEREAS, precise geographic delimitation would remove from the field of controversy a very disturbing element, this Congress is of the opinion that the precise delimitation of the boundaries of American states would be in the interest of international peace, and

WHEREAS, the North and Baltic Seas Conventions establishing the territorial status quo of those regions have proved the practicability of insuring territorial integrity by such means, therefore be it

Resolved, that this Congress calls to the attention of the United States government the advisability of including within the program of the Fifth International American Conference proposals to establish an international commission for the delimitation of the boundaries of the states of the two Americas and for the conclusion of a convention which shall maintain the integrity of the boundaries so delimitated.

17

Resolved, that in order to enable the executive and judicial departments of our government fully to discharge the international duties of the United States a thorough revision of the neutrality laws of the United States should be made.

18

Resolved, that the hearty thanks of this Congress be extended to the Johns Hopkins University for its very great hospitality.

MR. THEODORE MARBURG: The resolution relating to the organization of a national council is among the most important resolutions of the Congress.   You heard President Taft refer to the need of coördination among the societies whose aim is the peaceful settlement of international disputes.   The question was taken up at the Mohonk Conference three years ago, but unfortunately that body only meets once a year and has not been able to reach a decision.   Now, we have a living thing right here and we do not propose to let it die.   We represent the leading societies in America devoted to the settlement of disputes by means othert han war.   If we adjourn now *sine die,* we allow this Congress to go out of existence.   That we don't propose to do.   What we want is to make this a permanent congress with sessions once every two years and make it as established and fixed as the Congress of the United States, and then provide an Executive Committee which shall act for the Congress between sessions and likewise function as a national council or clearing house.   Let us make sure of a council and then, if necessary, merge it with others which may be created later on.   If the Mohonk Conference elects a national council composed of good men, we may appoint identical men so as to merge the two bodies.   If we find the Carnegie Endowment for Peace disposed to assume the office of a clearing house then we may work through them.

MR. EDWIN D. MEAD: I move the adoption of these resolutions.   I have been present at all three of the American Congresses. I think I was a member of the Resolution Committee of the first two Congresses, and I know the difficulty and care with which such a platform as this must be prepared, and I recommend these resolutions primarily because every one of them means something. Resolutions too often are merely rhetorical and seldom lead anywhere.   These resolutions are all necessary and are pregnant at this hour.   We heard that powerful address of Dean Rogers

this afternoon. There has never been a year in the peace movement when the United States took a more advanced position
than during the time between the Second National Congress and
the Congress in which we are gathered today. The President of
the United States has placed himself at the head of all the heads
of the great nations by standing for arbitration. The Congress
has placed itself at the head of all legislative bodies by moving
the reduction of armaments, and our secretary of state has placed
himself at the head of all foreign offices of the world by moving
for the organization of the International Prize Court and of the
International Court of Arbitral Justice, and finally the friends of
peace in this country have placed themselves at the head of all
benefactors by their donations this year. I rejoice that there are
resolutions here contained in recognition of these deeds. I rejoice
that there has been in this Congress such addresses as those of
the Hon. James Slayden and Hon. James Speyer.

Richard Cobden said what Mr. Speyer said, Oscar Straus has
also said it, but Mr. Speyer said it with power, and I am glad that
that was framed into a resolution and Congressman Slayden's
exhortation to us respecting the territories of our sister nations.

I notice that the Resolution Committee was a very representative one. We are not prepared to enter into detailed or technical
or fine discussions on these points. I hope that will not follow.
We have had a Resolution Committee that was entitled to our
trust, and I think we should trust it.

There was one resolution which, when I moved to adopt these
resolutions, I did so with misgivings, and that was the one touch-
ing the organization of all the societies represented at the Congress and with reference to future meetings. But I think it is
well to adopt this resolution as it stands, because its purpose is
excellent, and I believe that its details, in the main, are wise, and
I wish to express my great satisfaction in these most pertinent
and pregnant resolutions which are the culmination of this Congress.

REV. OLIVER HUCKLE: I rise for the privilege of seconding
this motion. Some of us believe, Mr. Chairman, that the periods
of human history have got to be thought of differently in the

future from the way they have been thought of in the past. Constitutional government is just coming into the midst of some of the nations of the earth. Daybreak is just coming in Turkey, and another epoch in international arbitration for the settlement of international disputes. We can date our modern history from the call of the First Hague Congress. These resolutions represent the best spirit and thought of these modern times. Some of us feel that the developments in the peace movement in the last ten years have been more momentous in the history of the human race than those of ten centuries preceding. One thousand years is sometimes with the Lord as one day, but sometimes a single day is as potential in its meaning as one year. These resolutions have something of the spirit of these on-rushing times in which we are living. We believe that the Third American Peace Congress has reached the high-water mark in the peace movement of the world, and these resolutions register the spirit and sentiment and something of what has resulted from the dignified and significant utterances of the distinguished men who have assembled here, things which will have influence on the history of the world. We believe these resolutions are such that we should give our hearty and unanimous approval to. Therefore, as a member of the American Peace Society and as vice-president of the Maryland Peace Society and as one who has something, at least, of the vision of the peace movement from the little house in the woods at The Hague, and as one being at Portsmouth and one also present as a delegate at the First National Peace Congress, I feel that it is a great privilege and an honor to second the motion made for the adoption of these resolutions.

MR. HARTMAN (of Lancaster, Pa.): I heartily coincide with the sentiments expressed. I was not able to be here at the opening of this Convention, but I have been at the previous conventions.

There is just one sentiment, however, that does not meet with my accord and that was what was said with regard to limited armament, which was brought up before the previous conventions and approved. But neither of the conventions—and I have not heard any sentiments expressed by these resolutions—stated a method by which the limited armament was to be achieved. I have forwarded to the president a copy of the two former resolutions, which I offered in New York and in Chicago, but which the president seems not to have received—that is the president of this Congress. I do not see how this country or the nations of the world are to achieve limited armaments except by some method by which the powers jointly will adopt some method by which the navies of all these nations now existing, and the armies, may be limited. I believe that whatever the powers agree to do they can do, but if they do not agree, you cannot achieve limited armament, so we must have a method—

CHAIRMAN TRUEBLOOD: Do you want to move an amendment?

MR. HARTMAN: Well, make it a resolution that this Congress recommends to The Hague Congress—because they are the legal body and we are not, and they represent the powers and therefore they can take legal action on the adoption of amendments or resolutions which we advocate; so I move that this convention adopt the method which I have suggested heretofore in previous resolutions, or some method equally as good.

CHAIRMAN TRUEBLOOD: I think I can explain just what Mr. Hartman means. He proposes that this Congress should recommend the adoption of an international patrol of war vessels on the sea in order to get a combination of the navies of the world for the protection of the commerce of the world. Is the amendment seconded?

(The amendment was duly seconded, and upon being put to a vote was lost.)

CHAIRMAN TRUEBLOOD: The question is now on the adoption of the motion of Mr. Mead, seconded by the Rev. Dr. Huckle, that these resolutions be approved and adopted as a whole.

REV. CHARLES E. BEALS: Nature has given to me a slow mind, if not a stupid one, and I would like to know what I am going to vote on with reference to this article about the coördination of all the different peace societies. This is the biggest question we have tackled yet. Now, these resolutions were not read until half past five, and we should be out of here at least by six o'clock.

I do not feel competent to form a snapshot opinion on this question. I would like to know how that Committee is to be appointed.

CHAIRMAN TRUEBLOOD: The Chair understands that this resolution is offered to continue the Executive Committee of this Congress until the next Congress, and if it sees fit, it can ally the various other societies, and whatever it wishes it may suggest to the next Peace Congress.

MR. HAYES: This has taken a form now that I seriously object to. I do not object to the organization of a committee, but I am a fervent believer that this movement should combine all these societies and the great mass of people to unify all these interests and I am not now ready to see a motion pass that we shall wait for two years. I am in favor of taking some steps now.

MR. ALFRED H. LOVE: We have been eminently favored in these resolutions, and as I must leave now, I do so leaving my vote for them.

REV. CHARLES E. BEALS: I must say that I cannot vote for that one resolution, and I move that the resolution that I refer to be withdrawn.

MR. HAMILTON HOLT: Let me read that resolution (reading):

"WHEREAS, there has been a manifest need for a central representative body which shall serve to coördinate the efforts of all the societies in America devoted to the settlement of international disputes by methods other than war, as emphasized by the President of the United States at the opening session of this Congress, therefore be it.

"RESOLVED, that this body of delegates declare that this National Peace Congress shall hereafter be known as the American Peace Congress, that it shall be a permanent institution which shall meet once in two years, and that while the Congress is not in session its Executive Committee shall be charged with all the powers of the Congress, provided that said Executive Committee shall have power to reorganize by enlarging its numbers so as to become representative and after its reorganization shall elect its own chairman. And be it further

"Resolved, that said Committee shall adopt a form of organization which will enable it to act as a clearing house for all the societies represented at this Congress."

That will have no effect unless the things which they suggest are agreed to by the other societies. It has no power to do anything except to perpetuate this Congress. That was done so as to continue a series of Congresses every two years. There had to be some permanent machinery, and as the matter was complex we thought that it would be better to leave it in the hands of the Executive Committee than to have another committee appointed.

MR. HARTMAN: Wouldn't it be better to have a committee composed of the presidents of all the other societies? The committee would know how to reorganize itself. The Mohonk Conference is working on a similar plan. We are all here officially representing different peace societies throughout the country. If we want to join with the Mohonk Conference, we can join with them, and if we find that they do something unwise we don't need to merge with them, but we simply continue this movement with the power to take advantage of these things.

A VOICE: Mr. Chairman, I call for the question.

CHAIRMAN TRUEBLOOD: It has been moved by Mr. Beals that this one resolution be stricken from the report of the Committee on Resolutions.

MR. EDWIN MEAD: I think that there is not such a difference of opinion as to that resolution about working out future conferences but as to its being a clearing house for all the other societies of the country. I think it would be better to take the votes on those two sections separately.

A VOICE: I second the motion.

CHAIRMAN TRUEBLOOD: The first part of the resolution simply perpetuates this Congress through this Executive Committee, giving it the power to call the next Congress two years hence and arrange a place of meeting and have the local committee appointed As I understand it, then, there is now a motion before the house to strike out this whole clause.

REV. CHARLES E. BEALS: Then I will withdraw my motion and the second will be withdrawn, and as I understand it, the function of this new body will be simply the holding of a Congress two years hence.

MR. HAYES: I submit that the Executive Committee ought to be constituted, but that the limitations should be taken off. Let them hold a meeting and form an organization and bring this body together again. Give them more power than they had.

CHAIRMAN TRUEBLOOD: The question is on the motion of Mr. Mead that the two parts of the resolution be divided.

(Mr. Hamilton Holt then read the first clause of Resolution No. 13.)

CHAIRMAN TRUEBLOOD: We will now take a vote on that portion of the resolution.

(Upon the vote being taken, the first clause of Resolution No. 13 was adopted.)

MR. HAMILTON HOLT: I will now read the second clause (reading).

MR. HUMPHREY: I move that every society or organization represented here should be included on that Executive Committee. I think a declaration of the Chairman to that effect will satisfy all of us.

CHAIRMAN TRUEBLOOD: That Executive Committee is given power to do just that thing, to enlarge itself and make it a committee of ten or fifty members.

MR. HAMILTON HOLT: That is what this resolution says here, and I think you can trust your committeemen.

MR. HUMPHREY: Well, I move that the Executive Committee be made up of representatives of the organizations represented in this Congress.

MR. EDWIN MEAD: I suppose there are fifty or a hundred organizations represented here.

CHAIRMAN TRUEBLOOD: Yes, sir; many of which are not peace societies at all. I think it would be unwise to adopt such a resolution. Let the Executive Committee work out its own extension.

MR. HUMPHREY: I will withdraw my motion. The Chair is a member of that Committee and will certainly exercise his personal influence in an effort to get that committee to enlarge itself.   I suppose that there are more than three=quarters of the societies represented here which are not peace societies.

CHAIRMAN TRUEBLOOD: The question is now on the second part of the Resolution No. 13.   All in favor of the second clause of the resolution will please say "Aye."

(Upon the vote being taken the second clause of Resolution No. 13 was adopted).

CHAIRMAN TRUEBLOOD: The resolution has been adopted. The question now is upon the adoption of the resolutions as a whole.

(Upon a vote being taken, the resolutions, as a whole, were adopted.)

ADJOURNED

SPEECHES AT THE BANQUET

FRIDAY EVENING, MAY 5, AT SEVEN O'CLOCK

Hon. Champ Clark, Toastmaster

MR. FRANK N. HOEN: Ladies and Gentlemen: We have now reached the time when it is my pleasure to call this session of the Peace Congress to order, that we may hear the distinguished speakers who will address us.

Before proceeding with the program, the usual Maryland custom is to offer a toast. I desire to offer, therefore, the usual toast to the President of the United States. I think you will agree with me that the address of the President at the first session of this Congress will perhaps be received more enthusiastically than any of his recent addresses. It was certainly a wonderful address at such a time. I therefore will ask all to stand and drink to the health of the President of the United States, Hon. William Howard Taft.

(A standing toast was then drunk to the President of the United States.)

MR. HOEN: I now have the pleasure and honor of introducing the Toastmaster of the evening, the distinguished Speaker of the House of Representatives, the Hon. Champ Clark, of Missouri.

HON. CHAMP CLARK: Ladies and Gentlemen: I thank the managers of this Congress for making me toastmaster. It is a great honor. The chief function of a toastmaster is not to make a speech himself, but to introduce the speechmakers, and it is much the easier part of the program. Introductions ought not to be long. When Max O'Rell was lecturing in this country some years ago, a president of a society in some town in which he was going to lecture consumed three-quarters of an hour in introducing him, and when O'Rell got up he offered a resolution of thanks to the chairman for the speech which he had made and sat down, and I always thought he treated him right.

I am the president or chairman or presiding officer of the greatest debating society on the face of the earth, barring none. The healthiest rule in that house on the subject of oratory is the confining of speeches on certain occasions to a five minute limit, and the best speeches ever made in that house are made under that five minute rule.

My good friend, David B. Henderson, the speaker of the house at one time, an approved soldier himself, who lost a leg at Corinth, several years ago began a speech to the Grand Army, at Indianapolis, with these words: "War is my theme, and I hate it!" All sane people agree in that sentiment. The vast majority of soldiers who have fought for a principle from a sense of duty join in that sentiment. We all hail this Peace Congress, not as a harbinger of the millennium, but as the prophecy of a better state of affairs than has existed on this earth since Cain slew Abel.

The United States ought to lead in this great peace movement. We ought to lead in this movement because of our happy geographical situation. Defended on the east and on the west by two great seas; with neighbors to the north and south perfectly friendly to us; with our immeasurable resources; with our vast population constantly growing greater and vaster, our position is impregnable in war. We have nothing to fear from any nation on the face of the earth in a war, and therefore of all the nations on this great earth we are in the best position to lead in the peace movement.

Our position in the world is—and it is historical—friendly, peaceful and honest with all the nations, with entangling alliances with none. We have no disposition to interfere with anybody, and no desire to encroach upon the territory or infringe upon the prerogatives of any other nation. Our desire is to be at peace with all the world.

I introduced a resolution into the last Congress and also in this one—and the chances are I can get it passed more easily in this Congress than in the last—to find out the cost of wars in the last one hundred years. And the more I study about it, the more difficult I know it is. You may ascertain approximately what the nations of the earth have spent in dollars and cents—that is the actual expenditure of money—but the property losses by reason of war, the loss of life, the shedding of tears, the hindrance of progress, no mathematics can explain and no mathematician can solve.

It is a strange thing, and those who have studied history know it full well, that the histories of the world are nine-tenths taken up with the description of wars between men. The soldiers have the monuments the wideworld over. Go to Washington. The town is full of equestrian statues to soldiers, and I give it as my opinion as a horseman, and one raised in Kentucky and living in Missouri, and representing the District where the highest priced saddler that the world ever saw was raised, that every bronze horse in the City of Washington, with the exception of two or three, should be broken up for old junk. But it is the soldiers that have the monuments in Washington as in every other capital in the world. I am not certain that there are statues in that town in public places to more than three or four statesmen, that is where the men did not happen to be both statesmen and soldiers. There is one to Daniel Webster and one to General Garfield, and an exceedingly poor one to Abraham Lincoln, and maybe two or three others. But it is all wrong. Soldiers are necessary in their time and place. They discharge the duties that devolve upon them, but I say that it is a crime for the civilized nations of the earth to be cutting each others throats in this day and generation. I am happy to give my mite, small as it is, to contribute it to this great movement for universal peace. I repeat it that we ought to lead in this movement, resolutely, constantly, unflinchingly until Tennyson's gorgeous vision is realized,

> When the war drum throbs no longer
> And the battle flags are furled,
> In the Parliament of Man,
> The Federation of the World.

I am rather inclined to believe that when the final account is made up, Andrew Carnegie will receive more praise from mankind

for the ten million dollars which he contributed to the cause of
peace than he will for the entire expenditure of the large remnant
of his fortune.

I am glad that President Taft and the administrative authorities of the United States are aiding in this cause. Congress ought
to coöperate with the administration in every good work, and the
administration ought to coöperate with Congress in every good
work. The thing is mutual. It is not one-sided, and we ought
to persevere in this matter, remembering and being encouraged
by John Milton's splendid utterance, "Peace has her victories
no less renowned than war." And my judgment of the matter is,
that as great a blessing as the Panama Canal will be as a commercial artery, its greatest blessing will be that it will bring the nations
of the world together more closely and make them better friends
and make wars scarcer.

I said I was not going to speak long, and I am not. This is
an historic city. Our national anthem was written here. Some
right lively war scenes were in this immediate vicinity. This is
called the "Monumental City." It has not only risen from its
ashes physically in recent years, after your great fire, but it is
rising otherwise. Originally this was the great convention city
of the United States. The first President ever nominated in a
national convention was nominated here, and for some reason—
I don't know who started it or how it happened—but gatherings are
coming here more frequently now than to the City of Washington,
and I rejoice at it.

The greatest problem of the century that is facing us is the
government of great cities. When our population was all rural,
government was easy. Everybody knew everybody. The
problems were not so complex. They get more complex every
year and are more difficult of solution. On that proper solution
of those problems depends, to a large extent, the prosperity and
glory of the Republic.

It is a great thing to be a member of Congress of either branch,
and it is a great thing to be the governor of a State or the mayor
of a city, and I now take pleasure in presenting to you His Honor,
J. Barry Mahool, the mayor of this city, who will respond to the
toast, "The City of Baltimore."

HON. J. BARRY MAHOOL: Mr. Toastmaster, Ladies and Gentlemen: I am sure that it is with a great deal of personal pleasure that I am permitted to come here tonight and extend a most cordial welcome to you on behalf of the people of Baltimore.

The Speaker has well said that the municipal problems which confront a city are even greater than those which confront a member of congress. The fact that $3\frac{1}{2}$ per cent of the population of this entire country one hundred years ago lived within the walls of a city made it comparatively simple at that time to administer municipal affairs. But at the present time, with 40 per cent of the entire population of the United States living and elbowing each other in these great aggregations of population which we call cities, it taxes the ability and efforts of our most public spirited citizens to enable people to live in these places and continue to thrive and prosper. And as mayor of a city which has done much, I think, in the last few years along the lines of progress and up-building in municipal affairs, I come here tonight and bid you Godspeed in the work of which you have undertaken in this Peace Congress. I am sure that a man who has served four years in the mayor's office is quite willing for peace to prevail all over the earth.

You, my friends, I am sure meet with the same thoughts that we all meet with, the same things that we meet with when we start to do a great thing, just as when we started out a few years ago to rebuild a city after a hundred million dollars were burned up within a few blocks of this hotel, when we meet with the idea that such a thing could not be accomplished, and just as we hear men say today that the time will never come when men all over the earth will live together in peace and tranquillity.

When the great railroad which was started from Baltimore, was first put into operation, they ran a race with an old gray mare, and the people said, when the mare beat the train, that it "would never amount to shucks," that it would never go, that it would never run. There are lots of croakers or knockers in the community, but they are getting fewer all the time. The story runs that the belt came off of the fly wheel and the engine stopped and the mare came in ahead of the railroad train.

When they started the great electric telegraph between Baltimore and Washington, and the message was sent, "What hath
God wrought," there were lots of people who were urged to give
their support to that movement, but they said that it could never
be, that it was impossible.   That message was sent, however, and
through the civilizing influences of the railroad and the telegraph,
the people of the world have been brought closer together, and I
believe that it is now almost impossible for two civilized nations
to come to war.

I am glad to come here as the mayor of Baltimore, after having
listened to the many splendid speeches which were delivered, and
I can tell you that any movement which starts out with the endorsement of the chief executive of this great nation, which has
the endorsement of men of finance, of the most learned, and of the
greatest statesmen of the country, must succeed, and when we
see what God hath wrought in the things that had the backing
of but a very few men in the past, I say then we can look forward
to that great result to which all the world looks, eternal peace.

I thank you most cordially for coming to Baltimore.   I am
glad our distinguished citizen, Mr. Theodore Marburg, has had
so much to do with the success of this Congress.   I am sure it has
inspired the hearts and minds of the people of this city and of this
country to better and nobler things in the future.   As mayor, I
extend to you a most cordial welcome on behalf of our city, and
I trust that you will see in the near future a fruition of your dreams,
of your ideas, your hopes and ambitions.   I thank you.

THE TOASTMASTER: This country contains about one-seven-
teenth of the people on the globe, and yet a nation as great as
this is cannot control the politics or the policies or destiny of the
world.   It takes coöperation, and this is preëminently the age
of coöperation.

A few years ago, when The Hague Court was established, a
great many people poked fun at it, but as the years have gone by
that Court has grown in strength and popularity.   I have no
doubt that it has already prevented several minor wars, and in the
days to come it will prevent a great many more.   I have said that

if I could pick the thing with which Colonel Theodore Roosevelt was to concern himself for the rest of his life, I would make him the perpetual president of The Hague Peace Tribunal. It would be a noble close to a phenomenal career.

We have with us tonight a distinguished gentleman who has devoted his life largely to this principle of the coöperation of nations. He won the Nobel Peace Prize in 1909. He was President of the International Conciliation Congress. He was a Delegate from France to the First and Second Hague Conferences. He is a life senator of France. His subject is "Coöperation of the Nations." I have the pleasure of introducing to you Senator Baron d'Estournelles de Constant.

COÖPERATION OF THE NATIONS

BARON D'ESTOURNELLES DE CONSTANT

Mr. Chairman, Ladies and Gentlemen: I would certainly, like my faithful and good friend, La Fontaine, prefer speaking French tonight. I think really it would be much better if we could express to you all that we feel, all that we have to say, in the best shape and best form possible. But I do not care so much for the shape of the words. I know now that you understand very well and support this feeling, so I shall do my best to express to you a few of the feelings which are very deep in my heart. First, I want to express my admiration and my gratitude for the organization of this splendid Congress. That is not at all a word of flattery. Having so few words to use I should not use them for flattery when I want them for explaining. It is not at all flattery.

I find here, as well as everywhere in the United States, such a fine organization, such fine elements for really good coöperation. Here, for instance, in this Congress you hardly can imagine, you Americans, what a success it is when we compare it to what the Peace Congresses generally are in Europe, although they are improving a great deal; but here the most ignorant people even can understand at once what great importance you attach and give to these manifestations. For instance, this banquet. It is organized not only in perfection, but our great, fine, devoted friend, who is one of these men that you always want in all kinds of work, not a man who does anything for show, but a man who really does for everybody, I mean Theodore Marburg, has given time and thought to its perfection. I say not only that, but what I admire beside the good will, beside the devotion of a man, you find the support of almost all the principal forces of your great Republic.

This banquet is presided over by the Speaker of the House of Representatives. That means a great deal. Your meetings have been more or less opened by the most eminent contributors which you could have, such as that of President Taft, and the mayor of your great city of Baltimore has expressed himself as being in sympathy, and has expressed the sympathies of his city for your work. So, I do not see what is missing in the support of all the forces of your country to our cause.

But perhaps I can bring you more than these feelings of congratulations and thanks. I can speak of my visit which I have made to your country and which I just finished today. This is the very last day, not of my journey, but of the long tour that I made all over the United States. I think now, that I am one of the men who know best about public opinion in the United States, from the mere fact that I have seen almost everybody in all your great towns and States. I am glad to see here tonight so many of the friends from the States that I had the great luck and chance of visiting.

There was one thing that struck me deeply. I went almost everywhere. I went to New York and Washington and Baltimore. I went from Baltimore to New Orleans, to Austin and to the Mexican frontier, to Arizona, to California, to Los Angeles, San Francisco, Oregon, Portland, Seattle, Colorado—I have seen Denver —then from Denver I went to your splendid, active, extraordinary Middle West, which is already so startlingly developed in almost fifty years, something which for a foreigner to see is almost a miracle. I saw all that. I went to St. Paul and Minneapolis and Cincinnati and finally to Washington and here. The one thing I noticed, the one thing which seems to me so striking, is that notwithstanding the great variety of all these cities and States facing the Atlantic Ocean or the Gulf of Mexico or the Pacific Ocean, and notwithstanding the fact that everywhere there is a difference in nature and everywhere you find differences in climate, culture, in everything, still in every town, in every State I found one feeling, one national feeling, uniting all these different states together, one same and quite definite aspiration for peace, against war and for eternal justice—against war not because they are weak people, but because they judge it exactly as we do in France. We are always and will be always glad to give our life and blood to the last drop in fighting for a good cause, for liberty or justice; but we are now more and more, just as you are, against war, because we understand that war is not only more and more disgusting, but that it only leads to catastrophies, that war is as bad for the victor as for the defeated.

Ladies and Gentlemen, I didn't give one minute from my time for pleasure or social entertainment, because I wanted to speak to the people of all kinds, I wanted to try to meet objections or contradictions. I did not try to escape conversation. Just the reverse. I wanted to find objections. I went to the Mexican frontier. I went to the California State, where I knew they spoke so much of the Japanese inevitable war. Everywhere I thought I might find difficulty I went, and I spoke to all the people I could. I spoke to the club men, to the preachers, to the business men, to the church men everywhere—I spoke to thousands of people, not leaving out the women, who can render such a great help to the cause of peace, and everywhere I found only one will, one aspiration. Republicans and Democrats, all people are supporting this one policy, the policy of international arbitration. They all understand that. Only five or six years ago, my friends remember it, this word "arbitration" was not so well understood. People did not know what it meant. Now they all understand, and one of the best proofs of what I say is that without any party lines, the Democrats and Republicans both speak with the highest gratitude and confidence of the initiative which was taken by President Taft in this great effort to make a treaty for obligatory arbitration.

So now, my dear friends, if we were men fond of having a rest, if we were something like this pacifist whom our adversaries are always laughing at, if we were not men who wanted to give all our strength, as La Fontaine does, and as many others do, if we were not ready to give our lives to our cause, then it seems we could now have a rest. But no, my dear sirs, you shall have no rest. That is life. That is the duty, the greatness of a cause. We shall not have a rest, because as long as ignorance will remain—and it will remain a long time in life—we will have to educate the people. They are ready and they are pleased to be educated, but still they may be taken by surprise every day. They may be deceived. They are deceived every day. They are deceived by people who do not know sometimes. Sometimes I suppose they do not know that they are deceiving. We have to follow them up and try to contradict the people who try to deceive, and we have to explain; and I assure you when we do it the country and the people are very grateful and will be very grateful, because they understand perfectly well where the truth is as long as we take the trouble to explain it.

I see here, just as in France or Germany or Great Britain, many people, perhaps with not so bad intentions, because sometimes they do not understand what they are doing, but they spread pessimism and alarming news. Some people are not satisfied unless they find something startling in their morning newspaper. They want to find something startling. "We are perfectly happy, so what is the use of having a newspaper except for that." They say that war is inevitable, that war is coming. They said that La Fontaine said that war was coming. That was very interesting, and they said that de Constant, for instance—because I read it myself—they said that they could build more dreadnoughts because Baron de Constant said that war with Great Britain and Germany was sure to come soon; but I had said just the reverse. I said that you could sleep quietly because there was no danger, but they said that I said to take care because war was coming. Of course, that is interesting, because I did not say it.

In California I spoke about what they called the inevitable

Japanese war with the United States, and I want to tell you that I found it was all a dream and not a reality, and I gave some explanation about it, and then I read in a paper—not there but at some other place—"Baron de Constant says that war between Japan and the United States is inevitable." Now this would be discouraging if public opinion was not educated, because such news is wired to Germany and France and Great Britain, and then what do they say? They say "You know we have to go to expense for military equipment because even the pacifist is speaking for war now."

But speaking of the Japanese question, I could demonstrate with the evidence given to me by all your people that it is not possible at all. There is no possibility of a war between Japan and the United States, unless you suppose the governments concerned are blind and all the other governments are indifferent and the people are ignorant and stupid. If you really take the facts, though, everything is against it. When I said that to my friends, they said that it was thought quite impossible for the United States to make war upon Japan, that nobody thought of the United States attacking Japan. But what else did they say—and we took it in France and Europe seriously—they said, "Everybody knows that there are plenty of Japanese spies in all the universities and hotels, in California and in Colorado and everywhere" and all these Japanese spies are ready, when they see that the government of the United States has some trouble or difficulty, to write or wire at once and the Japanese government sees its chance. Of course, all these people that talk this way know everything. They don't know it, but they are sure of it, which is worse. They say they will begin by seizing the Philippines, which is as easy as possible, and then the Hawaiian Islands and then after that the Pacific Ocean. Well, I found something still better. We French are imaginative, and I said that they would not stop at that but they would perhaps take San Francisco and make of that a Gibraltar, and that would be fine; and really the people looked as though they were pleased with the idea. But when I spoke of that I asked them if they thought of where they could find the necessary money for that plan. I heard Banker Speyer speak of a

splendid plan to do away with war.   I think it is very interesting
and fine; but of course all these people are dreamers and they
don't care about the question of money.   The danger is what they
care for—it is only the Japanese danger.   I said, "Very well,
suppose they can do all that, do you think they could really stop
there?   Supposing that they took the Philippines and the Hawaiian
Islands, and all the Pacific Ocean; very well, but the same moment
they attack the Philippine Islands, then the same moment they
tread on other possessions, the British possession; and they
threaten the Russian possession from Vladivostock and the
German possessions, and the Dutch possessions in Java."   And
they talk of it in Australia, this "yellow peril" and I said "Well,
Japan will have to attack Australia too."   I say it will be very
hard for one nation to do all that, and of course all the people
laugh, but that is because it is ridiculous.   I wish I could speak
in French now.   I wish I could say it in French.   I should like
to explain just exactly what it is that I find.   You know how it
is when boys make soap bubbles.   They do it in·France and I see
they do it here too.   In a few seconds it bursts by itself or you
can break it with your finger.   So it is really nothing.

In my country I can't open my mouth without someone saying
something about the masters of the sea.   Now the Japanese are
perfectly sane people.   They don't dream of such things.   Suppose they did!   They couldn't do it.   But they don't want any
masters of the sea.   The Pacific Ocean any more than any other
ocean doesn't belong to any nation any more than the sky,
which belongs to no nation but only to aviation and the air
men.

We want education, I should say daily education.   We have to
try now to undo what has been done sometimes very inefficiently,
sometimes very badly through ignorance or illwill.   We have to
undo all that.   We can do it and do it very easily because the facts
speak so eloquently.   Only in the last ten years have so many
good things been done, and you may be proud, ladies and gentlemen, in thinking how many things your country has done in all
this progress.   And when my honorable colleague, the Speaker of
the House of Representatives, speaks of the duty of America, of

the United States, of taking the lead in this movement, I say it is indeed your duty as it is your interest. It is your interest, because you are a great country. You have done a great many things, but you have still a great many things to do. I have seen all your country and I know many of the things you have still to do. You have not a dollar or an hour or a man to spare or waste for war. You have to give all your time, all your money, all your people and the natural resources of your country, you need all of your forces, for facing universal competition. They are speaking of the Japanese danger but I should say that if you enter the race you must not follow our mistakes—I mean of the great military powers in Europe. We are beginning to understand that we are wrong and have to abandon them, and if you just begin now to start these mistakes, you know who will be the winner of the race, who will be the winner of the fight? I should speak more of the Belgian terror or the Dutch peril, or the Scandinavian peril, or the peril of all the nations which seem so tiny, so modest, because having no military expenses, they can give all their efforts for the development of their natural resources, all their efforts for the great economic struggle. That is the real necessity. That is what you have to do. That is why you have to teach the people to understand that it is to your interest and it is your duty. You have given the world a good example. I said that very often. You did a signal thing in opening The Hague Court when no other government did it. My friend La Fontaine knows it well as a member of The Hague Conference, and I know it too, because we not only suffered from it; but we were deeply humiliated, my colleagues and I, who all gave the best that we had, and after having created this Hague Court, this institution which was the aspiration of all the world for so many centuries, no government would believe in that institution, no government wanted to use it, to try it and show that it was living. It was your government first, the government of the United States that gave not only this example but this lesson to the others in sending the first case to The Hague Court. This was the beginning, but it was not quite enough. The government of the United States gave the first case and it was a great beginning, a kind of attestation of confidence. But the governments refused to give the few thousands of dollars necessary to buy a house for the new institution. How could the people believe in this new court, when she had no house? Then came an American, which is very interesting. I remember very well that I was more and more distressed by this stand of the governments, when I had the pleasure of receiving at my country house one of your ambassadors, General Porter, and I said, "Is it not a pity to see this great thing almost stillborn, because they will give all their money for military expenses but nothing for The Hague Court." I said, "It is almost like a good young girl which you find in France"—of course I mean in France only—"when she has no money she can get no consideration or credit. Couldn't we find something like an American uncle for her, who could give her the money," and he said to me laughing, "Why don't you write to Mr. Carnegie?" I said, "I don't know him." "Well," he said, "I will give you a letter of introduction," and he did so, and I sent a letter to Mr. Carnegie saying that I heard he did so many good and fine things, and I thought really if he wanted to do something which was good that he should give something toward building a house for this poor girl. After a few weeks I received a letter from Mr. Carnegie saying he had the same idea and he was glad to tell me that he had given money enough not only to build a house, but a palace. Oh, my dear friends, how glad I was, but how humiliated I was afterwards when I saw that the government was so full of consideration for the girl after she had the money, that is the Court, I mean. Then the other cases came, the Casablanca case, and that is why I came to try to give you people the knowledge of the good you have done and to tell you how much you can do in the future. The people here have understood better than anywhere else that we must have coöperation. You are ready for it.

I shall go back to my country and other countries and tell them how you are feeling, how unanimous you are, and I am sure the people of all the world will give you thanks for the confidence you have shown and for what you have done.

Many thanks to you, my good friends, and many thanks to your good people who have done so much for me that I shall never forget the hearty welcome and hospitality of the United States.

THE TOASTMASTER: The Baron is not alone in having been misrepresented by a newspaper. There are others.

But as a rule they tell the truth. Sometimes they misrepresent through ignorance and once in a while through malice, but generally they are right. There is one thing I want to emphasize, and that is that there is nothing political in this peace movement. When Thomas Jefferson delivered his first inaugural, he said, "We are all Federalists, we are all Republicans," and if he were here tonight, he would say, taking into consideration the changes in the parties, "We are all Republicans, we are all Democrats," and this is as much Republican as it is Democratic and as much Democratic as Republican. It is American, that's what it is.

While politics are not allowed here, and I would not violate the proprieties, I will say this: I like to praise a Republican when I find one who deserves it, and it doesn't take me a long time, either. My judgment is that up to the present time President Taft will get more praise for his arbitration speech than anything else.

We have for the next speaker, the pastor of the Pilgrim Church in New York City, the editor of a Christian paper and the author of a book on the great subject of Peace.

I have the pleasure now of introducing Rev. Frederick Lynch of New York City.

SOME UNTABULATED SIGNS OF WORLD UNITY

REV. FREDERICK LYNCH

I shall not attempt to enlarge upon some significant facts of this new century, namely, the sudden and prolific production of books and pamphlets on the movement for international unity, world peace and international law. But I will turn to what is perhaps, after all, the surest promise of the federation of the nations, the unity of the races, the brotherhood of man, namely, those subtle, spiritual awakenings and movements of this century

—movements whose motion one cannot tabulate, but which are the most potent forces for the new world, as spiritual and ethical forces are always greatest. These movements are very pronounced. They show the mood, the temper, the trend of the century. The first and greatest of these new facts is this: we are at last passing up into that realm of ethics where we are seeing that the same ethic is binding upon groups of people that controls and determines the relations of individuals to each other. The trouble has been that we have been living under two standards of ethics—Christian for individuals, pagan for groups, communities, nations. We have demanded that individuals live as Christians towards each other, but corporations and nations as pirates. But there is no such thing as a double standard of ethics in the kingdom of God. That which is right for a man is right for the state; that which is wrong for a man to do is wrong for a corporation or nation to do. Taking things or land that do not belong to us is just as much stealing when done by a nation as when done by a man. If it is wrong for me to take revenge, it is wrong for a nation to take revenge. If it is wrong for me to settle my difficulties on the street with my fists, it is wrong for the nations to settle their difficulties on the seas with gunboats. Nations are under the same law of charity and forgiveness as individuals in any system of ethics that can last. The law of my country towards Japan is the law that governs me in my relations with my brother in my town. If it is wrong for me to kill my brother on the streets of my city, it is just as wrong for a nation to destroy a brother nation in this beautiful world. Both the church and the nation have been full of this spurious, double, unchristian morality. It has been largely responsible for rotten, thievish business methods of some corporations and insurance companies, for the corruption in civic and national life, as well as for the unchristian relationships of nations. It is passing very fast, and the most hopeful augury of a new internationalism is this arising in the race conscience of a morality really Christian and single, in which communities and nations are accountable at the same bar of righteousness as is a man.

Another movement gathering great headway in our century is the revival of the social gospel in the church and in the world of all good men. The gospel of the last century was directed towards saving the individual out of the evil of the world, and it laid great stress on the bliss awaiting the saved one in the world to come. The church can never neglect personal religion, for man's individual oneness with God is a great factor in his life. But the church is now seeing that its final object is not so much saving one man out of a corrupt society and social order into heaven as the redeeming of the very order itself, so that the will of God shall be done on earth as it is in heaven. This new, social consciousness is giving birth to a great revival of humaneness and is imparting to the church the determination to build the kingdom of God, the beautiful city of God in the earth. Consequently, she is driving out every evil that makes the kingdom impossible and degrades God's little children. A great campaign against child labor, the saloon, corrupt politics, unjust economic conditions, the exploitation of the weak and the foreigner, against all that makes the kingdom impossible and debases men has begun. Hatred between races, wars between nations, are the worst of these degrading forces. The moral damage of war is worse than the physical suffering it brings, as Rev. Walter Walsh, D.D., has shown in his recent remarkable book, *The Moral Damage of War*. Wars destroy the Christian nurture of centuries. They let loose again the worst lusts, passions and hatreds of men. They plunge nations back again into paganism. The new social gospel is already attacking it, along with all those evils that make the coming of the Christ-spirit into the social fabric impossible, for the kingdom of Christ must be built up on the law of love and not that of force. If the church should say tomorrow, "Wars must stop; arbitration must be resorted to," they would stop. But the whole logic of her present thinking will make her say it before the twentieth century is half gone.

The one word that is on all men's lips today is the brotherhood of man. It is passing up out of the world of sentiment into a working gospel. In America it is rapidly becoming a fact in spite of occasional relapses. It is seen in the mingling of all races in America. Dr. Edward Everett Hale used to call the United States the greatest peace society in existence. He had in mind the forty-six States living together without wars between each other. Perhaps he also had in mind the fact that fifty once hostile races now live, house to house in friendship and peace. What effect this can have on the peace of the world has been lucidly pointed out in Jane Addams' *Newer Ideals of Peace*. However this may be, brotherhood of man is attracting more response in our day than the older school of patriotism, which saw no good outside its own border. The many labor organizations and the social democracy of Europe, with all their shortcomings, are yet a groping towards brotherhood. Democracy is coming to its own in this century, and democracy, in its ideals at least, is brotherhood— a state where the ruling principle is, All for each and each for all. Democracy and war are incompatible, as this century will prove.

One other sign of the coming of the reign of law in this century is, to some minds, the most convincing of all, namely, that all our thinking today is gathering about the principle of evolution, and evolution is only nature's way of passing from brute to spirit. This law has *never* failed in any other field of operation. In every sphere of human action the brute, the physical, has passed on up into the spiritual and the realm of moral law. One instance will suffice: Once men settled all disputes by fierce, unregulated hand-to-hand fights. Then this single combat came to be regulated. This, in turn, was superseded by the duel. The duel is much higher than a fist fight, because the element of law comes in. But the duel was outgrown. Men had risen to courts, and as men have increased in virtue, courts are not used so much. Men are learning to forbear and forgive. Now, if war should show any signs of coming under the same principle, what sane man can believe the principle will break down here, where it has not in any other case? It will not. It cannot. Evolution does not break down! It is God operating, and when God begins, he finishes. But war has come under the principle. It has gone a long way under it. Once wars were the normal state of society. Now all agree they are abnormal and peace is normal. Once wars were continuous and peace occasional. Now peace is continuous and war occasional. The occasions are growing further and further apart all the time. Once war was the profession of all able-bodied men, except the priests. In the United States peace is the profession of everybody and soldiering thought less and less of as a trade. Once war was unregulated; now, there are a hundred humane laws, the two Hague Conferences having added many new ones to those which had already gradually grown up with the years. Once nations freely made wars for pillage and plunder. Today no nation would think of such a thing or dare carry it out if she did. A war today must at least have the semblance of rights defended or justice sought as an excuse. Once every dispute was settled by war. Now fully one-third of international disputes are put out of the zone where war is possible by existing arbitration treaties. And he who reads can see that the peace talk today is at least holding its own, and gradually displacing the war talk. Shall the law of evolution in this regard stop short here, let us ask again, when it has fulfilled itself in every other spiritual principle? Shall God fail here after having gone so wonderfully far? Who can think·so, especially today, when some think they even catch glimpses of that reign of law that is to supersede war?

THE TOASTMASTER: The next toast is "Woman's Part in the Promotion of Internationalism." It might have been entitled, "Woman's Part in Every Good Work." A good many American women have contributed to internationalism by taking foreign husbands. This topic is to be discussed by Mrs. May Wright Sewall of Boston, Massachusetts, a famous American woman.

WOMAN'S PART IN THE PROMOTION OF INTER-NATIONALISM

ABSTRACT

MRS. MAY WRIGHT SEWALL

The task before me is not easy. It is to pack the contents of a full wardrobe trunk into a diminutive suitcase. Were it possible to say something that has not been said during the previous sessions of this Congress, in which successive speakers have followed so closely upon one another, that only the last in each day's procession has escaped with ungrazed heels, that new word is what I should wish to say.   But as more than all has already been said, I can only hope to give a new form to some small fragment.

Although I appear in this Congress as the special delegate of the National Council of Women of the United States, as well as the Chairman of the Peace and Arbitration Committee of the International Council of Women, it is only the latter body that I shall attempt to represent.

What is the International Council of Women?   When and where was it formed?   What is its object?

It was founded in March, 1888, in the city of Washington. It is composed at the present time of the National Councils of Women of twenty-two countries.   These National Councils aggregate a membership estimated at between six and seven millions of women.   The object of the International Council as first announced, was to create an agency through which women of different countries might become acquainted with one another, since only in becoming acquainted did it seem possible to replace ignorance by mutual intelligence, and prejudice by reciprocal good will.

The first ten years of the Council's life were spent simply in getting acquainted, and in finding the other nations who wished to become acquainted with the nations that had founded the Council, and with one another.   This business of getting acquainted had attained a stage which enabled the Council in 1899. when its second quinquennial meeting was held in London, to adopt, or rather to begin to adopt, lines of work.

The first and only one voted at that time, and voted unanimously by the representatives of the ten National Councils of Women, then constituting the International, was the promotion of peace and arbitration.   The resolution then adopted committed the Council to working for the establishment of peaceful relations among the nations throughout the world everywhere, and by every means in its power.   This broad, inclusive resolution was reaffirmed by the unanimous vote of the nineteen councils of women, constituting the International at the time of its third quinquennial, which was held in Berlin in 1904.

At the fourth quinquennial reunion, held in Toronto, the same resolution was reaffirmed by the votes of the representatives of the twenty-two councils then and now in the International Council. Since 1899, beginning even before the quinquennial of that year, the Council had, through its Committee on Peace and Arbitration, attempted to promote internationalism by all friendly means; by annual executive meetings, held in the capitals of the different countries belonging to the Council; by maintaining headquarters at various international expositions; with most success at the Columbian Exposition in Chicago in 1893, the exposition at Paris in 1900, the Pan-American at Buffalo in 1901, and the Louisiana Purchase Exposition at St. Louis in 1904.

The Council stands pledged to the removal of prejudice, national and racial, and to the education of children, youth and the general public, in a proper estimate of what the different nations have successively contributed to the world's wealth and joy.

We are told that we must appeal to the hard-headed business man, and some members of our committee give an almost exclusive attention to the discussion of war and peace from the industrial and economic points of view.

As it is the policy of the International Council to work with all the agencies already organized for the promotion of peace in the different countries, the methods vary, according to the judgment, the ability, and taste of the representative of each of the National Councils, and according to the local conditions which they meet in the countries where they live. But in all these countries there are mothers and nurseries, and one part of our work is to remove from the nurseries all toys that bring into the child's mind the thought of military pomp and show, of warfare, with its contentions and its glories.

The National Council of our own country in 1895 began to attempt to modify and improve the character of the histories taught in our schools. We are still working in all countries, to endeavor to reduce the arrogance and excessive esteem of school children for their own land, and to increase their appreciation of the qualities of all other lands.

My own feeling is that in the United States the two most pressing needs are: two books; one a school history which can be studied with equal satisfaction by children in all sections of the United States. The theory that what is nearest must be first known by the child, has been so exaggerated in working it out, that the local map of the municipality or of the country township has been so large, and so much time has been spent in teaching every detail connected with it, that it is possible that the child, seeing a map covering an entire page of its geography devoted to his town, and all of Europe crowded into another page, shall get wrong ideas of their relative importance.

We also need in our country a book that shall teach the story of our industrial development, in connection with the story of the successive tides of immigration, through which alone this development has come about.

It is most inconsistent, and to a very large degree futile, for us to meet in peace congresses here and discuss with some degree of respect the great nations, and do nothing to abate the mutual ignorance and consequent mutual dislike, not to say hatred, of the representatives of the different races in the different cities in which we live. I sometimes hear peace workers deploring the admixture of so much sentiment with our peace work.

Why decry sentiment? Sentiment is not only much more universal, because much more spontaneous than sound judgment and trained reason, but it is infinitely more potent. I wish to increase sentiment; especially the sentiments that come only as the product of training the qualities of appreciation, power for admiration, for recognition and for gratitude.

To a large degree this seems to me woman's part of the work, but women are good organizers. There is probably no merely philanthropic society of men in the world better organized or more efficiently conducted than the Women's Christian Temperance Union, of which I am not a member, and therefore can mention it with no personal vanity.

The organizations that compose the National Council of Women of the United States include large bodies, thoroughly organized, local groups being brought into county, county into State, State

into national organizations. There are societies for mutual protection, for industrial advancement, including from thirty thousand to one hundred and fifty thousand members in our National
Council, which in their protective philanthropic work, collect and
expend hundreds of thousands of dollars annually. The ability
that women have already shown in organization should, from my
point of view, be made use of by the peace societies of our own country, who have the means with which to carry on organizations.

Our council work for peace and arbitration has always been done
at the expense of the individuals conducting it. So long as this
continues it must, of course, be very inadequate, because the
business of getting acquainted with people who live at long distances from one another, is one involving the exchange of frequent
visits and still more frequent correspondence. The appropriation per annum, made to the committee of which I am chairman,
is thirty shillings! I should be loath to confess this humiliating
fact, were women the purse holders of the world. I hope that by
mentioning it here some of the foundations now having millions
at their command, may see in the International Council an agency,
which wisely used, would be a most able auxiliary in the execution of their own purposes.

THE TOASTMASTER: The last toast on the program is "Internationalism as a Science." The name of La Fontaine is famous
in both hemispheres. It is especially dear to every boy who ever
tried to learn French. This toast will be responded to by Senator Henri La Fontaine, of Belgium.

INTERNATIONALISM AS A SCIENCE

HENRI LA FONTAINE

Internationalism as a science? Science is a method by which
the causes and the effects of kindred facts are discovered and determined. The facts we call internationalism happened about half
a century ago. More and more since 1840, the word "Internationalism" is applied to gatherings, organizations, institutions. It

was tried to find scientifically the origin of this movement and circumstances by which it was furthered.

Transportation has been the great and powerful factor: steam and electricity were the magicians, and railroads, steamers, automobiles, telegraphs and telephones were their tools. Transportation became rapid, secure, cheap: letters, commodities, persons in growing numbers traveled over the earth. Travel became a need and a pleasure.

Men of all races, religions, languages were obliged to intermix, their interests became international. Societies and bureaus, conferences and congresses were founded to discuss these material and moral interests.

Curiously, the first governmental conventions had for their aim the improvement of postal, telegraphic, land and maritime transportation and the improvement of our geodetic knowledge of the earth.

Since, in all the domains of human culture, congresses were held: more than two thousand until the end of 1910; more than eight hundred during the last decade, and one hundred and thirty four in 1910. There exist more than three hundred international permanent institutions.

What should now be done? The conclusion is obvious: improve, keep on improving the means of transportation; shorten more and more distances on land and on sea, render them as instantaneous as possible, as it was done for wireless telegraphy and as the aeroplane will perhaps do it in the near future; bring men close to men! Men who know one another are intended to love one another.

On the other hand, let us render internationalism more conscious. The most men engaged in international organizations ignore that other men are engaged in similar organizations to realize similar aims of international understanding. In the committees of these international institutions, each country's delegates are, of course, the cleverest men in the various branches of knowledge and activity: they are truly the upper ten thousand. To bring these men together was the aim of the Central office of International Associations which was created at Brussels in 1907, and which convoked in 1910 the first World's Congress of International Associations: one hundred and thirty six associations sent delegates and more than four hundred members were present. The reports made and the resolutions adopted were of the highest value. Truly it can be said that the sessions of this Congress constitute the intellectual parliament of men, the great consultative body of mankind.

The first session was, unfortunately, quite European. Its second session ought to be mainly American. It should take place on America soil. It is a necessary condition of progress that the best men of the new world should come in closer touch with the best men of the Old World.

Emigration, perhaps more than war, has deprived the old, historic countries of their most energetic and fittest sons, to build the progressive and wealthy people you are on this side of the Atlantic. You are, for us Europeans, the beloved brotherland. Do not forget that Europe is always and will still remain for you the beloved Motherland. Europe is now for the New World what Greece was for Europe. Europe has liberated Greece; America has to liberate Europe from its burdens, its prejudices, its hatreds. It is your duty, it is your highest duty to reconcile outside your borders the peoples you have reconciled within your borders.

But to reconcile the peoples, tribunals, parliaments and codes are not the most effective means. Not even the exchange of commodities and persons are sufficient factors. It is the intercourse of ideas, the same intellectual needs, the same ideals which unite men more than all other ties.

We have all—we should all have what I would call our elective international fatherlands: lawyers, physicians, astronomers, all over the world, are more attracted one by another than they are attracted by their own countrymen. All these international fatherlands have now their own parliaments, their international congresses. In these congresses, it is needful that men of all countries should attend as delegates of their compatriots engaged in the same studies, researches, professions or industries. In such gatherings, true brotherhood is fostered. Indeed international congresses and international associations are all peace congresses and peace societies.

Now, you can understand the greatness and the importance of the world's congresses of international associations. Now you are aware of the necessity to organize its second session on American soil. For indeed the American people is at present the true international people; it is the elected people which alone can further internationalism and transform all of the peoples of the earth into a family of nations—a brotherhood of men—an international people.

EIGHTH SESSION

Saturday Morning, May 6, at Ten O'clock

Hon. John Hayes Hammond, Presiding Officer

CHAIRMAN HAMMOND: Ladies and Gentlemen: Mr. Marburg does not wish to take up any time in introducing the chairman today. He told me to start right in, and my remarks will be brief.

The topic is "The Interest which Business Men have in the Peace Movement." Business men have an interest, both humane and pecuniary, in the peace movement, but nevertheless I believe that the great majority of business men do not favor disarmament or even a reduction in armament on the part of the nations to which they belong, unless accompanied by similar action on the part of the other governments of the world.

Indeed, I believe on the contrary that the average business man advocates the increase of armament so far as it is essential to the defense of his country. The business man believes that he does not evince a warlike spirit in this attitude, but is merely taking what he regards, from a business point of view, as ordinary precautions. The constant aim of men to conduct a business, in whatever line they may be engaged, is to obtain the minimum cost by the elimination of unnecessary operating expenses, and therefore business men regard war as a waste not only of life but of the revenues of a nation. They see that while war imposes onerous and unnecessary burdens on a nation there is but little change made in the relative strength of the powers. Business men cannot reconcile the altruistic endeavors of the present generation to conserve the natural resources of the country for the use of succeeding generations with the present great debt which is being piled up as a burden for posterity because of militarism.

Business men recognize the interdependence of the nations of the world, that the prosperity of a foreign nation develops in their markets the sale of the products of other nations, while impoverished treasuries and the condition of their people practically close those markets to foreign exploitation. Business men recognize the advantage in foreign trade of establishing amity among nations, and therefore are heartily in sympathy with the efforts of President Taft and Secretary Knox to establish a permanent tribunal for the judicial settlement of international disputes. Commercial relations between countries, especially when such relations are intimate and extensive, they believe make for peace and are not, as sometimes charged by opponents of the dollar diplomacy, provocative of war.

Business men are, as I have said, strenuous advocates of attaining economical results. They abjure wasted energy or wasted revenues. They see what can be realized through reclamation enterprises in agriculture, through the improvement and the extension of the navigability of our rivers and the building of a great mercantile marine. They see the amelioration of the conditions that might be secured for the community in the maintenance of eleemosynary institutions and in the provision of an old age pension system through the diversion of the present profligate expenditure of money for armed peace into these more profitable channels of industry and philanthropy. While unfortunately the peace men of the country leave to others the educational work in connection with this great peace movement—and in this I must admit they are remiss in the discharge of their civic duties—I am confident that when practicable measures are submitted they will zealously co-operate with you self sacrificing, indefatigable advocates of international peace. They appreciate your efforts and they congratulate you and mankind upon the results already achieved. I now have the pleasure of introducing Mr. John Ball Osborne, the chief of the bureau of trade relations of the Department of State.

HOW COMMERCE PROMOTES PEACE

JOHN BALL OSBORNE

My topic of "How Commerce Promotes Peace" might logically be reversed to read "How Peace Promotes Commerce," for commerce is completely dependent upon peace. The timidity of capital is proverbial; the mere suggestion of business disturbances frightens it into hiding-places from which it can be coaxed only when it is convinced that the danger is past. International commerce, representing as it does today the largest investment of capital in the world, with an approximate annual valuation of thirteen and a half billion dollars ($13,500,000,000), is extremely sensitive to whatever influences encourage or discourage capital. So long as peace prevails commerce flourishes and grows apace, registering in its development the growth of the wealth and prosperity of the trading countries; but the moment that rumors of coming war circulate commerce begins to seek new channels where it will be least exposed to attack, and, with the outbreak of hostilities, it dwindles rapidly. No matter how extensive and powerful the naval and military establishments may be which offer their protection, commerce is never sufficiently reassured to thrive while hostilities last. Thus it is that peace is vitally necessary to commerce.

Modern international commerce is very unlike that of earlier times. The student of history, in considering the influence of commerce on peace among nations, is apt to draw illustrations from the past where commerce has apparently furnished the provocation for war. This was particularly true under the old policy of colonial conquest and colonization pursued for several centuries by the leading European nations; at first by Spain and Portugal and later by England and France. Under this predatory system of commerce distant colonies, acquired by discovery or conquest, were exploited mercilessly and their resources drained with the sole purpose of increasing the wealth and power of the mother country, regardless of the welfare of the colonial possessions. Naturally the struggle for commercial supremacy based on such a selfish system resulted in a series of bloody and exhausting wars.

But today there are no new fields for colonial conquest; nor are there any extensive territories that remain unexplored. Practically the entire world is partitioned and the boundaries of the various political entities are well established and recognized by all civilized powers. Moreover, the spirit of conquest is no longer rampant; but has given way to the spirit of forbearance and mutual conciliation. Under these conditions commerce has become an eminently peaceful pursuit, mutually beneficial to the nations engaged therein. In fact, international commerce is the paramount power in the civilized world, and it furnishes the subject-matter of most of the questions that require consideration in the foreign relations of the various governments. Commercial diplomacy, therefore, has taken the place of the old political diplomacy, which means that the influences that make for peace are in control in the Foreign Offices of the world.

Modern commerce rests fairly and squarely upon the broad and equitable principles of reciprocity. Consequently, when we consider commerce as an agency in promoting peace we must look beyond the selfish viewpoint and narrow horizon of the old mercantilists or perhaps of even the modern ultra-protectionists and consider the movement of imports as well as of exports in our trade relations with foreign countries, for it is the principle of mutuality of trade interests that constitutes the best safeguard for the preservation of peace among trading nations.

By this reasoning we arrive at the basic proposition that the closer the commercial ties the better the outlook for permanent peace. It is obvious, I think, that the closer and more numerous the ties created between two nations by commercial relationship, the greater will be the reluctance on the part of either to begin a war against the other. These commercial ties make the damages possible by war so much greater than any gains derivable from it that the love of peace and the horror of war are both intensified, and thus expanding commerce furnishes an increasing security against war.

It may be of interest to take note of some of the various commercial ties which bind modern nations in a community of interest and a state of interdependence. Such a study of trade relations should include more than the movement of imports and exports of merchandise, although this is of course the largest item in the equation of international indebtedness. It should take account also of the navigation movement; the international railway traffic; cable and telegraphic communication between nations; the financial investments by citizens of one country in another country; the returns from these investments flowing from the debtor country to the creditor country; the remittances of money made by immigrants to families and friends in the fatherland, and numerous minor elements which enter into the general business relations between nations.

What we may term extraterritorial investments of capital constitute one of the most important phases of the business relations between modern nations. Although primarily classifiable under the head of finance, these interests are closely linked to commerce, for the investment of foreign capital usually promotes commerce between the lending and the borrowing country, particularly as regards the supply of machinery and other materials required in the industrial enterprises for which the foreign capital is employed. An eminent economist has said that "a cosmopolitan loan fund exists which runs everywhere as it is wanted, and as the rate of interest tempts it." Everyone knows, however, that money is too cautious to run into any foreign country unless peaceful conditions prevail there and are likely to continue. The foreign investments of capital among the nations reach a gigantic total, probably in the neighborhood of $40,000,000,000, of which Great Britain is represented by at least $15,000,000,000; Germany and France each by $8,000,000,000; and the United States by $1,750,000,000, of which at least $750,000,000 are placed in Mexico and $300,000,000 in Canada.

The international exhibitions, which are held at frequent intervals in all the leading countries of the world, are another effective means of extending international commerce and, at the same time, promoting the cause of peace. Take for example the International Exposition at Turin which is now in progress. Our Congress appropriated the sum of $130,000, which has enabled the United States to be officially represented with a creditable building of its

own. The industrial exhibits by American citizens at Turin
will surely lead to a gratifying extension of the sales of American
products in that part of the world and, what is far more important
the already friendly relations between the two nations will become
even more cordial than hitherto, for the participation of the United
States is highly appreciated by the Italian government and people.

The numerous international congresses that are held in various
countries each year, exercise the same salutary influence for peace.
They bring together leaders of thought and action in many countries and send them away inspired by the spirit of mutual conciliation and with a better understanding respecting the viewpoints
of the different nationalities represented at the congress.   There
were no less than twenty international congresses held at Brussels in 1910 in connection with the International Exposition.   The
moral atmosphere of some of these international congresses often
foreshadows, perhaps faintly but yet unmistakably, a universal
brotherhood of man.   I participated in such a gathering at London last summer—the International Congress of Chambers of
Commerce held under the auspices of the London Chamber of
Commerce.   It was attended by 450 delegates representing every
commercial power of any consequence in the world.   Great
Britain and her colonies sent representatives from 58 commercial
bodies; Germany from 17; France from 16; Austria from 12; and
so-on.   The American delegation at London brought forward
for consideration the proposal of Secretary of State Knox for the
establishment of a permanent court of arbitral justice for the
settlement of all disputes between nations.   This most important
proposition will undoubtedly be the subject of favorable action
by the International Congress of Chambers of Commerce to be
held·at Boston in 1912.

Another influence that is calculated to contribute to the cause
of peace relates to the increasing tourist movement between countries, favored by the improvement of the facilities for traveling.
This movement is rapidly breaking down the barriers that separate the different nations and the result is better trade relations
and closer international friendships. In recent years there have
been several instances where large parties of the business men of

one country have made a systematic tour of the commercial and industrial centers of foreign countries with which they were engaged in trade. A party of 100 business men from various parts of Germany made an excursion of this kind to Turkey in 1908. This example was followed by a party of 150 Roumanian business men. In 1909 a Turkish commercial delegation of 245 persons, representing the various branches of commerce in the leading cities of Turkey, visited the principal commercial and manufacturing centers of Austria-Hungary. It is reported that large orders were placed as a result of the visit. In 1908 a party of American business men, delegates from chambers of commerce on the Pacific Coast, visited Japan and were handsomely entertained by the Japanese Chambers of Commerce. A return visit to the United States was made a year or so ago by members of the Japanese commercial bodies. This exchange of visits by representative business men engaged in manufacturing for the commerce between the two countries has already been productive of good results in cementing the friendship between the United States and Japan. In the latter part of 1910 representatives of several Chambers of Commerce in the Pacific Coast States made a tour of China and were everywhere accorded a warm welcome. They are now making plans for the return visit which leading business men of China expect to make to the United States this summer. This exchánge of visits will undoubtedly result in increased trade and more cordial international relations. The Boston Chamber of Commerce, always progressive and always on the right side of every great moral question, is now making arrangements for a visit to European countries by a party of 100 American business men. The double purpose of the trip is to bring about closer industrial and commercial relations between the United States and European countries and to extend official invitations, on behalf of the Boston Chamber of Commerce, to European Chambers of Commerce to attend the International Congress of Chambers of Commerce which will be held in Boston in 1912. Everyone will admit that whoever goes on a business tour of this kind goes on a mission that contributes directly to the cause of international peace.

The principle that intimate commercial relations are an effective guarantee of peace is well illustrated by our trade relations with Great Britain, Germany, and France, the three best customers of the United States in Europe. Notwithstanding the comparatively limited area of the United Kingdom the total trade of the United States with that country amounted last year to more than $776,000,000, or 40 per cent of our total trade with Europe and about 24 per cent of that with the entire world. Of this vast amount our imports represented $271,000,000, or just about one-third of our total imports from Europe, while our exports were in excess of $500,000,000,or about 45 per cent of our total exports to Europe.

As regards Germany, our total trade was in the neighborhood of $450,000,000, of which Germany's imports of American products represented $300,000,000. Our total trade with France amounted last year to $250,000,000, of which our imports were somewhat in excess of our exports.

But, as I have already said, in order to obtain the true international perspective, we must look beyond the exchange of commodities, great as it is. Mr. George Paish, Editor of the *Statist* has recently estimated that the fixed investments of foreign capital in the United States reach a total of $6,000,000,000, of which Great Britain has furnished $3,500,000,000; Germany $1,000,000,000, and France $500,000,000. On the other hand, the fixed investments of American capital in England, Germany, and France, are relatively small. Another important consideration is that American tourists spend annually in Europe, particularly in the three countries mentioned, enormous sums of money, often estimated as high as $200,000,000.

The great mutual interdependence between the United States and the powers above mentioned is revealed by a study of the statistics of the commercial movement. England requires our cattle, wheat flour and other breadstuffs, meat products, raw cotton, copper, refined oil and unmanufactured tobacco. We need British chemicals, colonial India rubber and diamonds, tin, raw wool, certain classes of cutlery and machinery, and certain grades of cotton and woolen textiles, to supplement our own production.

Germany is vitally dependent upon our raw cotton and copper, and to a large extent on our breadstuffs, lard, refined oil, and un-manufactured tobacco.   On the other hand, we are absolutely dependent on Germany for potash as a fertilizer required in our agriculture to restore to the soil the properties that have been taken from it.   We require her colonial rubber and we find Germany an excellent source from which to supplement our requirements in cotton knit goods, laces, and toys.

France leans heavily on the United States for raw cotton, copper, refined oil, and to some extent for agricultural implements. Reciprocally, we are dependent upon France for many articles of high luxury, such as art works, laces and embroideries, silks, and champagne.

An endless procession of vessels is employed to carry this vast commerce to and fro across the Atlantic Ocean, and hundreds of thousands of producers in each country are dependent for their livelihood and the support of their families upon the uninterrupted continuance of this flourishing commerce.

The prosperity of the United Kingdom, Germany, and France, is our prosperity.   Anything that cripples their purchasing power must inevitably react adversely on our selling power and industrial welfare.   Similarly, whatever cripples their productive agencies must react unfavorably on the interests of the American consumers.   Industrial depression, financial disturbance, and popular distress with any one of them is sure to be reflected, sooner or later, in this country, and *vice versa*, as was demonstrated abundantly three or four years ago when the financial crisis in the United States had its reflex action in Europe.   These simple economic truths, predicated on the solidarities of commerce, show how desirable it is that the spirit of mutual conciliation should prevail in international relations.

CHAIRMAN HAMMOND: I now take pleasure in introducing Captain Charles C. Yates, of the United States Coast and Geodetic Survey.

THE IMPORTANCE OF THE GEOGRAPHIC DELIM-
ITATION OF INTERNATIONAL BOUNDARIES

CHARLES YATES

PRELIMINARY REMARK

For twenty-four hours, after I was informed that I was to present my subject at this meeting of your Congress, and after your Executive Secretary had drawn in a long breath as a fitting climax to the effort of writing down the somewhat ponderous title of my discussion, my mental machinery was engaged in an endeavor to manufacture, what might appear to you, a respectable subterfuge for connecting my subject with the topic of business which, according to the program, is the theme of the discussions of this session.

But being an engineer and not a lawyer, nothing would come forth from my mental factory except the axiomatic expressive expression that "business is business." Which means, if it means anything, that business is business.

But in the twenty-fifth hour, my long-sought subterfuge came into my mind, and I now present it for what it is worth.

If business is business, under what conditions does business cease to be business? And when we answer this question, we find that one of those conditions always exists when business reaches an international boundary line, *especially*, if its geographic delimitation is marked, as is that of our own country, by a great tariff wall. And you all know, that this wall presents an insurmountable obstacle to you business men when you attempt to extend your business into foreign realms, either going or coming, particularly the latter.

And having thus logically established a character for my theme that makes it appropriate to this occasion, I will now take up the *real* subject of my discussion.

INTRODUCTION

This brief discussion of the importance of the geographic delimitation of international boundaries, as a factor in the maintenance of peace, is presented from the point of view of a "geographic surveyor," who feels that the subject could have been better put before you by others in the Service to which he belongs; the notable example being the Honorable Otto H. Tittmann, Superintendent of the Coast and Geodetic Survey, who is also the representative of our country on the Commission now engaged on the demarcation of the boundary between Canada and the United States.

PAST HISTORY

It is thought that the meaning and importance of our theme in relation to peace, may be made evident without going into the history of the causes of past wars, and near wars, except in so far as it is covered by a brief mention of that still vivid incident of the Venezuelan boundary controversy.

President Cleveland in speaking of the end of the Venezuelan boundary controversy, has said, "the determination of the boundary between these two countries has (now) been fixed— perhaps in strict accord with justice—*but in all events finally and irrevocably.*"

DEDUCTIONS

And this quotation expresses the whole aim and object of this discussion, namely, the calling of attention to the great importance of final and incontestible geographic information in relation to international boundaries, whether this information be obtained prior to the beginning of such a controversy, and thus forestall a possible war as is our hope for the future, or whether, as so often has been the case in the past, it marks the end of a war where *might*, instead of right, is the determining factor in the establishing the boundary line.

FUTURE HISTORY

To dwell further on the lessons of the past in relation to our subject, would be to state what is already obvious; besides it is the future in which we, of the peace movement, are particularly interested.

To obtain a very convincing impression of the dangers to future peace which now lie hidden in boundary disputes, it is only necessary to cast our mind's eye over the maps of Asia, Africa, and South America and then pick out many a boundary which may occupy an evil place in the future history of the world, as the cause of a war.

And if we select for purposes of illustration, the great Chinese Empire, we find, that not only do her practically unmarked and geographically undefined boundaries, extend over the tremendous length of more than eight thousand miles, but that also, she has for her frontier neighbors the Asiatic possessions under the jurisdiction of the British, the French, the Germans, the Portuguese, the Russians, and the Japanese.

Speaking parenthetically, but with all seriousness, it would appear from this last statement, that the possibilities of China for war with the various countries of Europe would furnish these great powers an excellent future opportunity of demonstrating their claim, that a great army and a great navy are the best guarantees of peace. And it would also appear that it would furnish us, of the peace movement, a great opportunity of demonstrating the sincerity of our professions, by directing a part of our energies towards the elimination of those boundary disputes, which are likely to furnish the excuses for these potential wars which not only threaten the peace of China, but also the peace of the nations who are neighbors on the frontiers of that empire.

SUGGESTIONS

To dwell further on the subject of future wars that may be caused by boundary disputes, would be again to state what is already obvious.

And this directs our discussion to its next and final stage, which relates to the possibilities for constructive work that would make for peace by providing means for just and incontestible geographic determinations of international boundaries.

Knowing the exact object which it is desired to obtain, many different methods of procedure for accomplishing the result may be suggested to many different minds.

But from my point of view, as an individual and not as an official of the government, the most feasible suggestion is that of the establishment of an official International Geographic Institution which shall have for *one* of its main functions the gathering and compilation of authoritative geographic information relating to international boundaries.

As just indicated, the work of such an Institute would not be devoted entirely to those things which relate immediately to war and peace.

And consequently, our project would have the very practical advantage of gaining support from various national geographic bureaus which can not help recognizing the value of such an institution.

But however tempting it may be to me as a geographer, to discuss its other functions, it would be out of place to interject here more than a general statement on this point.

This International Geographic Institute, besides its boundary duties, would have other practical functions, such as providing for systematic geographic work, relating particularly to things that can be done most economically and efficiently by international coöperation.

These might include for example, the charting of the international waters of the high seas, and also the interchange of other navigational charts between the governments of the world, thus avoiding the great waste of overlapping energy and expense that now exists in this respect.

As it is now, with the very notable exception of the international committee engaged on the construction of a map of the world on a scale of one part in one million, the world is dependent for international geographic information on the splendid, but unsystematic efforts of nations, geographic societies, and individuals, who generously place the results of their geographic labors at the disposal of *all* who can read and understand that truly peaceful and truly great international language spoken by maps and charts.

RUFUS CHOATE ON BOUNDARY DISPUTES

This ends the discussion of my subject as originally planned, but as of necessity it has been rather technical, I can not resist the temptation of illustrating how it so often happens that boundaries are the cause of quarrels, by recounting an incident which was connected with a boundary dispute between two states of New England.

The great lawyer, Rufus Choate, represented one side of the question, and in his argument he referred to the elusive and unsatisfactory character of the original description of the boundary in the following scornful language:

"A boundary line between two sovereign states described by a couple of stones near a pond and a buttonwood sapling in a village! Why, the commissioners might as well have defined it as starting from a bluejay, thence to a swarm of bees in hiving time, and thence to five hundred foxes with firebrands tied to their tails."

CONCLUSION

As a practical engineer, whose training and experience have taught him to direct his energies towards obtaining those concrete results which can be accomplished in the present, I wish to say that I believe that this thing which I have proposed to you can be done. And when it is done, I believe it can be pointed out by us, of the Baltimore Peace Congress, as another one of those steps which, according to the words of warning of President Taft spoken to this Congress, must mark the progress of all practical peace movements.

CHAIRMAN HAMMOND: I may tell you a little discussion that I had on the subject of the armament of China a few years ago with the late Chinese ambassador, the Hon. Wu Ting Fang.

After telling me of the large sums which China contemplated spending in the development of her army and navy, I said, "That is truly deplorable." We Western nations regard it as money wasted, and from a selfish point of view wish that it could be obviated. If China could spend the money in the development of her natural resources and trade, she would open great markets of the world in which all Western nations would participate." He said, "That is quite true." Then I said, "Why not, following the example of the relation of Switzerland to the powers of Europe, why not reverse the position and have the great nations of the world protect China and obviate the necessity of her spending all this money for this insensate armament, because she will be a great power in this way and will threaten the nations." His answer was, "That is good policy, good diplomacy and good politics; but could we trust you Western nations?" I believe before long that with such meetings as this we could substantiate our claim that the great nations could be trusted and allow China and the other nations yet in the process of civilization to become a part of our great commercial development.

I now have the pleasure to introduce the next speaker, Mr. U. J. Ledoux:

THE BUSINESS MAN IN WORLD POLITICS

ABSTRACT

U. J. LEDOUX

Opening with the statement that if the commercial and industrial men would say the word, and do some of the work, there would be no more wars, and fully agreeing with President Taft that what is most needed in the Peace movement is better organization, Mr. Ledoux, an ex-American consul to Canada, France and Austria, in charge of the Department of Commercial Associations of the World Peace Foundation of Boston, said that over a year of professional study of internal conditions, both here and in Europe, had convinced him that what was most needed was the coöperation of commercial and industrial men in the application of more scientific methods of study, organization and general work—in short, a Taylor system of efficiency engineering.

The speaker said that he made the statement advisedly and without trembling—even in the presence of the Chairman, one of the most efficient engineers in his line the world had ever known, Mr. John Hays Hammond.

To him the purely sentimentalistic peace movement was an immense dove, all wings and no feet, which voraciously snapped at passing multi-colored butterfly-resolutions and then contentedly preened itself in the hot-air currents of its own preachlets and talklets.

But the dove was being brought closer to earth by such business men as Mr. Edwin Ginn and Andrew Carnegie, and, as announced by them and their lieutenants, feet were being grafted on the dear old bird. He was especially pleased at the tentative plans outlined at the Congress by Messrs. Ginn, Scott, and La Fontaine, which showed that we were measurably near the general application of efficiency engineering to the whole peace problems, to which solution the constructive and administrative ability of the commercial and industrial elements were of the greatest importance.

Requested to also represent the World Federation League, at the Congress, he cited the group of mainly business men, who were instrumental in the unanimous passage by Congress of the Resolution authorizing a Peace Commission as one of the best examples of what could be done by that strata of world society.

Mr. Ledoux opened his address with a happy quotation that "If men would permit their minds, like their children, to be associated freely together—if they could agree to meet one another with smiles and frankness instead of suspicion and defiance, the common stock of wisdom and of happiness would be centupled. Probably those very men who hate each other most and whose best husbandry is to sow briars and thistles in each other's path, would, if they had met and conversed familiarly, have been ardent and inseparable friends."

He applauded at the organizing ability and good sense of the promoters of the Congress, which had brought together the representatives of so many races, creeds, and ideas, at the common communion table of pacifism. For, as stated by a distinguished orator of the previous evening, Senator La Fontaine, tribunals, parliaments and codes are not the most effective means to reconcile people. Not even the interchange of commodities and persons are sufficient factors. It is the intercourse of ideas, the same intellectual needs, the same ideals, which, more than any other ties, unite men.

In a general survey of the progress of humanity, the speaker showed that from the appearance of man on earth, the tendencies have continually been in an ascendent line: the federation of mankind. By stages, has man evolved world organization from the establishment of family ties to those of tribes, clans, hordes, provinces and states, to end, thanks to alliance between provinces and states, into the creation of great nations, and in federations of nations, such as the British Empire, the United States, the German and Austrian Empire and the Pan-American Union.

Probably more than a century ago, man was of the village, within which was confined his wants and passions. The customs were local, the moneys varied in types and values, the roads were bristling with tolls and the stranger considered an unknown enemy or nearly so: Man was of the village.

But gradually was a national spirit evolved through political, social and commercial necessity and laws, moneys and customs made uniform and the tolls abolished: Man was of the nation.

Steam, electricity and a thousand other inventions have bound man to humanity with indissoluble ties of mutual interests.

These are the ties which can evolve a proper spirit of nationalism which, without shirking national and imperial duties, will assume a certain share of humanity's international responsibility.

This means strong, independent nations united through a proper spirit of brotherhood, united in one effort, the happiness of mankind.

The world was slowly but surely becoming divided into strata of interest instead of into races and creeds, and the one most pregnant of hope for the Peace of the world was certainly that of commerce.

With proper organization, business men have been able to secure for the world peaceful, systematic and rapid commercial organization through Chambers of Commerce, Boards of Trade, Merchants' Clubs, Manufacturers' Associations, etc., they could certainly secure for themselves and the world a relief from the heavy cost of international disorganization.

The speaker showed that though we may be far in advance of Europe as regards business systems and the combination of private and corporate interests for both public and private advantages, we are far from being as advanced as Europe in commercial associations for the protection of mutual interests and the advancement of the public welfare.

Britain, Germany, Austria, Belgium, Italy, Switzerland, etc., not only have strong commercial associations that protect the local interests of merchants, but also have very strong federations of Chambers of Commerce, which are generally consulted by the commercial and industrial departments of the Governments on matters within their sphere.

For instance, in Austria, the Chambers are entitled to four members in Parliament. The Chambers of Commerce of Berlin, Hamburg, Bremen, St. Petersburg, Vienna, Copenhagen, The Hague, Brussels, etc., not only control, the Bourses; but, in most cases, are invested with most extraordinary and practical rights of commercial official supervision, such as the Bourse industrial, commercial, vocational schools, building and control of public docks, the building and control, in certain cases, such as Havre and Marseilles, for instance, of telegraphic and telephonic communication, and the building of institutions of learning, connected with the furtherance of industry and commerce.

These, said the speaker, had federated into an International organization called the International Chamber of Commerce. These international organizations, when some plan matures, petition the Governments for a conference of nations. The organizations coöperate, but they don't command; they help but they don't handle the reins of power. Three such conferences have already been held in the matter of bills of exchange, the unification of class customs and the reform of calendar to secure a fixed date for Easter.

The speaker then outlined the international organization and the programs and stated that the Fifth Congress would be held next year in Boston when the question of the judicial settlement of international disputes promises to be one of the principal subjects for discussion.

He invited the largest possible American attendance in order to assure that practical coöperation with the Old World so necessary to international peace.

CHAIRMAN HAMMOND: The next speaker is Mr. Charles Mason Remay, whose subject is "The Bahai Movement and The Occident-Orient Unity."

THE BAHAI MOVEMENT: A TEACHING OF PEACE

CHARLES MASON REMEY

The Third Annual Convention of the Bahais of America, held in Chicago, Illinois, sends greetings to the Third American Peace Congress, assembled in Baltimore, Maryland, with the prayer that wisdom may advance, that all may be illumined, that there be no more wars and strife, that reconciliation and peace be established, that peoples of all religions and races be united, that the countries of this earth become as one land, and that all humanity may abide in unity and in peace.

WORDS OF BAHA'O'LLAH

"We desire but the good of the world, and the happiness of the nations . . . . That all nations should become one in faith, and all men as brothers; that the bonds of affection and unity between the sons of men should be strengthened . . . . These fruitless strifes, these ruinous wars shall pass away and the Great Peace shall come . . . . Let not a man glory in this, that he loves his country; let him rather glory in this, that he loves his kind."

Over half a century ago, before the attention of western thinkers had to any degree been directed toward the problem of universal peace, there was born in the Orient a movement for peace and

brotherhood, the call of which is now being heard in the Occident.

The Bahai movement has for its object not only international
conciliation, as considered from the political and economic view
points, but essentially the unification of the people of all races
and religions along spiritual lines.

Religious and racial hatred has been the chief cause of warfare.
Through the removal of these prejudices the followers of this
movement believe that peace will be established amongst nations.
Through it thousands of Christians, Moslems, Jews, Zoroastrians,
Hindoos, and Buddhists, of every race and nationality, are being
firmly united in the universal brotherhood of man under the
fatherhood of God.

In the month of May, 1844, there arose in Persia a teacher,
calling himself "The Bab," who proclaimed himself to be the
forerunner of "He Whom God would manifest." One who would
shortly appear with spiritual wisdom and power, through whose
teaching would be established the Divine Kingdom of Peace upon
earth. The ministry of "The Bab" lasted six years, and was
followed by his martyrdom, as well as the martyrdom of thousands of his followers, which was brought about by the Moham-
medan clergy upon the charge of heresy.

Shortly after the martyrdom of "The Bab," the promised one,
whose coming he had foretold, appeared in the person of Baha'o-
'llah. Under the most severe persecution Baha'o'llah, together
with some of his followers, was exiled to Turkey in Asia, then to
Turkey in Europe, and later on in 1868 was sent to the town of
Akka, a penal colony situated on the Mediterranean, just north
of Mt. Carmel, in Syria. Here in Akka he lived and taught until
he passed out of this mortal world in the year 1892. He gave his
teachings and spiritual instructions, yet during his ministry his
cause was not explained nor established in the world in general.
To this end Baha'o'llah commanded his followers upon his departure to turn their faces toward his son Adbul-Baha as their spiritual
guide, explainer of his teachings, one who would establish his cause
in the world, and one upon whose shoulders his mantle would fall.

Abdul-Baha, also known as Abbas Effendi, from 1868 until

1908, because of his teaching, was held a state prisoner in the town of Akka. At present he is in Egypt and there is a possibility that he may visit this country of America. He makes but one claim for himself, that of service in the path of God. His name, Abdul-Baha Abbas, means "Abbas the servant of God." He is the spiritual leader of the Bahais, and is their example to be followed in teaching this great faith in the world. He is making the spiritual life of Baha'o'llah possible, and bringing it within the reach of the poeple.

While there have been three teachers in this cause, Baha'o'llah is the central figure, about whom the other two revolve. It is from his name, Baha, that the movement takes its name. "The Bab" and his movement were but introductory to, while Abdul-Baha and his work are explanatory of, the Bahai movement.

This religious teaching is brief and simple. Each of the founders of the great religious systems of the world is looked upon as having been inspired by the one spirit of truth, which is God. The form and letter of the teachings of these various leaders differ because of the differing conditions of humanity to which they ministered, but in spirit each taught the fatherhood of God and the brotherhood of man. In the various religions the fundamental truths are one and the same.

Moreover each of the prophets taught of the coming of a great teacher, and of the establishment of a universal religion. The Jews await the coming of their Messiah, the Christians the coming of the Christ, the Moslems the coming of the Mahdi, the Buddhists the coming of the fifth Buddha, the Zoroastrians the coming of Shah Bahram, and the Hindus the return of Krishma.

The Bahai teach that the spirit of these promised teachers is one and the same, and they believe that in Baha'o'llah was manifested again this one spirit of truth, the Word of God. Therefore in his mission and teaching he has accomplished the hopes of the peoples of all religions. They believe that he was spiritually endowed with the wisdom and understanding necessary to found a new form of religion applicable to the needs of this day, one which will embrace within its fold people of all races and religions, uniting them in one human brotherhood.

The Bahai teaching is in no sense an eclectic philosophy. It is not a theology, nor does it put forward doctrine or dogma. It is essentially a religious faith. It seeks to change man's nature not by enforcing upon him laws from without, but by developing the higher nature of the individual from within.

Amongst the Moslems the Bahai teaching has had a phenomenal spread. The several recent progressive changes in the Islamic world in Persia have only been made possible through the introduction into that country of such progressive thought, and freedom from the superstitions of the past, as the Bahai movement stands for and takes with it wherever it goes. The progressive Moslem finds the Bahai teaching to be quite in accord with the spirit of the Koran and he accepts it as a new testament added thereto.

In like manner the Jew sees in this movement the fulfilment of the hope of the milennial age held out to him in his Bible and realizing this he finds himself at one with the Moslem, and the Christian.

In going farther into the Orient one finds staunch Bahais amongst the remnant of the ancient Zoroastrian faith. These received this message and believed its principles because in their ancient holy literature they find hidden away its simple truths.

Thinking Hindus are also being reached by the Bahai thought, and through its positive principle of action and service in bettering humanity they are working to free themselves from superstition and caste. Thus they are in sympathy with the progress of the world along material and spiritual lines together, whereas formerly their progress was limited because of the negative phase in which Hinduism has been during so many centuries.

The enlightened believer in Gauatama, the Buddah, finds in his own teaching the promise of peace and universal brotherhood on earth which makes it easy for him to detect and recognize the fulfilment of the same in the Bahai movement. To the Buddhist, therefore, the idea of this movement, for the readjustment of earthly conditions and the establishment of peace, is a welcome one.

Of all people, none have taken up the Bahai teaching with more fervor than those scattered here and there, where this message has reached, throughout Christendom. To them it fulfils and accomplishes the hopes of Christianity and they are taking hold of the teaching as a practical power in daily life. They are applying its principles and are holding out a helping hand to their co-workers in various parts of the Orient. Through this spirit of oneness with the Orientals a bond between the East and the West is established, a bond which will strengthen and grow until all peoples Occidental and Oriental will be as one people—until the great universal civilization, which is so rapidly casting its signs before it, shall stand accomplished.

The Bahais have no form of admission to their ranks, nor have they any enrolled membership. They do not form a sect. Those who sympathize with their aims they consider as friends and co-workers. As people work with them, they gradually imbibe the spirit and life inspiring the body of workers until they stand forth as exponents of this new faith. The Bahais have no outward institutions as barriers to differentiate nor to separate them from other people.

Some of the ordnances of this teaching touch upon the following subjects:

Religious Unity. All men are free to believe and to worship as they will, but they are exhorted to unite in faith for only through spiritual unity will mankind attain the highest development.

Tolerance. The Bahais should not separate themselves from people who are not of their belief, nor should they denounce nor antagonize those holding views other than their own. They should mingle freely with all people and show forth their faith through love and service to their fellow men.

Peace. Warfare should be abolished and international questions should be settled by arbitration. In order to facilitate international communication, one language should be chosen from those already existing, or one devised for that purpose.

Government. Representative legislation is most conducive to the welfare of the people. The Bahais should be loyal and law abiding citizens in whatever country they may dwell. They should not glory in that they love their country, but in that they love their kind.

Worship. Prayer supplemented by a pure and useful life in this world form the elements of true worship. Faith without works is not acceptable. Every one should have an occupation which conduces to the welfare of humanity, the diligent pursuance of which is in itself an act of worship.

Marriage. Celibacy and asceticism are discouraged. Man should marry and create a family and live in the world. Monogamy is ·taught.

Resistance. Harshness should be met with gentleness and hatred with love. With these weapons the Bahais will overcome all opposition.

The Church. In this cause there is no priesthood apart from the laity. Each one who receives the spirit should share it with those whom he meets in daily life. All are teachers, teaching is given without money and without price.

Religious Government. "The House of Justice" a central assembly the members of which are selected by general vote, is to preside over the affairs of the Bahai world. Its work has to do with charitable and educational matters and the general welfare of the people.

Temperance. In all matters moderation is to be observed. Man should not use intoxicating liquors as a beverage. The taking of opium and kindred drug habits are most emphatically denounced, and gaming is also forbidden. The use of tobacco is discouraged.

Admonitions forbidding mendicity, slavery, cruelty to animals, and various offences, together with rules regarding public hygiene, education of both sexes and other matters need not here be mentioned, as they are already provided by western civilization, though in the Orient the need for these is very great.

The effect of these ordnances cannot be overestimated. In the Orient, where religion is a far more potent factor in every day life than it is here in the West, religious exhortations and injunctions have inestimable weight in the lives of the masses of the people.

I have made a study of the Bahai movement, would like to add a few words of personal testimony regarding what I have seen amongst the Bahais in many parts of the world.

In Persia, where this movement had its birth, I found that the Bahais had not only overcome the hatred and antipathy which has for centuries existed between Christian, Jew, Zoroastrian and Moslem, but through the uniting spirit of their teaching this previously existing enmity had been replaced by a most binding fraternal spirit.   In the Bahai assemblies all differences of the past had been superseded by the strongest of ties.   In that country these people have suffered much because of the fanaticism of the surrounding people.   Thousands of their members have in the past been massacred, while in the present they are under many difficulties.   As recent as 1901 over one hundred and seventy Bahais were massacred in one town by the Moslems.

In Southern Russia and in Turkistan I have visited assemblies of Bahais.   In these territories the movement is protected by the Russian government, for it is understood that the Bahais stand for peace and are in no way connected with the many revolutionary movements which continually keep those countries in a state of unrest.

In Egypt and Syria, as well as Turkey I have met groups of Bahais working along progressive lines, but in those countries, as well as in Persia, the outward progress of the work is not as great as the unseen progress.   This is due to the prejudice and persecution of the Moslems which often lead to bloodshed.

In India the principal center of the Bahais is in Bombay. There I found many Parsees or Zoroastrians taking part in the work.   In Calcutta Baroda, Allahabad, Agra, Lahore, Poona and other cities there are assemblies and in these meetings Christians, Hindus and Moslems mingle as brothers.

In Burma there is a large Buddhist element amongst the Bahais. Last year I spent some time traveling in that country, and was most hospitably received by the Bahais in several towns and cities.   In Japan I found the Bahai teaching to be attracting some attention and in China too, the movement, to have a beginning.   Here in these United States as well as in Great Britain and Europe, I have visited many assemblies and found the work progressing amongst people of all classes and of varying religious thought.   Being essentially a spiritual movement this teaching appeals alike to the enlightened and to the uncultured as it does to people of various religions, races and nationalities.

Notwithstanding the previous attitude of the religionist, which is usually antagonistic to beliefs other than his own, the moment he becomes imbued with the spirit of the Bahais he no longer limits his interest to the mental confines to which he has been accustomed. He becomes a citizen of the world, freed from national, religious and racial prejudices. This is noticeable in the Occidental Bahai while in the Oriental Bahai it is many times more so, because of the surrounding background of ignorance, superstition and fanaticism against which he stands out emancipated in bold relief.

One who has lived in the Orient and known the Oriental people will at once recognize the importance of the religious factor in bringing about universal peace. It is the religious differences between the Oriental and Occidental which have created the great chasm between eastern and western thought, manners and customs. There being no religious thought in common between the East and West, there is no ground upon which their respective peoples can meet, hence the necessity for a common religion which only can solve the problem. The Bahai movement is working directly to bring about confidence, understanding and unity between the Oriental and the Occidental peoples. Baha'o'llah like all world movers, was far ahead of his time. A universal religion, international arbitration, peace, a universal language, universal suffrage, in fact a universal civilization, with all of its universal institutions, was unthought of by the world when he, over half a century ago first announced these principles. Now the world in general is awaking to the necessity for those very institutions to which thousands of Bahais have borne witness by persecution and martyrdom.

Progress is the resounding chord of this day. Progress in religion is needed more than progress in anything else. The world is now ready for a live and progressive faith of brotherly love which is broad enough to take in every race and every people; a faith which will lead and create progressive thought and progressive institutions; a faith which will actually produce a change in men's natures developing within their souls divine virtues; a religion which does not destroy but which fulfils the religions of the past; a religion free from dogma applicable to all races and conditions, the unique object of which is peace and the universal civilization. Such a faith is the Bahai teaching.

CHAIRMAN HAMMOND: The next speaker whom I wish to present is Dr. Charles E. Beals who was one of the organizers of the Second American Peace Congress at Chicago.

PATRIOTISM IN AN INTERNATIONAL WORLD

CHARLES E. BEALS

Patriotism is a large word—large enough indeed to cover a multitude of bad and good deeds. Many serious charges may be laid, all too justly, at its door. Dr. Johnson declared that patriotism was "the last refuge of a scoundrel." Mr. Emerson hesitated "to employ a word so much abused as *patriotism*, whose true sense is almost the reverse of the popular sense." Daniel Webster, in his day, lamented that a noble word was trailed in the dust. Even a secretary of war can affirm that a "demagogue . . . . is nothing if not loudly and aggressively patriotic." As one considers the follies perpetrated, the national injustices committed, the economic and moral devastation wrought under the name of patriotism, one is tempted to cry out, with Walter Walsh, "'patriotism' is a bait flung out by rogues to catch fools."

In spite of the wicked abuses of the word, however, patriotism stands for some of the finest loyalties, loftiest heroisms and noblest self-sacrifices the world ever has seen. Moreover patriotism plays no small part in the socializing of man. As understood in its crude popular sense, it may not teach the higher branches, but it serves at least as a good primary school teacher in the social education of mankind. And, with a clearer understanding of the possibilities of a new type of patriotism, it is capable of being keyed to service and universal brotherhood. I venture, therefore, to plead for patriotism, albeit for a just patriotism, for a rational patriotism, for a patriotism big enough and fine enough to fit the new conditions and the best thought and the highest ideals of the new day.

I. THE WORLD ALREADY PARTIALLY INTERNATIONALIZED

The patriotism which rightminded men henceforth will be willing to accept must state itself in the terms of an internationalized world. To speak of an internationalized world is not utopianism, not an "iridescent dream" of an improbable, if not impossible, millennium, not rainbow-chasing, but plain prose fact. For the world already is partially internationalized; and the evolution of mankind is headed, and can head, in but one direction, namely, towards a more and more complete internationalization. Ponderous volumes would be required to set forth in detail the progress already registered. But, in a rapid survey, we may hurriedly consider a few of the general forms in which internationalism is embodying itself.

1. We may begin by glancing at some of the unofficial international organizations existing at present. All sorts of learned societies are internationally organized. Scientific truth knows no geographical or political boundary lines. The binomial theorem is as true in Bombay as in Boston. When Japan entered upon the era of enlightenment a proclamation was issued, declaring that "knowledge shall be sought for throughout the whole earth" (DeForest: *Sunrise in the Sunrise Kingdom*, 25). The republic of science is world-embracing. Scientific investigators of all lands are doing team-work together, with microscope and telescope, test-tube and micrometer. Learned men meet together in the annual meetings of their international scientific societies. Professors are exchanged between some of the nations. Oriental students by the thousand are matriculated in American and European universities. Students of all nationalities live together in the Cosmopolitan Clubs. Engineers with their transit and level are at work under every sky, and engineering feats and facts are published in the engineering journals of all civilized lands. Agriculturalists, aviators, penologists, educators, electricians, geographers, linguists, artists, musicians, men of letters, doctors,

philanthropists, statisticians, zoölogists, etc., are banded together in their respective international organizations, and hold annual conferences, first in one land, and then in another. Many of these bodies maintain permanent headquarters and publish regular bulletins.

Labor is becoming more and more internationalized. Over thirty trades are internationally organized. The emblem of the American Federation of Labor is a pair of clasped hands upon a globe. The subdivision of labor makes class dependent upon class, nation upon nation. The mill operatives of Lancashire, England, were brought to the very verge of starvation by our American Civil War. Industrial migration and immigration play no small part in binding together the old world with the new. There is an international society for labor legislation, with sections in each land and publications in the various languages. (Comp. Graham Taylor in *Proceedings of Second National Peace Congress*, 168.) The permanent bureau of this society is at Basel (*American Journal of International Law*, Vol. I, Part II, 821).

Socialism too, is an international movement. It is probably more radical in its direct propaganda for internationalism than any other great organized movement of our day. It exposes the sophistries and wastes and wickednesses of competing and contending nationalisms with unrelenting mercilessness.

Business is coming to be more and more international. Great business enterprises seek world markets. I remember seeing in London, Paris, Lucerne and other European cities, branch-stores of great shoe manufacturing establishments of Brockton, Massachusetts. The International Harvester Company does business in many lands. If war should break out in any part of the world, the harvester business in Chicago would be affected. Even the short Boxer outbreak in China, though it lasted but a few weeks, affected the cotton-mills operatives in Fall River and New Bedford. A gentleman called at our peace office in Chicago not long ago and said, "I have just finished building bridges in Burmah and Egypt. My men are at work on one in St. Petersburg. I can't sell my bridges if war breaks out. So I think I'd better join the peace society and help on its work." I have been informed by a prominent London economist that during our American panic of 1907 the Bank of England came within a few days of suspending because of the financial situation in the United States. The Bank of England sought to obtain relief, at that crisis, from Berlin and Paris and other financial centers, but the great banking institutions of those cities were unable to render any assistance because they too were similarly affected by the American panic. Nor should we overlook the international investments, which are increasing year by year.   If one has not done so already, he should read that great little book of Norman Angell's, *The Great Illusion*, which has just been published simultaneously at London, New York, Paris, Leipsic, Copenhagen, Madrid, Borga (Finland), Leyden, Turin, Stockholm and Tokio.   There is an international organization of Chambers of Commerce holding annual congresses. The last congress was held in London last June.   Many international congresses of railroads have been held and a monthly bulletin in two languages is published.

There are various internationally organized law associations. The International Law Association held its twenty-sixth annual conference in London in 1910.

When one comes to study the philanthropic and reform movements of our day, he finds that many of these are of international scope.   For example take the Red Cross Society, which has its headquarters at Geneva.   Or take the peace societies of the world which have maintained a permanent international bureau of peace at Berne since 1891, said bureau issuing a fortnightly bulletin.

In religion we find not only the great missionary societies interlacing orient and occident, not only great world congresses of particular denominations (like Pan-Presbyterianism or the Oecumenical Methodist Conference or the World's Council of Congregationalists, or Pan-Anglicanism) but great interdenominational movements like the Y. P. S. C. E. and Y. M. C. A. binding continent to continent.   The World's Christian Student Federation held its seventh biennial meeting in Tokio in 1907, the first world conference ever held in Japan (See DeForest: *Sunrise in the Sunrise Kingdom*, 151–2).

We might continue almost indefinitely in an attempt to enumerate some of the voluntary and unofficial enterprises which are internationally organized. Probably during the last 75 years hundreds of international conferences have been held. Suffice it to say that, as Professor Reinsch tell us, "the world of international organization is an accomplished fact. The idea of cosmopolitanism is no longer a castle in the air, but it has become incorporated in numerous associations and unions, world wide in their operation. Nor are these merely manifested in Congresses where tendencies and aims are discussed, and resolutions voted. No, they have been provided with a permanent organization, with executive bureaus, with arbitration tribunals, with legislative commissions and assemblies of international unions composed of private individuals, united for the advancement of industry, commerce, or scientific work; there are no less than 150, all provided with a permanent form of organization" (Prof. Reinsch: Address delivered at Second American Peace Congress, report taken from *Unity*, May 20, 1909). There is now at Brussels a Central Office of International Associations, "whose purpose is to act as a clearing house for the national and international associations of the world, official and unofficial" (*Advocate of Peace*, 1911, 41).

2. Passing now from voluntary societies let us next consider the Interparliamentary Union. This is an international organization composed of members of the various national law-making bodies of the world, formed for the promotion of arbitration and better relations between nations. Its membership is now about 3000. It supports a permanent bureau at Brussels. Some of the governments are making annual appropriations for this bureau. For the first time in our history as a nation, the United States Congress in 1910 appropriated a small sum for this purpose. While, strictly speaking, the Interparliamentary Union is a voluntary organization, nevertheless being composed solely of lawmakers of the various nations, and receiving support from some of the governments, it is semi-official, semi-intergovernmental. Needless to say, an organization with such aims and personnel is highly significant and prophetic.

3. But, most important of all, are the official, intergovernmental enterprises which have been undertaken by governments. In the

82 years from 1826 to 1907, that is, from the Congress of Panama to the Second Hague Conference, there were convened 119 strictly international gatherings. Judge (and now Governor) Simeon E. Baldwin has enumerated these for us (*American Journal of International Law*, I, Part III, 808 ff). The comprehensiveness of these international meetings is revealed in a hasty survey. International congresses and conferences have been held by the various governments to consider Sanitation and Resistance to the Plague, A Uniform System of Meteorological observations at Sea, Statistics, Neutralization (on repeated occasions), Sound Dues (to Denmark), the Free Navigation of Rivers, the Universal Postal Union, Duties (on certain articles like sugar), Weights and Measures, Marine Signalling, Monetary Subjects, Telegraphy, The Rules of War, the Metric System, Submarine Telegraphic Cables, Geography, Protection against Plant Disseases, Industrial Property, Railroad Transportation, Fisheries, Exchange of Official and Scientific Documents, the Prime Meridian Commercial Law, Freedom of Grade through the Suez Canal, Literary and Artistic Property, the Liquor Traffic, Tariffs, The Working Classes, Maritime Law, the Slave Trade, Protection of Laborers in Factories, Pan-America, Private International Law, Telephony, Social and Economic Questions, Arbitration, the White Slave Traffic, Central American Peace, Wireless Telegraphy, the Unification of the Formulae of Potent Drugs, Agriculture, the Use of White Phosphorus in Matches, Night Work for Women, Morocco, and the First and Second Peace Conferences at The Hague.

More significant even than these international conferences are the permanent international bureaus and commissions which are in actual operation. According to Professor Reinsch; "There are in existence over 45 public international unions, composed of states. Of these 30 are provided with administrative bureaus or commissions."

Down in Washington, D. C., is the Pan-American Union through which 21 nations do business coöperatively. In Central America there is in operation the first permanent High Tribunal of Nations in the history of the world, an International

High Court which has full jurisdiction in all cases that may arise between the five contracting republics. Go to Berlin and you see an International Bureau of Weights and Measures. Paris is the seat of the permanent International Commission on Freedom of Trade through the Suez Canal. Go to little Berne, which globe-trotting tourists skip after a look at the famous Bears, and you find a whole group of international bureaus, the permanent Bureau for the Protection of Industrial, Literary and Artistic Property, which publishes a monthly journal; the permanent Monetary Diplomatic Bureau; the permanent Bureau of Telegraphy which publishes a gazette and is in official touch with 40 bureaus in as many countries besides 20 private corporations; the Bureau for Protection against Phylloxera (supported by five powers); the Tariff Bureau which publishes its bulletin in five different languages; and the Bureau of Railway Transportation which also issues a paper. Best known of all is the Berne Bureau of the Universal Postal Union, the executive body through which the postal systems of all the civilized, and some of the nations of the uncivilized, world are administered. Fifty different postal administrations use it and support it. Its congresses are held regularly every five years, and to these congresses the accredited and official representatives of the different powers are sent to legislate for the postal service of the world. As Judge Baldwin well says: "It can no longer be sneered at as impracticable, because it exists and has existed as a working force for a whole generation. Every man who sends a letter from New York to Tokio with quick despatch for a fee of only five cents, knows that he owes this privilege to an international agreement, and feels himself by virtue of it a citizen of the world."

"The first formal session of the International Institute of Agriculture took place in Rome. This institute is due to the initiative of Mr. David Lubin of California. Mr. Lubin's scheme was first presented to our national authorities at Washington, who were asked to initiate the Institute. It was rejected by them. The young King of Italy, Victor Emanuel, took it up, when asked to do so, and the Institute has been successfully inaugurated. The meeting in Rome was attended by delegates from 46 nations, including the United States. The purpose of the Institute is to promote the development of agriculture in all parts of the world, the restoration of worn-out lands, the redemption of the great still unused tracts of the earth's surface, etc." (*The Advocate of Peace*, December, 1908).

Similarly, within a few years, an International Health Bureau has been established with an international Office of Public Hygiene at Paris. Data concerning infectious diseases, notably cholera, plague and yellow fever, will be collected and measures taken to combat these diseases. Before long nations will wage a world-wide war on the rat as a bearer of diseases and then this pestiferous vermin will be wiped off the face of the earth.

In 1899 was held the First Hague Conference in which 26 powers participated, and three conventions, or articles of agreement, were adopted. Eight years later the Second Hague Conference convened in which 44 powers—practically the entire world—participated. There, through their official representatives, the nations of the world, by unanimous vote, adopted 14 conventions and made provision for a periodic re-assembling of the Conference and for the establishment of a permanent world court.

But in the face of these facts, I repeat that we have already entered upon the opening chapter of internationalism. We are even at present doing a whole lot of business together as a world. These different cities which are the seats of permanent international bureaus are virtually, with respect to certain specific functions, the capitals of the world. In due time, for economy's sake and for the sake of greater efficiency, all these separate functions will be transferred to one capital, where all affairs will be legislated upon and administered. The dozen Berne Bureaus, the Paris Bureaus, the Berlin and Brussels and Rome Bureaus, will then naturally be transferred to one place—probably The Hague. Thus, the internationalism which already has been born by the natural process of business evolution, will grow and wax stronger. To the question, whether internationalism would work, the answer is, it *is* working. The same irresistible evolutionary forces which forced the American Colonies on from a loose federation to a real nation, will, in a similar way, carry forward the world from its present loosely federated organization to a unified, simplified, economical, effective and universally just, internationalism. And this process will be more rapid than some of us think, perhaps more rapid than even the most radical and sanguine dare to dream.

Some one has said that the eighteenth century was a period of dependence; the nineteenth, a period of independence; while in the twentieth century the great word is interdependence. Certainly the race is just entering upon the final chapter of political evolution. I say this not in any alarmist spirit, not in any cheap, superstitious, catastrophic sense, but ground my glad statement on sober, scientific facts. Look back over the successive stages in the evolution of mankind. First, the individual was evolved, then the family, then the tribe, then the nation. The evolution process which has been going on from the beginning of man's existence will not stop now, and we shall go on and on to the next chapter and the next. And what will be the next thing? Internationalism. And beyond internationalism, what? Nothing, in the way of world political organization, unless, or until, Professor Percival Lowell shall succeed in annexing Mars. After such annexation panplanetism might become possible. But, until then, internationalism is the final chapter in the political evolution of man.

At the same time, we may say that while the complete realization of internationalism will be the last chapter in political evolution, in another sense it will be the first chapter in the higher industrial, educational, social, and moral evolution of man.

II. THE INADEQUACY OF THE OLD, DIVISIVE PATRIOTISM

Manifestly, if the world is already doing business internationally, the old divisive type of patriotism is inadequate to the needs of the new day. The older patriotism was characterized by three things—it was provincial and selfish, it was a patriotism of hatred of other nations, and it was largely a patriotism of military strife.

1. *The patriotism of provincialism and selfishness.* As Charles Sumner pointed out in his address on "The True Grandeur of Nations," our ideas of patriotism are largely inherited from the

ancients.   Cicero said of Rome that that country alone embraced all the excellences of all.   Greek and Roman conceptions of nations were intensely narrow, and a selfish type of patriotism resulted.   We moderns have only borrowed the older conceptions and attached them to our own respective nations.   The story is told of an American congressman who, when asked what effect a certain measure would produce abroad, ejaculated, "What have we 'to do with abroad?"   Stephen Decatur's atrocious toast, "My country, right or wrong," all too truly represents the general sentiment prevailing under the older patriotism.   How selfish the spread-eagle words of Daniel Webster sound to us today; "Let the object be our country, our whole country, and nothing but our country!" (Bartlett: *Quotations*, 530).   No wonder thoughtful people have protested against such barbaric selfishness.   Herbert Spencer heads one of his chapters, "The Bias of Patriotism."   (See Walsh: *Moral Damage* 53.)   George Eliot defined patriotism as the virtue of narrow minds (*Proceedings Second American Peace Congress*, 316).   Mrs. Browning argued that if patriotism means the flattery of one's nation in every case, then the patriot   .   .   .   is only a courtier (Mrs. Browning: *Poems*, II, 305).   This provincial, selfish patriotism often takes the form of a contempt for other nations rather than a reverence for one's own.   (Comp. Dawson: *Reproach of Christ*, 163).   Hence Charles Sumner uttered his noble protest against that form of patriotism which interferes with the spirit of humanity and is mere sectionalism of the heart (Sumner: "True Grandeur of Nations").   And Dr. Lyman Abbott exhorts us to "bid good-by to the provincialism that calls itself patriotism, and thinks it is patriotic because it sneers at every other nation but its own" (Abbott: "Address on International Brotherhood, *Modern Eloquence*, VII, I).   In trumpet tones Ernest Crosby sounds the same call to a better patriotism:

> Are these our patriots, these, the blind,
> Whose love of country is combined
> With petty hate for all mankind?
> Nay from their rule we pray release;
> Soon may such love of country cease.
> They know not love that love not peace.

Especially timely is the warning of Melville E. Stone concerning the dangers which are created by the race prejudices of Anglo-Saxons in the Orient (*National Geographic Magazine*, December, 1910).

2. *The patriotism of hate.* Naturally, and all too easily, a patriotism of provincialism and selfishness heads up into a patriotism of hate. All down through the centuries true patriotism has been thought to imply an intense hatred of other nations. To the Greeks, all foreigners were barbarians. Only until a comparatively high state of civilization is attained are foreigners regarded otherwise than as enemies. Especially in those cases into which war has entered, is the test of hatred passed on from decade to decade.

For generations the *sine qua non* of British patriotism was hatred of the French. Nelson's motto was, "Trust in God, and hate the Frenchman like the devil." During the Boer War any Briton who did not emphatically declare his hatred of the Boers was set down as a traitor, labelled "Pro-Boer," and, in many cases, mobbed. In the last decade British patriotism has taken the form of anti-Germanism.

So, too, in Germany. Revenge on France for humiliation by Napoleon was for over half a century the one patriotic purpose nursed by Germans. This sentiment became incarnated in a group of statuary on one of the Berlin bridges, in which a stalwart warrior is teaching an ardent youth the art of war (Stoddard: *Lectures*, VI Berlin, 18.) A famous Berlin teacher used to make a practice of leading his pupils out through the Brandenburg Gate, invariably asking them, "Of what are you thinking"? Usually the answers were not entirely satisfactory and the teacher would upbraid his pupils saying: "You should be remembering here that you are the children of the vanquished; and that your first resolve, as men, must be to march to Paris, and bring back thence the car of victory stolen from this gate by the robber Napoleon" (the same). Even Francis Lieber, whose *Rules of War* almost may be considered as the nucleus of a code of international law, never could rise above his hatred of France, thus inculcated. Germany's humiliation by Napoleon rankled in his memory. When Germany triumphed in the Franco-Prussian War the great publicist could not refrain from writing to friends in Germany advising that the most stringent terms be imposed upon the conquered nation. His love of Fatherland was animated by what Charles Sumner characterized as "Gallophobia" (*American Journal of International Law*, January 1911, 87, 89).

For a century or more American patriotism consisted of hatred of mother country—Anglophobia. In 1898, however, "Remember the Maine" became the slogan. During the war with Spain a school teacher in Washington, D. C., asked what patriotism meant. The reply given by one of the girl pupils was, "To kill Spaniards" (Warner: *Ethics of Force*, 40–41). Today, if we are to accept the brainless jingoism of scheming demagogues, the very quintessence of American patriotism is an intense hatred of Japan.

Even this brief historical survey convinces one that there is too much ground for the charge that patriotism, as popularly understood, "requires us, off and on, to hate all foreign governments, especially such as are called monarchies, and to pursue our own interests and ends with lordly indifference to the opinions and interests of mankind. It glories in the immensity of our population, our vast resources, and our assumed ability to thrash the united world. It relates, in fact, wholly to war, actual or prospective" (Warner: *Ethics of Force*, 40).

Thinking people, however, refuse to accept any longer hatred as a criterion of patriotism. Hatred is mere negativism. It proves nothing. A man's fidelity to his wife is not demonstrated by his hatred of a neighbor. In religion men are coming to see that old hatred tests are insufficient. We should no longer accept Sancho Panza's plea that he hated the Jews as valid and sufficient evidence of being a Christian. The story is told concerning a little girl who applied for admission to an orthodox church. When asked by the examining committee why she thought she was a Christian she replied, "I just hate the Universalists and Unitarians." She was admitted. No other evidence was needed at that time. But today something more than hatred is required in religion. And as for patriotism, mere hatred of a sister nation, is altogether too negative and barbarous to satisfy the citizens of an internationalized world. A patriotism of hate is too small to fit even the present civilization, to say nothing of the finer civilization of tomorrow.

Even now the words of Ernest Crosby do not sound so treasonable as they did when penned by him:

> I am no patriot.
> I do not wish my countrymen to overrun the world.
> I love the date-palm equally with the pine-tree, and each in its place.
> I am as true a friend to the banana and orange as to the pear and apple.
> I thank the genial breath of climate for making men different.
> I am glad to know that, if my people succeed in spreading over the face of the earth, they will gradually differ from each other as they attune themselves to every degree of latitude and longitude.
> Humanity is no air to be strummed on one note or upon one instrument.
> It is a symphony where every note and instrument has its part, and would be sadly missed.
> I do not take the side of the cornet against the violin, for the cornet needs the violin.
> I am no patriot.
> I love my country too well to be a patriot.
> (Ernest Crosby: *Swords and Plowshares*, 15–16.)

3. *The old patriotism was too largely a gun patriotism.* Mrs. Mead, in one of her pamphlets, tells of a child's paper which, some time ago, contained a picture of an old man showing a boy a gun, while beneath the picture were the words, "Teaching Patriotism." And Mr. Mead, in his introduction to Sumner's *Addresses on War*, says, "Every war gives new life to that old notion which dies so hard. . . . that patriotism is somehow bound up with war—the patriotic war man, the man who fights or wants to fight for his country." One of our American college presidents says, "The gateway to social service is no longer alone by way of West Point or Annapolis, but it comes through service to humanity in the arts and in the marts and in the manufacturies and the labor and the home rather than upon the field of battle." There is a world of truth, too, in these words from Scotland: "To risk life on the battlefield is not the only form of patriotism; it may not be that bespattered thing at all, but only adventure,

excitement, pugilism, mercenariness, social outlawry, moral cowardice or other squalid impulse." Certainly, as Mr. Bryan points
out; "One of the things we should try to cultivate is the idea that
it is not necessary for a man to die on the battlefield in order to be
a patriot."

When one studies the budgets of the various nations one comes
to realize the extent to which the gun type of patriotism prevails.

The chief and sufficient indictment against gun patriotism is
this, that it is the one thing which obstructs the progress of an
evolving internationalism. We have pointed out that learned
societies, reformers, educators and even governments are organizing and coöperating internationally. While scientists, reformers, philosophers, educators, teachers, churchmen and government commissioners meet together as co-workers, form genuine
friendships with men of their own group, and look upon each other
as brother toilers in a common holy cause, the one man who is
out of joint with all this increasing international comradeship
is the gun patriot. The gun patriot is not loyal to his own class.
The gun patriot of one land looks upon the gun patriot of another
land as a menace to his own nation.

Such was the older patriotism, provincial and selfish, animated
with hate, and with a gun for its emblem. With justice Edward
Eggleston characterized such patriotism as "a virtue of the half-
developed, higher than tribal instinct and lower than that great
world benevolence that is to be the work of coming ages" (Edward
Eggleston: "The New History; "See *Modern Eloquence*, VIII,
404). But competitive internationalism has had its day and is
even now obsolescent. A new patriotism is being born.

III. THE NEW PATRIOTISM SYNTHETIC

An internationalized world requires a patriotism that shall be
synthetic, instead of divisive; coöperative, instead of competitive,
constructive, instead of destructive. Pretty rapidly we are learning to enlarge tribal sentiment and national loyalty until our
patriotism shall be world-embracing. This does not mean the
destruction of patriotism, but its completion.

1. *The new patriotism is loyal to internationalism.* We know that it is possible to be a loyal citizen of the city of Chicago and of the State of Illinois, and of the United States of America. So, while remaining loyal to all these it is possible at the same time to yield allegiance to an internationalized world. As Goldwin Smith so beautifully said, "Above all nations is humanity." [When the New England Peace Congress of 1910 devoted a day to the honoring of the memory of Elihu Burritt, a mammoth banner bearing this noble sentiment of Professor Smith flung across the principal square of New Britain, Connecticut. These words have been adopted as the motto of the Cosmopolitan Clubs. They express the creed of the new and greater patriotism— "above all nations is humanity."]

Hence the new patriot will loyally support all movements for the internationalizing of the world. He will especially be faithful to the efforts to complete the machinery of international justice at The Hague. He will discountenance and oppose all reactionary policies which would mean infidelity to, and the thwarting of, the Hague movement. He will go in for less hate and more service, for less "world-politics' and more world organization. Macaulay's noble verse some day will be re-written. In place of his:

> Then none was for a party;
> Then all were for the State;
> Then the great man helped the poor
> And the poor man loved the great;

Some new Macaulay will be able to sing:

> Now none are for a nation,
> But all for a world-state;
> Great lands and small together
> Live in justice and not hate.

2. *Then shall it be possible for a patriot to be loyal to loyalty.* Professor Royce in his admirable little volume, *The Philosophy of Loyalty*, shows that in war-time one man's loyalty clashes with the loyalty of the citizen in the hostile state. This is the moral

condemnation of the war system.   Patriotism in an internationalized world will harmonize and unify these competitive loyalties.
Then shall it be possible to apply Kant's rule to citizenship:
"Act so that the immediate motive of thy will may become a
universal rule for all intelligent beings."   In the not distant future
it will be commonplace for instructors of children to teach that
the true patriotism is that which will form a fraternal bond between the nations and strengthen their loyalty to the world state.

3. *The new patriotism will enable a man to be loyal to morality.*
The old war patriotism oftentimes forced men to do things against
their judgment and convictions.   Certain prominent American
statesman protested against our treatment of Mexico, which at
last headed up in the Mexican War.   But when war was once
declared, their protest ceased and they contributed their sons to
the army of conquest.   Now, as a New England divine pointed
out, a thing which was wrong for statesmen up to 1846, and wrong
after 1848, could not have been right from 1846 to 1848.   (Theodore Parker).

The old war patriotism forced men and nations to violate all
the higher laws of kindness and brotherly love to which man's
highest allegiance is due.   In spite of the fact that today emphasis is laid chiefly on the financial, economic and biological arguments against war, nevertheless it still remains true that its chief
condemnation lies in the moral ruin which it produces.   Fortunately the new internationalism is leading us on to a broader
patriotism in a warless world-family, so that it shall be no longer
necessary for a man to separate his patriotism from his prayer life.
More and more it is becoming possible to be a patriot and at the
same time to be loyal to one's highest moral convictions.

Little by little a new type of citizen and patriot is being evolved,
namely the socialized individual.   Now once let a man become
socialized and it is then forever impossible to get him to hark
back to the old patriotism of hate.   To such a temptation the
socialized patriot replies in the noble words of Charles Sumner:
"Man was made to love his neighbor and not to despise him.   I
detest the words of Dr. Johnson who boasted of loving 'a good
hater.'   I like the man who loves his neighbor.   A favorable

appreciation of the character and position of nations and individuals exercises the best influence." Or he replies in the words of one of our New England poets:

We owe allegiance to the State, but deeper, truer, more
To the sympathies that rise and burn, within our spirits' core.
Our country claims our fealty, we grant it so, but then
Before men made us citizens, great nature made us men.

It is to this type of patriotism that social evolution is carrying us forward. The industrial and economic and political necessities of men are irresistibly driving us on to a larger patriotism than that of selfish provincialism, hate and military spread-eagleism which has too long cursed the world.

IV. FULFILMENT OF THE DREAM OF BRAVE DREAMERS

This evolution which history makes so evident enables us to see that the dream of brave dreamers is being fulfilled.

1. Great men, in all the centuries, have dreamed of world organization and brotherhood. Cosmopolitanism was a part of the creed of the Stoics (Eucken: *Problem of Human Life*, 91-2). Horace declared that "the brave man is at home in every land, as fishes in the ocean" (*Modern Eloquence* VII, 176). Marcus Aurelius likened nations to members of the body, saying: "We are made for coöperation like feet, like hands, like eyelids, like the rows of the upper and lower teeth. To act against one another, then, is contrary to nature" (Marcus Aurelius: *Thoughts*, 95, 175). Jesus, though of Jewish descent, rose above the narrow nationalism of his times and people. As Dr. Darby says, "Jesus, though of Jewish descent. . . . was not a Jew—but just a *man*, untrammelled by race limitations or prejudices, unwarped by so-called patriotism" (Darby: *The Christ Method of Peace Making*, 63). It was Bolingbroke who declared that "a wise man looks upon himself as a citizen of the world; and when you ask him where his country lies, points, like Anexagoras, with his finger to the heavens " (*Masterpieces of Literature, Ancient and Modern*, III, 1477). Over his door, during his exile, Edmund Ludlow wrote,

Every land is my fatherland
For all lands are my Father's.
(See Walsh: *Moral Damage of War*, 404.)

William Lloyd Garrison headed the very first number of his *Liberator* with this motto:

Our country is the World
Our countrymen are mankind.
(Crosby: *Garrison, the Non-Resistant*, 15.)

Mr. Emerson, who possessed a world-soul, if any man ever did, wrote: "We have no sympathy with that boyish egotism, hoarse with cheering for one side, for one state, for one town; the right patriotism consists in the delight which springs from contributing our peculiar and legitimate advantages to the benefit of humanity" (*Emerson*, XI, 328). Elihu Burritt, setting himself to prepare a lecture on the anatomy of the earth, was struck by the interdependence of the various nations. It was this which lead him into the peace movement. His lecture grew into a peace lecture, and thenceforth he became a prophet of world citizenship (Northend: *Elihu Burritt*, 23). Professor Bovio describes the internationalized patriot as "the man of the future;" Jules Simon, as "the patriot of humanity" (*Concord*, January 1911, 5). When society is completely internationalized, and individuals thoroughly socialized, then shall the noble prophecy of Tennyson be fulfilled:

When the schemes and all the systems,
Kingdoms and republics fall
Something kindlier, higher, holier,—
All for each and each for all.
(See Tennyson: *Enoch Arden*.)

These are the dreams of some of the dreamers. It is only a question of a comparatively short time, now, when the dream of a world-state and a pan-human patriotism will be commonplace actuality. In his day when internationalism is being consummated, as never before, it is "bliss to be alive" (See Dawson:

Makers of English Poetry, 45–46). If, as Horace declared, "a pleasant and a noble thing it is to die for fatherland" (Horace: *The Odes, Old Roman Character* (Bohn edition, 46) how much nobler and sweeter and more glorious it is to put in a life for an internationalized humanity!

CHAIRMAN HAMMOND: The last speaker of today will discuss peace as a preventive of poverty. I have the pleasure and honor of introducing to you Mr. J. W. Magruder, secretary of the Federated Charities of Baltimore.

MR. J. W. MAGRUDER: Mr. Marburg, in his letter inviting me to speak upon this subject, enclosed a circular letter containing a statement which, to those who are uninformed, must be nothing short of astounding; that, "for the fiscal year ending July 1, 1910, the United States expended on the navy, the army and on pensions, which are the result of past wars, $447,620,723 constituting 68 per cent of the ordinary disbursements of the government, including postoffice deficiency." This means nearly five dollars per capita for every man, woman and child in the United States, Alaska, the Philippines and all our colonial possessions. It means for every family of five an annual tax of nearly twenty-five dollars. It means for the average wage-earner with a family of six or seven a tax of thirty or thirty-five dollars or more.

Nor does this tell the whole tale; for the enormous expenditure of more than two-thirds of the nation's income goes into an absolutely non-productive, I need not say destructive, business; the men who are engaged in it are or should be the natural breadwinners of families; and yet every one of them is a consumer and not a producer of wealth.

The only inevitable effect of this superimposed burden upon the rank and file of the nation is to depress below the poverty line and sink to the level of dependency that marginal contingent of the population which, but for this fixed charge upon their narrow income, would escape the sting of having to accept alms and themselves becoming an additional burden upon the already burdened community.

That the contingent of population on this border line is by no means small is evidenced by the fact that in a city as unusually prosperous as Baltimore undoubtedly is, there has been for the last three years and is likely to be for some time to come, an average of one in twenty of the population in such straitened circumstances that one-third of them are in need of material relief and two-thirds barely escape from dependency. This too in an era which, as Professor Patten has recently pointed out, furnishes a new basis for civilization in that it is characterized not by deficit, but by surplus.

In other words, there are hundreds of thousands of people in these United States who are suffering from underfeeding, overcrowding, ill-health, debility, inefficiency, discouragement, failure—all because of an army and navy consuming $447,620,723 annually of the people's wealth.

This is not a matter of dollars or cents, it is a matter of flesh and blood; it is a human concern; it affects women and children as well as men; it affects the poor vastly more than the rich or well-to-do. To narrow it down to the tax-payer is to overlook the fact that the taxes of this country are paid not by the taxpayer technically so-called; only the smallest fraction of the burden falls upon him. The real incidence of taxation is upon every man, woman and child who eats a mouthful of food or wears a stitch of clothing or uses a stick of furniture or lives under a roof or lives at all. Even a nursing baby has to pay tribute; and to this exaction is chargeable some of our excessively high mortality rate. The ultimate consumer pays the bills either in the coin of the realm or in his own life blood.

How is it that we have been so long coming to this Peace Conference and to the judicial settlement of our international differences? Is it not largely because our war taxes are indirect? "My people perish for lack of knowledge." The man in the streets does not know he is paying these bills. Even intelligent wage-earners, the bread-winner with a family to support, does not realize how much of his money, if any of it, is going into the nation's war chest. Were it a direct tax upon us, there would be 101,100,-000 thoroughly aroused Americans praying with their faces towards this Baltimore Peace Conference and enlisting for the war against war.

Let us turn on the light, let us educate our children. Let them see what it all costs, not merely in treasure but in human life and blood even in piping times of peace. Let them come to understand that to disarm means to transform an army of consumers into producers of wealth. It means the deliverance of one more entire stratum of the population from poverty and dependence, and the permanent enlargement of the area of self-dependence and self-respect. It means more and better food, clothing, housing, education, leisure for everybody—it means life, liberty and the pursuit of happiness for more of the poor.

CHAIRMAN HAMMOND: Ladies and Gentlemen, the sessions of the Third National Peace Congress are at an end, and in accordance with the provisions of the Committee on Resolutions we are now

ADJOURNED

PROGRAM OF MEETING FOR SCHOOLS

Preceding the regular sessions of the Third American Peace Congress, peace meetings were held for the teachers and students of the public schools of Baltimore. At the first meeting, held on Tuesday, May 2, at 3 p.m., in the Assembly hall of the Western High School, Hon. M. Bates Stephens, State Superintendent of Public Instruction, presided. After a few words of explanation, he introduced Mrs. Lucia Ames Mead, of Boston, who delivered the following address:

ADDRESS TO TEACHERS OF MARYLAND

LUCIA AMES MEAD OF BOSTON

The twentieth century child may be taught the three "R's" in the same way as was the nineteenth century child, but if he is to be fitted for twentieth century politics and business, he must be taught literature, geography, history and patriotism by a teacher who comprehends the new internationalism.

Since the last generation, business and world politics have been revolutionized as much as medicine and agriculture and sanitation. The teacher who is in touch with the history that is in the making and who has the spirit of internationalism is alone fitted to lead today. He must be in advance of the text book. No book records the most significant word uttered for a decade by the chief executive of a great nation—that word uttered by President Taft, declaring that all difficulties between nations, including those involving national honor should be settled by peaceable methods. Only one text book that I know—Meyer's *Mediaeval and Modern History* chronicles under the chapter, "The World State," the most significant facts in modern history.

The average teacher, overburdened with examination papers and all the new requirements of manual training, physical culture

472

and nature study, looks askance at any new subject that is imposed on the crowded curriculum. He fears that we are doing
nothing well in consequence of congestion. Let it be understood
that what is needed is not more work, but work modified by a
different point of view and different spirit, which, illuminating
the lesson in history or literature or geography, shall inspire
the feelings of the Latin poet who said: "I count nothing human
foreign to me," a spirit which shall banish caste, race prejudice,
class prejudice, national prejudice and enable the child to deal
justly with all mankind.

An honorable, national self-interest must be a great incentive
in the new movement to justly formulate national interdependence. The twentieth century youth who is putting money into
Siberian railroads, Peruvian mines, South African bridges, or
who will be employed in filling orders for reapers and ploughs in
Russia, for plumbing in Turkey and electric engines in Persia and
China, must be taught that his prosperity depends on peace and
peace depends on justice and justice depends on farsighted organization and treaty provision. He must learn the commerical value
of imagination and sympathy as well as its higher ethical value.
In the lowest grammar grades, as soon as he can study what our
"little cousins" are doing in the Philippines or in Holland or
Greece, he must read stories that develop his power to put himself "in the other fellow's place." The Golden Rule would be
oftener applied were our complacent eyes able to see how the world
looks to the man with the black skin, or brown skin, or yellow
skin, or to the man of our own Caucasian race who, driven by
military oppression in the Old World, finds refuge in our shores
and sends his little daughter to a Triangle shirt-waist factory to
earn her bread. German success in obtaining trade in South
America is due to that power of imagination and shrewd sympathy
which studies the customer's language and gives him what he
wants when and as he wants it. Our failure thus far in those
regions is largely due to assuming that our way of doing is good
enough for other people, whether they like it or not. Our business men and drummers lack the requisite imagination and sympathy to make the success they might.

War depends upon the psychology of nations. What are those people thinking in the Mikado's or Kaiser's or Tsar's capital and how many American militarists or men eager for contracts are going to foment mysterious war scares? How many credulous readers can we count on believing these war scares valid? That is the main problem, not how many dreadnoughts have we or they. As a nation fears or suspects, so is its burden of military taxation. As the boy stores up impressions, prejudices, sympathies, so the man legislates and the nation makes friends or foes. The responsibility of the teacher was never so great to do what both church and home often neglect—to inspire a friendly instead of a suspicious attitude toward the world.

Patriotism may be so mistaught as to develop the worst instead of the best impulses. It may encourage arrogance and pride in our country instead of humble readiness to serve it, which is the only test of patriotism. It may be so taught as to distort the lessons of history and forbid seeing any fault in our past. Every young patriot should learn that, in the words of General Grant, who fought in our Mexican war, "It was one of the most unjust wars ever fought by a strong people against a weak one." Love of country like love of our brother must not imply blindness to defects. Let every child learn that patriotism has no more to do with a gun than with a broom and that Colonel Waring, reducing New York's death rate 15,000 with his brooms, did a far greater service for his country than if he had left as many of the enemy on a battlefield.

Every child should learn, when studying the history of the Revolution, that it was a war between the progressive and retrogressive forces on both sides of the Atlantic. He should be taught that all English text books teach admiration for Washington and criticism of George III. Had this been known in 1895, when a Venezuela boundary line was the occasion of a week of belligerent talk on our part, it might have saved us the one hundred million dollars in foregin investments which it was said our little war-scare cost us. Generations had grown up here crudely considering Englishmen as hereditary foes and politely refraining from mentioning July 4th in their presence as if they were still sensitive. Such ignorance, due to bad teaching, is costly.

The teacher must know far more than he can definitely teach of internationalism, if the school is to have the right atmosphere and his pupils get the right point of view that will stand them in stead when national hysteria prevails. If possible he should read two books,—David Starr Jordan's *The Human Harvest*—a complete refutation of the fallacy that *War promotes virility*, and *The Great Illusion*, by Norman Angell, an epoch-making book published in many tongues which presentes the new economic facts that when realized will end forever all attempt at foreign war.

The main thing is to secure a teacher whose patriotism will put conscience and enthusiasm into teaching those character-building lessons of infinitely more value to every child than any technical booklore the schools can give him. In the primary grades, stories of knights fighting dragons, of firemen fighting flames, of heroes saving life should be substituted for tales of wars. Later, in history classes, wars must be studied, but if the emphasis is laid on causes and cost and results of wars and not on campaigns; if copies of Verestchagin's mournful pictures of war and clear statement of its squalor and horrors are presented briefly, the glamor of the "Splendid Charge" will not dim the child's insight into the true nature of war. Statistics of huge losses mean nothing to immature minds. A few pathetic or realistic stories of individual loss are more impressive. But some faint conception of the appalling cost of armaments may be given the arithmetic class by setting them to figure out how many schools like theirs could be built at the cost of one short-lived dreadnought, costing $12,500,000, or how many children could have suits of clothes for one shot costing $1700 at target practice.

May I now offer a few practical suggestions?

First: Give clear-cut definitions of those words about which there is much confused thought even in editorial chairs and naval colleges. Do not let pupils define *war* so as to put it in the same category with wholesome struggle, as do Captain Mahan and many other clever writers. Show how there is no war in the animal world, only occasional, impromptu duels and getting dinner by killing other animals for food. War is always the work of human beings, organized and authorized by certain men who do

not themselves fight.   Man deliberately practises to learn the
art of killing in far more fiendish fashion than anything devised
by sharks or wolves.   Man is the only creature who practises
systematically in order to destroy *his own kind.*

Second: Refute the fallacy that "Government rests on force."
All governments use force, but no government, even a tribal
government, rests so much on force as on the consent of the governed.   The weakest government, like the Tsar's requires the
most force to bolster it up.   A government like ours rests on the
broad basis of the peoples' will and needs but little force to but-
tress it.   A republic rests on courts, on law, on schools, on means
of communication, on a free press, on money, on police, and on
the peoples' will.   Our army of school teachers is doing more to
perpetuate our republic, by defending it from the rule of an illit-
erate mob, than are all our army and navy.

Third: Sharply distinguish between war *within* nations and
war *between* nations.   Hague Courts and Conferences cannot
affect Mexican rebellions, though they are sure in time to end war
between nations as completely as our Supreme Court has since its
beginning prevented any war between one State and another
State, and this without any change of human nature.   Show how
peace through organization can be obtained long before murder,
intemperance, vice, poverty, and ignorance, deep rooted in heredity and social conditions, can disappear.   It is the most hopeful
of all reforms.   International war must end a thousand years
before we can talk of a millennium.   It is a prerequisite to all
advance in civilization.

Fourth: Emphasize justice.   Differentiate clearly between the
kinds of force which aim to secure justice, and the kinds that do
not.   Police and militia alone aim at justice and use the minimum
of force to get criminals to court or to disperse rioters.   Rival
armies and navies, on the other hand, never aim to secure justice, never take any one to court and are but the tools of nations
engaged in gigantic duelling.   They achieve justice only acci-
dentally, incidentally and then with a long train of injustices
behind them.   There never was a war that was just upon both
sides.

Besides giving clear-cut definitions let me suggest your giving certain definite facts that should be taught and memorized.

First: Show that in our one hundred and twenty-two years of history our Republic has never yet been attacked. We began our war with England in 1812, the war with Mexico and the Spanish war and it was an American who fired the first gun upon a Filippino, after the real first gun had been fired from Washington in December, 1898, in a message which General Otis, knowing its dangerous import, in vain attempted to delay. We hear much of "danger of invasion" and attack, though we are strong and vastly more self-sufficient than we were a generation since when we had a small navy and no fear. The more dreadnoughts the nations build, the more their panic about attack.

Second: Teach in simple outline the result of modern banking and investment. Under the new conditions no nation can conquer another and not lose more than it could gain. This was not always so, but modern investments and banking, which depend so largely upon credit and confidence, have altered all former conditions. Should a German army ever invade England (Von Moltke said he knew three ways of getting in, but not one of getting an army out) and should destroy the Bank of England and soldiers confiscate its gold, a "run" would presently follow on every bank in Great Britain and they would suspend payments. Merchants the world over would face ruin and call in their credits in Germany and thus undermine German finance. German trade would be paralyzed and a thousand marks lost for every one confiscated. If twenty-five years ago the rumor of a probable failure of the Barings created consternation and was a theme for special prayers in American churches, how vastly more would the much talked of war between Germany and England bring chaos on Wall Street today and affect every village in the land. That war can never be permitted if for no other reason than for the business world it spells disaster. The thought of it would never have gained ground, had the business world not been under the obsession of antiquated notions of economics. It repeats naively an old phraseology about defense, which today does not apply.

The youngest child should be taught Franklin's adage that

"The poorest thing you can do with a customer is to knock him on the head." We are all customers and sellers today and the world is our market. We can no more separate our success from others' success than hand and foot or lungs and heart can ignore each other. Trade does not follow the flag as every economist knows. England's huge navy does not avail to sell one more screw driver. Her carrying trade per capita is hardly more than one-third of Norway's. She has become land poor in taking, within a generation, as much territory and population as that of the whole United States. She must police most of this, yet gets not enough revenue to pay for the policing. No foreign nation can gain anything today by conquest of colonies, and no people in a protectionist country can gain by a war indemnity. Preposterous as it may seem, the French indemnity demoralized Germany and brought financial depression from 1872 to 1880. Ten years after Sedan, France was more prosperous than Germany.

Third: In view of the wanton, vicious talk so prevalent and persistent about danger from Japan, older classes should be explicitly taught the following facts:

Japan is crippled by a crushing taxation for past war. With two bloody wars within a generation, she has no desire for another. She has her hands full with her new acquisitions, Formosa and Korea, which require guarding and development. She has just put forty million dollars into railroads in Korea. Should she embroil herself with us, she would lose her greatest trade, which is with us, and expose herself to Chinese and Russian aggression in the rear and lose these two possessions. The Japanese are now ambitious to develop intensively and not be diverted by outside matters. With their new manufacturing interests they could sustain twice their present population. Moreover the Japanese nation has always kept its faith with us; it looks to us as teacher and guide and its people are sincerely friendly to us, as one hundred missionaries who have long been there recently testified. Ambassador Luke Wright well said: "The talk of war with Japan is not even respectable nonsense." It is deliberately and maliciously manufactured by certain special interests. It has cost us upwards of eight hundred million dollars to get and hold the Philippines, though the natives have paid all the cost of their education and civic government. For Japan to try to wrest them from us would cost vastly more and would mean national suicide, and this her astute statesmen well know. Moreover, if she had them they would be a costly burden to her as they are to us. It is evident that special private interests are fomenting the iniquitous rumors of danger from Japan and that a detective should ferret out the origin of our war-scares.

Fourth: Show how our only dangers are from within. In all our three foreign wars we lost less than fifteen thousand men— one-tenth the number killed annually by tuberculosis! In four recent years of peace we lost sixty thousand more citizens by accident than were killed in our four years of civil war and last year we burned up eight times as much property as was burned in all Europe.

Fifth: Present the prime facts which pupils need to know concerning the epoch-making achievements of the two Hague Conferences. Picture that surprising call from the Tsar in August, 1898, to the twenty-six nations that had ambassadors at his court and his appeal for a limitation of the stupendous increase in armaments, which were "bringing about the very cataclysm they were designed to avert." Describe that meeting of one hundred representatives with fifty attachés in the "House in the Wood" at The Hague on May 18, 1899; of the work in those committees behind locked doors; of America's happy influence in removing Germany's obstruction to progress; of the social daily intercourse which made friends of these men from China to Austria, who spoke in the official language, French. Tell of the great result, the agreement for a Permanent Tribunal of Arbitration for whose building Mr. Carnegie gave $1,500,000; of the provision for Inquiry which shortly after prevented war between Russian and England over the North Sea attack on English fishing vessels; of the third provision for Mediation which enabled President Roosevelt to mediate between Russia and Japan and end their bloody conflict. Describe the Second Hague Conference, first called by President Roosevelt in 1905, and convened by the Tsar in 1907, to which forty-six nations, practically all the civilized world—were invited. Show how it prohibited bombardment of unfortified places, throwing bombs from balloons, removed various barbarities of war, prevented war for collection of debts and recommended the establishment of a Prize Court and a court of Arbitral Justice, which is to have fifteen judges, and will be opened to settle questions by international law, as soon as a method of selecting these judges can be agreed on.

Show how this will supplement the existing Arbitration Tribunal with its panel of one hundred and thirty-eight judges from which five are chosen to repair to The Hague whenever a case is tried. President Roosevelt and President Diaz sent the first case to this in much less time than it took our United States Supreme Court to receive its first case.

Show that over one hundred arbitration treaties of limited scope have been signed in the last eight years, twenty-four of which have been with the United States. The first Peace Society in the world was started in New York in 1815. In 1915, on the centennial of that event, the third Hague Conference will open. Two years before that in 1913, its programme will be agreed on. Upon the work which can be done between 1911 and 1913 will depend the scope of that programme, and probably the wasting or the saving of upwards of several thousand million dollars of the hard-earned taxes of the world.

What can our country do to make 1915 mark an enormous step forward in human history? First of all, ask for complete arbitration treaties with all nations and then, beginning with this Congress, refuse until 1915 to build more battleships. This will not mean disarmament or even reduction of armaments, but the halting of an increase in armaments by the one nation that can afford to lead. If this saving of two battleships this one year alone and their cost of running during the next ten years, which amounts to about forty-five million dollars, were put into a peace budget, providing annual interchange of visits of editors and legislators beyond seas, into scholarships for the future leaders of the Orient; into translations, medical missionaries, into teachers and to giving friendly help where plague and famine are driving men and women to despair, is it not certain that we should do vastly more to de-

fend ourselves from a conceivable "yellow peril," to dispel suspicion from Latin Americans of our intervention, and to secure
friendly treatment in Europe, than if we spent those colossal
sums on steel and dynamite!

The teacher's function is to show the moral of the old fable
as applied to twentieth century problems and to teach the scientific fact that the genial sun is more effective upon a perverse
neighbor than is the harsh and bitter wind.

A second meeting in connection with the schools was held on
Thursday, May 4, at 3 p.m., in the Assembly Room of the West-
ern High School (for Girls). The Presiding Officer, Dr. James
H. Van Sickle, City Superintendent of Schools in Baltimore, and
President of the American School Peace League, delivered the
following address:

OPENING REMARKS AT YOUNG PEOPLE'S MEETING

J. H. VAN SICKLE

Young men and young women, delegates to the Third American
Peace Congress, I have the honor and pleasure of welcoming you
to this meeting. This I do most heartily. In your capacity as
delegates, you represent approximately ninety thousand pupils
in the public and private schools of elementary, secondary, and
collegiate grade in Baltimore City and County. It is expected
that you will report to your several classes a summary of the points
made in the addresses of the distinguished speakers to whom you
are to listen this afternoon.

For the city of Baltimore, there can be no question that this is
the most important session of the week. This is easily seen when
we realize that the attitude of people toward peace and war depends upon the state of mind of the people. In a very few years,
pupils now in the schools of various grades will exert a decided
influence in determining what the state of mind upon this subject
is to be; for you will be the thoughtful citizens and will be guiding
the affairs of the state and city, and you and the seventeen mil-

lions of others in schools throughout the land will determine what the state of mind upon this subject shall be throughout the country. This question will be settled in the schools. The boys and girls in this very audience will be leaders in bringing about correct thinking on the subject of how disputes may be settled without resort to war. Through the influence of the schools, twenty years from now the question will be settled and will not be open to debate or doubt.

Even the younger ones among you have studied United States history for a year or more. You have read of the voyages of discovery, of the colonization of this country, of the federation of the thirteen colonies, and of their more perfect union into a nation. Columbus, Magellan, Lord Baltimore, William Penn, Washington, Hamilton, Jefferson, and other prominent figures of early days seem only half real to you, they were making history so long ago; but how important that history was! More and more, as time goes on, you will realize the significance of the struggles of those early days. It was by no means easy, as you know, to form the original thirteen colonies into a union. After they, as States, had increased in number and had become more and more varied in their interests, it was by no means easy to keep them together. We rejoice that they *are* together as a nation, more compact, more united than before, and more effective in all the glories and arts of peace—and the glories of peace are greater than the glories of war. In the development of nations, wars have been necessary; but the questions at issue between nations are no longer such as need lead to war. They are industrial or commercial; and just as questions between individuals and between States are settled in courts so questions between nations are even now beginning to be settled by a similar tribunal. We have honored and shall continue to honor the heroes of righteous wars. But our future heroes will be heroes of peaceful achievement. They will diminish poverty, they will devise means to stop the ravages of preventable disease; and better than all, they will devise ways of preventing the destruction of human life in wars by putting into effect plans of judicial settlement of questions of dispute. There is a world-wide movement now going on in this direction in which our own country is taking a leading part. You are to hear about that movement this afternoon. It is history that is making right now in our own times. As, years ago, the American colonies united for the common good, so the nations of the world are moving toward such a union as will insure justice and peace throughout the world. As surely as we are here today, the time is not far distant when there will be a world court to settle difficulties between nations, just as there is a Supreme Court in our country which settles difficulties between States. It is to enable you to realize that just as in the days of Washington and Jefferson momentous steps were being taken that made the history set down in your books, so in your own day—this very day—a world-wide movement is in progress which you should understand. Three of the most distinguished delegates to the Third National Peace Congress are here to inform us of the world history now in the making.

Chairman Van Sickle then introduced Mrs. Lucia Ames Mead, who delivered an address on "The Family of Nations."

THE FAMILY OF NATIONS

LUCIA AMES MEAD

In Washington's day, if there had been a war between Russia and Japan, the small four-page newspapers in our sparsely settled States would have told little of it. Six months after Port Arthur had fallen a slow sailing vessel arriving in New York might have given the bare fact. But all that reporters, photographers and Red Cross nurses would now add to that would have been missing. We should have had no commerce, no missionaries, no money in Manchuria and consequently little knowledge of or interest in the war that filled its people with misery and gloom. Today all this has changed—when Mr. Roosevelt reaches Central Africa easier than Washington could go to Cincinnati. During the Russo-Japanese war, 1200 Poles, escaping military service, arrived in Boston and necessitated the citizens getting them work to keep them out of jails and hospitals and asylums. Today, sooner or later every nation is affected when any nation suffers. Once, nations at the antipodes of each other were as independent as so many marbles in a box. Today they are like heart and lungs and hands and feet, all united as closely by steam and electricity as our bodily members are by nerves, and through all, like red blood, flows the world's trade. Nearly every land has helped to make the food and clothes, the furniture and ornaments of our homes.

Our forty-page newspaper this year gives us yesterday's news from Tokio and Rio Janeiro and New Zealand. Your fathers are making reapers to send to Siberia, iron bridges for South Africa and sewing machines for Egypt; they are putting money into coffee plantations in Brazil, into mines in Bolivia, and irrigation in Arabia. People from the ends of the earth are flocking to our shores. We are not only New England but New Ireland, New Germany, New Italy, and in New York we have more Hebrews than ever congregated in any city upon earth. Today we are giving the best we have, and alas, also the worst we have to the black-eyed boys in China and Japan. We are teaching them to heal men scientifically in hospitals and to kill each other scientifically by machine guns at frightful cost.

It is a wonderful time to live in, a time of opportunity and responsibility. Life changes so fast, like a kaleidoscope, that more has happened in your short lifetime than in all dull Methusaleh's or strenuous Julius Caesar's. There never was so romantic, so fascinating a time to live in, when even a common, poor boy might grow to such influence that he could help shape the course of nations around the globe.

The knowledge that was sufficient for the nineteenth century will not suffice for us. We must have not only more knowledge of electricity and aviation and apple raising, but a great deal more knowledge of that very complex thing—human nature. Lack of knowledge of how other people think and feel, means loss of trade and often fearful cost for armaments. Lack of knowledge that God meant this world to be a family of nations has been as costly as the lack of knowledge in old times that dirt and flies and bad milk meant disease. This is getting to be an age of scientific management and it is high time that we learned not only to lay bricks scientifically, so as to save enormous time and strength, but also learned how to govern, how to live together and how to carry on the world's business by scientific management.

Sometimes we have acted in a scientific way but not usually. It is never scientific to ignore the fact that people keep the peace, if preparation is made beforehand for it. In 1817, in time of peace, Great Britain and the United States prepared to keep the peace by removing all battleships from the Great Lakes and all forts along our border. We might have kept them on both sides, renewing them every few years as they became out of date and spent a fabulous amount of money, but we should not have had the safety and peace along that 3000 miles of border line that we have had since. Two or three times, in the Civil War and again in 1896, it would have been very easy to have come to blows had we had frowning guns and sentries facing each other. We have kept the peace for nearly one hundred years and now President Taft means to keep it forever by signing an arbitration treaty with the English government, pledging both parts of the great family of English-speaking people never again to shed each others' blood.

If we can by right management ensure perpetual peace with each other, we shall soon see that we can likewise forever keep peace with France, our old ally, and then with a long line of other nations who are our friends. There is no nation which is not our friend. Let us never forget that since we became a republic we have never yet been attacked but have begun every war we have ever had.

There is as yet no scientific management that will prevent all murders or riots or civil wars but, our United States has the glory of having worked out a practical, scientific method of keeping the peace between forty-eight States, by which the world as well can keep peace between forty-eight nations. Little Palestine taught the world that there were not many Gods but only one. Great America, the "melting pot" of nations has to teach that in His eyes there is but one race, the human race, and that all His children are brethren. There are differences between them but the likenesses are greater than the differences. Let us write on the walls of every school room Garrison's motto: "My country is the world, my countrymen are all mankind." As our families make a State and our family of States are federated to make a nation, so the nations, learning their lessons from the States, must make a federated world, a family of nations.

Washington and Franklin and the less than one hundred men who worked behind locked doors that summer of 1787 in Philadelphia to make a Constitution for thirteen quarrelsome colonies, did a far greater thing than they realized. They were unconsciously working out a method to federate forty-eight States and forty-eight nations. They invented a Supreme Court, without which we should probably have had several wars between one State and another. But for one hundred and twenty-two years every quarrel between one State and another State has gone to that Supreme Court to be settled; though the feuds and riots within the States it could not touch.

In 1898, Russia had a terrible war budget. Moreover, a rich, imperial councillor, named Jean de Bloch, had written a marvellous book entitled—*The Future of War*, which greatly impressed the Tsar. It showed how machine guns and smokeless powder were changing the whole chances of success in war and making it possible, as we saw a few years later, for 50,000 peasant Boers to hold off two years and a half an English army of 250,000 men. The Tsar felt that something should be done and issued a letter in August of that year that amazed all Europe. He asked the twenty-six nations that had ambassadors at his court to send delegates to a peace conference. He showed how the increased cost of armaments was "bringing about the very cataclysm they were designed to avert." That is, preparations for war were getting nearly as ruinous as war itself. All the winter following his invitations, meetings were held all over England and, in the United States as the time approached, clubs and churches and chambers of commerce met and passed peace resolutions.

On May 18, in 1899, one hundred representatives from the twenty-six countries met in a great circular hall which Queen

Wilhelmina of Holland, had offered them at The Hague. Some of them joked and some of them sneered as of it were all a farce. But there were among the hundred some earnest men with hearts on fire, and among them, the distinguished senator from France, who will address you.

Presently they began work in three committees. The public was locked out and the whole world waited and prayed and guessed what the result would be. At one time, the Conference came near collapsing, as Germany seemed unwilling to coöperate. At this crisis, our great ambassador, Andrew D. White, sent Mr. Holls, the secretary of the delegation, to Berlin, to see the diplomats, who were amazed to find Americans cared so much about the Conference. Among the piles of letters and telegrams from America which he showed them, was a prayer written by a bishop of Texas for the Conference, to be prayed by thousands of worshippers every Sunday while the Conference sat. This made those Germans pause. They saw that we really cared as to what was being done there at The Hague; they consequently told the Kaiser and he removed the obstructions.

The result of those two months of hard work by the delegates speaking in French, the official language of the Conference, was not what the Tsar asked for, i.e., discovery of a way to lessen armaments, but rather provision for what must logically precede that. This was a Permanent Tribunal of Arbitration with a long list of judges from different countries, five of whom would be selected to hear any case that any two of the nations wanted to send to it. Shortly afterwards, our "star spangled Scotchman," as Mr. Carnegie is sometimes called, gave $1,500,000 to erect a handsome building for the Tribunal and, though the sceptics began to scoff because no nation sent a case for many months, President Roosevelt and President Diaz had the first case arbitrated in much less time than it took our Supreme Court at Washington to get its first case.

The Tribunal was opened in 1910 and the terrible war in the East soon followed, although the Tsar had not expected it. Had the world been a little better organized it might have been prevented. In the midst of it the Russian fleet fired, one dark night,

upon some poor English fishermen in the North Sea and so en-
raged England that many shrieked for war.   But France reminded
England and Russia that at The Hague, in 1899, they had provided for inquiry as well as arbitration and it invited the Russian
admiral and the surviving fishermen over to Paris to tell their
stories to an impartial commission.   The latter decided that this
"Doggerbank" disaster was a blunder, but asked the Russians to
pay $350,000 to the widows and orphans.   They gladly did it,
though nothing but public sentiment compelled them to.

A few months later, President Roosevelt, recalling that at The
Hague, in 1899, provision was also made for mediation, played
the mediator and brought the Russian and Japanese diplomats
over here to sign the Portsmouth treaty of peace.   In half a
dozen years after the prophecy by a distinguished American that
"no one living would live long enough to ever see a Permanent
International Tribual of Arbitration," that Tribunal was doing
business and one war had been prevented, one war ended, and the
nations were beginning to sign arbitration treaties!   Today, about
one hundred treaties have been signed agreeing to arbitrate everything but "honor" and "vital interests," and a few of the small
nations have agreed to arbitrate everything with each other as
President Taft earnestly desires America to do with Great Britain.

In 1904, President Roosevelt, at the request of the Interparliamentary Union, a great body of the legislators of the world who
meet yearly to promote better relations between nations, invited
the nations to a Second Hague Conference.   But this conference
was delayed for several reasons until 1907, and then the Tsar
asked if he might invite them and President Roosevelt said he
would be delighted to have him.   When the Second Hague Conference was called, forty-six instead of twenty-six nations were
invited, including the South American republics; all the civilized
world was represented.   Clutching my precious ticket which gave
me admission to the little gallery over-looking the ancient stone
Hall of the Knights where they assembled, I looked down one
September day in 1907 on the most august assembly that had
ever met in human history.   I have seen many brilliant, spectac-
ular displays but none that made the heart beat and the eyes fill

as did this.   Those quiet men, without uniforms or badges, were
largely helping to shape the future of the world.   Had they accomplished nothing more than get acquainted and keep perfect courtesy it would have been much.   During cold, rainy, summer days
they labored and dined together and telegraphed constantly to
their governments.   They accomplished much that did not show
in the final result but which evinced great progress in ideas.   Practical unanimity was needed to pass any resolution but sometimes
two-thirds or three-fourths agreed and this marked a great stride
forward, even though some nations still held back and prevented
the signing of an agreement.   Many barbarities of war were
lessened.   All agreed that unfortified places could not be bom-
barded, and that force must not be used to collect contractual
debts.   Germany had learned much since 1899 and in 1907 went
further than some other nations.   A prize court, to settle prizes
captured in war, and a new supreme court of the nations to settle
questions by international law were decided on, but as the strong
and weak nations could not agree how to select its fifteen judges,
it has not yet opened.

One great decision was to have a Third Hague Conference not
later than 1915.   That Third Conference will go much further
toward organizing the world.   The ice is broken and the world
is well on the way to accomplish four things before you are a
grandfather or a grandmother.   These four are:

1. *A regular world parliament.*

2. *A supreme court*, settling all quarrels between all nations
whenever they can not settle them peaceably otherwise.

3. *Executive commissions.*   There will probably never be a
world president but many executives will carry out the laws.
We already have a Universal Postal Union.

4. *An international police.*   Our present rival armies are not
a police and will gradually diminish, and a few soldiers and war
ships of the different nations will unite to keep in order any nation
that attacks another and thus act as real police.

When this is achieved, we shall be ready for the first time
to have a fair chance for civilization.   If you want to share in the
most inspiring and hopeful work the world has now on hand,

just study how you can help our country do a prodigious work of peace education in the precious four years before 1915.

Chairman Van Sickle then introduced Senator La Fontaine of Belgium, President of the Permanent International Peace Bureau, who spoke of the "Relation of Education to the Cause of the World's Peace." The presence of this distinguished visitor, and his illuminating address, were of advantage in directing the attention of teachers and students to the peace movement.

· Music was furnished by the public school choruses.

In conjunction with the Third National Peace Congress, a special session was held on Friday, May 5, at 8.15 p.m., in McCoy Hall, of the Johns Hopkins University, at which time an Interstate Oratorical Contest was conducted under the auspices of the Intercollegiate Peace Association. The Presiding Officer was Dean William P. Rodgers, of the Cincinnati School of Law. The Judges, appointed, to determine the winner of the First Prize of $75, and the Second Prize of $50, given by the Intercollegiate Peace Association, for the best original speech on some subject bearing upon the general question of Peace, were: Hon. Henry Stockbridge, Judge of the Maryland Court of Appeals; Professor Charles W. Hodell, Ph.D., of Goucher College; Mr. James A. C. Bond, of Westminster, Md.; Mr. Alpheus H. Snow, of Washington, D.C.; President Thomas Fell, of St. John's College, Annapolis, Md.

The following persons spoke on the subjects announced: C. L. Saxby, Beloit College, Wisconsin, "The Evolution of Peace;" Stanley H. Howe, Albion College, Michigan, "The Hope of Peace;" Wayne Calhoun, Illinois Wesleyan University, "War and the Man;" Charles M. Anderson, University of Notre Dame, Indiana, "America and Universal Peace;" C. M. Lodge, Dickinson College, Pennsylvania, "The Proposed Court of Arbitral Justice;" L. B. Bobbitt, Johns Hopkins University, "Patriotism and Peace."

The first prize was awarded to Stanley H. Howe, of Albion College, Michigan.

The second prize was awarded to L. B. Bobbitt, of the Johns Hopkins University.

The meeting of the Third American Peace Congress in Baltimore was coincident with the meeting of the American Chamber of Commerce in Paris, France, and a telegram was received in Baltimore setting forth resolutions adopted by the American Chamber of Commerce in Paris favoring the proposal of the President of the United States in favor of the submission to arbitration of any difference which the United States of America may have with any other nation. Those resolutions are as follows:

Resolved that the Chamber of Commerce of the State of New York urges the negotiation of treaties with Great Britain, France and other leading nations, such as shall establish (to use the language of President Taft) "positive agreements to abide the adjudication of an international arbitral in every issue which cannot be settled by negotiation, no matter what it involves, whether honor, territory, or money;" and be it further

Resolved that this Chamber believes that such treaties are the necessary step toward a material reduction in the size and cost of national armaments, and that such reduction is imperatively needed for the relief of heavy burdens and the doing away of causes of social unrest; and be it further

Resolved that copies of these resolutions and the accompanying report be transmitted to the President and Vice-President of the United States, the Secretary of State, the Committee on Foreign Relations of the Senate and the British and French Ambassadors at Washington; and that the coöperation of leading Chambers of Commerce in England and France be solicited. And

Whereas recently the President of the United States has again recommended the high desirability of making international treaties for the purpose of establishing international arbitration *in every issue which cannot be settled by negotiation, no matter what it involves, whether honor, territory or money;* now therefore be it

Resolved that the American Chamber of Commerce in Paris, assembled in general meeting this third day of May 1911, welcomes the proposal of the President of the United States in favor of the submission to arbitration of any difference which the United States of America may have with any other nation, and records its earnest and sincere hope that treaties may be concluded embodying the affirmation of this method of securing the peaceful solution of international disagreements; and be it further

Resolved that copies of these Resolutions be transmitted to the American Ambassador in Paris and to the Chamber of Commerce of the State of New York.

Paris, May third, 1911.

    (Seal)   (Signed) WM. S. HOGAN,
                                           Honorary Secretary.

The International Medical Association Against War conveyed by telegram through its President, Doctor Riviere, greetings and best wishes to the Peace Congress in Baltimore.

The National Society of the Sons of the American Revolution, meeting in Louisville, Ky., conveyed through its President-General, Mr. Wm. A. Marble, greetings to the Peace Congress.

The American Peace Society of Japan cabled greetings and good wishes from Yokohoma, Japan.

The Japan Peace Society cabled greetings and best wishes from Tokio, Japan, signed by Count Okuma.

The Pacific Coast Peace Conference telegraphed from Riverside, California, a message of greeting.

A similar message was received from the Denver Convention League, signed by Hon. John F. Shafroth, Governor.

The National Council of Jewish Women through its President telegraphed from Providence, R. I., a message of greeting.

A similar telegram was received from the Baltimore Section of the Council of Jewish Women.

The Commercial Association of Cincinnati through its Secretary, and the Manufacturers' Club through its President telegraphed greetings, and expressed interest in the work of the Congress.

The Military Order of the Loyal Legion presented through its Commander and Recorder a complimentary minute which was read at the Congress. This endorsement of Peace by such an organization was encouraging.

The North Carolina Federation of Women's Clubs sent a message of greeting, and pledged support.

The American Federation of Labor through its President, Mr. Samuel Gompers, extended greetings, and promised coöperation.

The President of the Brotherhood of St. Paul, Baltimore, presented the following resolutions:

1. That this Brotherhood favors the negotiation between the United States and Great Britain of an unlimited arbitration convention as proposed by President Taft.

2. That this Brotherhood favors the beginning by our Department of State of a revision of the existing arbitration conventions of the United States with other nations with a view to securing such unlimited arbitration treaties with all.

The British National Peace Council through its Secretary expressed cordial greetings, as follows:

"Your Congress meets at an important moment in the Peace Movement. America has, through President Taft, given a striking lead warmly reciprocated in this country. The work which the peace organizations have been doing through many years is, we trust, to be crowned with a great success. The permanent and full treaty between the States and Britain will, when established, be the first, we hope, of a long series to be formed with all the civilized nations of the world. I earnestly hope you will have the most successful of gatherings."

INDEX

Abbas Effendi, teachings of, 444.

Abbott, Lyman, address of, 247; Presiding Officer, 247, 252, 267, 275, 288; patriotism, 460; quoted, xviii.

Abdul-Baha Abbas, 444.

Abolition of trial by battle, 275.

Adams, Samuel, peace instructions of, 362.

Addams, Jane, on peace, 416.

Address to teachers of Maryland, 473.

Advocate of Peace, The, 186.

Alabama Claims, 32, 196, 377.

Alaska, maps of, 202; Panhandle of, 204; concession of part of, 204.

Aliens, status of, 100.

America, arbitration and, 410; duty of, xxvi.

America as peacemaker, 354, 359.

American Chamber of Commerce in Paris, resolutions of, 492.

American Federation of Labor, 494.

American Journal of International Law, 211.

American Peace Commission, 115.

American Peace Congress, 389, 395.

American Peace and Arbitration League, 227.

American Peace Society, 353; duties of field secretary, 229.

American Peace Society of Japan, 493.

American School Peace League, 482; education by, 268; teaching and, 270; articles concerning, 272; international council of, 273.

American Society of International Law, 210.

Andrews, F. F., address of, 267; quoted, xxxv.

Angell, Norman, on commercial relations, 337; on war, 476.

Anglo–American leadership for peace, 134.

Anglo-Japanese alliance, 307.

Appropriations for war by Congress, 366.

Arbitration, all-inclusive, 386; contract debts and, 167; definition of, 30; growth of, 97; Hague Conference and, 488; interdependence in, 102, 251; Latin-American and, 27;

limitations of, 100; no reservation in, 102; objections to, 144-146; panacea of, 249; resolutions on, 492; scope of, xxiii; theory of, 143; treaties of, 481.

Arbitration treaty of 1897, 335.

Arbitration treaty with England, 2, 11, 12, 21, 134, 213, 262.

Argentina and Uruguay, relations of, 27.

Argument from Hobbes' *Leviathan*, an, 147.

Armament as a guarantee of peace, 119.

Armaments, cost of, xxxiii, 253, 357; increase of wealth and, 369; limitations, xxxiv, 5, 388; purpose of, 68.

Argentine and Chile, peace between, 376.

Army life, attraction of, 71-73.

Army and Navy Journal, on School Peace League, 339.

Asquith, on peace, 365.

Aurelius, Marcus, on cooperation, 467.

Bahai, The Movement: a teaching of peace 443.

Bahai, The teachings of, 445; spread of, 446; ordinances of, 447; influences of, 448-451.

Bahai'o'llah, words of, 443; life of, 444.

Bahais of America, greetings of, 443.

Baker, T. S. address of, 88; quoted xxxvii.

Baldwin, Judge, on postal service, 457.

Baltimore, 402.

Barrett, John, address of, 181.

Bartholdt, Richard, address of, 142.

Battleship circular, 241.

Beals, C. E., addresses of, 229, 451; remarks of, 394, 396.

Behring Sea Arbitration, 32.

Belgium, neutrality of, 373.

Berthing, Karl, on conscription. 70.

Bismarck, on a God of battles, 279.

Black, Mrs. Elmer E., address of, 226

Black Sea, neutralization of, 373.

Blackstone, on war, 279; excuse of, 280.